Methodist Connectionalism

Methodist Connectionalism

Historical Perspectives

Russell E. Richey

General Board of Higher Education and Ministry
The United Methodist Church
Nashville, Tennessee

This project was supported by a generous grant from the Alonzo L. McDonald Family Agape Foundation to the Center for the Study of Law and Religion at Emory University, and was prepared by the author as a Senior Fellow of the Center. The author wishes to thank especially Alonzo L. McDonald, Peter McDonald, and the other McDonald Agape Foundation trustees for their support and encouragement. The opinions in this publication are those of the author and do not necessarily reflect the views of the Foundation or the Center.

The General Board of Higher Education and Ministry leads and serves The United Methodist Church in the recruitment, preparation, nurture, education, and support of Christian leaders—lay and clergy—for the work of making disciples of Jesus Christ for the transformation of the world. Its vision is that a new generation of Christian leaders will commit boldly to Jesus Christ and be characterized by intellectual excellence, moral integrity, spiritual courage, and holiness of heart and life.

The General Board of Higher Education and Ministry of The United Methodist Church is the church's agency for educational, institutional, and ministerial leadership. It serves as an advocate for the intellectual life of the church. The Board's mission embodies the Wesleyan tradition of commitment to the education of laypersons and ordained persons by providing access to higher education for all persons.

Copyright © 2009 by the General Board of Higher Education and Ministry, The United Methodist Church. All rights reserved.

No part of this book may be reproduced in any form whatsoever, print or electronic, without written permission, except in the case of brief quotations embodied in critical articles or reviews. For information regarding rights and permissions, contact the Office of Interpretation, General Board of Higher Education and Ministry, P.O. Box 340007, Nashville, TN 37203-0007; phone 615-340-7383; fax 615-340-7048; e-mail hpieterse@gbhem.org. Visit our Web site at www.gbhem.org.

All Scripture quotations unless noted otherwise are taken from the *New Revised Standard Version of the Bible*, copyright 1989, Division of Christian Education of the National Council of Churches of Christ in the United States of America. Used by permission. All rights reserved.

Scripture quotations noted KJV are taken from the King James or Authorized Version of the Bible.

ISBN 978-0-938162-85-8

Produced by the Office of Interpretation

Manufactured in the United States of America

Contents

Abbreviations	vii
Acknowledgments	xiii
Foreword	xv
Introduction: History, the Methodist Mode of Self-Identification	1

Connectional Order

Chapter 1:	The First Word about Methodism: History in the *Discipline*	17
Chapter 2:	Connectionalism: Defined in Conflict	34
Chapter 3:	General Conference: A Retrospective	49

Connectionalism and Ministry

Chapter 4:	Itinerancy in Historical Perspective: "A Wandering Arminian Was My Father . . ."	65
Chapter 5:	Extension Ministries	83
Chapter 6:	Organizing for Missions	98

Self-Presentation—Ritually and Apologetically

Chapter 7:	Connecting at the Table	117
Chapter 8:	A Study in Conference Self-Preoccupation	129
Chapter 9:	A Methodist Doctrine of the Church?	141

Conceptualizing the Connection

Chapter 10:	Family Values: A Connectional Concern	155
Chapter 11:	Methodism as Machine	172
Chapter 12:	Methodism and Providence	183
Chapter 13:	United Methodism at 40: Taking Stock	208

Conclusion: Reforming the Connection: Breaching Four Walls	234
Notes	249
Index	291

Abbreviations

For Methodist Denominations

AME   The African Methodist Episcopal Church (1816–)
AMEZ   The African Methodist Episcopal Church Zion (1820–)
CME   The Christian [originally Colored] Methodist Episcopal Church (1870–)
EA   The Evangelical Association/Church (1803–1946)
EUBC   The Evangelical United Brethren Church (1946–1968)
MC   The Methodist Church, USA (1939–1968)
MEC   The Methodist Episcopal Church (1784–1939)
MECS   The Methodist Episcopal Church, South (1844–1939)
MPC   The Methodist Protestant Church (1830–1939)
UBC   The United Brethren Church (1800–1946)
UMC   The United Methodist Church (1968–)

For Denominational Periodicals and Journals

CA   *Christian Advocate*, New York (MEC)
MQRS   *Methodist Quarterly Review* of the MECS
QR   *Quarterly Review* (UMC)

For Other Publications

Annual Report/Board or Institution/Church
Annual reports, however titled

Asbury/Coke *Discipline*
The Doctrines and Discipline of the Methodist Episcopal Church in America, with Explanatory Notes by Thomas Coke and Francis Asbury, 10th ed. (Philadelphia: Henry Tuckniss, 1798; reprint: Rutland, Vt.: Academy, 1979).

Bangs, *History*
Nathan Bangs, *A History of the Methodist Episcopal Church*, 12th ed., 4 vols. (New York: Carlton & Porter, 1860).

Barclay, *Missions*
Wade Crawford Barclay, *Early American Methodism, 1769–1844, The Methodist Episcopal Church, 1845–1939: Widening Horizons, 1845–95*, vols. 1–3 of *History of Methodist Missions*, 4 vols. (New York: Board of Missions of the Methodist Church, 1949–73), vols. 1–3 by Barclay, vol. 4 by J. Tremayne Copplestone.

Behney/Eller, *History*
J. Bruce Behney and Paul H. Eller, *The History of the Evangelical United Brethren Church*, ed. Kenneth W. Krueger (Nashville: Abingdon, 1979).

Buckley, *History of the Methodists*
James M. Buckley, *A History of the Methodists in the United States*, 4th ed. (New York: Charles Scribner's Sons, 1890).

Curts, *General Conferences*
The General Conferences of the Methodist Episcopal Church: From 1792–1896, edited by Lewis Curts (Cincinnati: Curts & Jennings, 1900).

Discipline/Church year
Book of Discipline (under slightly varying names) for the denomination cited; e.g., UMC *Discipline* 1996.

Emory, *Discipline*
Robert Emory, *History of the* Discipline *of the Methodist Episcopal Church*, rev. W. P. Strickland (New York: Carlton & Porter [1857]).

Abbreviations

Frank, *Polity*	Thomas Edward Frank, *Polity, Practice, and the Mission of The United Methodist Church* (Nashville: Abingdon, 2006).
HAM	*The History of American Methodism*, ed. Emory Stevens Bucke, 3 vols. (New York: Abingdon, 1964).
JGC/Church year	*Journal of the General Conference of the Methodist Episcopal Church* for the church and year indicated. Includes citations rendered discretely though from the aggregated *Journals of the General Conference of the Methodist Episcopal Church, 1796–1856*, 3 vols. (New York: Carlton & Phillips, 1856). Vol. 1, 1796–1836; Vol. 2, 1840–44; Vol. 3, 1848–56.
JLFA	*The Journal and Letters of Francis Asbury*, ed. Elmer T. Clark, 3 vols. (London: Epworth; and Nashville: Abingdon, 1958).
Lee, *Short History*	Jesse Lee, *A Short History of the Methodists* (Baltimore, 1810; Rutland, Vt.: Academy, 1974).
Mathews, *Slavery*	Donald G. Mathews, *Slavery and Methodism* (Princeton, N.J.: Princeton University Press, 1965).
MEA	*The Methodist Experience in America*, ed. Russell E. Richey, Kenneth E. Rowe, and Jean Miller Schmidt, Vol. 2 (Nashville: Abingdon, 2000; Vol. 1 in preparation).
Minutes/church/year	Annual or General Minutes, however titled and aggregated. Reference for the early years of the MEC is to *Minutes of the Annual Conferences of the Methodist Episcopal Church for the Years 1773–1828* (New York: T. Mason and G. Lane, 1840) unless alternative edition indicated. For example, reference for 1784 in *Minutes of the Methodist Conferences, Annually Held in America from 1773 to 1813, Inclusive* (New York:

	Published by Daniel Hitt & Thomas Ware for the Methodist Connexion in the United States, 1813) as *Minutes*/MEC/1784 (1813).
Richey, *Conference*	Russell E. Richey, *The Methodist Conference in America* (Nashville: Kingswood, 1996).
Simpson, *Cyclopaedia*	Matthew Simpson, *Cyclopaedia of Methodism: Embracing Sketches of its Rise, Progress, and Present Condition with Biographical Notices and Numerous Illustrations*, 5th rev. ed. (Philadelphia: Louis H. Ewerts, 1882).
Sweet, *Methodists*	William Warren Sweet, ed., *Religion on the American Frontier, 1783–1840: The Methodists, A Collection of Source Materials* (New York: Cooper Square [1964]; reprint of 1946 edition).
Tigert, *History*	Jno. J. Tigert, *A Constitutional History of American Episcopal Methodism*, 3rd ed., rev. and enl. (Nashville: Publishing House of the Methodist Episcopal Church, South, 1908).
Wesley, *Journal* (Curnock)	*The Journal of the Rev. John Wesley, A.M.*, ed. Nehemiah Curnock, 8 vols. (London: Epworth, 1909–16).
Wesley, *Letters* (Telford)	*The Letters of the Rev. John Wesley, A.M.*, ed. John Telford, 8 vols. (London: Epworth, 1931).
Wesley, *Works*	*The Works of John Wesley*; begun as *The Oxford Edition of The Works of John Wesley* (Oxford: Clarendon, 1975–83); continued as *The Bicentennial Edition of The Works of John Wesley* (Nashville: Abingdon, 1984–); 16 of 35 vols. published to date.
Wesley, *Works* (Jackson)	*The Works of John Wesley*, ed. Thomas Jackson, 14 vols. (London, 1872; Grand Rapids: Zondervan, 1958).

For United Methodism and American Culture Volumes

CEMI *Connectionalism: Ecclesiology, Mission, and Identity*, ed. Russell E. Richey, Dennis M. Campbell, and William B. Lawrence, United Methodism and American Culture series 1 (Nashville: Abingdon, 1997).

PCM *The People(s) Called Methodists: Forms and Reforms of their Life*, ed. Russell E. Richey, Dennis M. Campbell, and William B. Lawrence, United Methodism and American Culture series 2 (Nashville: Abingdon, 1999).

DD *Doctrines and Discipline*, ed. Dennis M. Campbell and William B. Lawrence, and Russell E. Richey, United Methodism and American Culture series 3 (Nashville: Abingdon, 1999).

QTCC *Questions for the Twenty-First Century Church*, ed. Russell E. Richey, William B. Lawrence, and Dennis M. Campbell, United Methodism and American Culture series 4 (Nashville: Abingdon, 1999).

MARKS *Marks of Methodism: Theology in Ecclesial Practice*, ed. Russell E. Richey, with Dennis M. Campbell and William B. Lawrence, United Methodism and American Culture series 5 (Nashville: Abingdon, 2005).

Acknowledgments

"The First Word about Methodism," originally published as "The Role of History in the *Discipline*," *Quarterly Review* 10 (Winter 1989): 3–20; and *Doctrine and Theology in the United Methodist Church*, ed. Thomas A. Langford (Nashville: Kingswood, 1991), 90–202.

"Connectionalism: Defined in Conflict," originally published as "Francis Asbury, James O'Kelly and Methodism's Growing Pains," published in *Southeastern Jurisdiction Historical Society Proceedings*, 2001; and *Virginia United Methodist Heritage* 27 (Fall 2001): 24–40, but under Russell E. Richey copyright.

"General Conference: A Retrospective," appeared in *Quarterly Review* 20/1 (Winter 2000): 50–65.

"Itinerancy in Historical Perspective," originally published as "Itinerancy in Early Methodism," in *Send Me? The Itinerancy in Crisis*, ed. Donald E. Messer (Nashville: Abingdon, 1991), 23–38, 175–79.

"Extension Ministries," originally published as "Are Extension Ministries an Opportunity to Reclaim a Wesleyan Understanding of Mission?" in *Questions for the Twenty-First Century Church*, ed. Russell E. Richey, Dennis M. Campbell, and William B. Lawrence, United Methodist and American Culture series 4 (Nashville: Abingdon, 1999), 175–85.

"Organizing for Missions," published as "Organizing for Missions: A Methodist Case Study," in *The Foreign Missionary Enterprise at Home: Explorations in North American Cultural History*, ed. Daniel H. Bays and Grant Wacker (Tuscaloosa: University of Alabama Press, 2003), 75–89.

"Connecting at the Table," originally published as "Three Ecumenical Agendas: A Methodist Approach," in *Quarterly Review* 11/4 (Winter 1991): 47–62.

"A Study in Conference Self-Preoccupation," published as "And Are We Yet Alive: A Study in Conference Self-Preoccupation," *Methodist History* 33 (July 1995): 249–61.

"A Methodist Doctrine of the Church?" appeared as "Ecclesial Sensibilities in Nineteenth-Century American Methodism," published in *Quarterly Review* 4/1 (Spring 1984): 31–42.

"Family Values: A Connectional Concern," originally published as "Family Values: Two Centuries of Southern Methodism," in *SEJ Historical Society Proceedings* (1997): 1–22; and in *Virginia United Methodist Heritage* 24 (Spring 1998): 9–27, but under Russell E. Richey copyright.

"Methodism as Machine," appeared in *Church, Identity, and Change: Theology and Denominational Structures in Unsettled Times*, ed. David A. Roozen and James Nieman (Grand Rapids: Eerdmans, 2005), 523–33.

"Methodism and Providence," appeared as "Methodism and Providence: A Study in Secularization," in *Studies in Church History 7: Protestant Evangelicalism: Britain, Ireland, Germany and America, c. 1750–c. 1950*, ed. Keith Robbins (Essex, England: The Ecclesiastical History Society, 1990), 51–77.

"United Methodism at 40: Taking Stock," published as "The United Methodist Church at 40: Where Have We Come From?" in *Methodist Review* 1 (2009): 27–56.

"Reforming the Connection: Breaching Four Walls" is based on an unpublished lecture, delivered at Drew Theological School Tipple-Vosburgh Lectures and Alumni/ae Reunion: "The World Is My Parish: Church, Academy and Civic Engagement" (Tuesday, 14 October 2008).

Foreword

Once again, we are reminded why Russ Richey is one of United Methodism's preeminent historians. By chronicling the notion of connectionalism through American Methodist history, this latest book affirms the profound value and relevance of the concept for The United Methodist Church today.

One of my own theological mentors, systematic theologian John Cobb, once admitted that much of current reality could be understood primarily through the lens of history. Through his entire book, Dr. Richey reminds us of this fact. As United Methodists look at our current situation as a denomination and, more importantly, gaze into our future, *Methodist Connectionalism* provides critical insight through a sustained, multifaceted look at our own history.

With adept analysis, Richey explores the hallmarks of our denomination as they have traversed our long Methodist history. Church order; General Conference; itinerancy; extension ministry; mission; the ideals of justice, evangelism, and ecumenism; hymnody; doctrine—these form the core of who we are as United Methodists. Mining our rich history, Richey reflects on how these central United Methodist values have been shaped and how they form our religious identity.

Richey's treatment of each of these areas deserves extensive study and comment, not just by scholars of Methodism but also, and *especially*, by United

Methodist church leaders at all levels of the connection. For the historic transitions that are reconfiguring the shape and expression of Christianity in our time confront The United Methodist Church with challenges that touch the heart of our identity today. As we seek to discern the contours of faithful United Methodism for our time, Dr. Richey's seasoned reflections on the core and the central values that have guided Methodist mission and ministry throughout American history are an invaluable resource. His narration of Methodism's understanding and practice of mission provides a good illustration.

In the beginning, he points out, mission was fundamental to American Methodism—an almost ontological state of being, deeply ingrained in our structure and identity. However, as the denomination grew in numbers and organizational complexity, mission became *a* function among others. Perhaps predictably, in its third phase, mission became the purview of a national bureaucratic machinery. Not surprisingly, the original consciousness of mission as core identity faded more and more.

I feel profound sadness at this evolution. This growing bureaucratization of our mission and ministry, I believe, lies at the heart of United Methodism's present woes. Who would disagree with Richey's lament that a "polity suffocating from over-structure," an "itinerancy collapsed into congregationalism," a "discipline transformed into a praxis of regulation and hyper-accountability," and a "mission confused with numbers and notions of Christendom and a Christian America" are draining the lifeblood from our being as a church?

Yet this historical trajectory may provide United Methodists with just the insights we need both in understanding our current crisis, at least in part, and in offering hope for the future. In reading these chapters it ought to be clear that United Methodism's current malaise, our continuing slide into irrelevancy and even oblivion, is directly related to the loss of mission as central to our identity. Yet, like our forebears, United Methodists can retrieve our dynamism as a missionary movement and so regain the direction and confidence we need for faithful ministry in our day. In recovering our missional identity, we can discover anew our United Methodist reason for being.

Grant Hagiya
Bishop, Seattle Episcopal Area
The United Methodist Church

INTRODUCTION

History, the Methodist Mode of Self-Identification

In North America, Methodism presented itself to the ear. It represented itself by the printed word. It was an aural/oral movement. It prospered through publications. Adherents took pride in their evocative hymns and lusty hymn singing, in their vibrant preaching, in their converting testimony. These singing, testifying, shouting Methodists carried pocket hymnbooks, preached from the Bible, and shared witness through letter and publication. The circuit-riding preacher needed, so it was said, a horse and strong lungs. He rode with books—Bible, *Discipline*, hymnbook. And soon after becoming an independent church, the denomination commissioned the circuit rider to function as colporteur for its growing book business, the proceeds from book sales augmenting meager salaries (quarterage).[1] Employing their dual resources—voice and publication—American Methodists patterned themselves after John and Charles Wesley and the Wesleyan movement generally. Preaching the Word and pushing books, that was the Methodist way.

A Methodism for Ear and Eye

The dual commitment had been prefigured in the very first gathering of the Methodist preachers in conference. Its one page of actions indicates that they agreed to adhere to the Wesleyan doctrine and discipline, to remain a renewal movement within the church (of England), to refrain from administering the sacraments, and to accept their preaching appointments. Thus began the commitment to the oral/aural side of the itinerant preaching movement. Three of the six rules to which they bound themselves pertained to the other side, to the written word—also "agreed to by all the preachers present."

> 4. None of the preachers in America to reprint any of Mr. Wesley's books, without his authority (when it can be got) and the consent of their brethren.
> 5. Robert Williams to sell the books he has already printed, but to print no more, unless under the above restriction.
> 6. Every preacher, who acts as an assistant, to send an account of the work once in six months to the general assistant.[2]

The preachers felt themselves obliged to set forth such rules because one of their number, Robert Williams, had appointed himself publisher and proceeded to put basic Wesleyan resources into print. Maintaining denominational control over publications—and especially over hymnbooks and other devotional items—proved a challenge then and thereafter, and remains such to this day. A challenge it was and is because individuals such as Williams, and Methodists generally, grasped the point that a dynamic, fissiparous, expansive movement that prospered on shouting preachers, hymn singing, class meetings, and testifying love feasts needed the ballast of the written word—the Bible, John's standard sermons, Charles's hymns, and the "Large Minutes."

Instructions for Independence

When, after the American Revolution, John Wesley recognized that the American movement needed to function as a church with full ministerial orders, he pronounced them "now at full liberty, simply to follow the Scriptures and the Primitive Church." He continued, "And we judge it best that they should stand fast in that Liberty, wherewith God has so strangely made them free."[3] To exercise that freedom rightly and orient them correctly to tradition and Scripture, he provided both a guide and detailed road maps. The former came in the office and person of Dr. Thomas Coke, ordained as superintendent by Wesley himself, and sent over with two other ordained preachers (the ordinations much to the consternation of brother Charles). The latter would be books.

The directive letter, "To Dr. COKE, Mr. ASBURY, and our Brethren in NORTH-AMERICA," presumed that the new church would retain the style and substance of the Wesleyan reform movement but take the form and offices of the Church of England. Hence the salutation to the two whom he desired to be superintendents and who would later take the more conventional title "bishop" (to the consternation of both Wesleys). Among the books that Wesley supplied (the Bible requiring transmission only by mention) was a revised and digested *Book of Common Prayer* (*BCP*), a book very dear to the Wesleys. Retitled the *Sunday Service of the Methodists in North America*, it provided the full array of rituals—morning prayer, evening prayer, weekday litany, Sunday service, Eucharist, two baptismal rites, marriage, and orders for Communion of the Sick, burial, and ordination services for deacons, elders, and superintendents. It also included a brief lectionary and twenty-four Articles of Religion, excerpted from Anglicanism's Thirty-Nine.[4] The American preachers, "long accustomed to pray extempore," as Jesse Lee explained, "fully satisfied that they could pray better, and with more devotion with the eyes shut, than they could with their eyes open," soon laid the book aside.[5]

Not to be laid aside was Wesley's "Large Minutes," the governing instrument of the Methodist movement. Revising it to constitute a quasi-constitution or *Discipline*, carrying out further ordinations (including that of Asbury), and establishing a church according to its strictures was the work of a specially called Christmas Conference.[6] Compiled somewhat hodgepodge by Wesley out of the decisions of his conferences, the Large Minutes, and now the American version thereof, the *Discipline*, provided rule and structure for the reformist Methodist movement, specified its distinctive practices and gatherings, and outlined tasks and duties. Revising and updating the *Discipline* would thereafter be the regular work of American conferences, initially its annual conferences, later its General Conferences.

Appended to the *Discipline* (in its first, 1785 edition) was *A Collection of Psalms and Hymns for the Lord's Day*.[7] *A Pocket Hymnbook* appeared the next year, one in a long series of hymnbooks for the Methodist people. The Wesleys had selected verse from Charles and structured and organized the collection to guide the faithful in the way of salvation.[8] Rich in scriptural citation and allusion,[9] it put biblical motif and Wesleyan doctrine on Methodist lips. By reference, inclusion, and allusion, these books pointed to other standards: Twenty-five Articles of Religion (adapted from the Thirty-Nine and one added to the twenty-four that Wesley had isolated), Wesley's *Sermons*, his *Explanatory Notes upon the New Testament*, and the

General Rules, a set of injunctions and disciplines by which Methodists might hold themselves and one another accountable for the ethical life and chart their way.

So the preachers called Methodist and the aural/oral movement they headed got their riding orders—by the book(s). With two exceptions, these standards from Wesley remained fixed as received. In both official and unofficial versions, the hymnal would be augmented with verse appropriate for revivals, camp meetings, and other aspects of American life. And, as noted, revision of the *Discipline* would become the regular work of the Methodist conferences. In 1787, in the first major revision, the Americans reordered Wesley's hodgepodge, announcing it "Arranged under proper HEADS, and METHODIZED in a more acceptable and easy MANNER." Brought to the fore in this version was a brief historical introduction that would remain fixed there for the century to follow. It spoke of origins, of emphases, of purpose, of identity:

> *Of the Rise of Methodism (so called) in Europe and America.*
> *Quest.* 1. What was the Rise of Methodism, so called, in Europe?
> *Answ.* In 1729, two young Men, reading the Bible, saw they could not be saved without Holiness, followed after it, and incited others so to do. In 1737, they saw likewise, that Men are justified before they are sanctified: but still Holiness was their Object. God then thrust them out, to raise an holy People.
> *Quest.* 2. What was the Rise of Methodism, so called, in America?
> *Answ.* During the Space of thirty Years past, certain Persons, Members of the Society, emigrated from England and Ireland, and settled in various Parts of this Country. About twenty Years ago, Philip Embury, a local Preacher from Ireland, began to preach in the City of New-York, and formed a Society of his own Countrymen and the Citizens. About the same Time, Robert Strawbridge, a local Preacher from Ireland, settled in Frederick County, in the State of Maryland, and preaching there formed some Societies. In 1769, Richard Boardman and Joseph Pilmoor, came to New-York; who were the first regular Methodist Preachers on the Continent. In the latter End of the Year 1771, Francis Asbury and Richard Wright, of the same Order, came over.
> *Quest.* 3. What may we reasonably believe to be God's Design, in raising up the Preachers called Methodists?
> *Answ.* To reform the Continent, and spread scripture Holiness over these Lands. As a Proof hereof, we have seen in the Course of fifteen Years a great a glorious Work of God, from New-York through the Jersies, Pennsylvania, Maryland, Virginia, North and South Carolina, even to Georgia.[10]

In Connection

In the chapters that follow we explore the import of this first word, this historical first word, this introduction through history. We focus as well on the peculiar ecclesial self-understanding implicit in the historical introduction, the presumed connection with Mr. Wesley, and the notion that the church is a connection. The early minutes of the American conferences, kept by the preachers in manuscript from 1773 on and published as a collection in 1785, bore the curious title "Minutes of Some Conversations Between the Preachers in Connection with the Rev. Mr. John Wesley." And at several points in the 1773 "Minutes," that first conference identified the commitments that kept them, individually and collectively, "in connection with Mr. Wesley."[11] The constitutional historian John Tigert commented on the import of title and reference, explaining that "connection," "connectional," and "connectionalism" acquired technical significance for Methodists.

> Thus from the beginning, in both England and America, Methodism has been a "Connection." The term is technical, and characteristic of the denomination. Connectionalism is of the essence of the system, equally opposed to congregationalism in the churches and to individualism in the preachers. Mr. Wesley, in America no less than in England, was, at the first, the center of union. Connection with him was the living bond that held incipient American Methodism together. He was the foundation of authority, acknowledged by all as rightful, original, and supreme. Through him a closer organic union subsisted between the Methodism of America (recognized at home as scarcely more than a needy but promising and fruitful mission field) and that of England, than among the colonies, now on the eve of revolt, and the mother country. Mr. Wesley was the patriarch and apostle, the founder and creator, of ecumenical Methodism.[12]

From the beginning, as the chapters that follow will in various ways indicate, *connection* and *connectionalism* developed multiple, complex, interlacing, changing meaning. The terms designate Methodism's origins, as Tigert noted. They refer to the relationships that existed among the preachers and peoples and between them and Mr. Wesley. The words acquired technical force in specifying ordained ministerial status and full conference membership. They could be used generally to apply to the conference or agency structures that governed. I have used them and found them used to refer to whatever the actions or measures or processes that held the denomination together, that is, that connected. They serve then to describe the evolving movement as institution or polity.

At times Methodists made efforts to give the terms theological or ecclesiological force. More frequently, those employing the words *connection* or *connectional* left the theological import or dimension at best implicit. Common usage nevertheless conveyed the presumption that Methodism and Methodists would adhere or connect. So Tigert rightly insisted that the terms function as a denominational self-understanding. However, *connection* and *connectional* lost something of their ecclesiological force when, in 1816, at the death of Bishop Asbury, the General Conference of the Methodist Episcopal Church directed that the more common word *church* be substituted throughout the *Discipline* for the Wesleyan terms *society* and *connection*. However, as I note below, we have come full circle with regard to the latter, the *Discipline* according it specific attention. And from the days of Wesley and Asbury to the present, Methodists have popularly referred to the Methodist connection, have recognized the connectional nature of the conference structure, and have employed the phrase "in full connection" to specify a preacher's status and prerogative.

Recently, commentators on the North American religious scene have begun to use the term *connectional*, in its various forms, as an organizational classification. So employed it distinguishes denominations with centralized authority, governance, and structure from those that lodge such prerogatives in the congregation. The term makes a useful contrast, especially a legal contrast, between churches with strong corporate, centralized, or hierarchical polities and ownership policies and those with systems that function self-consciously or operationally as congregational, independent, or free church and vest property in local hands. A word search through electronic databases—for "religion," "sociology," "American history"—will show a few such usages (many of them to publications in which I have had a hand).[13] However, the term has not acquired technical significance for sociologists and other interpreters of organization and polity. And the two communions that use the term *connectional* routinely in self-description are Presbyterians and Methodists, especially United Methodists. The latter's current *Discipline* references "connectional enterprises," "connectional ministries," "connectional ministries director," "Connectional Table," and "connectionalism." Among the thirty-two paragraphs cited, one in Part 3, Section 2, both titled "The Ministry of All Christians," the one bears quotation. Labeled "The Journey of a Connectional People," it affirms:

Connectionalism in the United Methodist tradition is multi-leveled, global in scope, and local in thrust. Our connectionalism is not merely a linking of one charge conference to another. It is rather a vital web of interactive relationships.

We are connected by sharing a common tradition of faith, including our Doctrinal Standards and General Rules (¶ 103); by sharing together a constitutional polity, including a leadership of general superintendency; by sharing a common mission, which we seek to carry out by working together in and through conferences that reflect the inclusive and missional character of our fellowship; by sharing a common ethos that characterizes our distinctive way of doing things.[14]

And General Conference, in 2004, also created a new coordinating entity for the denomination to which it gave the name "Connectional Table."

The best official definition of *connectional* occurred in an earlier *Discipline*, that of 1988, which devoted not just two paragraphs (as above) but three pages and eighteen paragraphs to "The Journey of a Connectional People."[15] With this statement, repeated in the 1992 *Discipline*,[16] United Methodism began to use the term more frequently in self-description, both officially, as in the *Discipline*, and in popular discourse. Indeed, even as the paragraphs explicitly devoted to the concept shrank, giving way to emphases on disciple making, servant leadership, and globalism, connectionalism became more useful as a term to gather in the entirety of the United Methodist system. We have, as it were, undone the work of the 1816 General Conference and made *connectional* again a word with ecclesiological import.

Connection and History

The chapters that follow explore historically various dimensions to Methodism's connectionalism, particularly Methodist efforts to make their system work, and their endeavors to understand who they were and what they were about. In some respects, Methodists said a lot about themselves. They did so with their publications, the "Book Concern," as they termed it, being the first of their connectional agencies. It generated tracts, Wesleyana, *Discipline*s, hymnals, devotional biographies, and other materials in quantity. And eventually its *Christian Advocate*(s) rivaled secular papers in distribution, and its *Methodist Magazine* compared with clergy journals of other denominations.[17] In all such pages, Methodists said much about being Methodist. Yet they struggled in the area that serves theologically to define what a church is and is about, namely, ecclesiology (but see chapter 9, "A Methodist Doctrine of the Church?").

To be sure, as several chapters will indicate, Methodists said what they were about more effectively in the doing, in their circuits and conferences, in what they accomplished, in their building of an effective organizational structure, in practice and practices. Their connectional enterprise functioned to enact or embody an ecclesiology. Seldom, however, were Methodists capable of teasing out and specifying what their connectionalism implicitly said about themselves. Seldom did connectionalism cash out as an articulated ecclesiology. The enacted understanding of the church remained just that—enacted, structured, practiced.

It is perhaps in its history that Methodism came closest to letting its many words about itself describe its connectional nature in quasi-ecclesiological terms. That, at least, is what this book argues. Methodist history, rendered for the eye, captured and captures what was heard and done. In looking at and describing the Methodist connection in its detail, history rendered a kind of phenomenological ecclesiology. So I have argued, and in these chapters bring the subject of "the connection" into view, from various angles. I do so mindful that historical accounts can exhibit Methodism's connectional nature but had to enter the theological realm to make the implicit ecclesiology explicit. And, as the last chapter indicates, the trajectory of historical treatment of Methodism has veered away from the theological. Getting history to reclaim its theological responsibility is part of what this book is about.

I admit, then, to having a constructive, personal interest in getting Methodists—United Methodists, particularly—to recognize that their connectionalism has expressed and does express their best ecclesiology, to help them make that explicit so as to become ecclesiologically self-conscious as a denomination, and then begin to think critically with and about that more formalized ecclesial understanding. Becoming ecclesiologically more self-aware should, I believe, allow Methodists to fashion connectional praxis, program, and structure more faithful to their sense of mission, to their Wesleyan heritage, to Scripture, and to the leading of the Spirit. That is my programmatic gesture toward United Methodists. And what is said about the Methodist Episcopal/Methodist/United Methodist legacy applies, to some extent, to the larger family of communions that share common rootage in American Methodism (African Methodists, Holiness churches, and, to some extent, Pentecostal bodies).

In this book I have a word as well for the non-Methodists. What is here for readers outside the Wesleyan family? Those from the more confessional or liturgical communions should find these chapters helpful in understanding why Methodists sometimes have seemed so opaque about or uninterested in certain areas of doctrine, inarticulate at times about ecclesiology, and yet fervidly committed to "connectional" polity and practice. To reiterate, such behavior attests a commitment to a practice of ecclesiology about which Methodists could be more articulate. Until they achieve more theological self-awareness, the effort in this volume should help non-Methodists understand why Methodists remain so fixated on themselves and their polity system. For the non-Methodist, then, this volume might be seen as an effort in translation.

An Overview of the Book

Each of the chapters in this volume explores some dimension, aspect, institution, or representation of Methodism's connectionalism, of its practiced theology, its structure, or its institutionalized ecclesiology.

The first three chapters are grouped under the theme "Connectional Order." Pursing the issue already noted—that United Methodist *Discipline*s introduce the church's order and its doctrine, its practices and ethics with historical accounts—chapter 1, "The First Word about Methodism: History in the *Discipline*," asks why there is the prominent positioning of the denomination's history. One answer is that American Methodists introduced a historical self-presentation and a self-*re*presentation into the *Discipline*, very early, as we observed above, and that such introductions have become a Methodist signature, appearing in the first *Discipline*s of virtually all Methodist movements. The chapter then notes the utility of such Disciplinary narratives in stating Methodist purposes, explaining divisions and warranting union. And now historical accounts function as well to ground and interpret United Methodism's key doctrinal formulations.

Chapter 2, "Connectionalism: Defined in Conflict," argues that American Methodist connectionalism did not and could not replicate the monarchical-like, Wesley-centered and Wesley-controlled ordering of the British movement. Under Asbury, and especially during the American Revolution, an American style of governance emerged, an indigenizing that preceded and set terms for the reception of Wesley's 1784 provisioning for ordination, polity, liturgy, and authority. Examining

Methodism's most important early schism, that led by James O'Kelly, the chapter suggests that conflict, spontaneous development of offices and practices, and sprawling growth fixed (rigidified) certain connectional aspects and furthered the development of new polity practices and patterns.

Chapter 3, "General Conference: A Retrospective," ties together the stories of the first two chapters. It treats the governing conference, which for Methodism has functioned as well as its teaching office, as a role inherited from Wesley but only gradually defined. The chapter then traces key stages in the evolution of conference power and authority, from its prehistory and particularly from the 1784 Christmas Conference through the development of General Conference and the safeguarding of its authority with the Restrictive Rules to the late twentieth century.

The three chapters in the second section explore the relationship between connectionalism and ministry in Methodism. In chapter 4, "Itinerancy in Historical Perspective: A Wandering Arminian Was My Father. . . ," I show that itinerancy, perhaps the defining feature but certainly the dynamic principle of Methodist connectionalism, has, like connectionalism as a whole, been lived, described, and celebrated but insufficiently analyzed. This chapter pursues analysis of the rich complexity in Methodist itinerancy by looking at its several dimensions in various contexts.

Chapter 5, "Extension Ministries," looks at a clergy category, that of elders serving in appointments known as "special" or "extension." Assignments to noncongregational or non-parish roles, the chapter argues, emerged early in the movement to care for needs and functions of the connection as a whole. Recognizing such duties and responsibilities (as these had been exercised by John Wesley) as appropriate and connectional must have come relatively easily. Acknowledging that extension ministries now seem peripheral to the system and a compromise to the principle of itinerancy, the chapter wonders why and what might restore these roles to a more appropriate place within the connectional system.

Another ministry sometimes contrasted with itinerancy and/or viewed as external to the connectional system, or perhaps even as a specific form of extension ministry, is that of missions. In treating this topic, chapter 6, "Organizing for Missions," however, focuses not on the missionary but on mission structures. It shows mission organization to be a key element in the development and evolution of Methodism's connectionalism. The chapter also treats some of the ironies in the unfolding of Methodism as a missionary movement.

The three chapters in the third section of the book are devoted to Methodism's modalities of self-presentation, both ritually and apologetically. In chapter 7, "Connecting at the Table," I identify three ideals of today's United Methodism—justice, evangelism, and ecumenism—that bid for attention, commitment, and dominance. I argue that the church needs all three; I do so with a distant mirror on the present, that of the practice not unique to but certainly energetically promoted by Methodism, namely, camp meetings. Although never formally incorporated into the connectional order, camp meetings nevertheless became an important strategy for being present in American society. Three camp meeting meals, each in its way essential, can be viewed as "sacramental" and expressive of deeply imbedded Wesleyan commitments, distinctive aspects of Methodism's connectional practice, and metaphors for today's ideals and their necessary interconnection.

Chapter 8, "A Study in Conference Self-Preoccupation," considers one of Wesleyanism's connective tissues—hymnody—and specifically an important Charles Wesley hymn, "And Are We Yet Alive." It shows the adoption of the practice of singing this hymn at the opening of annual conferences to be revelatory of changes in Methodist connectionalism in the Civil War era, such as self-preoccupation, formalization, liturgical awareness, tradition-creation, and memory making.

Entertaining the question "A Methodist Doctrine of the Church?", posed and probed by Albert Outler, chapter 9 concedes that early American Methodists lacked the theological talent to work the church-founding provisions that Wesley had sent them into a formal ecclesiology. I suggest, however, that Methodists recovered and transmitted something of Wesley's ecclesial and catholic sensibilities as they found themselves drawn into apological skirmishes with Presbyterians, Episcopalians, and Baptists. The focus here is on seminal works by the historian/theologians Nathan Bangs and Abel Stevens.

In the four chapters in the final section, I examine the complex, at times convoluted, ways in which Methodists have conceptualized the connectional bonds and structures they have created to bind them together around common values, vision, and mission. Chapter 10, "Family Values: A Connectional Concern," takes snapshots of the church in 1797, 1897, and 1997 (the century-apart dates selected to capture a specific homosexuality decision), proceeding on the assumption that Methodist ethos and ethics are connectionally inscribed in practices and polity. The snapshots catch in the single frames what had been the gradual evolution of Methodist values from a pietist/sectarian to a missionary/denominational to a churchly/congregational system. The chapter focuses on Southern Methodism and on connectional social (familial) codes and practices.

In chapter 11, titled "Methodism as Machine," I put present-day indifference toward, hostility to, or rebellion against denominational corporate structures and centralized authority (boards, agencies, bishops) into historical perspective. I posit that Methodists have both agonized about but also gloried in the church's connectionalism, polity, and organization. The chapter exhibits concepts of and attitudes toward connectional machinery at several points in Methodist life.

Chapter 12, "Methodism and Providence," revisits the theme of the first chapter, that is, the representation of Methodist connectionalism in its historical writings. Here, however, I focus on the notion, initially widely held, that the Holy Spirit or Providence created, sustained, and perfected the connectional system. Through examining important denominational histories, I seek to trace the subtle changes in Methodist understanding of Providence and in Methodist self-understanding. The histories of Methodism treated were recognized as authoritative for their respective days.

Chapter 13, the final chapter of the section and of the book, originated as a plenary address delivered at a conference held in August 2008 in Atlanta, Georgia, to commemorate the fortieth anniversary of the formation of The United Methodist Church. Hence the title of the chapter, "United Methodism at 40: Taking Stock." Conventionally, we attribute United Methodism's numerical decline, institutional rigidity, leadership-bent-in-on-maintenance, and internal conflict to the social turmoil of the 1960s and to structural-ideological arrangements reached in the 1968 union. This chapter argues instead that the strains and problems root deeply in the Methodist past—in the organizational revolution of the nineteenth century, the regionalization of the church in 1939, long-term patterns of professionalization, Methodism's efforts to stay the course in the cities, and a diocesan episcopacy.

I conclude the book with a set of reflections under the theme "Reforming the Connection: Breaching Four Walls." Here I take up issues implicit in the volume as a whole, namely, membership decline, culture war divisions, revolts against "headquarters," and the slippage of mainline denominations (United Methodism among them). It employs Martin Luther's image of walls that imprison the gospel and the church. Luther saw three walls; this chapter envisions four walls as entrapping Methodism: a polity suffocating from overstructure, an itinerancy collapsed into congregationalism, discipline transformed into a praxis of regulation and hyper-accountability, and mission confused with numbers and notions of Christendom and a Christian America. The chapter and book end with some suggestions about ways forward in reformation.

Historical Self-Presentation: Windows or Walls?

Employing testimony, narration, and history, rather than creed, confession, liturgy, or doctrine to render its ecclesial and connectional self-understanding has given Methodism extraordinary rich, varied, multilayered, and complex accounts of itself. Discerning readings of the movement's firsthand literary self-imagings, its formal histories, or its structured or institutionalized expressions of its self-understanding can provide a theology—and specifically an ecclesiology—comparable to that of more confessional churches. Methodism, and particularly United Methodism, need not apologize for its relative lack of formal ecclesiology. On the other hand, the church and its leadership need to know where to turn to interpret its connectional self-understanding when in dialogue with more confessional bodies. It needs to evidence its own take on the church's oneness, holiness, catholicity, and apostolicity.[18] A high level of comfort with Methodism's history and the ability to read it critically and imaginatively is a theological imperative for Methodism's interpreters.

The church's story, and its self-understanding as imbedded in its policy—as the following chapters should show—does not necessarily always speak theologically and doctrinally with clarity, uniformity, concession, and precision. Indeed, as ways of doing history have changed, as the church has divided, united, grown, and become more diverse, as its structures have developed complexity, and as its record keeping has been magnified and multiplied, so Methodism's historical documents and historical accounts represent both openings deep into its mission and identity and barriers to understanding them aright. Or, to sharpen the image a bit, the church's messy record and layered histories feature both windows into its connectional self-understanding and walls that deny present members and interpreters from seeing Methodism's true and full nature. Given that difficulty—given that reading ourselves through testimony, narration, and history is hard work—our temptation is to go bookless. We do so readily, in policy as well as worship, defending the practice as following the Spirit or as Wesleyan pragmatism. But Wesley gave us both voice and text. His books to us—Sunday Service, Bible, *Discipline*, hymnbook—invite us to look into the windows of our past to grasp our full integrity as a church. If we neglect or refuse this invitation, we threaten to cut ourselves off from our genius, our mission, our rich contribution to the church catholic. Our history, our polity, our texts, our connectionalism—are these encumbrances from the past, barriers to effective mission, walls that entrap us? Or are they windows through which we see, with God's guidance, a vision of our calling as a church?

Connectional Order

CHAPTER 1

The First Word about Methodism: History in the *Discipline*

*T*he *Book of Discipline of The United Methodist Church*, that of 1988 and those issued quadrennially thereafter, provides two historical accounts of Methodism, one in the prefatory "Historical Statement," another in the section titled "Doctrinal Standards and Our Theological Task." The first introduces the *Discipline* as a whole. The other frames the church's doctrinal commitments. These historical sections are not inconsequential. The first extends to nineteen pages (including a chronologically arranged list of bishops, United Methodism's gesture toward the historic episcopate, a broken succession with Mr. Wesley but continuous thereafter). So also the church dedicates the first nineteen pages of the Doctrinal Standards section to history. This latter narrative treatment introduces important items of historical as well as current doctrinal import, notably "Our Doctrinal Standards and General Rules." If we include these historical documents, we add another sixteen pages to a running total. In addition, the *Discipline* devotes thirteen pages to a discussion of the Quadrilateral and therefore to history in relation to tradition.

Why these historical statements? Why do Methodists introduce themselves historically? Why do they render their doctrine historically? What explains this appeal to history? What should one make of the historical self-estimate United Methodists render in their *Discipline*? A series of further questions might sharpen the issue:

- Why do Methodists need two such historical accounts, one prefatory to the *Discipline* as a whole, the other introductory to the section "Doctrinal Standards and Our Theological Task"?
- Why would Methodists grant history such a privileged place in their book?
- Why do Methodists introduce themselves historically?
- Why do they explain their doctrine historically?
- Why would they commit such a proportion of the *Discipline* to history?
- Why such an upfront, substantial, significant attention to history in the *Discipline*'s first eighty-six pages?
- Why, in a doctrinal section, would a church, its highest authority, and its theologians appeal to history at all? And why would they set the doctrinal section within a historical framework?
- How is history functioning in the *Discipline* as a whole and within the section on doctrinal standards and theological task?
- In that discussion, what do the structure of the narrative, the starting point, the topics covered, and the topics omitted indicate about how Methodism understands itself, its doctrine, and its authority?
- What does one learn about Methodism by recognizing its dependence upon history, by acknowledging that at critical junctures it turns to history?
- What does this use of history suggest about what *really* functions as authority for Methodism?
- Why does the church need this historical statement?
- For that matter, why in this whole section does it need anything more than the doctrinal standards themselves? Why all the explanation? Do not the history and the explanation infringe on the standards?

This chapter endeavors to address these questions. In brief, it posits that in turning the Large Minutes—the strange document by which John Wesley governed the people called Methodist—into a *Discipline*, American Methodists found they needed to begin with a providential or pneumatological narrative of the movement.

The First Word about Methodism   19

Ever since, American Methodists have prefaced the *Discipline* with history. Such a narrative introduction or self-declaration has been and continued to be a Methodist practice, taking a great variety of forms. The Disciplinary appeal to history, both that for 1972–84 and that for 1988 and thereafter, including the section that frames Methodist doctrine, makes sense against this long-standing "use" of history. However, the appeal to history, plausible perhaps when seen in a Methodist context, is by no means an obvious or standard prolegomenon, as comparison with the practice of other denominations will show. And, by such comparisons, we can see the theological statement of 1988 (and thereafter) and the longer Methodist Disciplinary appeal to history as a peculiar and important Methodist trait—doing theology with history and expecting theological value from history.

Early Methodist Disciplines

Almost from the beginning, American Methodists have made Disciplinary appeal to history. Positioning the account in some prefatory fashion, they have made the first word to be said about themselves a historical one. The exceptions to this pattern were the first two *Discipline*s. These *Discipline*s, those of 1785 and 1786, followed in style, substance, and order the loosely constructed, question-and-answer document derived from John Wesley's conferences with his preachers, and known as the Large Minutes.[1] The *Discipline* began where the Large Minutes began, with the question, "How may we best improve the Time of our Conferences?" It was, even a Methodist might concede, a curious way to begin, a curious introductory statement. So American Methodists found it.

Two years later, in 1787, the church restructured the volume, announcing it to be "[a]rranged under proper HEADS, and METHODIZED in a more acceptable and easy MANNER." In this new format, before it said anything about what it believed, about Scripture, about sacraments, about authority, or about polity, it said something historical. Still honoring Wesley's question-and-answer style, the church asked first, "What was the Rise of Methodism so called in Europe?"; second, "What was the Rise of Methodism, so called in America?"; and third, "What may we reasonably believe to be God's design in raising up the Preachers called Methodists?"

The answers to these three questions provided a short history of American Methodism. The first two answers sketched the very beginning of Methodism in Britain and America. The third answer, which Americanized Wesley's original formulation, placed a most significant construction on the first two. It was continuously cited and is still cited as the central definition of Methodist purpose. It epitomized Methodism. God's design was

> [t]o reform the Continent, and spread scripture Holiness over these Lands. As a Proof hereof, we have seen in the Course of fifteen Years a great and glorious Work of God, from New York through the Jersies, Pennsylvania, Delaware, Maryland, Virginia, North and South Carolina, even to Georgia.[2]

Thus, the *Discipline* gathered the entire Methodist movement into Providence, turned mundane into sacred history, and conceived of history in redemptive terms. History rendered the work of God. History made a statement of Methodist belief. History said what no other part of the *Discipline* could quite so directly affirm—God worked through, and God works through, the Methodists.

Although Methodists do not seem to have drawn out its implications, they carefully preserved both the precise wording and the placement of this formulation. It continued to be their first statement about themselves. Even when they changed the character of the *Discipline*, they retained this providential history and its prominent placement.

So when, in 1790, they departed from Wesley's question-and-answer format, bishops Thomas Coke and Francis Asbury recast this historical-providential self-understanding into a prefatory episcopal address. Two years later, in further recognition of history's priority, the church added a new section, placed it immediately after the episcopal address, titled it "Of the Origin of the Methodist Episcopal Church," and brought the account of Methodist beginnings up to 1784.

This historical addition functioned to legitimize the church as an institution, particularly its orders and sacraments. Each statement—the historical episcopal address and the section "Of the Origin of the Methodist Episcopal Address"—amounted to only one page of text.[3] These two pages sufficed. By them, Methodism introduced itself, said what it was, and defined itself.

This self-definition proved to be concise and sufficient. So for the rest of the nineteenth century, the church left these formulations intact and in place. History said the first word about Methodism. History declared Methodist meaning and purpose. History functioned appropriately to introduce Methodism's constituting documents. History provided the definition of Methodism, or, to be more precise, The Methodist Episcopal Church (MEC). History sufficed.

Behind the American Methodist appeal to history lay that of John Wesley. Wesley's apologetical use of the Methodist story, which lies beyond the purview of this chapter, obviously informed these early American efforts. Asbury, Coke, and others of the American leadership would have known Wesley's 1748 "A Plain Account of The People Called Methodists"; the historical appeals made elsewhere in Wesleyan apologetics; the premium Wesley placed upon his own and his itinerants' diaries and journals and his efforts to publish them; the place of history in the recently launched *Arminian Magazine*.[4] Accounting for themselves historically came naturally to Methodists generally, for reasons we will pursue below and elsewhere in this volume. Here we note the American Methodist penchant for making it their first word.

History Justifies Methodist Division

When the movement fragmented, the new Methodist bodies recognized their divergence from the MEC, but preserved its sense of historical self-identification. They did so in the way that Methodists claim legitimacy. They also began their *Disciplines* with history. So the *Disciplines* of the AME Church, the AME Zion Church, the Evangelical Association, The United Brethren in Christ, The Methodist Protestant Church, the Wesleyan Methodist Connection, The Methodist Episcopal Church, South, the Free Methodist Church, and the Colored Methodist Episcopal Church—all feature some sort of historical preface.[5] Each Methodist movement defined itself, introduced itself, by way of an account of how it had come into being. Like the MEC, each focused on beginnings. And, typically, they explained, in some cases at great length, why departure from the MEC (or, in the case of the CME, from the MECS) had been necessary. Conflictual origins produced apologetical tones to these accounts. Hence these later Methodist movements were less prone to discern Providence in events connected with their founding and to frame their narrative introduction doctrinally. Still the accounts registered their loyalty to Wesley and the Wesleyan witness. And they clearly recognized the value of history as a self-definition. For them also, the first word had to be historical.

Comparative Polity

A comparison underscores the distinctive character of Methodism's appeal to history. Two sister denominations, the Episcopalians and Presbyterians, make interesting comparative case studies. Both produced constitutions in the 1780s. Both did so, I would argue, with a clearer sense than the Methodists of what goes into a constitution. Presbyterians and Anglicans possessed then and continued to possess a keen sense—even a theology—of polity (though they differ sharply on its nature, source, and limits).[6] For them, as for the Methodists, the American Revolution called for new constitutional arrangements:

- American independence put them in a situation calling for clarity about the nature of authority.
- Their status in the new nation required a new orientation to the British authorities upon which they had depended.
- They could no longer depend upon the bishop of London or the Scottish Kirk for legitimacy, the adjudication of disputes, ordination, and the like.
- They needed to make provision for their own authority, and furthermore through a national rather than just a colonial, provincial, or state authority structure.
- Hence, each required a formal constitution that carried its own warranty of authenticity.

Constitutionally, their situations resembled those of the Methodists. In the 1780s, then, Presbyterians, Anglicans, and Methodists shared in a constitutional crisis.

The documents that resulted were titled *Constitution and Canons for the Government of the Protestant Episcopal Church* and *The Constitution of the Presbyterian Church*. Like the Methodist *Discipline*, both have persisted to this day, serving as the rootstock for two centuries of growth and successive grafts and pruning.

Neither the Episcopal nor the Presbyterian constitution, either initially or in later years, made significant appeal to history.[7] Neither introduces itself historically. Neither prefaces polity with narrative. Neither legitimates the new church by recounting its story. That could scarcely constitute an oversight. Both Presbyterian and Anglican traditions are quite self-conscious about the nature and bases of authority. Neither accorded or would accord history such a place of privilege.

The Episcopalians prize tradition. But tradition for them does not mean the recent saga of God's work in their midst. Instead, it means patristics. History is no companion to tradition in the warranting of a constitution. Instead, tradition apparently expresses itself immediately in canon and liturgy. It is apparently unnecessary, perhaps unthinkable, to render a historical account of that which the church has accepted.

Similarly, Presbyterians put too high a premium on Scripture and its perspicuity to suffer any mediation or dilution of its authority. To explain themselves, or what they believe, historically would be unthinkable. If a warrant were needed for Presbyterian practice, they would look to Scripture and Scripture alone. The Book of Order translates Scripture directly into structure and procedure. Creeds put Scripture into the mouths of the people. Here, too, a historical preface to either Confessions or Order would be unthinkable.

A Methodist Experience

There is something very Methodist, then, about a constitutional appeal to history, an initial historical statement of legitimacy. At any rate, Methodists, children of Providence by their own estimation, turned to history for the frame for their church, the *Discipline*. Why did Methodists turn to history in this fashion?

It would be too much to argue that these prefaces represent self-conscious exercises in theological prolegomena. I think and am trying to show that they performed that function. But intentionally so? Probably not. Rather, they seem to be more spontaneous, instinctive movements of the Methodist spirit. Methodists seem drawn to tell how it is with their spirit, collective or individual. Such statements take journal, confessional, conversionist, autobiographical, biographical, or historical shape. The root form seems to be the conversion narrative, a powerful account that warrants its own authenticity and has the power to induce a similar experience in others. Each of the other accounts is also self-authenticating, but typically less so and with less capacity to induce religious experience. The early Methodist histories clearly betray their origins in these outpourings of the Methodist spirit. At their root lie the conversion narratives, the dramatic encounters with God that must be related as a personal story. The first histories were little more than a string of accounts of conversions and revivals, the gathering of religious experiences into the narrative of God at work, the church's story as conversion writ large.[8] History attests that God works through the Methodists.

So why history? Perhaps, the claim must finally be confessional. Our fascination as Methodists with history has to do with the dynamics and character of our movement—the prominence we allowed and allow to both tradition and experience in our epistemology; the premium we (along with other evangelicals/pietists) put on the inward experience of salvation; the place we have given to testimony in class meeting and later in Sunday school; the emphasis we place (following Wesley) on popular media (magazine, tract, newspaper), which both necessitates and accommodates narrated experience; the confidence we have had that God works providentially in our corporate life as well as savingly in our individual lives; the recognition we consequently gave to Wesley's demand that we record (and share) our stories, our histories; the apologetical use we found for appeals to history and tradition; and the obvious value and impact that we (members and prospective members) discovered in the story of conversion, revival, and missionary encounter.

Human interest, Methodists learned, displayed the divine interest. Personal testimony disclosed the spiritual identity of an individual; history evidenced corporate identity. So we Methodists did theology in our own way. And one way we did and do theology is by telling our story, the narrative of God's work in us and among us. History became a Methodist mode of theologizing. We began and begin our *Discipline* with a historical word about ourselves, and we publish history because we know we need to tell God's modern story.

Despite their brevity, the historical prefaces rendered existence as story, as a narrative construction of the Methodist reality. They shared the Methodist religious experience—hence the appropriateness of their placement and their function as introduction. Just as the individual Methodists formally began their sojourn in the movement by telling their stories, by relating their conversions, by recounting God's saving work in their lives, so also Methodism as a movement began by narrating the salvation story—God at work in its midst. The shared individual experience—in class meeting, love feast, quarterly meeting, and camp meeting—quite literally constituted the movement. What better way to constitute the movement formally than with the shared corporate experience! A historical or narrative genre of discourse composed the movement. Appropriately, a historical reflective maneuver shaped the prefaces. It also expressed itself in the writing of Methodist history generally. Methodists paid tremendous attention over the years to historical endeavor. They did so, in part, because of history's power to define the movement. History represents a kind of proto-theology for Methodism, a lay theology, a witness of Methodism to and for itself.

Experience and Not the Quadrilateral?

So, although the Methodists were not as self-conscious as the Presbyterians or the Episcopalians about how their "Book" should be constructed, they had, in fact, discovered an appropriate methodological starting point. History belongs at the beginning because the shared religious experience belongs first. The *Discipline* appeals to experience.

Yet, the lack of self-consciousness about this appeal—the instinctive rather than reflective use of history—would prove troubling over the long haul for at least two reasons, one having to do with other sources of Methodist authority, and the other having to do with the capacity of this historical genre to sustain its richer theological and experiential meaning.

First, early and nineteenth-century Methodists would have been greatly troubled had it been suggested to them that their appeal to history and experience implied that Scripture did not take first place. Had the framers of these *Discipline*s been pressed with a query "Why history and not Scripture?" they doubtless would have quickly asserted the primacy of Scripture. Indeed, when Coke and Asbury produced an annotated version of the *Discipline* in 1798,[9] they made Scripture's primacy the primary appeal. And one can find there, and indeed in these historical prefaces themselves, the other elements of what we know as the Quadrilateral.

I would note parenthetically that to accent the experiential bases of the prefaces should not imply that other resources of Methodist reflection were wholly absent. Reason functions in any ordering of discourse. It was obviously at play in the conference's reordering and "methodizing" of the *Discipline*, construction of the historical narratives, and decision to place them first. The historical statements expressed Methodism's dependence upon reason. So also they represented an appeal to tradition—in their retention of the Wesleyan queries and answers, in their identification of a tradition that was passed along, in their focus upon the constitutive phases of the movement (in both Britain and America) that had "traditioning" value, in their function as the memory of the church, and in their definition of the *Discipline* as a living past. The appeal to Scripture is less obvious but also operative in the representation of Methodism as a scriptural way of holiness.[10]

To recognize the appropriateness of a historical, and, therefore, an experiential starting point, is not to suggest that Methodists would not have profited from a more self-conscious theological prolegomenon. They would have. It would have been helpful had Methodists been more theologically self-conscious in these prefaces.[11] The fact is that early American Methodism could call upon few persons with formal theological training, and its most eminent resource, Bishop Coke, was not regarded as fully committed to the American movement. The church made do with the intellectual leadership it could trust. In retrospect, one could argue that it would have been preferable for Methodism and for the *Discipline* to have had greater theological clarity about the warrant for doctrine and polity.

Second, had the church been more self-conscious about these historical prefaces, it might have chosen to deal with them in a different way in later years, particularly in the twentieth century. The church, as we shall see momentarily, has sustained the *genre* of the historical preface but lost the *sense* of it as mediating the work of God. The form is there. But it no longer evokes the conversion experience, the recounting of God's work among us. The preface had lost its ability to bear its richer theological and experiential meaning.

History Justifies Methodist Union

Prior to the 1939 union, the *Discipline* of the MEC began in a fashion that bishops Coke and Asbury would have easily recognized: a very short episcopal address, followed immediately by a four-page "Historical Statement." That statement spoke of the "Rise of Methodism so-called in Europe" and the "Rise of Methodism so-called in America." To be sure, the quaint language of the early *Discipline*s had long since disappeared. But the gist of the early *Discipline*s was there. Quite striking is the fact that the account came no farther than 1784. The statement legitimated the church that had been formed that year (i.e., 1784). These historical statements did not even pretend to carry the church's history toward the present. Their function was actually the reverse, namely, to claim that the present remained faithful to the past. By the twentieth century, the MEC *Discipline* had added an additional page that identified, celebrated, and apologized for the Methodist system. It affirmed of the denomination: "While its polity and administrative rules have been modified from time to time to meet changing conditions and opportunities, it remains unchanged in doctrine and ministerial offices."[12]

The next *Discipline*, that of 1940, had to make sense of a new church, The Methodist Church, formed by the union of The Methodist Episcopal Church, The Methodist Episcopal Church, South, and The Methodist Protestant Church. And for that, where else would the church turn but to the historical statement? The prior MEC statement gave structure and bulk to the text. The MPC and MECS contributed two paragraphs each.[13] The resultant account devoted attention primarily to the origins of the three churches but referenced the stages toward union and its consummation.

This continued to be history in the spare, gospel-like mode, nothing more than what was needed to establish the legitimacy of The Methodist Church. So that each church contributed a brief sketch of its origin, the origin of the new Methodist Church was added, and the mix constituted the new history. The new history was in the old mode. Why?

One would be hard pressed to argue that the appeal to history at this late stage in the church's life partook of the experiential immediacy and instinctiveness of the early prefaces. General Conferences gathered the theologically trained and included the best theological minds of the denomination. Why history first? If the church still believed its history to be providential, it was reluctant in an ecumenical age to be so self-congratulatory. History's placement here doubtless had more to do with precedent than anything else. And yet that very habit is not unimportant. Narrative had become an established pattern for Methodist reflection.

And Union Again

The 1968 union of The Methodist Church and The Evangelical United Brethren (EUBC) required yet another effort at self-definition. Here, too, the new church found no more appropriate self-declaration than through history. The statement took up the old task afresh. It established the new entity, The United Methodist Church, as in legitimate continuity with its predecessors.[14]

In regard to the 1968 *Discipline*, three points are in order. First, that *Discipline* gave almost equal treatment to The Methodist Church and The Evangelical United Brethren Church—four full pages to the former and slightly less than four to the latter. The separate sagas of the MEC, MECS, and MPC and the earlier union consumed one small paragraph. The distinct histories of The United Brethren and of The Evangelical Church each loomed larger than that of the MECS. The 1968 account established the legitimacy of The United Methodist Church; it was no longer burdened with legitimating the prior union of 1939.

Second, this *Discipline* also carried a list of United Methodist bishops.[15] That, too, functioned to integrate the separate traditions. After Asbury and Coke came

Martin Boehm and Philip William Otterbein; after Richard Whatcoat came Jacob Albright; and after William McKendree came Christian Newcomer. Here also the endeavor to legitimate the 1968 union obscured the prior union and the sensibilities of the Methodist Protestants, who did not think so highly of bishops.

Third, this *Discipline* prefaced "Doctrinal Statements and General Rules" with a terse, two-page discussion of standards. Its primary function seemed to be to establish the congruence of the Methodist Articles of Religion and the Evangelical United Brethren Confession of Faith (which followed immediately). It did not yet press history into the service that the 1972 *Discipline* would.

All three sections—historical statement, list of bishops, and doctrinal preface—seemed to serve the same general purpose: as had earlier statements, they conferred legitimacy on the new creation, The United Methodist Church.

Thus, for almost 200 years, from 1787 to 1968, there persisted a rather striking continuity in the church's appeal to history. The historical statements conferred legitimacy on the church by connecting the church of the present with its origins and Mr. Wesley; by locating its purposes in those that had animated the church from the start; and by construing Methodism as a design of Providence.

And yet, as we have seen, the last purpose and the theological force of the prefaces collapsed. The form remained but the content eroded. The 1972 *Discipline* represents a dramatic addition to that tradition. In continuity with the tradition, an important new appeal is made to history. In enrichment of that tradition, it brings to self-consciousness the theological force and value of historical prefaces.

History and Doctrine

The *Discipline*s up to and including that of 1988 retain the historical statement of 1968.[16] In the *Discipline*s of 1972 and later there appear also very substantial interpretive sections both before and after the doctrinal statements and general rules. The authoritative "Landmark" documents are sandwiched between a fourteen-page "Historical Background" and a fifteen-page section titled "Our Theological Task." Here, for the first time really, something akin to the constitutional self-consciousness of the Presbyterians and Episcopalians is at work. After 200 years of relatively instinctive or habitual appeal to history as the warrant for its *Discipline*, Methodism gives deliberate (surprisingly also, historical) and substantial attention to what is constitutive. These sections should be viewed against the backdrop of what has been described and assessed here as an important new venture for Methodism, an innovation in the tradition of Disciplinary historical reflection. That sense of both continuity and innovation is well symbolized in the fact that these *Disciplines* carry both a historical statement prefatory to the *Discipline* as a whole and historical segments that frame the important and long doctrinal section.

The questions initially posed and the issues of concern they raise invite reflection on this venture. For the most part, they apply to the 1972 *Discipline* as well as that of 1988. It will be most useful to bring them to bear upon that of 1988. So, finally, let us review the 1988 *Discipline*, and particularly paragraph 66, beginning with "Our Distinctive Heritage as United Methodists" and continuing through paragraph 67. Several points are in order, each of which draws out the implications of the inclusion within the *Discipline* of a historical treatment of doctrine.

1. In assessing this section, readers should keep in view its several possible functions and uses, including some that may have not been anticipated by its drafters or General Conference. It may be seen as

- an exercise of General Conference's teaching office;
- a midrash, or commentary, on United Methodist texts;
- an effort at doctrinal restoration and conservation;
- a judicial finding on the Landmark Documents, as though rendered by the Judicial Council;
- an instruction in the reception of Methodist teaching;
- a constitutional history in the tradition of James Buckley, Thomas Neely, or John Tigert;
- an essay on the evolution of Methodist doctrine; and, insofar as it has been written over against the 1972 statement,
- a revisionist recasting of the history of doctrine.

This section has purely historical utility, as the last three items suggest. But its value extends beyond mere history, as have the prefatory historical statements over the years. History has consistently played an important legitimating role for Methodist polity. Here it is pressed into a similar service for Methodist doctrine. So though this use capitalizes upon an established Methodist habit of mind, its full implications may not be clear.

2. The reader who compares this section of 1988 and later *Discipline*s with that of the 1972 version cannot help being struck by the differences in shape, tone, structure, and emphasis of the two. A detailed accounting and evaluation of those differences might better be left to another hand, perhaps to someone closer to the process.[17] However, a comment on change itself would be in order. As the discussion above should indicate, such a pronounced recasting of its historical self-understanding has not been the church's way. On the contrary, Methodism left the historical prefaces largely unaltered until changed circumstances dictated a new account, that is, after a division or union. Furthermore, change to a narrative explanation of Methodist doctrine would seem to be of greater moment than change to the historical prefaces. That, after all, was the point of the Restrictive Rules, namely, to inhibit change that touched those things most precious to Methodism. There is at least an irony or incongruity, if not at problem, in such a thoroughly revised narrative whose purpose is the preservation of Methodist doctrine. Ends and means, intent and vehicle, are mismatched.

3. Another impression is of the overwhelmingly Wesleyan character of this Methodist history.[18] To be sure, it locates United Methodist teaching within "Our Common Heritage as Christians" and honors the Reformation's contribution, notably in the Anglican Articles (through the MEC) and the Heidelberg Catechism (through the EUBC). However, in the decisive transitional section—"Our Distinctive Heritage as United Methodists"—Wesley figures, implicitly or explicitly, in every paragraph. And Wesley's spirit hovers over the remainder of the Methodist discussion and even that of the EUBCs. Here, also, the contrast with the prefatory historical statements is instructive. In those, the American developments claim center stage and Wesley figures primarily as a point of departure. The accent falls on the American character of Methodism. In the 1968 prefatory account (for United Methodism), Wesley looms larger than he had in previous prefaces; but even there the combined Methodist and Evangelical United Brethren sagas yield a very American story. So the strongly Wesleyan motif of the doctrinal historical statement contrasts sharply with the more American theme of the prefatory account. One must wonder about the appropriateness of two such variant constructions within the *Discipline.*

4. That contrast serves also to underscore the fact that there are less "Wesleyan" ways of construing Methodist doctrinal history. What does the church intend to say by such an exclusively Wesleyan interpretation? Furthermore, one can ask whether the heritage should be envisioned as a self-contained Wesleyan stream

and whether its theological purity at any point in time should be assessed by its proximity to the source. There are, after all, other historical readings of the development of Methodist doctrine.[19] Should not the *Discipline* take account of other factors that impinge upon the formation of doctrine and acknowledge alternative ways of construing its development?[20]

5. The governing metaphor of this account—declension—would strike many historians as suspect and certainly bears scrutiny.[21] The notion of an original Wesleyan purity, its dissipation, and the gradual resultant declension of Methodism doubtless serves what such jeremiadic history typically serves, namely, to build a case for reform through recovery. It is a strategy of primitivism, a prophetic call to return to the covenant. This may be exactly the note that the church wishes to sound. Clearly, some within the denomination have struck this note repeatedly. A challenge at this point serves as more than a reminder that this is not the only way of explaining historical and doctrinal change. A challenge is also a way of asking whether the church really has committed itself to jeremiadic politics and to the dynamics and implications that jeremiads unleash.

6. The historical discussion clearly evidences Richard Heitzenrater's interpretation of the Restrictive Rules.[22] Such a textual nuance (and the Albert Outlerian tone of the prior *Discipline*) may be the consequences of employing top-flight Wesley scholars in the drafting process. Drafters will inevitably put their own stamp on the text. Clearly, the church has been blessed by the services of such qualified scholars. Still, there may be some problems in according Disciplinary status to what remains a controversial historical argument.[23]

In this last question, as in those preceding, the premise is that the historical account functions as a claim of the church about itself. As such, then, this is not mere history but in some sense ecclesiology. It may well be that the historical discussion in the doctrinal section will have more value to the church than the documents it purports to introduce. Certainly, one could argue that case for the 1972 historical/interpretive statement—thus the controversy around it. That statement, its affirmation of pluralism, and the notion of a Quadrilateral claimed attention as United Methodist belief—so much attention that the present revision was demanded. Pluralism was made almost creedal. The Quadrilateral slighted the unique witness of Scripture. And so on. The interpretation of the doctrinal statements had become the doctrine. And so now the historical/interpretive statement of 1988 may well be read and critiqued as a faith statement. If so, United Methodists will (1) sustain a long tradition of employing history for self-definition, but (2) become far more self-consciousness about the doctrinal implications of that appeal.

The History in the *Discipline* and the Doctrine in That History

This chapter first examined the *Discipline*'s historical prefaces. A rather spontaneous effort to introduce the new church, drawing on an established pattern of Methodist narrative reflection, not developed as self-conscious prolegomenon, nor ever mined for its theological implications, the preface nevertheless functioned successfully to locate Methodism in the economy of Providence. History made a statement of Methodist belief—belief about God at work, belief about Methodism itself. Methodist history was sacred history. At least, it was so initially. And even as the nineteenth century wore on and historiography became more objective and scientific, the prefatory histories continued to recall that God works in and through the Methodists. Without ever discussing the matter formally, Methodists of various stripes seemed to know that a historical preface appropriately opened their *Discipline*s. So at every point when new forms of Methodism emerged, history served as prolegomenon.

Since 1972, United Methodist *Discipline*s have also placed history to work in introducing the church's doctrine, polity, and discipline. On the assumption that here, too, the church's act may speak and may, perhaps, say more than the church has self-consciously willed, this chapter has endeavored to begin the process of exploring what this new historical statement means. Clearly, the history has been written to explain the doctrine. What, it may be asked, are the doctrinal implications of undertaking such history? Why, in a doctrinal section, would a church, its highest authority and its theologians, appeal to history at all, and particularly to a history rendered with little sense of God's hand in human affairs?

One answer, as this chapter and this volume suggests, is that when Methodists need to say something introductory about themselves, their vocation, and their mission, they reflexively turn to narrative, to testimony, to the work of God in their lives. They do so as individuals. They once did so as a movement. What is missing in the more recent versions of Methodist self-introductions is a deeper sense of the theological import of their story and a willingness to be forthright about where and in what they deem the Spirit to be at work. Such a providential account need not succumb to what my colleague Kenneth Rowe terms "happy history," the aggrandizing of the Methodist story or even the apotheosizing of a history rife with racism, conflict, self-aggrandizement, bigotry, sexism, homophobia, and class prejudice. Indeed, a right telling would, in good prophetic style, name the places where the church has failed to live the covenant and so set the agenda for change. But a historical preface rendered in such fashion might once again address the question, "What may we reasonably believe to be God's design in raising up the Preachers called Methodists?" and might say, "God's design was To reform the Continent, and spread scripture Holiness over these Lands. As a Proof hereof, we have seen in. . . ."

CHAPTER 2

Connectionalism: Defined in Conflict

In explaining his leadership role in the 1792 General Conference legislative fight that produced schism and a new denomination, the Republican Methodists, Presiding Elder James O'Kelly, wrote a local preacher friend:

> What have I done? Overturned government? What? the Council—not Methodism. I only say no man among us ought to get into the Apostle's chair with the Keys, and stretch a lordly power over the ministers and Kingdom of Christ. 'Tis a human invention, a quicksand; and when my grey hairs may be preserved under ground, I may be remembered. We ought to respect the body before any mere man. A consolidated government is always bad. We have published that we believe a General Conference to be injurious to the Church. District Conferences have lost their suffrages; men of wit will leave the travelling connection. Boys with their Keys, under the absolute sway of one who declares his authority and succession from the Apostles—these striplings must rule and govern Christ's Church, as master workmen; as though they could finish such a temple. People are to depend on their credibility. These things are so; I know what I say; I am able when called upon to answer it. I am a friend to Christ; to his Church, but not to prelatick government.[1]

Here O'Kelly enunciated key principles for which he and his movement stood:

- wariness against arbitrary, "monarchical" power, especially as lodged in bishops;
- high valuation of the "republican" rights and liberties, to be cherished in church as in the new nation;
- affection for the fraternity within conference and within Methodism; and
- a primitivist hermeneutic that recognized only the principles, praxis, and polity explicitly mentioned in Scripture.

Not mentioned here by O'Kelly but equally a commitment of the new movement was fervid antislavery.[2] These principles had much to do with the schism and even more with the conflict thereafter; but, as is so typically the case in church fights, personalities played as important a part as principles.

James O'Kelly faced off against Francis Asbury repeatedly, almost from his acceptance on trial in 1778. O'Kelly had some role, typically an adversarial one, in five major events through and/or against which Asbury consolidated his authority and power within the little Methodist movement: the Broken Back, or Fluvanna, Conference of 1779, which made provision for the sacraments and ordination; the 1784 Christmas Conference, which created the new church; the 1787 Rough Creek (Virginia) Conference, which mounted a frontal challenge to Wesley's, Asbury's, and Coke's authority; the 1789 and 1790 experiments with a Council; and the 1792 General Conference, which produced schism. Each deserves some comment. Each contributed to the definition of Methodism, and O'Kelly indeed provided some of the pain in Methodism's growth.[3]

Declarations of Independence

In 1779 the Methodist movement experienced its first division. Histories usually represent this as Virginian impetuousness—precipitous declaration of independence and impatience with John Wesley's inaction on American requests for enabling recognition. This reading, the one imbedded in the later published version of the *Minutes*,[4] gave "official" standing to the conference that met, for Asbury's convenience and safety, at Thomas White's in Delaware. In quite a number of respects, it, rather than the later Broken Back, or Fluvanna, Conference, was the schismatic affair. Or, at the very least, each had problematic aspects.

How was Asbury's conference schismatic? First, it convened irregularly. Second, it presumed to act on matters constitutional in the name of the conference. Third, it appointed a president without regard to the existence of one, naming him (Asbury) general assistant in America. Fourth, it established Asbury's role on the basis of its own constitutional specifications and construal of Mr. Wesley's actions. The latter action, in Asbury's own hand, the "Leesburg Minutes," conveyed in Wesleyan fashion as an answer to a query about why Asbury should be the general assistant: "A. He Ought because Originally Appointed by Mr. Wesley to Act Jointly therein with Mr. Rankin & Mr. Shadford." The published version elaborated and refined that: "Ans. He ought: 1st, on account of his age; 2d, because originally appointed by Mr. Wesley; 3d being joined with Messrs. Rankin and Shadford, by express order from Mr. Wesley."[5]

Fifth, this conference took two further actions, which their (later) published minutes just somehow omitted: making provision for successors "in case of Br. Asbury's Death or absence" and providing for their own subsequent meeting:

> When and where Shall our next conference be held? Ans. Whereas it is thought that without some Extraordinary change in affairs it will not be possible for all the Preachers to attend in Virginia let it be in the Baltimore Circuit the last Tuesday in April.[6]

The regularly called conference met as appointed at Fluvanna (*MEA*, 1779),[7] undeterred by the Asburian cabal and its actions. It proceeded as though the Delaware Conference had not met or acted. It did what conferences were supposed to do. It made provision for presidency during its sessions, so authorizing Philip Gatch, as indicated by his standing first in several key listings. It did the movement's business. It examined its members. It collected and disbursed monies. It stationed the preachers. It attended to discipline.

Recognizing the Episcopal Establishment as dissolved by the Revolution, it adopted measures through and by which the necessary rites and offices of a Christian church might be provided for the Methodist faithful. In particular, it conferred to a committee of four, elected by the preachers and listed by name, the authority that had been vested in Wesley or his general assistant—legislative and administrative authority—including presumably Wesley's power to appoint. To a presbytery, similarly constituted and composed of the same four individuals, it transmitted the right to administer the sacraments, to ordain, and to determine who else should receive sacramental authority. The preachers undertook these acts, of course, without the confirming episcopal touch or that of any regularly ordained person. It was, so to speak, a fresh start of the Christian church (*MEA*, 1779), contravening Wesley's wish and precept and implicitly discounting the historic succession. Combining features from Wesleyan, Presbyterian, Anglican, and republican practice, the Fluvanna Conference opened a route that American Methodism would follow, albeit very slowly, but that O'Kelly would traverse more quickly.

Asburian Order

The dramatic healing of this two-year schism will not concern us here. Suffice it to say that it occurred on the basis of stipulations that the Asbury wing promulgated in Baltimore the following year:

> How many preachers do now agree to Sitt in Conference on the Original plan as Methodists let all there names be enter'd upon the minutes. . . .
> Does this conference acknowledge Francess Asbury as Mr. Wesleys representative to exercise the same pour [power] and travel in the same manner when circumstances will admit.[8]

So Mr. Asbury became the symbol and guarantor of Wesleyan and ecclesial integrity and the American counterpart of Mr. Wesley. On this premise the 1781 Conference(s) reunited the movement, stipulating as the disciplinary and doctrinal standards of an emerging American connection those of Wesleyanism: "How many of our preachers are now determined after mature consideration, close observation and earnest prayer to preach the old Methodist doctrine, and strictly enforce the discipline, as contained in the notes, sermons, and minutes published by Mr. Wesley. . . ."[9]

Thirty-nine signed, according to the published minutes, an additional five in the Leesburg version. On neither did the name James O'Kelly appear. He was apparently not present. Others who were, Jesse Lee reported, would not concur in disavowing the separation or suspending the sacraments. The spirit and style of Fluvanna lived on. Later that year, Asbury encountered Virginia preachers eager for the ordinances. Preparing to fight the "spreading fire of division," Asbury began reading and marking Richard Baxter's *Cure for Church Divisions* for possible abridgment. An American Wesley he?

The 1782 conference endeavored to counter such continuing independence by blotting out reference to the enabling conference activities and ordering the removal of reference to such (the sacraments) in the *Minutes*.[10] The 1784 Christmas Conference achieved the ecclesial transformation that Fluvanna had sought. It brought a Wesleyan episcopal order through an instrumentality, Thomas Coke, that seriously undercut Asbury's role as symbol and guarantor of Wesleyan and ecclesial integrity. It also introduced Coke as the American Mr. Wesley. Coke was Wesley's chief lieutenant, had been university educated, ordained an Anglican priest, and appointed as superintendent for America. He was charged to ordain Asbury, and in so doing, he carried his own and Wesley's plans for the new church, and prepared explanatory discourses and sermons while on the ship's voyage so that he was ready to execute this new church start on Wesley's authority. Thus, he symbolized and guaranteed Wesleyan and ecclesial integrity. He wore Mr. Wesley's mantle. Asbury countered, we have been told, by insisting on the convening of a conference and the election of any to be recognized as superintendent, himself most particularly. By that plebiscite Asbury regained a good measure of the authority "lost" in the presence of Coke. He eventually took control through making appointments, effectively leaving Coke with symbolism and little power. Coke might have a Wesley style. Asbury would settle for the substance. He would be the operative guarantor of Wesleyan and ecclesial integrity and the American counterpart of Mr. Wesley, if not the symbol.

Witnessing these Christmas Conference maneuverings, James O'Kelly made his signal contribution to the event much later. Long after the fact he sought to undercut Asbury by denying that any episcopal election took place. More immediately, O'Kelly emerged from the conference designated as elder in the new church. He became a presiding elder as that superintending function evolved quickly out of the elder's office and became clearly a significant and even beloved leader.

Contending with Authority

Coke returned to Britain after the 1785 conferences. He came back in 1787 with a number of directives from Wesley, including the convening of a general conference and the appointment of Richard Whatcoat as "Superintendent with Asbury." These orders accorded with the "binding minute" to obey Wesley's commands and with Wesley's vision of a global connection. They hardly accorded with American sensitivities.[11] Some 3,000 gathered for conference at Rough Creek, Virginia, where O'Kelly and Lee led the opposition to Coke, to Wesley's exercise of authority, and to the nomination of Whatcoat. Of the subsequent conference, held on May 1 in Baltimore, Asbury noted, "We had some warm and close debates in conference; but all ended in love and peace." Thomas Ware reported, more candidly, that many of the preachers took great offense at the presumption of resetting the conference date, at the implicit conferring of decision making to the superintendents, at the appointment rather than the election of superintendents, and at the fear that Whatcoat's elevation might produce the recall of Asbury. The fear doomed Whatcoat's episcopal chances at that juncture. The conferences responded more formally by qualifying Coke's authority, stipulating in the Annual Minutes to the first question about who are the superintendents the answer "Thomas Coke, (when present in the States), and Francis Asbury." Coke responded with a certificate promising not to exercise superintending authority when absent and limiting it when present to ordaining, presiding, and traveling. They also rescinded the binding minute of loyalty to Wesley from the *Discipline* (*MEA*, 1785*a*, Q. 2), sometimes described as dropping Wesley's name from the Minutes.[12]

If the Methodists did not want a monarchical episcopacy—that is, a superintendency with authority like Wesley's—then how would they have a common mind? As the little movement expanded, the problems of cohesion and direction increased. Distances necessitated the convening of multiple conferences. Six were appointed for 1788, but according to Lee seven were held. For 1789, eleven conferences met. That year the bishops proposed a small executive body, a council. Lee, who reproduced the entirety of the enabling legislation, complained that the council was new, dangerous, unworkable, and not genuinely representative:

> This plan for having a council, was entirely new, and exceedingly dangerous. A majority of the preachers voted in favour of it, but they were soon sensible, that the plan would not answer the purpose for which it was intended. The council was to be composed of the bishops, and the presiding elders: the presiding elders were appointed, changed, and put out of office by the bishop, and just when he pleased; of course, the whole of the council were to consist of the bishops, and a few other men of their own choice or appointing.[13]

The council possessed two other features well devised to doom it. Its enactments required unanimity, in effect allowing Asbury veto power. And legislation would be binding only in concurring conferences—a "dangerous clause" Lee thought, prone to divide the connection.[14]

In its first meeting, the council adopted a constitution that remedied these three glaring defects. It provided for election of its members, a two-thirds majority rather than unanimity for legislation (plus, however,"the consent of the bishop"), and only the concurrence of "a majority of the several conferences." Even in this revised form, many experienced the council as what Neely terms "a dangerous centralization of power."[15]

Contending for Power

Irish-born O'Kelly was outspoken on the issue of centralized power and led the charge against the council. Asbury reported:

> I received a letter from the presiding elder of this district [South Virginia], James O'Kelly; he makes heavy complaints of my power, and bids me stop for one year, or he must use his influence against me. Power! Power![16]

Others shared O'Kelly's concern. The conference at Charleston sought to constrict the council's power to "advice only" and to make the "consent of the conference decisive." At Petersburg Asbury reported, "Our conference began; all was peace until the council was mentioned. The young men appeared to be entirely under the influence of the elders, and turned it out of doors." James Meacham, a young preacher at that conference, noted in his journal for September 1, 1790, the opposition to the council in southern Virginia, an opposition that he thought would lead either to expulsions or separation. Four days later he reported receiving "4 Letters from the Travelling Preachers, they are much oppos'd to the Council." William McKendree, later to be Asbury's colleague as bishop, then possessed great confidence in O'Kelly, whose word "was next to gospel with me." Asbury is reported to have said: "Ye have all spoken out of one mouth. Henceforth you are all out of the union." Following the Leesburg Conference, where similar agitation prevailed, Asbury backed down and made yet another concession:

To conciliate the minds of our brethren in the south district of Virginia, who are restless about the council, I wrote their leader a letter, informing him, "that I would take my seat in council as another member"; and, in that point, at least, waive the claims of episcopacy. . . .

Not satisfied, the southern Virginia preachers met under O'Kelly's leadership at Mecklenburg and resolved "to send no member to Council."[17] The second meeting of the council did not stem the tide of opposition. O'Kelly had, in fact, rallied Coke to that side. Lee also played an important oppositional role.

On Coke's return to the United States in early 1791, Asbury discovered "the Doctor's sentiments, with regard to the council, quite changed." Sizing up the situation, Asbury continued, "James O'Kelly's letters had reached London. I felt perfectly calm, and acceded to a general conference, for the sake of peace." So at the Petersburg Conference of that year, as Asbury reported, "the affair of the council was suspended until a general conference."

A general conference had been proposed by both Lee and O'Kelly but dismissed when the plan for a council was initially introduced. Lee reiterated that proposal on July 7, 1791, submitting the matter in writing, as also may have Coke in May, just prior to his return to England. "This day," recorded Asbury, "brother Lee put a paper into my hand, proposing the election of not less than two, nor more than four preachers from each conference, to form a general conference in Baltimore, in December, 1792, to be continued annually." Lee's conception of delegation or representation would have to wait its time, and his notion of an annual meeting did not prevail. But he, O'Kelly, and Coke had their way. The first General Conference met in Baltimore November 1–15, 1792. When it gathered, the council proposal was given a very unceremonious burial. "For soon after we met together," Lee reported, "the *bishops* and the preachers in general, shewed a disposition to drop the *council*, and all things belonging there. And the bishops requested that the name of the *council* might not be mentioned in the conference again."[18]

An Issue over Which to Divide and Conquer

The second day of General Conference, O'Kelly placed a motion giving preachers who thought themselves "injured" by the bishop's appointment the "liberty to appeal to the conference" and the right, if the appeal was sustained, to another appointment.

Unfortunately, the "long" debate that followed was not minuted. Lee indicated that "the arguments for and against the proposal were weighty, and handled in a masterly manner." He continued: "There never had been a subject before us that so fully called forth all the strength of the preachers. A large majority of them appeared at first to be in favour of the motion."[19] Ware concurred, "Had Mr. O'Kelly's proposition been differently managed it might possibly have been carried. For myself at first I did not see any thing very objectionable in it."[20]

The motion, and doubtless much of the affirmative argument, self-servingly enunciated in O'Kelly's account of the event (*MEA*, 1792*a*), made appeal to what we would now term the language or ideology of republicanism—the rhetoric of the American Revolution and the early American republic. Republicanism held and O'Kelly preached a radical Whiggery that bifurcated social reality into a people with real but fragile rights, on the one hand, and hostile, "kingly" authority whose natural tendency was to tyranny and usurpation of rights, on the other. The liberties of the people, if they were to be preserved, demanded collective resolve on the part of the people—a unity founded in virtue, watchful monitoring of authority, forceful response against authority's inducements, and resistance to luxury. Liberty and virtue were easily corrupted and the people's resolve dissipated. Authority was ever encroaching. Freedom's hope demanded vigilance. Unless liberty were defended, the people would be reduced to slavery. So taught the history of republics and so O'Kelly discovered in the tyrannical behavior of Asbury and, to a lesser extent, of Coke.[21]

McKendree, who sided with O'Kelly, lodged with him at General Conference, but later reverted to the Methodist Episcopal Church (and even later was elected bishop), caught the republican resonances in a retrospective assessment: "Evil was determined against the Connection, justified by the supposition that the Bishop and his creatures were working the ruin of the Church to gratify their pride and ambition."[22]

When the motion failed,[23] O'Kelly walked out with a party of supporters to form a rival movement that took the republican banner into its name. James Meacham made this entry in his journal:

> [H]e has taken his fare well of conference. I think my poor heart scarcely ever felt the like before, I could not refrain from weeping deeply I hope God will still direct aright, & give us our dear old bro. & yokefellow back again—if he comes not back, I fear bad consequences will accrue.[24]

As Meacham's affection and fear suggest, the Republican Methodists had considerable appeal, some of it based on O'Kelly himself, some on what would be the movement's efforts to create a polity protective of liberty, grounded in Scripture alone, and explicitly antislavery. Enunciating such principles in his preaching and in his apologetical writings (*MEA*, 1792*a*), O'Kelly initially garnered considerable support, particularly in lower Virginia and upper North Carolina.

The O'Kelly Stamp on American Methodism

The Asbury–O'Kelly interaction produced or helped to produce the identity of the Methodist Episcopal Church. Through this contest and others, the church came into being, resolving some issues, pushing others off the table, setting priorities, developing sensitivities about certain questions, creating taboos and instinctive responses, and leaving some matters for later attention.[25]

What choices did Methodism make? How did its choices shape it? What got ruled in? ruled out? What future did it chart with respect to practices, policy, connection, structure, governance, fraternity? What did it learn about itself in this conflict? And how did the experience with O'Kelly affect later, or more gradual, forms of Methodism's self-discernment?

Connectionalism: Five Conflictual/Conflicted Gifts

Itinerancy

First and most immediately, the rejection of O'Kelly's motion and the association of it with schism committed the new church to a very rigid conception of itinerancy. His motion opened up some very basic issues. Perhaps some of the following were debated in 1792 but then shelved for a century or so: Do itinerancy, appointment, and connectionalism have fundamentally to do with *missio Dei*? Or are they primarily tactical? If about the ministry, the church, and the world, how might wisdom be gained about deployment and who could contribute to that wisdom? Might a circuit or a preacher have a useful word to add to that conversation among bishop and presiding elders? If so, how might appointments be effected and who might participate? Should appointments require some degree of consent or assent by preachers? By circuit? And if there must be some Wesley surrogate, some central agency for appointments, should that be bishop, committee, or conference? Should itinerancy remain national or become conference based and therefore regional?

The O'Kelly schism left something of a taboo on itinerancy. It was not to be opened for interpretation, exploration, reconsideration, or refinement. It became the defining Methodist tactic. And if one had problems or issues with itinerancy or one's fate within it, one expression of discontent or dissent remained: location. And so, into the ranks of the local preacher would fall many of Methodism's most able and effective ministers. And two decades later their plight would contribute to another schism.

The Episcopal Teaching Office

Many forces and factors shaped Methodist episcopacy. Voices other than O'Kelly's protested monarchical tendencies in Asbury and Coke. Still O'Kelly rallied those so concerned, and doubtless played an important part in moderating and checking such tendencies, in creating the instrumentality of General Conference as the central authority, and in lodging there constitutional and doctrinal prerogatives. Even in schism, O'Kelly continued this moderating function, his movement providing an alternative should Methodist episcopacy prove insufferable.

By his opposition and schism, O'Kelly forced or enticed Asbury into exercise of the teaching office, becoming thereby guarantor of Wesleyan and ecclesial integrity and the American counterpart of Mr. Wesley. In contending with O'Kelly, Asbury found that he could and must find ways to speak on behalf of the church. Asbury did so most consistently and effectively orally, on the road, in camp, in conference, by prayer, by counsel, by sermon, by admonition, by exhortation. Asbury's success—and he did, in fact, contain the O'Kelly schism—we infer from the journaled remarks of his compatriots. Asbury did teach orally. He also taught by guiding early Methodism's publication efforts, a remarkable gesture given the quite meager talent the movement possessed. So Asbury taught by:

- launching periodicals, such as the *Arminian Magazine* in 1789 and 1790 and *The Methodist Magazine* in 1797 and 1798;
- publishing his own journal therein in serial form and later by itself;[26]

- encouraging and directing the publishing of other Methodist materials—standard works, Wesley items, hymnbooks, *Disciplines*, and especially *Minutes*;[27]
- crafting a book on schism, a volume he intended as a balm for Methodism's wounds, initially that of Fluvanna but later and particularly that of James O'Kelly and titled graphically *The Causes, Evils, and Cures of Heart and Church Divisions, Extracted from the Works of Mr. Jeremiah Burroughs and Mr. Richard Baxter*;[28]
- annotating, with Coke, the *Discipline* (in 1798), *The Doctrines and Discipline of the Methodist Episcopal Church in America with Explanatory Notes, by Thomas Coke and Francis Asbury*,[29] instructing the Methodist faithful through and about Methodist belief and practice (*MEA*, 1798);
- endeavoring his own overview of the movement, in the *Extracts of Letters Containing Some Account of the Work of God Since the Year 1800*.[30]

Asbury also exercised the teaching office by encouraging the development of Methodist apologetics, being forced into this by O'Kelly's published critique of the church, *The Author's Apology for Protesting Against the Methodist Episcopal Government*.[31] He and Coke took on that task directly in 1798 with the production of *The Doctrines and Discipline of the Methodist Episcopal Church in America with Explanatory Notes*. For intellectual defenses Asbury also called upon his sometime traveling companion, Nicholas Snethen. Snethen produced two apologetic works against O'Kelly: *A Reply to an Apology for Protesting Against the Methodist Episcopal Government* and *An Answer to James O'Kelly's Vindication*.[32]

The Church

O'Kelly, the conflict that he occasioned, and Methodism's experience of his schism helped shape ecclesial policy, practice, and polity. In particular, Methodism's connectionalism emerged from the O'Kelly fights as a governance structure with unmistakable federal potentialities. Until the development of General Conference, the shape, style, feel, and procedure of Mr. Wesley's connectionalism remained fluid.

How would Methodism's connectional nature be expressed best in this new, dynamic republic? In a single Wesley surrogate? In some small group of trusted elders? In the fraternity, or brotherhood, of conference? Of the conferences collectively? Or less structurally, in the affectionate bonds between and among the preachers? Or more inclusively, in the revivalistic dynamisms of conference that pointed downward to the wells of Methodist corporate spirituality of quarterly meeting, society, and class? Should Methodism hang together in its revivalistic mission, through its intense affectionate "fraternal" or communal bonds, or by governance structures? Many forces, including its very growth, led the church to shape connectionalism politically, as polity. Gradually, policy pressures and legislative functions resolved Methodist connectionalism into a series of politically defined conferences—quarterly, annual, and general. And the church would spend the next century and a half determining who had voice and who had membership in these structures, structures that alone had say on matters Methodist. The political definition that O'Kelly helped give to conference gradually crowded out its spiritual and fraternal aspects, robbing its incredible theological and ecclesial substance but permitting it to function legislatively. The church experienced an immediate fraternal hurt when the beloved O'Kelly walked. It experienced a long-term incalculable fraternal and spiritual hurt in the political walk its connectionalism took.[33]

If O'Kelly shared in damaging Methodism's connectionalism, he took greater responsibility for distorting its catholicity. His protest and schism patterned conflict and division for at least a century. Another schism, that led by William Hammett in South Carolina, occurred at the same time as O'Kelly's. And every decade saw yet another split. The nineteenth century was for Methodism a century of division. Each had its just cause. But in subtle ways the O'Kelly fight created fault lines, sensitivities, taboos, and instinctive protective responses, particularly on episcopacy and presiding eldership. These reactive tendencies hampered Methodist flexibility in dealing with conflicts, and thereby made subsequent divisions easier. Again and again Methodists would, following O'Kelly, focus divisive issues around episcopacy and the exercise of the appointive office. And the experience with O'Kelly affected Methodism's capacity for creativity with other reformist impulses, permitting loyal Methodists to dismiss quickly any attacks on these tabooed issues. One wonders, for instance, whether the church would have been so inflexible with Richard Allen and the AME impulse, or later with the AMEZ, had it not been so badly and recently burned with O'Kelly. And what opportunities for unity in diversity might the MEC have pursued more vigorously with the UBC and EA if it had been less preoccupied with a singular understanding of office and structure? Methodism's catholicity, its ecumenical sensibilities, would have to wait for another day.

Scriptural Holiness

O'Kelly's outspokenness on certain principles doubtless also affected how the MEC could entertain them. How, for instance, would the church read Scripture? What appeal would it make to the biblical witness? To what extent would it seek to conform practice, polity, and policy to the word of Scripture? This was as live an issue in the early Republic as it is today. O'Kelly enunciated a very radical primitivist posture, an insistence our initial quotation indicates, that the church's life and structure should copy the Bible's. This primitivism in the O'Kelly impulse may well have inoculated the MEC against the Bible-only contagion that ran through American Protestantism in the early nineteenth century. Instructive in this regard was the appeal that Asbury and Coke made in their annotated *Discipline*, a publication designed to answer O'Kelly.[34] They were no primitivists; they employed all the elements of what we now term the "Quadrilateral" and put a high premium on Wesley, the longer Christian tradition, and the Bible as exegeted (*MEA*, 1798).

If O'Kelly's primitivism elicited a more nuanced hermeneutic and broader understanding of authority, what reactions might his fervent antislavery and republicanism have occasioned? What tendencies might such activism have encouraged with regard to holiness? Could it have influenced the tempering of enthusiasm for the doctrine of perfection? Might it have nuanced the church's notions of perfection? Could it have discouraged the structural, societal, and systemic understandings and encouraged more individual understandings?

Similarly, with regard to Wesley's reforming mandate, might the republicanism, the democratic spirit, and the commitment to antislavery have undercut the MEC's resolve? Might O'Kelly have drained off into his movement many of the most fervid Virginia and North Carolina opponents of slavery? And might that exodus have made it easier for the southern wing of the MEC to press for the compromises that seemingly came so relentlessly?

What about the implications of O'Kelly's commitments for the MEC's key doctrine, Arminianism? O'Kelly seemed to merge republicanism and Arminianism so that free will meant freedom, liberty, equality *for all*, for black as well as white, for slave as well as free. The MEC certainly continued to speak of liberty and freedom. But increasingly these came to be free response to the invitation, to liberty in preaching, and to equality before God. And when Arminianism was so spiritualized, was it surprising that the MEC came down where it did on who could preach, be ordained, and be admitted into full connection? Or that it had so much difficulty in deciding whether Africans and women could hear God's call to ministry?

Discipline

The evolution of discipline from an activity and set of practices into law and structure, from discipline to *Discipline*, came through many large and small genetic changes. O'Kelly's part in these developments was doubtless small. Nevertheless, as a reformer, he understood that response to God's grace did entail the disciplining of self, family, servants, neighbors, and church. Partially in defense against him, the MEC accelerated the processes that would accent *Discipline* as structure and procedure of governance. Efforts at governance through conference (fraternity) yielded to an experiment with council (aristocracy) and then to General Conference (representative clerical democracy). The gains in this "progress" have always seemed clear. Less obvious were the ways that accent on governance sidelined precious Wesleyan patterns, principles, and practices that would thereafter struggle for their proper forum.[35]

A Concluding Note

Conflict, schism, and threatened schism would continue to be generative of Methodist self-understanding and productive of significant changes in its polity. Reformers, like O'Kelly, sometimes remembered only as disruptive and self-aggrandizing irritants, have had both short-term and long-term impact. They have occasioned defensiveness, rigidity, and self-preoccupation. They have also led the church to a richer grasp of its Wesleyan heritage, prodded Methodism to change governance and decision making, shaped the movement's social ethic, and put ideas into play that the church would eventually embrace.

CHAPTER 3

General Conference: A Retrospective

Francis Asbury and Jesse Lee, two of the primary shapers and interpreters of American Methodism, termed the 1784 Christmas Conference a "general conference." They were wrong, technically and properly speaking, as John Tigert long ago showed. The Christmas Conference had the status of neither a General Conference nor an annual conference.[1] Instead, it was an irregularly called constitutional assembly. Not anticipated in the procedures that governed the American movement or authorized by John Wesley, it made no provision for its own continuance or succession. It gave itself no place in Methodist polity. Though irregular—a gambit on Asbury's part to alter the authority and governance relations among him and Coke and Wesley—it nevertheless set the pattern for regular General Conferences from 1792 and thereafter; for the succession of annual conferences between 1784 and 1792, which carried on the "general" work; and for one conference specially called by Wesley in 1787 to elect Richard Whatcoat bishop. It also set the pattern for similar bodies in the family of Wesleyan or Methodist denominations.[2]

The Template

"We were in great haste," said Asbury, "and did much business in a little time." In their hurry, the preachers at the Christmas Conference cared for some aspects of what a general conference would be and do, and rather neglected others. It spent most of its sessions amending Wesley's Large Minutes into the first *Discipline*, a task nicely captured in the title *Minutes of several Conversations between the Rev. Thomas Coke, LL.D., The Rev. Francis Asbury and others, At a Conference, Begun in Baltimore, in the State of Maryland, on Monday, the 27th of December, in the Year 1784. Composing a Form of Discipline for the Ministers, Preachers and Other Members of the Methodist Episcopal Church in America.*[3] This—its central, church-establishing task—the Christmas Conference performed but neglected to define in legislation. For this basic work, it made no provision in the *Discipline*. And in the absence of any conveyance of or limits on the amendment process, of any theory of governance, of any warrant—in Scripture, tradition, experience, or reason—for such periodic "constitutional" overhaul, the collectivity of Methodist annual conferences after 1784, of General Conferences from 1792, and of similar bodies in the larger Methodist/Wesleyan/EUB family have presumed that their work was to alter the *Discipline*. Taking this amendment prerogative for granted, Methodists seldom stop, or stopped, to reflect how very strange, how very presumptuous, how irregular it is to for church bodies that convene only periodically, sit for a short period, and typically find new faces in their midst to set about reconsidering the entirety of the movement's constitutive document.

A second task undertaken by the Christmas Conference, no less constitutive and precedent setting, was the selection of the church's episcopal leadership. Asbury had insisted that it be elective. So it became. So the *Discipline* mandated. The ordination, later consecration, of the bishop also became a conference event. Bishop Thomas Coke published his sermon on that occasion as *The Substance of a Sermon Preached at Baltimore, in the State of Maryland, before the General Conference of the Methodist Episcopal Church, . . . at the ordination of the Reverend Francis Asbury, to the office of a superintendent.*[4] Coke apparently did much of the preaching at this particular conference. And conferences thereafter featured the best of Methodist preaching—a third trait reenforced by, if not created by, the Christmas Conference. Preaching would be "appointed" both for and in the conference proper, but also for and throughout the larger community, in all pulpits opened to the conference and whenever the break of business made preaching possible. Conferences would be preaching festivals and, at least in the case of the General Conference of 1800, produced widescale revival. And Henry Boehm, son of one of the founders of The United Brethren Church and traveling associate of Asbury, reported extensively on the preaching at the General Conferences of 1808 and 1812, explaining "I need not give an account of the doings of the General Conference, which the reader can find in the printed journals."[5]

Pronouncement, Program, Precept, and Polity

Fourth, the Christmas Conference took some strong ethical stands. Of particular note, it prohibited "Ministers or Travelling-Preachers" from drinking "spirituous Liquors." And it passed even more courageous and extensive legislation against slavery, mandating that all Methodists, laity as well as preachers, emancipate their slaves; set timetables and ministerially administrated procedure for that process; and prescribed excommunication for refusal.[6] From this strong pronouncement the church would back away quickly and steadily. However, the action set an important socioeconomic-political precedent.

Fifth, the Christmas Conference sanctioned program for the new church. Specifically, it accepted the proposal from Coke and Asbury for an academy and apparently acquiesced in the naming of it for the two superintendents—Cokesbury College. It also launched the missionary enterprise, sending Freeborn Garrettson and James O. Cromwell to Nova Scotia.

Sixth, and no less vital than the 1784 gathering's crafting of the *Discipline* and of electing bishops, was its defining the faith. It did that explicitly by adopting Wesley's recension of the Anglican Articles of Religion and implicitly by understanding itself as bound to Wesleyan doctrine—Mr. Wesley's "Sons in the Gospel." Accordingly, it published with the *Discipline* as one volume Mr. Wesley's circular letter, "To Dr. Coke, Mr. Asbury, and our brethren in North America," the "Sunday Service," the Articles, and Wesley's "A Collection of Psalms and Hymns."[7]

Seventh, the Christmas Conference engaged itself, throughout its work, in the care of and regulation of ministry. Like Wesley's conferences and the American ones that preceded and long followed it, the 1784 event gathered only preachers. Using Wesley's record of conversations with his preachers—the Large Minutes—as its template, the American preachers inserted pieces of Anglican ministerial order and practice. They established American Methodism as episcopal, so naming it; accepted Wesley's modification of *The Book of Common Prayer* (*The Sunday Service*); and forced Methodist patterns of conference membership into awkward relation to Anglican orders and sacramental praxis. These preachers hadn't time, trained personnel, or constitutional wisdom for thinking fundamentally and philosophically about how to transform an autocratically run movement into a church governed properly according to scripturally based and culturally accepted norms, how a new church in a new nation should be ordered, or where the voice of the laity would be heard or their consent garnered. And it wasn't that the British hadn't been thinking for two centuries about the proper ordering of the church or that the American Methodists lacked for available models. They made provision for no British-like parliamentary role, no Scottish-like or New England-like ruling elders, and no Virginia-like governing lay vestries. Their oversight can certainly be understood, either because most of those gathered had been only the day before themselves laity (save for Thomas Coke, Richard Whatcoat, and Thomas Vasey), or because they thought of themselves as one with the people, or because the Methodist impulse had drawn and would continue to draw its leadership immediately out of the folk. For a variety of reasons, then, the Christmas Conference established the precedent for the church's practice of shaping polity and policy guided by little in the way of biblical, theological, or other warrant.

Finally, the positive side of the Christmas Conference's omission of the laity from the church's government was its preservation of the fraternal character of conference. Conferences, both annual and General, would be for the next century great, colorful gatherings of the brotherhood of preachers. Conferences resisted inclusion—of nonwhites, of local preachers, of women, of laity. Such intransigence would shake—indeed, split—the entire denomination, and do so repeatedly. The resistance would be energized, if not excused, by the deep feelings, even affection, that the preachers had for one another, and the range of emotions that their gatherings elicited. Conferences were fraternity.[8]

To 1792 and 1808

These several tasks—revising the *Discipline*, electing bishops, exhibiting preaching, making pronouncements, guiding program, defining the faith, ordering the ministry, gathering the brotherhood—proved more difficult in the years immediately after 1784. Then the annual conference served as The Methodist Episcopal Church's highest assembly but met in multiple sessions, three in 1785, seven in 1788, and eleven in 1789. Through the succession of conferences, any important decisions had to be carried, with attendees hoping for consensus. The chaos prompted Asbury's venture with a council, which was workable but unpopular because it was composed of his appointees, the presiding elders. Pressure from Lee and O'Kelly, effectively applied on Coke, led to the calling and convening of the first General Conference in Baltimore in 1792. Like the Christmas Conference, 1792 was open rather than delegated or representative, though limited to those in full connection. Also like the Christmas Conference, 1792 undertook its basic task, revising the *Discipline*, with less constitutional self-awareness than one might want. It took no minutes nor made a journal of its work.[9] Like 1784, it left its record in the *Discipline* itself, as Lee reported:

> At that general conference we revised the form of discipline, and made several alterations. The proceedings of that conference were not published in separate minutes, but the alterations were entered at their proper places, and published in the next edition of the form of discipline. . . .[10]

The reflex that went into such wholesale constitutional tinkering was well captured by a motion of 1804: "Brother G. Roberts moved, that this conference revise the Discipline of our Church, and that in revising it, it shall be read chapter by chapter, section by section, and paragraph by paragraph. Carried."[11]

The year 1792, then, established the institution. General Conference claimed for itself the legislative power for the church, established itself as a permanent body, and agreed to convene again in four years in a conference "to which, all the preachers in full connection were at liberty to come." That plenary definition of itself, its claim to a future, and its assumption of the authority to legislate for the church, specifically to revise the *Discipline*—a two-thirds majority being required for new actions or total rescission of existing legislation but only a majority to amend—provided what Asbury had sought through the council, namely, a politically competent and sovereign center to the movement. General Conferences of the United Brethren followed in 1815 and of the Evangelical Association in 1816, taking on themselves the range of tasks enumerated above. (The Evangelical Association adopted a quadrennial pattern only in 1839.)[12]

Limiting the Membership

The composition or membership of such bodies became problematic very quickly because of whom General Conferences excluded (all but the traveling elders in full connection, i.e., no African Americans, no other local preachers, no women, no laity) and because of whom they included (all the traveling elders in full connection). The latter surfaced first as an issue, a product of the church's growth. As the denomination expanded numerically and geographically, too many preachers were eligible to come and too many came from areas proximate to the General Conference site. That complaint acquired political force after the MEC General Conference of 1796 defined annual conferences geographically and preachers came to understand themselves as members of a specific conference. A restriction, in 1800, of General Conference membership to those in full connection who had traveled four years, helped with the problem of numbers but not with distribution. In 1804 it looked like this:

Philadelphia	41
Baltimore	29
Virginia	17
New York	12
South Carolina	5
New England	4
Western	4[13]

Lee, who had initiated the idea of a delegated or representative General Conference in the 1780s, opposed it in 1804, 1806, and 1808. But its time had come, and when reported out of committee in 1808 and from the pen of Joshua Soule, it was framed with a set of provisos, known as the Restrictive Rules, that effectively guarded essential elements of Wesleyan practice and belief from casual General Conference emendation while reasserting General Conference's plenary authority: "[T]he General Conference shall have full powers to make rules and regulations for our Church, under the following restrictions." The rules that established representation—one for each five members of an annual conference—and that protected "itinerant general superintendency" also changed the relation of bishop to General Conference, giving them presidential but not membership roles.

Enlarging the Membership

Delegation solved one horn of the membership dilemma, that of limiting the number of those constitutionally included and establishing proportionality. It did not resolve other issues of representation and membership, as for instance, that of:

- the free African Americans whose leadership was locked on the local level;
- the local preachers more generally into whose ranks, as the 1816 Committee of Ways and Means reported, had fallen many of the church's "experienced, trained and pious 'ornaments'," including persons who had served in General Conference;[14]
- laity who had great concern over the church's handling of slavery, finances, salaries, publications, and the like.

Several schisms resulted, each creating a new denomination with its own General Conference. African Americans found General Conference membership in The African Methodist Episcopal Church (1816) and The African Methodist Episcopal Zion Church (1820). The latter two bulleted issues above and the related representational issue of selection procedures for presiding elders (district superintendents) produced a powerful reform movement in the 1820s. Finding their concerns resisted or suppressed, the reformers founded in 1830 The Methodist Protestant Church (MPC), which dealt with the latter two issues by composing its delegated General Conference of equal numbers of ministers and lay*men*. It dealt with the first issue by qualifying membership with the word *white*.[15]

Expansion of membership in episcopal Methodism came several decades later and after the 1844 division over slavery. In 1856, the MEC authorized missionary bishops, and Liberia elected Francis Burns, the MEC's first black bishop, in 1858. He apparently did not attend the 1860 General Conference and died prior to that of 1864. The General Conference of that year authorized the bishops to organize missionary conferences among African Americans within the United States "where in their godly judgment the exigencies of the work may demand it."[16] The same conference denied representation in General Conference to these missionary conferences, an action rescinded, however, in 1868. That year the first two of the then eight black conferences, Delaware and Washington, sent clergy delegates to General Conference. The MEC General Conference would wait a long time before giving itself and these conferences black leadership, electing its first black bishops (not in missionary capacity), Robert E. Jones and Matthew W. Clair, in 1920.[17] It should be noted that the 1864 conference that established black annual conferences also created German annual conferences, the first of what would be a plethora of language conferences. Racial-ethnic-linguistic conferences would function thereafter both to separate and to empower.

The 1868 MEC also established a commission to explore union with the AMEZ and other bodies open to such overtures, legislation that eventuated, ironically, not in meaningful discourse between black and white "separated brethren" but between the two white episcopal churches. The Methodist Episcopal Church, South (MECS) dealt with the potential of black membership in its ranks and conferences by setting off its African American adherents into the Colored Methodist Episcopal Church (1870).

The General Conferences of the MECS authorized lay delegations in 1866; the MEC in 1868. The latter opened the question of whether women qualified as "laity" and might be delegates by allowing women to vote in the referendum necessitated by such a change in the Restrictive Rules. In 1888 MEC Conferences tested the male definition of laity by electing five women delegates to that year's General Conference. They were not seated and the issue boiled in the church press and assemblies for the next decade. Similar controversy stirred in other Methodist bodies. The MPC General Conference received women delegates in 1892 and seated them only after two days of debate and against the recommendation of its Credentials Committee. The United Brethren accepted lay delegates for the first time the next year, two women among them. Both bodies had earlier authorized the ordination of women, the MPC by 1892 and the UBC in 1889. The UBC seated its first female clergy delegate to General Conference in 1901. The MEC relented in 1900, authorizing election of women to General Conference and seating twenty-four as delegates, and recognizing thirty as reserves in 1904. Women were seated in the MECS in 1922. The churches in the Evangelical tradition—The Evangelical Church and the Evangelical Association—admitted laity in 1898 and 1907, but excluded women, even after their merger in 1922, and admitted them only on the eve of union with the United Brethren in 1946.[18]

Connectional Oversight

The first delegated General Conference, that of 1812, also experienced the novelty of William McKendree's episcopal address, a surprise for the elderly Asbury but not for others with whom the junior bishop had taken counsel. This conference saw as well much more consistent use of committees. The two initiatives would thereafter structure General Conference affairs. The 1816 conference referred the addresses of the recently deceased Asbury and his surviving colleague, McKendree, to a committee "whose duty it shall be to report to the conference the different subjects in them proper to be committed to district committees." That body reported out recommendations establishing six committees—episcopacy, book concern, ways and means, review and revision, safety, and temporal economy. It further proposed that two, episcopacy and review and revision, be "of nine members, one from each annual conference."[19] That precedent would be followed for important committees thereafter, a policy that made sense in a church of nine conferences. The shaping of committee agenda through the widescale submission of petitions developed slowly until the slavery debates of the 1840s, and then ballooned into the active overturing by the entire church to General Conference that continues to the present.

Oversight through committees, by a body meeting quadrennially and then only briefly, made sense, because the program of the church remained largely what it had been from the beginning and manageable through the conference apparatus derived from Wesley. And the members of General Conference were also the program—all of Methodism being simply one great missionary system and all the preachers being missionaries. The preachers who voted initiatives in General Conference simply saw to their implementation on their circuit, district, or conference. Actually, then, General Conference exercised a quadrennial review but delegated its management and oversight. It continued such patterns even as the church launched the *Methodist Quarterly Review* for clergy and *Christian Advocates* for the people, formed a Missionary Society to guide far-flung outreach, established colleges, and plunged into mass education through Sunday schools.

General Conferences would elect the specialists who operated such programs, in elections quite as competitive and with stakes as high as those for the episcopacy. Then General Conference made these specialists—book agents, *Advocate* editors, (executive) secretaries—accountable to specific annual conferences; and the latter, in turn, would further delegate day-to-day oversight to the preachers of the city from which that program operated. In addition, several of these program ventures, beginning with the Missionary Society, functioned as voluntary societies, attracted their own members, encouraged auxiliaries at every level of the church, developed patterns of accountability to their dues-paying constituents, and held annual meetings in conjunction with annual conferences.

As the church's agencies and institutions grew, this system of limited and delegated accountability and of designated giving proved more and more problematic. So, in 1872 in the MEC and 1874 in the MECS, the respective General Conferences put the agencies then functioning as voluntary societies, legally reconstituted as corporations, under their control, with boards as well as executive secretaries to be elected by General Conference.[20] This pattern continued until 1939, at which point the General Conference of reunited Methodism surrendered its power to elect the general secretaries to the agencies themselves and much of its power to approve their boards to the jurisdictions.

General Conferences experimented over the years with various mechanisms for coordinating the work of the several agencies, a challenge made more acute by General Conference's loss of direct control and by the reshuffling and combinations resultant from merger(s). Prior to the 1968 merger, two agencies in The Methodist Church provided oversight, achieved accountability, and reported directly to General Conference. These were the Co-ordinating Council and the Council on World Service and Finance. After the 1968 merger, and guided partially by EUB experience, the new church established two oversight agencies, the General Council on Ministries and the General Council on Finance and Administration.

Special General Conference commissions have a long history in the church. They have seemingly grown in importance since 1939 as *ad interim* bodies more directly responsive to General Conference than the agencies.

General Conference Accountability

General Conferences have "full legislative power over all matters distinctively connectional," but how does the connection check the exercise of such power? And who or what can assess or determine the constitutionality of General Conference's actions? That issue came to the fore in the General Conference of 1844 and in the division of episcopal Methodism. The conference raised a number of fundamental issues: What would the church do about slavery and particularly a slave-holding bishop? What force and continued applicability remained in its ethical commitments? What really was meant by itinerant general superintendency and what compromised it? What power did General Conference have over the bishops? Could it remove a bishop from office other than through prescribed judicial action? Or was the episcopacy, as Southerners argued, a coordinate branch of the church, not an office of or under the control of General Conference? Was General Conference to judge the constitutionality of its own acts?

On the final point, the MECS thought not, and made provision in 1854 for the bishops to challenge the constitutionality of a General Conference action. A challenged action then required a two-thirds majority.[21] The MEC, consistent with its understanding of General Conference supremacy, created its own Judiciary Committee in 1876, initially limiting its jurisdiction to appeals from annual conferences. In 1884, the MEC General Conference extended the Judicial Committee's authority to include "all records of Judicial Conference, appeals on points of law, and all proposed changes in the Ecclesiastical Code," but not the ability to arrest legislation.[22] The creation of a judicial council with such plenary and arresting power became a recurrent ultimatum of the MECS in the several decades of negotiation that produced the 1939 union.

Another instrumentality of accountability, not often noted as such, also derives from the 1844 General Conference. That conference and its heated, sometimes eloquent debates were the first to be covered in a *Daily Christian Advocate*, a responsibility exercised that year by the Western Book Concern (Cincinnati); the Book Concern was given the added responsibility of publishing the conference's *Journal*. Thereafter, both delegates and the reading Methodist public had a reliable, direct, immediate way of keeping tabs on General Conferences.

Jurisdictioned and Re-Jurisdictioned

The union in 1939, which brought together the MPC, MECS, and MEC, wrought more changes in the fabric of General Conference life than the institution of a judicial council. The most signal change and another ultimatum from the MECS was for the creation of a national conference structure—the Central Jurisdiction—that would separate the black membership of the MEC, much of it in the South, from the white churches, districts, and conferences of the MECS, and thereby also protect the (white) minority's interests and capacities for self-direction in the new church.[23] The new church featured six jurisdictions, five of them regional, the sixth an all–African American entity putting together the black membership from the MEC and MPC.

To the jurisdictions the 1939 plan assigned what had been key General Conference powers—in particular, the election of bishops, the determination of annual conference boundaries, the hearing of clergy appeals, and the approval of slates of directors to denominational boards. (The duty of electing the general secretaries of the boards, the Uniting Conference surrendered, as already noted, to the boards themselves.) In addition, the jurisdictional conferences were empowered to care for "evangelistic, educational, missionary and benevolent interests" and requisite to such endeavors to elaborate administrative machinery.

The 1939 plan also provided for equal lay and clergy representation on the several conference levels, with the delegates to jurisdictional and General Conferences being elected by lay and clergy annual conference members voting separately.[24]

Criticisms of jurisdictions, and especially of constitutionalized racism, surfaced when early versions of the plan were introduced in the 1920s, greeted the final version, and followed it after implementation. The 1956 General Conference approved provisions for transfer of churches and conferences between jurisdictions, but only with the 1968 merger of the Evangelical United Brethren and the Methodists was full dismantling of the Central Jurisdiction voted. Its abolition and the union of the once-German denomination (EUB) and The Methodist Church ended over two centuries of accommodating racial, ethnic, and linguistic interests in conference structures and thereby channeling and defining participation in General Conference and national affairs.

Almost immediately, racial, ethnic, and linguistic interests *re-jurisdictioned* themselves in caucus form, their needs hardly satisfied in the two ethnic-language conferences allowed to continue (Rio Grande and Oklahoma). The Black Methodists for Church Renewal (BMCR) formed in 1968, the Native American International Caucus (NAIC) in 1970, the National Fellowship of Asian American United Methodists (NFAAUM) in 1971, and Methodists Associated Representing the Caucus of Hispanic Americans (MARCHA) in 1971. Other caucuses formed soon thereafter, some from preexisting movements. And some caucus-like impulses found board expression. General Conference had defined away particularity in one form to find it reasserting itself in a new guise. Thereafter, caucuses would become important features of General Conference life. And the church would launch and fund new programs, like the Ethnic Minority Local Church, to sustain ministries once cared for through conference structures. Despite such efforts, the case for language conferences, specifically for Korean communities, would be heard again.

And in the period after 1968, delegates, board members, and bishops from central conferences came to play an increasingly active role in the affairs of General

Conference, to register unhappiness with the marginal role previously accorded them, and to put their needs and accomplishments to the fore.

Bookmaking: Is That It?

Over the years, the General Conference has altered, increased, reshaped, and delegated the duties inherited from the Christmas Conference—revising the *Discipline*, electing bishops, exhibiting preaching, making pronouncements, guiding program, defining the faith, ordering the ministry, ingathering the brotherhood. Much of its work, as always, has focused on its first task, revising the *Discipline*. There it would lodge its mandates and pronouncements, there prescribe program, there define the faith, there order the ministry, there prescribe how bishops would be elected and where they would be assigned and what would they do, there define who belonged to the brotherhood and, eventually, the sisterhood. Even the preaching would be shaped by what General Conference did within the *Discipline* in relation to courses of study and seminaries.

General Conferences could not squeeze all they did and wanted to convey into the *Discipline*. So they began to publish their *Journals* and the *Daily Christian Advocate* (1844). In the twentieth century, the Advance Edition of the *DCA*, with proposed legislation and significant petitions, would become important. And after 1968, General Conferences would pull together their social witness into *The Book of Resolutions*.

Also after 1968, General Conferences would increasingly restructure early portions of the *Discipline* so as to display "upfront" and to interpret Methodism's basic commitments and beliefs. Further, recent General Conferences have had to deal with and approve a new *Hymnal* and *Book of Worship*, tasks that, thankfully, come infrequently. But to making book there seems to be no end. Beginning in 1996, General Conference put its activities, speeches, reports, and actions on a Web page, that year's materials remaining as a resource until now—a rich cyber-book for all to read who would and could.

A Concluding Note

"We were in great haste," said Asbury, "and did much business in a little time." The worry implicit in Asbury's early report, at some point, might be worth hearing.

Perhaps, General Conferences and Methodism would benefit from less production, less preoccupation with machinery, less bookmaking, and more Christian conference, more reflective conversation, more effort to discern the work of God.

If conference is a distinctive Methodist way of being church, if conferring can be a means of grace, if holy conferencing can really be business, then perhaps Methodism needs to worry a little less about what is on the page and more about what is in the heart.

Connectionalism
and Ministry

CHAPTER 4

Itinerancy in Historical Perspective: "A Wandering Arminian Was My Father . . ."

"I am a travelling preacher of the Methodist persuasion, and have come in order to preach in this place." So Jesse Lee announced himself.[1] So Methodism introduced itself. So Methodism has understood itself—a movement led by wandering Arminians, traveling preachers.

> *Our grand plan*, in all its parts, leads to an *itinerant* ministry. Our bishops are *travelling* bishops. All the different orders that compose our conferences are employed in the *travelling line*; and our local preachers are, *in some degree*, travelling preachers. Every thing is kept moving as far as possible; and we will be bold to say, that, next to the grace of God, there is nothing *like this* for keeping the whole body alive from the center to the circumference, and for the continual extension of that circumference on every hand.[2]

As this explanation and exegesis of the *Discipline* by bishops Thomas Coke and Francis Asbury illustrates, American Methodists have not been bashful about itinerants and itinerancy. They have often taken itinerancy to be the most distinctive and distinguishing feature of the movement.[3]

The great, vital feature of the new church was its itinerant system. There had been itinerants before in the world's history, and missionaries of nearly every creed . . . ; but never before did a church destined to become great and powerful in the family of Christ establish as its main working force a body of men devoted to a perpetual pilgrimage, yet held strictly to the rules and discipline of ecclesiastical government.[4]

In itinerancy Methodists gloried; in it they believed. Some thought it providential, as Robert Paine insisted in the nineteenth century: "The *itinerant* system of preaching is of divine appointment, and unquestionably John Wesley, and his sons in the gospel, may justly claim in this respect to be in the *apostolic succession.*"[5] But so also proclaimed Wallace G. Smelter and E. Dale Dunlap more recently:

It is a signal evidence of divine providence that the instrument was at hand for the evangelizing of the moving frontier. This instrument was the Methodist Circuit System. . . .

The origin of the itinerant ministry in Methodism was incidental and providential. It certainly was not a premeditated and carefully projected design in the mind of John Wesley.[6]

Others less confident of itinerancy's divinity have been no less persuaded of its "uniqueness." Matthew Simpson took it to be "a peculiar feature of Methodistic economy." "It does not claim for its peculiar order a direct Divine sanction; and yet it does claim that it follows essentially the example of Christ and of his apostles; as no one of them, for any considerable time, remained in charge of a single congregation, or preached to the same people."[7] Others have insisted on its centrality to Methodism and key to the church's growth. So said James Porter: "There is no feature of our economy more highly prized among us than its *itinerancy.* It is believed by many that much of our extraordinary success in saving souls is attributable to this peculiarity of Wesleyanism, more than to any other one thing."[8] For Gerald Kennedy, it was "the rock on which we have built our connectional system."[9] Its foundational character was well summarized in *The Methodist Magazine* in 1843:

The grand feature by which the polity of the Methodist Episcopal Church is characterized; that feature to which the others are in a great degree subordinate; and that feature which constitutes the main difference between ourselves and other evangelical denominations, is *an itinerating ministry*. From this arrangement flows the necessity of episcopacy, of conferences, of the office of presiding elders; and hence is perpetuated the unity of the church itself.[10]

If the character, performance, and health of the church are tied to itinerancy as much as these citations would imply, what happens when itinerancy changes? What happens to the *church* when itinerancy changes? United Methodism is, after all, a long way from the days indicated in the first *Minutes* by the stationing orders:

New York	Thomas Rankin	⎱ to change in
Philadelphia	George Shadford	⎰ four months.[11]

Has the itinerancy transmuted itself into something else? Has it, for instance, become like the parish ministry of Wesley's day? Has Methodism lost that which distinguishes it? In answering such questions, we need to look at more than temporality and locality, though those will, in fact, be important considerations. Several contextual constellations gave itinerancy its initial coloration and remain important in understanding its appearance in successive periods:

- the social/cultural context within which Methodist ministry (itinerancy) found itself, including the leadership styles prevalent in other denominations and the society at large;
- the web of other Wesleyan practice (e.g., connection, appointment, superintendency) in its current expression, meaning, and operation;
- the leadership structure of the movement, and in particular the way functions and roles were differentiated and allocated on the local level;
- the rhythms, calendar, and geography of the movement.[12]

If we take only the last, we might move quickly to remark how a mobile office became stationary, how a national ministerium became local, and how an extraordinary office became ordinary. But that perhaps oversimplifies the story.

Itinerancy in Social Context

In Britain, George Whitefield and John Wesley's practice of itinerant preaching and Wesley's regularization of it into a precept for ministerial order broke with both custom and law. The established church functioned with offices graded like the chain of being, from national down to parish level, each geographically defined. The parish priest or curate was a communal figure, a leader whose whole career might well be exercised in one town or in one parish of a city and whose work was confined therein. Reinforcing that Medieval pattern, by Wesley's day, were the memories and experiences with Puritanism, attitudes codified in the so-called "Clarendon Code," which proscribed enthusiasm and set very narrow limits for non-Anglican or dissenting religious practice—limits that Wesley successfully defied but that nonetheless affected how both he and the society viewed what he was about. Recognizing its deviance from established patterns, Wesley termed the ministry of his itinerants "extraordinary," a designation he freighted theologically, as we shall see in a moment, but which had also ecclesiastic and social force. Itinerancy was quite irregular; it did not belong; it violated communal norms. So also it was in New England, as Whitefield's example proved. There, as in old England, the vernacular and itinerant style violated custom, elicited imitators, and unleashed new patterns of religious leadership and communication.[13]

Itinerancy has been frequently seen in old or New England perspective, an appropriate viewpoint given both Methodist origins and the terrific conflict into which Methodism plunged itself in the early nineteenth century when it penetrated Calvinist Congregationalist strongholds. By happenstance, our early Methodist historians—notably Jesse Lee and Nathan Bangs—played key roles in that conflict with Congregationalism, so rendered the historical record, and so viewed itinerancy, that is, as unique and to be contrasted with an essentially congregational norm. However, that perspective, though illuminating, may not be the most accurate or helpful portrayal of American reception of and reaction to Methodist itinerants. Early American Methodism was primarily a movement of the Chesapeake, Middle Colonies and upper South, not of the North.[14] In those contexts, itinerancy was a way of life, necessitated by widespread settlements, very few settled clergy, religious and linguistic diversity, and parishes or a sense of religious responsibility defined in square miles, not by village squares. Some of that itinerating was doubtless modeled on the grand itinerant, George Whitefield; but much emerged spontaneously as scattered settlements cried for religious service and the few clergy responded. So we see in the work of Charles Woodmason, the South Carolina Anglican itinerant.[15] Similar itinerating patterns among the Reformed, Lutherans, Presbyterians, Mennonites, Moravians, and other Pietist groups—undertaken often in response to desperate pleas from unled communities—produced the widespread religious ferment, organization, and excitement that we recognize as the Middle Atlantic phase of the Great Awakening.[16]

The earliest itinerancy among groups that now constitute United Methodism probably occurred in such spontaneous fashion among those communities that coalesced into the United Brethren. Philip William Otterbein and Martin Boehm both traveled to conduct services and meet the various religious needs of scattered Reformed and Mennonite communities. In addition, Boehm made use of the already established pattern of great meetings, which, like Methodist quarterly meetings and the later camp meetings, aggregated thinly settled believers into an assembly and met for several days for preaching.[17] Before British Methodism made its entry, before even the unappointed lay pioneers initiated Methodist preaching, itinerancy was an American and a German "Methodist" practice.

Thanks to Mr. Wesley, Methodists put into precept, pattern, and policy what for others had been only practice. And in reflecting on itinerancy, Methodists rightly refer to Wesley, for it was his program and not the existing but inchoate colonial practice that defined early American Methodism. Indeed, the earliest preachers show virtually no awareness of prior itinerancy, save that of Whitefield. So Wesley was the origin for its theory. And yet its prevalence in the colonies was not unimportant in the success that Methodist itinerancy enjoyed and the reception that it found. It was already ordinary and not extraordinary, customary and not abnormal—a practice if not a precept.

When we look at itinerancy in Chesapeake, rather than New England, perspective, we see that from the start Methodist ministry closely approximated existing cultural styles. In the decades and centuries after 1784, Methodist itinerancy continued to look remarkably like ministry in other communions and indeed like the leadership patterns exercised generally in American history. The former connection has been brilliantly traced by E. Brooks Holifield.[18] In each period of ministry, the Methodist itinerant closely resembled his or her Protestant counterpart. Itinerancy found some way of accommodating the remarkable changes in tenure, role, self-understanding, training, function, and status through which American ministry has evolved. That evolution also approximated significant stages in the leadership of American society: "booster" in the early nineteenth century, "cultured communal elite" in the latter nineteenth, "progressive" or "prophetic reformer" in the early twentieth century, "corporate manager" up through the 1950s, and, more recently, "medical-style professional."[19] Through these various metamorphoses, Methodists continued to speak of their ministry as itinerating. But with each adaptation, the meaning of itineration changed significantly.

The cultural adaptation of itinerancy has produced two dominant assessments, one valuing positively the consequent increase of freedom, democracy, inclusiveness, consultation, and lay prerogative,[20] and the other viewing the dramatic changes as having fundamentally violated Methodist principle. In adjudicating that debate we need to look at other indexes of Methodist change. We also should note, though we cannot explore the point fully here, that in the interaction with culture, Methodism contributed as well as received, shaped the culture as well as was shaped by it—a point suggestively elaborated by Nathan O. Hatch and a recurrent theme in Methodist treatment of itinerancy.[21] In particular, Methodist ministry resembled that of other Protestant leadership because other Protestants mimicked the Methodists. That was especially true in the nineteenth century and in the conquest of the frontier for which itinerancy proved the premier form of evangelization.[22]

Itinerancy in Wesleyan Context

Though Methodist ministry has resembled that of other communions more than Methodists have sometimes wanted to admit, itinerancy was nonetheless characteristically and unmistakably Wesleyan. Itinerants were initially, in both Britain and America, "extraordinary messengers"; persons gifted in the Spirit to preach scriptural Christianity; Wesley's sons in the gospel; chosen and directed by him and accountable to him; under appointment sent to a circuit and to travel that circuit; bound together with other such helpers into the connection and in recognition of Wesley's superintendence over them and the people called Methodist.[23] They were explicitly not ordinary ministers, not appointed to administer sacraments, not ordained to the priestly office, not parish-bound.[24] Their nature and tasks Wesley outlined in the Large Minutes:

> Q. 24 In what view must we and our *Helpers* be considered?
> A. Perhaps as Extraordinary Messengers (i.e. out of the ordinary way) designed 1. To provoke the regular Ministers to jealousy. 2. To supply their lack of service, toward those who are perishing for want of knowledge.
>
> Q. 25 What is the Office of an *Helper*?
> A. In the absence of a Minister, to feed and guide the flock: In particular,
> 1. To preach Morning and Evening . . .
> 2. To meet the Society and the Bands weekly . . .
> 3. To meet the Leaders weekly . . .[25]

Itinerancy, then, was defined by its relation to Wesley (the appointive power), through its purposes and over against parish ministry, but ostensibly within the Church of England. It was extraordinary.

The year 1784 changed itinerancy in essence, though not initially in manifestation. As an episcopal church, American Methodism was now to offer the ordinary ministrations—most notably the sacraments but with them those offices and functions that fall to presbyters and for which Methodists had previously and theoretically resorted to the parish church. Fittingly, the new church recognized its ministry with proper ecclesial titles—deacon, elder, and bishop (initially superintendent). The church also retained the Wesleyan procedures and terminology—the distinction between traveling and local preachers, admission on trial, conference membership—juxtaposing the ecclesial and the Wesleyan, the ordinary and the extraordinary, and leaving the integration of elder with traveling preacher and the relation of deacon to "on trial" to be worked out. As the next section will indicate, the meshing of those offices and functions would take some time, a process completed only as stations displaced circuits and Methodism made the station its norm.[26] Nevertheless, we need to underscore the obvious point, namely, that Wesleyan itinerancy had not been designed to bear the ordinary offices and serve the congregational needs that over two centuries it was increasingly to assume. (German Methodists, less reliant upon Wesley, and heirs to ecclesial principles from the Lutheran and Reformed traditions, seem to have been less troubled by this puzzle.[27] Their lack of commitment to itinerancy as a principle may have made such adjustments easier.[28])

Corresponding to changes in itinerancy were developments in appointment and connection; indeed, itinerancy at any point in time is intelligible only in relation to these other Wesleyan essentials. They, too, defined the "extraordinary" office and were gradually and subtly altered by the assumption of "ordinary" episcopal and ecclesial roles. The appointive power was one that itinerancy and itinerants knew well. Asbury summed up ministry under the appointive power in his 1813 Valedictory:

> [I]t is the traveling apostolic order and ministry that is found in our very constitution . . . ; and all are movable at the pleasure of the superintendent whenever he may find it necessary for the good of the cause.[29]

In accepting the call to itinerate, the prospective minister placed himself (and not until the mid-twentieth century, herself) at the disposal of the connection, to be sent where the bishop and those who shared in the bishop's appointive functions, the presiding elders and those in charge of circuits, determined. Self-sacrifice and obedience were requisite:

> When a man takes upon himself the obligations of a Methodist preacher he identifies himself with the system. The question is not, then, whether he will go to this or that appointment, but whether he will hereafter obey the voice of the Church, and go to such fields of labor as the judgment of its constituted authorities may determine. . . . This mode of making appointments is called by some *the tyranny* of the system. If so, it is a tyranny that each one voluntarily assumes, and with which he voluntarily remains.[30]

Methodist preachers knew their ministry and that of the connection to be determined by that appointive power. Complaints about the exercise of that power recur through our history. And virtually every political fracas and division has, at one level or another, challenged episcopal authority, some like the Republican Methodists, the Methodist Protestants, and the Free Methodists explicitly, others implicitly. The split in 1844 also turned on the nature and exercise of the appointive power (though the basic issue was slavery). The exercise and evolution of the episcopal office is a central part of the story of itinerancy, a point to which we will return briefly below.

In theory, then, bishops made appointments in the interest of the connection (though that fact was not always obvious to those sent or to the receiving charge). The connection, originally those literally in connection with Mr. Wesley, took social form in America in a hierarchy of conferences, each responsible, with the appointive authority, for the ministry of a given area. The most basic, though not the smallest, of these was the annual conference, which eventually stabilized itself as the Methodist counterpart to the state. In that conference, the traveling preachers held their membership. Conference became family, fraternity, and community for the preachers. The great intensity of this bond is well illustrated in Lee's account of his first, in 1782, a gathering of some thirty preachers:

> The union and brotherly love which I saw among the preachers, exceeded every thing I had ever seen before, and caused me to wish that I was worthy to have a place amongst them. When they took leave of each other, I observed that they embraced each other in their arms, and wept as though they never expected to meet again. Had the heathens been there, they might have well

said, 'see how the Christians love one another!' By reason of what I saw and heard during the four days that the conference sat, I found my heart truly humbled in the dust, and my desires greatly increased to love and serve God more perfectly than I had ever done before.[31]

Two aspects of this conference gathering deserve comment. First, the intense fraternal display defined a community, a body of preachers, who labored together to serve the connection. Lee entered a collective service that, as E. Dale Dunlap indicates, functioned as a covenant between the body of preachers and the Methodist societies, a covenant mediated by the appointing power.[32] Itinerants served, deliberated, and acted, as bishops Asbury and Coke explained, for "the good of the whole," with "an enlarged, apostolic spirit, which would endeavour, whatever might be the sacrifice, to make all things *tally*."[33] Preachers dramatized and experienced the corporate character of that sacrificial service in conference gatherings.

Second, as the above statement by Lee also indicates, conference was and remained through much of the nineteenth century a very intense fraternal experience. Much of its intensity derived from conference's inquiry into the character, gifts, beliefs, and religious experience of its members—those being received on trial and continued on trial and those under appointment. Methodists understood and conducted those processes as the exercise of discipline, understood themselves to be under discipline, understood itinerancy to be a disciplined life (and fittingly constituted themselves with a *Discipline*). That disciplined life and the disciplining of those who failed to live it—disciplining that employed trials as the last resort—gets frequent treatment in discussions of itinerancy. Here we would remark on its ordinary power, the way that the intense scrutiny produced fraternal (male) bonding, camaraderie, and family feeling. Initially conducted in camera, the review of character functioned to build close relations among the preachers and make conference a covenanted community.[34] James Mudge described it well:

> Two items occupy nearly all the space of the early minutes; one is the examination of character, and the other is the adjustment of the receipts. The marked thing about the former is the perfectly free, frank, fraternal comment and criticism offered on the young men as they severally come up for admission on trial or in full connection; and a very similar sort of remark was indulged in by the members regarding each other when the passage of character was in question.[35]

Intimacy and bonding came also from traveling together, a practice far more common than our image of the lonely itinerant would suggest, and undertaken routinely in the apprenticing of new itinerants, as the following account by William Burke indicates:

> In the fall, at the beginning of October, brother Lowe insisted that I should accompany him round New Hope circuit. Accordingly, I arranged my business so as to make the tour of six weeks. We went on together, preaching time about, till he was taken sick and returned home, and left me to complete the round.[36]

For a glimpse of the operation of this seminary of the road, note the following entry of Lee's from Tuesday, November 24, 1795:

> I rode to New-Milford, and held forth in the new meeting-house, on Rom.ii.6. I had but few to hear; . . . The young candidate rode with me a few miles after meeting, and was not satisfied with my inviting all to Christ, and persuading them to choose religion and turn to God. I asked him if he did not believe that God had decreed that some men should not be saved? He said he did. I then asked him if he did not believe that Christ opened a way, by his death, whereby all might possibly be saved? He said he did. Then I told him, according to what he said, Christ had opened the way whereby God's decrees might be broken, and wished him to try and clear up the contradiction: he did try, and tried it often, till he was quite confused—and so we parted.[37]

The bonds were cemented by such shared apprenticing experience, also by common adversity and a common wage, by the peculiar transitory relation they enjoyed with the Methodist people, by the equally peculiar continuing relation they enjoyed with the appointive power, by the stories they shared, by correspondence, and by the intense engagement with one another in conference.[38] Itinerants traveled a common road, both metaphorically and literally.[39]

Male bonding has negative as well as positive features. Fraternal feeling among the brethren doubtless explains, in some measure, the difficulty white preachers found in accepting into full membership their black "brethren," the necessity they found for separating out ministries to linguistic and ethnic groups into separate conferences, and later the great resistance they showed in recognizing the call to preach that women experienced.[40] In fact, women did preach and did itinerate, in both Wesley's England and Asbury's America,[41] but were not accorded until well into the twentieth century full standing in the "traveling" ministry.

Fraternity was vulnerable to the various ills that beset human community, including prejudice, shortsightedness, and self-interest. It proved especially vulnerable to aging, death, conflict, growth, novelty, and social change. Though a sense of "brotherhood" continues to this day—despite the radical pluralization of ministry, the admission of women into the ranks of the ordained, and the transformation of conference from a preacher's order into a body with roughly equal proportions of clergy and laity—conference has radically changed, and with it the Wesleyan context for ministry. Very early on the fraternity gathered to itself legislative and judicial functions, and around the mid-nineteenth century conference had become a political entity. Conference's political potentialities were especially sharpened by the conflicts around the reform movement that resulted in Methodist Protestantism and over slavery and abolition. Pressures for lay and female participation furthered that political development. In the early twentieth century, conference took on certain features of the modern corporation, as did the denomination as a whole. In the middle decades of the century, conferences increasingly behaved like professional societies, and like the American Medical Association or the American Bar Assocation (though on regional rather than national levels), concerned themselves with matters of professional status, credentialing, salary, authority, competence, and prerogative. The evolution of conference and the connectional principle affected and was affected by the evolution of itinerancy.

So also the evolution of the appointive power, of the episcopacy, affected and was affected by the changes in itinerancy. For instance, both episcopacy and itinerancy, once national in character, became gradually parochial offices. In theory and self-understanding, the bishops remained and remain itinerating general superintendents, but found themselves made first sectional and then, in the twentieth century, virtually provincial officers. The limitations put on episcopal horizons accelerated the collapse of itinerancy from a national to a conference ministry.[42]

The national character of early itinerancy was well illustrated by Thomas Ware of New Jersey. Converted in Mount Holly (ca. 1780), he became active in filling appointments on that circuit. Then, in 1783, Asbury sent him to Dover circuit as an assistant. Present at the Spring and Christmas conferences of 1784, he had served that year on Kent, eastern shore (Maryland). The years following found him on Salem, New Jersey (1785), Long Island (1786), Holston (1787), East New River (1788), Caswell, N.C. (1789), Wilmington, Delaware, (1791), and Staten Island (1792). The next year he became a presiding elder, an office he held until 1808, on

Susquehanna (1793), Albany (1794), Philadelphia (1796), Peninsula (1800), Philadelphia (1802), New Jersey (1803), and again Philadelphia districts. Supernumerary in 1809 and superannuated in 1810, he returned later for active work in Lancaster and Long Island.[43]

Asbury valued such national appointments and warned in his valedictory "against the growing evil of locality in bishops, elders, preachers, or Conferences."[44] Asbury's warning could not withstand the variety of forces that impelled the church toward confining itinerancy within conference. The sectional spirit of the land had much to do with this; the geographical stabilization of conferences played a role; marriages made itinerants more eager for shorter moves; and a delegated and elective General Conference put a premium on nurturing a conference constituency. The result was that a national ministerium became parochial. The regionalization of the ministry contributed, according to both nineteenth-century contemporaries and twentieth-century interpreters, to the sectional divide that led eventually to the Civil War.[45]

Leadership Structure

Itinerancy was defined by its place in the leadership structure of the movement, and in particular by the way ministerial functions and roles were differentiated and allocated on the local level. In the earliest years, the defining relationships were with the presiding elder, on the one side, and with the local pastor and class leader, on the other.

The presiding elder emerged in the late 1780s[46] as an extension of the appointive office with charge over the circuits gathered into a district. However, from the start and by Wesley's intention the eldership functioned ordinarily as well; initially, the few ordained as elders circulated to celebrate the sacraments.[47] In both their extraordinary and ordinary capacities, the presiding elders fulfilled or completed the local ministerial office.

That fulfillment and completion occurred most clearly and dramatically at quarterly meeting (quarterly conference). Those two-day dramas had become great religious festivals and intense revivalistic occasions well before 1784. At them (after the 1780s), and with the presiding elder "presiding," the circuit did its extraordinary business, including reckoning financial accounts; scrutinizing class leaders, stewards, exhorters, local preachers, and those who had begun to travel;

exercising discipline, including hearing appeals from class and society cases; overseeing "the spiritual and temporal business of the societies in his district"[48]; in short, exercising "within his own district, during the absence of the superintendents, all the powers invested in them for the government of our church."[49] Quarterly meetings performed ordinarily as well. They gathered large crowds, particularly for the third, in late summer, and offered the full range of religious services, including love feasts, preaching, the Lord's Supper and baptism or memorial services as appropriate.

This 1788 report by Robert Ayers was entirely typical, save for the presence of Asbury:

> Saturday, July 26th: We held a Quarterly Meeting, and I suppose there were not less than one thousand people there. I opened the Meeting with an exhortation, and Brother Conaway followed with another, and then Mr. Asbury preached from Revelation 3:20, and Brother Whatcoat followed with an exhortation, and then Brother Phoebus concluded. . . . Sunday, July 27th: We held a love feast early in the morning. At ten o'clock Brother Matthews began with an exhortation, and Brother Lurton and Brother Simmons followed. Then Mr. Asbury preached, and Brother Whatcoat concluded. Then the ordination of a Deacon and the administration of the Lord's Supper was performed. I tarried at the Widow Murphys.[50]

The point to underscore here is that at the quarterly meetings both the extraordinary (itinerant) and ordinary (sacramental) offices were completed or fulfilled by the presiding elder or, at least, under the presidency of the presiding elder. In the early nineteenth century, the church found a vehicle for that completion of ministry, namely, the camp meeting. Thereafter, presiding elders appointed quarterly meetings for camp meetings.

The itinerant looked to such occasions and depended on such occasions for a range of ministerial functions that he did not or could not perform as he made his two-week or four-week or six-week circuit. The camp meeting, as we well know, became a stable and popular aspect of Methodist ministry. So that dependence was not resisted; it was rather by design and by *Discipline* that dependence existed whether the itinerant in question was on trial or a deacon or an elder. Still, the presiding elder crowded the itinerant from the top, as it were.

That crowding lessened dramatically when the itinerants assumed stations. Then preachers, typically elders, routinely performed the offices, both ordinary and extraordinary, that had earlier awaited the quarterly meeting and the gathering of the circuits. They did so because they remained present through the week, and week to week, and were therefore present to deal with the congregation's various religious needs, ordinary and extraordinary. Bangs celebrated this development:

> Whatever may be said against this policy in other parts of our work, it is certain that its adoption in many portions of this country in the eastern and northern states has had a beneficial influence upon the interests of our Church. By this means the people have been able to meet the expense of sustaining the worship of God, and also to secure permanent congregations; and the preachers could more fully and effectually discharge *all* the duties of pastors, in overseeing the temporal and spiritual affairs of the Church, such as visiting from house to house, attending upon the sick, burying the dead, meeting the classes, and regulating sabbath school, tract, and missionary societies. And who will say that these things are not as important to the well-being of the Church, or the prosperity of true religion, as it is 'to preach so many sermons'?[51]

For the panoply of pastoral offices, stations did not need to wait for a presiding elder every quarter; they had an elder on site. For stations, quarterly meetings became occasions for the connection to intrude on congregational life and the congregation to honor its connection. Quarterly conference or charge conference remained, and remains, an important connectional event, but it no longer crowded, completed, or fulfilled the ministry as it had for circuits.

Similarly, itinerancy depended on the offices "below" it. In the earliest period, both the class leader and the local preacher functioned very much like the parson of Wesley's England or the parish minister in contemporary United Methodism. They served local ministerial needs, whether appointed to do such according to Disciplinary procedure, simply by default, or through community request. They often initiated and typically sustained the ministry on the local level.

Local preachers proved to be an immensely important cog in the Methodist machinery. A stable office in the received Wesleyan order, exercised under the traveling preacher's authority, ordained deacon by 1789, regulated by a distinct Disciplinary paragraph by 1796, and in 1812 made eligible for elder's orders,[52] the local ministry was a point of entry to itinerancy for some, a permanent local office for others and, perhaps most important, the station to which traveling preachers, unable or unwilling to itinerate, resorted. The latter category included some of the most able of the itinerants, many choosing not to travel and to leave the conference on marriage.⁵³ Asbury complained repeatedly that marriage ruined Methodist ministry: "Marriage is honourable in all—but to me it is a ceremony awful as death. Well may it be so, when I calculate we have lost the travelling labours of two hundred of the best men in America, or the world, by marriage and consequent location." Asbury's sentiments prevailed within the traveling ranks as this comment by Finley concerning Benjamin Lakin's 1797 marriage indicates:

> Such was the prejudice that existed in the Church, at that day, against married preachers, that it was almost out of the question for any man to continue in the work if he had a wife. They were not exactly obliged to take the Popish vow of celibacy, but it almost amounted to the same thing; and there being such a high example for single life, as exhibited in the cases of the bishops, if a preacher married he was looked upon almost as a heretic who had denied the faith. Besides, no provision was made for the wife, and she was regarded, on all hands, as an incumbrance.⁵⁴

For much of our history, the local ministry also outnumbered the traveling ministry three to one, according to Lee in 1799⁵⁵—850 local to 269 traveling, maintaining that proportion still in 1812, according to Bishop McKendree, and slipping to two to one by the 1830s.⁵⁶

The local ministry affected, and one might say, defined itinerancy. It did so by its sheer numbers. It did so, more important, by the fact that until the itinerants began to settle into stations, the local minister provided for congregational needs. A good illustration is provided by Mudge of his own kinsman, Enoch Mudge, who, after traveling with Lee and supervising Maine for six months in 1796, located at Orrington in 1799 "where he had married two years before."

> He remained there eighteen years. He became at once the teacher of the winter school (for a long time the only one in the place), he was the local pastor, whoever might be the circuit preacher, he administered the sacraments, solemnized marriages, and conducted funerals throughout the surrounding country, and was emphatically *the* man of the whole region, sent repeatedly to the Legislature at Boston, and looked up to as one of the fathers of the town, although still young, so that his name became a household word there for a generation following.⁵⁷

Essentially the same point can be made, and has been made by Norwood, on the relation of class leader to itinerant. When the traveling preacher really traveled, the community relied on class leaders for local ministerial needs. "The class leader was needed to perform those pastoral functions which are part of a balanced ministry. But when the preacher settled down in a parsonage as a stationed pastor, the class leader (and along with him the local preacher and exhorter) became, at least so it seemed, an unnecessary wheel."[58]

There were interesting ironies and real tensions in the relations between the itinerant and these local officers, as also between the itinerant and the presiding elder. The itinerant performed extraordinarily, to use Wesley's term, but possessed by the *Discipline* some authority for and oversight of the ordinary, pastoral duties. The local preacher, class leader, exhorter, and stewards performed ordinarily, but, of course, lacked full authority and conference membership. Not surprisingly, the church felt pressures for local preacher and lay participation in annual conference, pressures that played into the Reform movement and the emergence of Methodist Protestantism.

A similar set of ironies and tensions characterized the relation between the itinerant and presiding elder. The traveling preacher might be in charge, on both extraordinary and ordinary levels, but yielded to the presiding elder at quarterly meeting time, when the business of the circuit would be completed and many of the ordinary ecclesial rituals performed. This tension also vented itself politically in the debates over election of the presiding elders.

These tensions were not entirely resolved but they were reframed when the itinerant did settle. Then, the so-called traveling preacher could and did gather in and exercise the ordinary functions, offering those on a more regular basis than quarterly and in so doing preempting the roles previously played by local preacher and class leader. The settling into ordinary functions occurred at different rates in different places through the latter half of the nineteenth century and early twentieth century. So Methodist ministry reconfigured itself and reimaged itself in terms of the new set of "ordinary" parish duties. But it continued to be defined by its place in the leadership structure of the movement, and in particular by the way ministerial functions and roles were differentiated and allocated on the local level. It simply had to do with the new structures that emerged during that period and the roles played by both men and women in the Sunday school, missionary society, temperance organization, and the various congregational offices.

The "location" of the itinerant raised questions then and it raises questions now about the extraordinary purposes for which Wesley intended the office. To understand that, we need to conclude with a few statements concerning the temporal and spatial changes in itinerancy.

The Rhythms, Calendar, and Geography of Itinerancy

"All the Preachers to change at the end of 6 months," the *Minutes* stipulated in 1774, an expectation reiterated in 1794.[59] Quarterly changes had also been tried. The terms gradually lengthened.[60] What had been an extraordinary ministry—a regimen suited for young, unmarried, mobile, healthy men, to be deployed on a national basis and moved frequently—evolved slowly in ordinary directions. This evolution had something to do with the changing Methodist calendar, as quarterly, biannual, annual, biennial, triennial, quadrennial, and eventually variable terms became the norm. The length of terms and the debates on setting or lengthening thereof certainly focused the church's concerns about the change in its ministry.

The changes were indeed quite dramatic. United Methodist theological students and conference personnel now speak about parish ministry as *the* norm with no sense of the ambiguity and irony inherent in that self-description. The rhythms and geography of today's ministry differ radically from those of early American Methodism or of Wesley's England. Today's does indeed look much more like the ministry of the parish parson of Wesley's day than of his itinerants.

Yet before United Methodists fix on some aspect of change as the culprit—perhaps now on the required consultation—they should consider how much of the dramatic alterations was prefigured by the decisions made in 1784, how closely the evolution tracks that of other American ministry and indeed styles of secular leadership, how the changes in itinerancy cohere with those in the overall leadership structure.[61] Reformers often wish to turn back the clock and recover the vitalities of an earlier day—certainly a laudable and, in some instances, an effective ploy. The appeal to the past can indeed focus issues about the nature and purpose of the church and its ministry. Before we fix on itinerancy, or some aspect thereof, which should be returned to the style of Wesley or Asbury or some latter day, we should remind ourselves that the clock has run also on the several contexts within which itinerancy defines itself. American ministry has changed; the web of other Wesleyan practice has changed; the leadership structure of the movement has changed. Itinerancy really cannot be returned to an earlier day; at least, it cannot be returned to an earlier day without corresponding societal, ecclesial, and administrative reversals.

More needful than such hindsight is a compelling vision for the future. In that, the memory of our wandering Arminian fathers and mothers should figure. Memory, including the memory of our own tradition, constitutes an important source of Methodism's self-understanding, a point reinforced in the *Discipline*'s theological guidelines and its own appeal to history.[62] We do need to be reminded of our forebears' visions *and* their perplexities. That can be a stimulus for today's ministry—but it will not suffice. History can inform but cannot provide the vision.

CHAPTER 5

Extension Ministries

Section X. Appointments to Extension Ministries
¶ 343. *Appointments Extending the Ministry of The United Methodist Church*—1. Elders in effective relationship may be appointed to serve in ministry settings beyond the local United Methodist Church in the witness and service of Christ's love and justice. Persons in these appointments remain within the itineracy and shall be accountable to the annual conference.[1]

With the notion of "extension ministries," General Conference has made some real progress in rethinking what it previously termed "appointments beyond the local church" and even earlier "special appointments." As it has found more apt ways of understanding such ministries, capturing their relation to the connection, and providing for more regular accountability, has General Conference exposed something of the poverty in its/our conception of the regular or non-extension ministry? To put the matter bluntly, one might ask, Has General Conference ascribed to those in special appointments what Wesley expected of himself and his itinerants and ascribed to those in regular appointments what he knew to be the task of the parish clergy of the Church of England? Was not extension the mandate of Wesley's itinerants? And was not "beyond the local church" where they were charged to position their work? And were not he and they special, providentially given, rescuers of a stagnant parish system?[2]

The Argument: Historical but Self-Interested

This chapter attempts three things. First, it explores the ambiguity of connectional appointments, showing the church's indecision—from the start—about how to handle tasks that lay beyond the normal circuit assignments. The chapter makes a case, second, for special appointments as indeed continuations of roles played by Mr. Wesley, for their exercise amid the appointments held by their "fellow" itinerants, for their connectionalism as genuinely conference in character, and for an appropriate oversight of such special appointments by annual conferences. All that changed in the latter part of the nineteenth century, as connectionalism increasingly restructured its operations in corporate boards and such centralization eroded the close ties between the special appointees and their conferences. Third, the chapter suggests that those of us in such "special" or "ABLC" (appointments beyond the local church) or "extension" ministries have responsibility for defining and enhancing our place within Methodist connectionalism—a responsibility we (or, I should say, I) have not been always very eager to exercise. Ought we not to be helping the church envision how our special assignments serve the connection as a whole? Underlying the presentation and each of these points is the conviction that our connectionalism is at risk and that we, United Methodists generally, and the church at large, have much to lose from selfish localism.

I should indicate (though I think it will be obvious) that I am an elder in full connection serving in extension ministry. I have enjoyed "special" appointment for four decades, as did my father. Since I began full-time ministry as a theological educator, I have never heard the "leaving the ministry" charge or joke at which those preparing to undertake extension roles are supposed to muster a smile. Nor did I find myself, as have a number of gifted students, turned down by a district or conference board of ordained ministry that judged my intended ministry not worthy of conference membership and ordination. But long tenure in theological education, several terms of service on conference boards in two conferences, and four series of speaking engagements with chaplains have made me painfully aware of how very marginal some in extension ministry are made to feel. Some United Methodist clergy, who ought to know better, have mentally collapsed real ministry into the local church. They have inverted John Wesley and, as some wag observed, made their parish the world. But I have gotten us ahead of the story.

The Ambiguity of Connectional Appointments

The *Minutes* for 1799 answered the standard query "Where are the Preachers stationed this year?" as follows:

> Jesse Lee travels with Bishop Asbury.
> Ezekiel Cooper, Editor and General Book Steward.

And for 1801 the answer was:

> Thomas Coke, by consent of the general conference is in Europe.
> Nicholas Snethen travels with Bishop Asbury.
> S. Hutchinson travels with Bishop Whatcoat.
> Ezekiel Cooper superintends the printing and book business.[3]

The provision for a traveling companion for the bishops was not new—nor was the arrangement for a book steward.[4] What *was* new was the organizational or conceptual treatment of the special appointment for Ezekiel Cooper. The *Minutes* that year made provision for what we now term "extension ministries" or appointments "beyond the local church," and visualized Cooper's appointment as not just "within the connectional structures" but also in relation to the connection as a whole. Specifically, the *Minutes* isolated Cooper, as book agent, along with the episcopal companions, as in service of the connection, though continuing in the traveling relation and serving under appointment. The 1799 and also the 1801 *Minutes* lodged that assignment first, right after the question and before the long list of other appointments. The next year, in 1802, the *Minutes* buried that connectional assignment in the list of appointments, listing it as one of the assignments on the Philadelphia District: "Ezekiel Cooper, superintendent of the Printing and Book-Concern."[5]

The following year, in 1803, the *Minutes* struggled with another special assignment that it nevertheless located within the conference listings. That year four persons carried the designation "missionary" after their names—Shadrach Bostwick on the Deerfield circuit of the Pittsburgh District, and Samuel Merwin, Elijah Chichester, and Laban Clark on the Montreal and St. John's and Soreille circuits of the Pittsfield District.[6]

By 1804, the church had arrived at something like the present arrangement. That year the *Minutes* listed Ezekiel Cooper and John Wilson as editor and general book steward and assistant, respectively, and listed them in New York along with the others assigned there—N. Snethen, M. Coate, and S. Merwin.[7] By 1809, the *Minutes* struck something of a compromise, listing the book agents in relation to the conference (New York) and above the districts. The *Minutes* privileged that special appointment above others. It listed the missionaries and the person traveling with the bishop (Henry Boehm for that year) in relation to a specific district, though without a circuit or station designation.[8]

Accountability

Very early, then, the church recognized: (1) it had duties, tasks, and roles of a connectional nature—in service to the entire connection—and that those needed staffing; (2) the exercise of such responsibilities belonged to or were appropriately undertaken by the traveling ministry; (3) the persons under such appointment had to be made accountable to the connection.

What was unclear then and has remained unclear to this day is how best, substantively and structurally, to care for that connectional accountability. How were and how are those of us in special appointments to exercise those ministries in truly connectional fashion? How should they and we be connected and where should we report—on the most general level, primarily to the annual conference, or most directly to local Methodism?

In 1799 and 1801, the church achieved and represented the accountability as to the connection as a whole by depicting Cooper with the bishops and those traveling with the bishops. In 1802, the *Minutes* displayed the accountability to the conference as primary by lodging Cooper immediately behind the presiding elder of the Philadelphia District. In 1804, the *Minutes* accented local accountability by visualizing the book agents as on the circuit. In 1809, the *Minutes* again isolated the placement of the agents, but in relation to the New York Conference as a whole.[9]

In each of these depictions, the church, we would have to concede, understood such persons in special appointments—the book agents, the missionaries, those traveling with the bishops—to be accountable at every Methodist level. But where would that primary accountability lie—to the general church, to the conference, to local Methodism? The church visualized the problem in the *Minutes*, but doubtless faced it more personally with those exercising these special roles. Publishing raised the issue of accountability and responsibility from the very start. The very first

American conference, that of 1773, had to contend with a book concern that in the person of Robert Williams had proceeded—by himself—to pursue denominational publication. The conference halted that presumption, decreeing:

> None of the preachers in America to re-print any of Mr. Wesley's books, without his authority (when it can be gotten) and the consent of the brethren. . . . Robert Williams to sell the books he has already printed, but to print no more, unless under the above restrictions.[10]

Where would the primary accountability be lodged? Early Methodism struggled to achieve a multilayered accountability with respect to the Book Concern. Always the bishops, and especially Asbury, took a hand in its operations. So also did the short-lived Council and later General Conference. But such general oversight had, perforce, to be episodic and epistolary. Some local body was designated to work along with the book agent or book agents. And then, in 1796, General Conference[11] assigned oversight to the Philadelphia Conference, and that body delegated the responsibility to the presiding elders and elders of Philadelphia, a body of seven, in 1797.

The *Minutes* specified that new agency:

Quest. 14. *What regulations have been made in respect to the Printing-Business, and the publication of books?*

Ans. The Philadelphia conference, in whom the management of these affairs was invested by the general conference, and who have not time during their annual sittings to complete this business, have, by the advice and consent of Bishop Asbury, unanimously appointed the following persons to be a standing committee, viz.

Ezekiel Cooper, *Chairman*

Thomas Ware
John M'Claskey } Presiding Elders
Christopher Spry

William M'Lenahan
Richard Swain
Solomon Sharp } Elders
Charles Cavender

. . . [T]he general book-steward shall lay before the committee, all manuscripts, books, and pamphlets, which are designed for publication, except such as the general conference has authorized him to publish.[12]

When the book concern was moved to New York, the same provision applied. The New York Conference assumed oversight and "[v]oted that the stationed preachers in New York and Brooklyn be a committee on the Book Concern."[13] Thus the church set a pattern of conference oversight of special ventures. Missions, colleges, theological schools, hospitals, and a variety of other ventures would be handled similarly. Individual conferences, or several conferences together, would oversee efforts that served the connectional common good and would oversee those *specially* appointed to serve in these efforts.

Special Appointments: Heirs to Wesley

That American Methodism would struggle to find ways of structuring these connectional roles should come as no surprise. After all, the roles had inhered in an office that American Methodism had never fully replicated, namely, that of John Wesley. Although both Thomas Coke and Francis Asbury aspired to his mantle, the American conferences proved unwilling to countenance such benevolent autocracy. Wesley had personified the connection. He served as publisher (as well as author). He directed the mission of the movement. He served as its primary fundraiser. He directed the organizational life of Methodism. He constituted the faculty for the preachers, though delegating that role for lower schools to others. He was chaplain.

These were the roles that American Methodists gave "special" status over the course of the nineteenth century:

- publisher
- missionary and director of that cause
- fund-raiser for colleges
- secretary of Methodist and interdenominational Bible
- tract, Sunday school, and missionary societies
- faculty in Methodist schools
- chaplains (prison or army)

The "special appointments" in American Methodism really institutionalized and divided offices held by Wesley. So several points:

- Special appointments structured offices or roles that Wesley played as connectional.
- The century saw the gradual expansion of the number and character of these.
- The church increasingly struggled to find ways to centralize such offices.
- Methodists recognized these offices as essentially connective for Methodism as a whole.

Both the array of such offices and the continuing oversight played by conferences for the connection as a whole can be exhibited by the Philadelphia Conference. By 1862 that conference enjoyed the special responsibility of appointing and reviewing the character of the Corresponding Secretary of the Missionary Society (the nineteenth-century counterpart to general secretary), John P. Durbin. He was accountable to the North Philadelphia District. Three other persons joined him below the regular appointments: A. Manship, Agent of Philadelphia Conference Tract Society; S. Higgins, Sunday School Agent; and J.Y. Ashton, Agent of Home Mission and Sunday School Society. South Philadelphia listed two faculty members from Dickinson College. Reading, Easton, and Snow Hill Districts had none in such special connectional roles. Wilmington carried two faculty members of Wesleyan Female College.[14] By 1865 the conference listed more such appointments, the additions primarily serving as chaplains in the United States Army—one for North Philadelphia, six for South Philadelphia, one for Reading, three for Wilmington, one for Easton, and two for Snow Hill.[15] Four special appointments per district continued to be a common pattern, as also was their role, mainly to carry out and represent the work of the conference itself. For instance, by 1886 Northwest Philadelphia still carried four special appointments:

James Neill, Financial Agent of the Methodist Episcopal Church Hospital
    J.B. McCulough, Editor of the *Philadelphia Methodist*
    T.A. Fernley, Corresponding Secretary of the Philadelphia Sabbath Association
    E.I.D. Pepper, Editor of the *Christian Standard and Home*.[16]

By this point, as my other chapters in this volume indicate, Methodism had restructured and reincorporated its boards as corporate bodies accountable to and appointed by General Conference. A new kind of connectionalism eventually emerged out of these special appointments—a connectionalism defined by boards and agencies, anchored on the national level and establishing corporate power centers that would serve but also compete with General Conference and the episcopacy.

This new corporate structure, eventually but only gradually bureaucratized, had several implications for special appointments. In the first place, it necessitated ever more of them. Second, and perhaps more important, by centralizing and nationalizing denominational decision making, program development, and staff leadership, and by making accountability primarily to General Conference, the boards eviscerated the reporting and accountability that special appointments had had to annual conferences. The John Durbins of the twentieth century remained theoretically in "effective relation" to the annual conference, but that relation did not register the connectional value of the appointment as it once did. The connectional meaning of the "special" appointments—often clear intrinsically in what such persons did for Methodism and typically registered in some national fashion—lost its salience and visibility within the annual conference. And so ministers serving in circuits and stations gradually and naturally came to think of those taking special appointments as "leaving the ministry."

Conference Connectionalism

The loss of conference-level meaning to special appointments or extension ministries has something to do with the loss of the connectional and missional value to conference itself. In early American Methodism, conferences served as the primary agent of all that the movement attempted. Conference was the spiritual home of the itinerants, their class or band. Conference was also spiritually alive. Conferences featured testimony, relation of experiences, preaching, counsel, and prayer. Their spiritual vitality drew lay observers, and conferences often had a revivalistic quality. That quality Richard Whatcoat captured in entries for conferences over which he presided. First, for 1800:

> On the 1st of June we held a Conference at Duck Creek Cross Roads, in the state of Delaware. This was a glorious time; such a spirit of faith, prayer, and zeal, rested on the preachers and people, that I think it exceeded any thing of

the kind I ever saw before. O, the strong cries, groans, and agonies of the mourners! Enough to pierce the hardest heart; but when the Deliverer set their souls at liberty, their ecstasies of joy were inexpressibly great, so that the high praises of the Redeemer's name sounded through the town, until solemnity appeared on every countenance: the effect of which was, that on the Thursday following, one hundred and fifteen persons joined the society in that town, while the divine flame spread greatly through the adjacent societies.[17]

For an 1802 Virginia conference, he reported:

Our Conference began at Salem, March 1st, and closed the 4th. I ordained seven travelling, and five local preachers to the Deacon's office; it was thought that ten or twelve were converted during the sitting of our Conference. . . .[18]

And for a conference of 1804 in March at Edward Droomgoole's, he noted:

I ordained five travelling, and four local preachers to the Deacon's, and three to the Elder's office; Sabbath-day was a great day: after the love-feast the public service continued from 11 o'clock, until 9 at night, in the woods: it was thought twenty, if not thirty were converted.[19]

To facilitate their own revivalistic endeavor for a time, particularly in the Midwest, conferences actually appointed a camp meeting to sit concurrently during their sessions.

Conferences were revivalistic in themselves and clearly also in their outreach. The ministry was sent out from and returned a year later to conference to be sent again. Conferences expanded their circuits to encompass newly settled or unmissionized territory and then divided when growth made further effective strategizing and missionizing difficult. Methodism quite literally conferenced the frontier and conferenced the nation.[20] Ministry was missionary, and conference the agency, framework, and resource for mission. That is what Abel Stevens meant when he said, "Though American Methodism was many years without a distinct missionary organization, it was owing to the fact that its whole organization was essentially a missionary scheme. It was, in fine, the great Home Mission enterprise of the north American continent."[21]

Methodism was indeed a "missionary scheme" and conferences the working element of the scheme. Only as conferences and the church as a whole began to confront missionary situations that demanded more than elaboration of new circuits—as, for instance, the challenging work with the Wyandots or sending a person to work with the French in the Louisiana Purchase or commissioning evangelists for Liberia—did Methodism create a Missionary Society (and the women their counterpart).

But even those persons, if in full connection, remained accountable to conferences. And conferences exercised the supervisory, report-receiving, monitoring roles with great effectiveness through much of the nineteenth century and over the myriad of activities and institutions represented by special appointments. In particular, conferences oversaw Methodism's colleges and, later, her theological schools. They did so with visiting committees, through institutional reports, by close connection, with presence on boards, by sending students, and by episcopal appointment and oversight. Conferences also commanded a peculiar kind of oversight, a sinew of connectionalism, which made conference work as an agency of accountability and conference's special appointments as genuinely conferenced connectional endeavors. It was called the review of character. Today that is a routine, largely ritual gesture, with the district superintendents, saying with a straight face "nothing against the preachers on the Raleigh District." In early Methodism, each preacher's name was called individually and his character reviewed.

Early Methodism functioned like a series of classes—or at least a series of conferences, each the size of a class. In reviewing the character of the preachers, the conference did for its members what the class did for its. The review of character was a classlike, a covenant-discipleship-like exercise. Through the annual review, conferences exercised theological, ministerial, ethical, and familial accountability. And when they found deviance, they conducted inquiries and trials, meting out judgments as the case demanded. The process held Methodism's institutions accountable by holding those of its people in special relation accountable. To illustrate, Methodism worried from the start about theological education and whether it would serve Methodism's purposes well. Among its worries was the issue of theological accountability. In a remarkably insightful statement in 1872, William F. Warren noted a variety of checks on the then three Northern theological schools (Boston, Garrett, Drew). Key among them was the following: "At the Annual Conference examination of character, every professor—save one who chances to be a layman—is each year liable to arrest if even a rumor of heterodoxy is abroad against him." This was the fourth of Warren's seven points. Here is the list, and it spells out tight connectional webs binding extension ministry to the church and its various authority structures:

1. Each is officially placed under the direct supervision of the bishops of the Methodist Episcopal Church.
2. No professor can be appointed to any chair in either of the three institutions without the concurrence of the bishops.
3. In at least two of them no professor can take his chair until, in the presence of the Board of Trust, he have signed a solemn declaration, to the effect that so long as he occupies the same he will teach nothing inconsistent with the doctrines and discipline of the Methodist Episcopal Church.
4. At the Annual Conference examination of character, every professor—save one who chances to be a layman—is each year liable to arrest if even a rumor of heterodoxy is abroad against him.
5. Each institution is inspected, and its pupils annually examined as to what they have been taught, by visitors delegated from adjacent annual conferences.
6. Each has ecclesiastical qualifications affecting the appointment of trustees.
7. Each is required to report to every General Conference.[22]

With the review of character, as well as through these various offices and activities oriented toward the life and work of those in extension roles, conference kept in touch with and in oversight of those in special appointments; and it was, in turn, enriched and informed by those extension ministries. So conferences kept as their own the various roles or offices that had belonged to Wesley.

Change

Over the course of the twentieth century, conference's structures of accountability have eroded or been delegated to boards of ordained ministry or committees or special offices. And until recently the special ministries have gravitated out of conference life. The forces making for both changes are many and diverse. They include:

- the sheer growth of annual conferences
- the admission (for other than Methodist Protestants) into conferences of laity in equal numbers
- professionalization of the ministry and particularly of special ministries
- the routinization of review of character

- further centralization of the program and initiative-taking activities of the denomination
- the jurisdictioning of the connection
- the drift of special appointments into accountability to other institutions
- the explosion of numbers of those in such special situations
- the apotheosis of the local church and the consequent gravitation toward understanding "real" ministry as within a local church and everything else as "beyond the local church"

Recent General Conferences indeed improved our understanding, and the last several have clearly worked at the relation of those in extension ministries to the conference. We still have not recovered structures and processes that once claimed special ministries, those once exercised by Wesley, as belonging to conference and as intimately connected with all ministry. And the reports, special meetings, and attendance at annual conference seem less as significant, substantive accountability than as acts of compliance.

Our Responsibility

To this point, those of us in extension or ABLC or special appointments seem to have waited for General Conference to discern and remedy the problem we present to the appointive process and for connectionalism. What if we were to exercise some responsibility in raising the issue and proposing solutions? Posing such a question seemed to me novel when I drafted the first version of this chapter several years ago. Having lectured to and heard from chaplains several times and having conferred with my colleague John Patton, I am aware now that he, Patricia Barrett (former assistant general secretary at the General Board of Higher Education and Ministry), and others have tried for a long time to put remedies on the church's agenda. So what follows draws on good counsel from others and poses some queries, intended to work at connection and connectivity. They move in different and not necessarily compatible directions and are not meant as a series or a set of closely related recommendations. Instead, each might be taken as a thought experiment.

Some proposals in query form:

1. Would the *Discipline* be more faithful to our Wesleyan heritage if it more consistently employed the new rubrics "appointments extending the ministry of The

United Methodist Church" or "appointments within or appointments beyond the connectional structures" and removed entirely the remaining, repeatedly used, and clearly congregationalist or parish notion of "appointments beyond the local church"? And might it help as well to expand the missional arena in which we conceived disciple making to be undertaken, and recognize that camping, campus, hospital, and social ministries bring persons to Jesus Christ? Or is our ministry really cramped into parish and our ecclesiology into congregation?

2. Should offices wholly within present conference structures and fully determined by episcopal appointment (as, for instance, the district superintendents or conference staff posts) be removed from the extension category and recognized as they should be—as genuinely itinerant appointments? Here, too, have some practical considerations confused us theologically and made us forget that we understand both district superintendent and bishop to be superintendents, and understand superintendency to be itinerant?

3. Might the notion of "location" be reclaimed to serve, as it once did, for persons who would remain elders but who elect a long-term extension career; whose job or vocation involves them regularly in Word, Sacrament, and Service (but not Order, or at least not ordering roles within the UMC); whose hospital, hospice, camp, prison, military, or educational setting regularly requires sacramental duties; and who therefore might function appropriately in their vocation and vocational setting as local elder? Should such persons, as they surrender their full connection status, be transferred to the district within which their ministry is exercised and to a charge conference in that district (and across conference lines, if appropriate, but making some allowance for mobility in military chaplain assignments)?

4. Should those of us, once ordained and securely established in what appears to be a long-term extension career

- be invited to or perhaps even obliged to waive guaranteed appointment;
- retain membership and voting privileges in the order and in clergy executive sessions;
- be available for service on conference committees and perhaps even eligible to stand for election to General Conference and to the episcopacy;
- but otherwise enjoy *voice but not vote* in annual conference?

5. Might either location or waiver of guaranteed appointment be combined in some fashion with creative use of both deacon's and elder's orders to sort out which functions and roles ought to be recognized as extensions of the church's witness, mission, and service and which as extensions of the church's Word, Sacrament, and Order and to determine the degree to which either requires full-connection conference membership? Might the church provide for easy transfer between deacon and elder tracks during the probationary or provisional period as persons find vocational clarity and find opportunities for permanent roles?

6. Should new conference structures be elaborated into which those within the connectional structure and those beyond the connectional structure would be appointed? And should new conference structures lump together all those who serve beyond the local church, that is, define structures negatively in relation to local church? Or should any new entities array kindred ministries, that is, campus ministries, chaplains, teachers, missionaries, administrators, social workers?

Might the structure of "central" connectional units again be utilized or some similar rubric generated?

- Might some appointments be made within annual conferences but in central districts—when the ministry in question has a translocal but not transconference range and has a strong nexus with district superintendents (hospital chaplains)? So, for example, the healthcare chaplains district?
- Might others be made within new central conferences—when the ministry has a transconference range and has a strong nexus with one or more bishops (military chaplains, theological educators)? So, for example, the seminary conference?
- And might truly national or transdenominational conferences (missionaries) be made within a central connectional unit? So the missionary conference and military chaplains conference?
- Might such central bodies have rights of representation in the higher regular conference structure (district within the annual conference; annual within a jurisdiction; national/transdenominational within the General Conference)?

7. Should the point of such central bodies be not the segregation of those in such special appointments but rather the creation of structures of mission and accountability appropriate to the range and character of their ministerial service? Indeed, might the primary utility of such conferences for persons in special appointments be to recreate something like the review of character, some accountability appropriate to the role, something that would give those conferences a covenant discipleship dimension? Might oversight, at least initially, be rendered by retired bishops or by retired leaders from the respective extension role?

8. And whatever might be done in relation to the above queries, should those of us currently included in the extension, ABLC, or special category, and however continued under any new rubrics be zealous in making the Disciplinary accountabilities and affiliations work?

- How might we relate to conference and bishop through our special ministries and in collaboration with others in ways that strengthen and further the church's mission?
- How might we organize, and around what goals—perhaps through our specialties on local, district, conference, or connectional level—so as to make the church more faithful?
- What might we do to bring reporting functions, forms, and questionnaires expressive of the distinctive ministries we exercise?
- What ought we offer a local church out of expertise? As part of our ordination?
- What can or might we do that would make Mr. Wesley proud of his true heirs?

CHAPTER 6

Organizing for Missions

> Methodism was essentially a missionary movement, domestic and foreign. It initiated not only the spirit, but the practical plans of modern English missions.... Though American Methodism was many years without a distinct missionary organization, it was owing to the fact that its whole organization was essentially a missionary scheme. It was, in fine, the great Home Mission enterprise of the north American continent, and its domestic work demanded all its resources of men and money.[1]

Abel Stevens, one of the "ablest" nineteenth-century observers of Methodism, saw clearly, perhaps as clearly as any, the importance of the Protestant missionary impulse. The centrality of missions on a national level within Methodism Stevens both discerned and effected. He had a role in the great celebration and capital campaign that gave title to the volume from which the above statement derived, *The Centenary of American Methodism: A Sketch of Its History, Theology, Practical System, and Success.* This event might be seen as American Methodism's coming of age (that is, the Northern church's—The Methodist Episcopal Church's—coming of age), a campaign hesitantly launched for $2 million, which elicited $5 million in pledges, and eventually produced $8.7 million in receipts. Much of this the church dedicated to education, specifically theological education; but a portion of the monies raised went to mission, including a new missions building.

On the place of missions in Methodist endeavor Stevens had earned the right to comment.[2] Indeed, he served as Methodism's official mid-century spokesperson. Its historian and apologist, he produced, in addition to the "Centenary" assessment, a four-volume history of American Methodism, a three-volume history of the larger Methodist movement, two single-volume overviews, two books on the introduction of Methodism into the eastern states, defenses of Methodist polity, and a history of Methodist women.[3] And Stevens took these longer views not from the isolation of an academic's study but from amid the turmoil and conflicts of a church torn asunder by sectionalism and slavery. He held, by the church's election in General Conference assembled, a series of the most vital and important editorships in the denomination—those of *Zion's Herald*, the New England Methodist paper; then of *The National Magazine*; and finally of *The Christian Advocate*, Northern episcopal Methodism's national paper. For his day, then, Stevens represented one of the most respected and discerning observers of the Methodist scene. He thought Methodism a missionary movement. Was it? If so, in what sense? And did it maintain its "missionary" aspect once it created is own distinct missionary organization and when some, if not all, of its missionary impulse was channeled through that structure?

Phases of Missionary Organization

To test Stevens's judgment one might focus on the national missionary agencies, denominational (male) and female, which sent out foreign missionaries.[4] The obvious alternative might seem to be the local congregation. However, in Methodism the intervening structure, today spoken of in colorless terms as "the middle judicatory," constituted the real engine, the drive wheel, for missions,[5] particularly in the nineteenth century. Methodists term that middle judicatory "conference," and recognize it as the basic body of the church.[6]

The focus on conference permits us to differentiate three phases of Methodist missions in the nineteenth century and to observe, from an interesting angle, how organizing for missions transformed the denomination. On the first, pre-1820, pre-missionary society phase, I will comment only briefly. In this period, before Methodist encounter with the Wyandots, Methodism as a whole, the system itself, was indeed missionary in the sense of which Stevens spoke. This "Wesleyan" phase followed the founder's precept in making the people the instrumentalities of their own evangelization. Leadership, including the preachers, emerged out of those missionized—poor whites, Germans, African Americans, and occasionally women (white and black). Methodism drew boundaries of class rather than race, language, or ethnicity. Turning the world upside down—denouncing worldliness, gentility, and especially slaveholding—Methodists embraced those not privileged by society. Methodists undertook missions in intrinsic, local, face-to-face, and inclusive fashion.

By contrast, Methodist missions became extrinsic, distant, mediated, and exclusive in what we will term the third, post-1872, national, proto-bureaucratic, centrally administered, accountable-to-General Conference phase. Then the church drew clear boundaries of race, language, gender, and ethnicity. Missions would not be left to those missionized but would be run by quasi professionals—paid national staff and recruited and trained missionaries. The church embraced the "other" in totally separate, non-interfacing systems—schemes of organization and order that put distance between people, even those who lived close together. The missionary system and the church extension system ran on their own tracks, distinct from those of regular conferences. The church designated bishops as "missionary" to distinguish them clearly (in power and prerogative) from regular bishops. Methodist preachers increasingly behaved less like evangelists called from the folk and more like clergy of established churches, as "pastors" to a parish.

Much of the chapter will concern the transition to the third phase from a second 1820–72, conference-based and conference-administered but centrally funded phase. With respect to the qualifiers—intrinsic-extrinsic, local-distant, face-to-face or mediated, inclusive-exclusive—Methodist missions during this middle period were clearly hybrid or in transition. If looked at nationally, missions might still seem intrinsic, local, direct, and inclusive. If looked at in relation to local Methodism, missions would seem extrinsic, removed, delegated, and exclusive. By focusing on the conference we can observe the transitions through which Methodism was going, transitions having essentially to do with missions but affecting every aspect of Methodist life. Evangelization might be undertaken close at hand or across international borders, but in either case the new communities would be socially segregated in some fashion from those mounting the mission. The church increasingly respected boundaries of race, language, and ethnicity, but on a local level and not always through formal recognition or legislation. Methodism put regular preachers into missions still, but on special assignment. It termed them "missionaries." The church still embraced "the other" within the society, the camp meeting, the quarterly meeting, but often in separate classes, in distant or distinct parts of the camp meeting (separate camp meetings for Cherokees or for Germans), through distinguishing treatment. Missions carried Methodism slowly and gradually toward an interesting, worldly or world-respecting set of distinctions, transforming in so doing the basic structure of the church, the annual conference.

Hence, when thinking about missions and the church, or missions in the church, one appropriately focuses on missions in relation to annual conference. It was initially the agent of missions. And it remained, and remains to this day, the basic structure of the church. By Stevens's time, however, the role of conference in missions was shifting. It had been both the locus and agent of missions. Then it became the primary collection agency for more distant missions. And eventually it became the cheerleader for missions at a distance, and primarily a conduit for monies raised and allocated locally. By focusing on conference, we can observe (1) the changes through which Methodism went in the effort to conduct missions; (2) how conferences themselves evolved in order to cope with the increased fiscal responsibility; (3) how perceptions of mission gradually altered as it became less a regular aspect of conference life and more a sponsored and specialized distant operation; (4) and the way Methodism's understanding of itself as missionary altered. Those transitions will be the exploration of this chapter.

Conferences as Missionary

Stevens rightly termed Methodism "essentially a missionary movement." Its conference-based structure had functioned in missionary fashion from the start. The effective beginnings of Methodism date from the calling of the first conferences, though, to be sure, spontaneous efforts to witness in a Methodist manner and carry on religious life in a Methodist spirit anticipated Wesley's sending of missionaries and their convening a conference. The first conference, bearing the quaint title "Minutes of Some Conversations Between the Preachers in Connection with the Rev. Mr. John Wesley," committed itself to obedience to Wesley, his rules, doctrine, and discipline; adherence to conference minutes (the British at this point); and acceptance of the Methodist pattern of sending or appointing the preachers to circuits.[7] Thereafter, American Methodism followed the missionary scheme established by Wesley.

In conference, the assistant, later the superintendent, and still later the bishop stationed the preachers for the following year. Conference and bishop sent out the ministers into mission. They returned a year later to conference, only to be sent out again. Missions constituted the business of Methodist ministry. Methodist structure also functioned on missionary behalf and in missionary fashion. In early American Methodism, conferences expanded their circuits to encompass newly settled or unmissionized territory and then divided when growth made further effective strategizing and missionizing difficult. Methodism quite literally "conferenced" the frontier and "conferenced" the nation.[8] Ministry was missionary, and conference the agency, framework, and resource for mission. That is what Stevens meant when he said:

> Though American Methodism was many years without a distinct missionary organization, it was owing to the fact that its whole organization was essentially a missionary scheme. It was, in fine, the great Home Mission enterprise of the north American continent, and its domestic work demanded all its resources of men and money.[9]

By the time Stevens wrote, conferences were less intrinsically the missionary "scheme" that they had been originally. Indeed, from 1819 Methodism recognized that

- special situations, as for instance, the evangelization of the Wyandot Native Americans, did not lend themselves to the standard formulas of conference expansion through enlarged circuits and revolving itinerants;
- some efforts at Christianization would require specialization and sustained commitment; and
- these special missionary settings required financial underwriting quite beyond the capacity of those receiving the evangelistic efforts or even of the sponsoring conference.

So the church founded a Missionary Society to provide "pecuniary aid . . . to enable the Conferences to carry on their missionary labours on a more extended plan" and "to extend the influence of divine truth, by means of those missionaries which may, from time to time, be approved and employed by the Bishops and Conferences for that purpose."[10] Around the same time, Methodist women, led by

Mary W. Mason, formed an auxiliary society to the Missionary Society of the Methodist Episcopal Church.[11] Conferences created their own auxiliaries; and both denominational and female auxiliaries were encouraged at local levels as well.[12]

National Society—Conference Activity

Through such auxiliaries and their collections; through the fees paid for membership in its own ranks, $2 annually, $20 for a life membership; and through special larger benefactions, the Missionary Society raised funds to support work among the Wyandots; among the French in Louisiana; in the territories, including those on the West Coast; in Liberia; and eventually throughout the world. The founding of the Society did not remove mission from conferences. Indeed, conferences still carried on all those missions, except those few beyond the bounds of existing conferences and abroad. Initially, the Missionary Society functioned to promote and finance, to raise and distribute funds. The Society had no staff, and neither selected nor sent missionaries; it did not even authorize its own disbursements. The bishops drew on its funds to support missionaries whom they appointed, as they appointed others within conferences.[13]

Conferences played the major role in supporting missions financially, but given how the monies were disbursed, conferences may well have been tempted to cut out the middleman and expend their own resources locally. Certainly, the Philadelphia Conference, a body to be focused upon for the rest of this chapter, initially hesitated to support the Missionary Society. It had good reason for hesitation

- competing as it did with New York for preeminence in denominational affairs;
- objecting to the way the Missionary Society was originally structured as a combined Bible and missionary endeavor;
- wanting to retain its and the denomination's affiliation with the American Bible Society; and
- preferring to conduct missions through its own "Mite" society.[14]

However, the Philadelphia resistance, doubtless unique, underscores the nature of the missionary enterprise. The "national" society was less a denominational agency than a New York-based and -controlled voluntary society. That was the pattern of denominational endeavor. Lacking any central apparatus for oversight, possessing itinerating bishops, gathering in General Conference only every four years, Methodism found it necessary—and had from the beginning of the century—to assign supervisory responsibility for agencies like the Book Concern and Missions to a specific annual conference. It must have been galling to Philadelphia, where the Book Concern had been originally sited, that New York had now gotten both missions and publications.

Given such competitive and differing conference stake in the ostensibly denominational endeavors, it is not surprisingly that the conference auxiliary societies functioned variously. And yet, it was their responsibility, as also auxiliaries at any level, to raise funds for the national society.

The monies flowed slowly. So, beginning in 1832, General Conference decreed that annual conferences were to monitor and report the monies raised for these "voluntary" commitments the church had made. Specifically, General Conference added a mandate in the Methodist manner, namely, by the addition of a question to those inherited from Wesley by which conferences conducted their business and made annual report. The *Discipline* then directed for the conduct "Of the Annual Conference" in a new Question 6: "What is the method wherein we usually proceed in the yearly conferences?" The following report and mandate were made: "What has been contributed for the support of missions, and what for the publication of Bibles, tracts, and Sunday schools books?"[15] Steadily from 1832, the church, and particularly the Missionary Society, sought to achieve greater stability and larger resources and a more effective outreach by drawing in and mandating support from the primary agency of Methodist life: the conferences.[16] We will chart that progress from 1832 to 1872, the point at which focus shifted again to the national scene.

The Philadelphia Conference

The Philadelphia Conference well serves our purpose as a test conference. As indicated earlier, it was initially reluctant in its support of the Missionary Society. As an East Coast and older conference with mostly settled circuits and stations, by the 1830s it no longer functioned in the older Methodist missionary fashion that Stevens outlined. By 1837 it had only six missionaries functioning within its bounds—in Southwark, Susquehannah, Fairchount, Easton, German, and Longneck missions.[17] At that point, it was a huge conference encompassing much of

Pennsylvania, all of Delaware, and the eastern shore of Virginia and Maryland.[18] The Philadelphia Conference was typical in generating initially modest support for the Missionary Society. For instance, in the first year after 1832, when General Conference had mandated the query "What has been contributed for the support of missions?" Philadelphia failed to report its contributions. Its receipts then grew gradually as follows:

1833	no report
1834	$2,129.60
1835	$2,838.13
1836	no report
1837	$2,892.65
1838	$3,417.70
1839	no report[19]
1840	$1,814.31*
1841	$3,000.00*
1842	no report
1843	$4,403.23
1844	$4,399.00
1845	$4,409.33[20]
1846	$6,062.51
1847	$5,584.97
1848	$6,374.98
1849	$6,050.51
1850	$7,994.73
1851	$9,121.32[21]
1852	$11,246.71
1853	$14,492.43
1854	$18,371.40
1855	$19,085.58[22]
1856	$19,438.52
1857	$25,863.62[23]

By the late 1850s Philadelphia led the denomination, exceeding all other conferences in the amount given. For 1834, Philadelphia raised $2,129 of the total

$35,700 raised nationally; for 1857, $25,863 of a total $268,890; for 1882, $46,500 of a total $751,469. By that point, Philadelphia produced the most for missions of any conference, being followed by New York and New York East, both over $32,000, and then Baltimore, at $26,500. The rest of the then ninety-nine conferences obviously trailed.[24] There were, as we shall discover, good reasons for Philadelphia's growing affirmation of missions.

Through the 1830s, the conference's efforts for missions remained primarily financial. And the money must not have flowed automatically. In 1839, the Philadelphia Conference listed as the first of six resolutions: "That it is the duty of every member of this conference to take up the conference collections in every principal congregation in his circuit and station. . . ."[25] To underscore that responsibility, the conference restructured its *Minutes* to make the efforts of individual preachers and charges toward that duty highly visible. Beginning with 1839, the conference arrayed its "Statistics of the Philadelphia Annual Conference" by individual charges (circuits and stations), including in table a line for "Missionary Money." The other lines for that year were Sabbath Scholars, Library Books, Teachers, Superintendents, and Local Preachers.[26] Since by that point the conference was printing the *Minutes*, the whole conference saw what individual preachers and churches did for missions. The display at once individualized or localized duty and registered the corporate or conference performance as an aggregate.

Persuading charges of the importance of such stewardship remained (and remains) one of conference's challenges. In 1842, Philadelphia "[r]esolved, That we heartily concur in the recommendation of the Missionary Board of New York, that all our members contribute one cent a week, towards the support of our Missions, and that all our ministers be requested to use their best efforts to get this plan into speedy operation."[27]

This effort to regularize benevolences went hand in glove with efforts to stabilize the entire financial machinery of the circuits and stations. At the same time, conference also adopted a fairly intricate "uniform and efficient plan, for the management of the temporal supplies of the preachers." It recommended working out apportionments for support of the ministry of the church and provided for collections *by class* and through *Class Collectors*.[28]

The next innovation in Philadelphia's encouragement of contributions was the establishment throughout the conference of specific times of collections for each of the benevolent objects. So in 1846, conference

Resolved, That the public collections ordered by this conference be taken at the following periods of the Conference Year, viz:

    1, The Bible collection in June; 2, the Sunday School Union in July; 3, the Educational, in October; 4, the Missionary in November, December and January; 5, the Conference and ten cent, in January, February and March.[29]

This became then a way of distributing the benevolences over the year, avoiding some competition between and among the causes, and providing for some regularity of funding. In 1848, for instance, Conference again set "Times of Collections":

1. The Bible collection in June; 2. the Sunday School Union in July, August or September; 3. The Education in October; 4. The Missionary in November or December; 5. The Philadelphia Conference in February and March; 6. The ten cent collection during the year at the discretion of each preacher.[30]

Missions from Conference: Special Appointments

Conferences so encompassed Methodist life and work that the church had no way of visualizing ministry other than in relation to conference, no other way of achieving supervision or oversight than through conferences, no way of assigning persons to outreach than from conference. In 1839, the Missionary Society had been incorporated in New York as a voluntary society with a self-perpetuating board.[31] In effect, however, it remained under the New York Conference. Its resident corresponding secretary, Nathan Bangs, was under appointment through New York,[32] and its ministerial board members were accountable to the denomination through that or some conference.

Missionaries were also under conference appointment—those obviously so who worked within the bounds of the conference but also those sent abroad. In 1847 the last item under Snow Hill District appointments in the Philadelphia Conference was "Buenos Ayres, D.D. Lore, Missionary."[33] Of course, the *Minutes* also listed the domestic missions, as, for instance, that year, a North Philadelphia Mission and a South Philadelphia Mission.[34] However, from this point on Philadelphia had a special attachment to the global missionary cause. One of its own was abroad under support from the Missionary Society. Envisioning missions overseas in this new way, the conference seemingly saw local efforts afresh as well. The next year it carried "German Mission" in the *Minutes* in brackets with Union under the South Philadelphia appointments. D.D. Lore continued in Buenos Aires.[35] By that point, the denomination had a paper dedicated to representation of missions alone, a *Missionary Advocate*, by 1848 in its fourth year. The same year, General Conference adopted and outlined in the *Discipline* a multipoint program to enhance missions—a program that would give much higher visibility to and involvement in missions for conferences.[36]

Dramatically changing Philadelphia's visualization of and investment in missions was an individual who rose to prominence within the conference, then to prominence in missions for the denomination, who put the new Disciplinary expectations into operation, and who, perhaps more than any other, transformed missions from a voluntary into a denominational endeavor.[37] This man was John Price Durbin.[38] Durbin served for a short time as chaplain of the United States Senate and also briefly as editor of the *Christian Advocate* (New York), the paper later edited by Stevens. In 1834, he became Principal (later President) of Dickinson College.[39] He transferred to the Philadelphia Conference in 1836 and eight times earned the conference's token of highest respect: election to represent it at General Conference. Five of those times he led the delegation (being elected first), the highest accolade that conferences then or now accord their own.[40] Philadelphia turned to him at every point. The 1845 Conference appointed or elected him to preach the Conference Sermon (for 1846). Also, he served as examiner in the Committees for Examination of the second-year exam on the "Bible as to ordinance or Sacraments."[41] Durbin also headed the Visiting Committee to Dickinson College in 1846 (the agency through which the church exercised its oversight of institutions).[42] In 1849, the bishop concurred in the conference's high estimation of J.P. Durbin and made him presiding elder of North Philadelphia.[43]

A year later, in 1850, Durbin succeeded Charles Pitman as secretary of the Missionary Society.[44] The Philadelphia *Minutes* registered that change with yet another special appointment: "Cor. Sec. of Miss. Soc. of M.E. Church" and carried the new national or denominational role under the North Philadelphia District appointments.[45] Thereafter Philadelphia had a very personal and direct connection to the mission enterprise. Durbin found a way of making missions personal for other conferences as well.

Organizing for Missions

Durbin clearly began his new work with a fresh vision of what conferences might be and do in missions and set out immediately to make conferences a more significant instrument in the missionary cause. His efforts, really endeavors to translate the *Discipline*'s mandates into conference operations, came apparently too late to catch the 1850 Philadelphia Conference. They drew responses elsewhere. For instance, the Troy Conference for 1850 passed an eight-point program, one apparently outlined in a communiqué from Durbin. It called for missionary organization at every level, annual missionary meetings, appointed collectors in "every class or neighborhood," reports and publication of the amounts collected—all muscled by the presiding elders who were to meet with the preachers and preach on missions.[46]

Other conferences passed very similar sets of programs for missions, often with some such introduction as "The Committee to whom was referred the papers from Dr. Durbin, Corresponding Secretary of the Missionary Society of the M.E. Church, presented their report, which was adopted. . . ."[47] Each conference seemed to configure the program to suit its own taste. But they typically included the above ingredients, often adding an item that Troy omitted and that must have been part of Durbin's program, namely, promotion within the conference of *The Missionary Advocate*.[48] The following year Philadelphia got on the program. It adopted a "Report of Committee on Missions," which called for a nine-point program: (1) monthly missionary prayer meetings or lectures in each church; (2) promotion of "our *Missionary Advocate*"; (3) annual missionary collections in November or December; (4) appointment of local missionary collectors; (5) publication annually of donors, collectors, and officers; (6) the establishment of a missionary sermon at conference and holding of the anniversary during conference; (7) use of the Sunday schools as "a powerful auxiliary to the Missionary cause"; (8) and their formal organization as auxiliaries where feasible; (9) and the creation of the category of life membership in the denominational society, a recommendation that the conference made to "the Parent Society."[49] By then, Philadelphia had further incentive for missionary enthusiasm. In addition to Durbin at the helm, it boasted two missionaries from its ranks: J. Calder, missionary to China, and D.D. Lore, missionary to Buenos Aires.[50]

In 1852, Durbin and the Missionary Society pushed a revised constitution through General Conference and the New York legislatures. Among other things, it provided for board rather than New York Conference responsibility for removal or replacement of the corresponding secretary between sessions of General Conference. It also allowed each annual conference a "vice-president from its own body."[51] Also by this point the Missionary Society had recognized the strategic value of moving its annual meetings out of New York and around the connection, Philadelphia already having been the first of the alternative anniversary meeting sites, followed by Boston and Buffalo.[52]

In 1856, Philadelphia passed a resolution of approbation for African colonization, calling for sermons and a collection "on or about the 4th of July." By this point as well, the conference, in establishing what was becoming an increasingly complex committee structure, gave missions unusual prominence by appointing as its members, "The Presiding Elders."[53] Complexity, order, priority, regimen, reporting, and numbers had become, by that point, important to Methodists. And conferences displayed their concerns with elaborate statistics and their values with money. By 1859, Philadelphia needed two committees to deal with missions, one with that title, another titled "Missionary Statistics." And, appropriately, conference projected for itself in the future a "Plan of Statistics for Annual Minutes," a thirteen-item report expected of each charge, including the "Missionary Report for Philadelphia Conference."[54] Thereafter, the *Minutes* showed very clearly just how each circuit and station performed on this and other points of religious vitality.

War, Race, Missions

As Methodism embroiled itself in the Civil War, missions competed for conference attention with matters of loyalty, support for the war effort, supplying of chaplains, stands on slavery, and the like. Philadelphia, though continuing its active support of missions, had to worry about its own slaveholding members and the care of its African American membership, free and slave. In 1861, by official action, it actively supported the war cause but initially not the "New Chapter," the stronger stand against slavery passed in 1860 by the denomination.[55] In 1864, "On motion of G. Quigley, the Presiding Elders were instructed not to employ as supplies, any person who is either disloyal or pro-slavery." That year's "Report on the State of the Country" reaffirmed previous stands, supported the war, issued a declaration of loyalty to the government and the Constitution, urged it as "a religious duty not to speak evil of ministers and magistrates," and denounced slavery as against the law of God and the principles of the Revolution.[56]

This same conference took another action that had to do with its own life and work, but had implications for missions. It passed a resolution calling for the bishops and presiding elders to organize "our colored people into district Circuits . . . with a view of furnishing them with ministerial service by preachers of their own color."[57] The General Conference of that year indeed authorized the establishment of mission conferences "for the benefit of our colored members and populations."[58] For "their benefit" Bishop Edmund Janes that year organized the African Americans—previously members, churches, circuits, and ministers of the Philadelphia Conference—into a new Delaware Conference.[59] While African Americans also requested this action, the segregation distinguished within the church a large population (black) that had long been the recipient of missions from another large population (white) that thought of itself as the supplier of missions. Some peoples would thereafter be the objects of missions, others the agents of missionary endeavor. And across the boundary between the two only the missionaries would cross. Conferences, white conferences at least, would need fewer missionaries in their midst, because the objects of mission would be given their own ecclesial organization. That had been permitted since 1856 for Germans and now from 1864 it would increasingly characterize Methodist activity with African Americans as well. Missions externalized certain peoples from Methodist society. It did so mostly at a distance. It could do so nearer at hand.

At the same time, perhaps not coincidentally, support for missions took on more of a social character. By 1862, the Philadelphia Conference, still an all-male and clergy-only affair, featured a whole set of "Anniversaries," annual meetings set to coincide with or follow conference, sometimes evening affairs—the Female Bible Society of the M.E. Church, the Philadelphia City Home Mission, the Young Men's Central Home Mission, the Philadelphia Conference Tract Society, and the Philadelphia Conference Missionary Society. Including laity as well as clergy, women as well as men, these affairs transacted necessary business, heard annual reports, and featured multiple addresses.[60] Speakers would often be the key denominational players in the cause of the day; for missions that would be the conference's own John Durbin.

"First Place in Our Affections"

At the end of the war, Northern Methodism geared up for larger conquests, a capital campaign among them. Clearly, missions also claimed the church's heart. That was made most visible, perhaps, by the new priority the Conference Missionary Society had in conference affairs. For starters, beginning in 1867, the conference published the *Annual Report of the Missionary Society* as part of its own *Minutes* and numbered it sequentially.[61] The *Minutes* also gave a new prominence to the society, listing its officers second after the stewards among the Conference bodies. Two years later it would stand first. The presiding elders still served as the standing committee on missions.

The 1867 Conference, meeting in Harrisburg, took such symbolic gestures seriously. It heard fraternal addresses from other denominations, notably the A.M.E. Zion Church, the Presbyterian Church, and the Lutheran Church, and introduced members of other denominations. It welcomed an invitation to "visit the rooms of the Young Men's Christian Association."[62] It received communiqués from the various denominational agencies and responded appropriately. It invited to sit with it the members of the Senate and House of Representatives then in session, and welcomed the reciprocal invitation to hold services in the House. It passed various resolutions, including one dispatched to the U.S. Senate and House.

Missions claimed further ritual gesture. J.B. McCullough "appointed at the last session to preach the Annual Missionary Sermon before the Conference" did so to "marked attention." That evening, the fifth night of its meeting, the conference celebrated the Missionary Society's anniversary, completely packing "with ladies and gentlemen" the Locust St. Methodist Episcopal Church (the site for the conference as a whole). After opening devotions and the treasurer's report, the Reverend S. Pancoast, of Upper Iowa, spoke. The society then sung "From Greenland's icy mountains." Next, the Reverend Dr. De Hass of the Metropolitan Church, Washington, spoke. After a hymn, Dr. Durbin spoke and "sketched the field of missions as it now exists and is occupied by the M.E. Church, in an elaborate and eloquent manner, for which he is so peculiar." The assemblage then nominated and elected the board of managers for the following year and were dismissed.[63]

The next day, "J.P. Durbin addressed the Conference in behalf of the Missionary Cause." Following his speech, the conference resolved "[t]hat the Missionary Cause in the future, as in the past, shall hold the first place in our affections, and that we hereby pledge ourselves to do our full part in paying any indebtedness that may be incurred by our Parent Board in maintaining our Missionary work at home and abroad." The Conference then passed a resolution thanking "Bro. McCullough" for his missionary sermon and requesting a copy for publication.[64]

Another ritual action focused attention away from leaders and the pulpit to every member. When passing the character of its members—the annual review by and through which the church assessed and guaranteed orthodoxy, effectiveness, integrity, and conformity—the conference did so with an interesting formula: "The names of all the effective Elders on this District were called, their collections reported, and their character passed."[65] This action, which connected approval of the individual's standing as a minister to his charge's collections, put into dramatic form what the *Minutes* and the *Report* accomplished by table and statistic. It identified the mission of every station and circuit with what it contributed. It made clear that holding "the Missionary Cause . . . first . . . in our affections" meant organizing Methodism around collections. Missions, once the activity of conferences, had become a benevolence.

A New Chapter

In 1868, Philadelphia recognized the half-century of Durbin's service by a motion "requesting J.P. Durbin, D.D., to preach a semi-centennial sermon at our next session, [which] was adopted by a rising vote."[66] It was a fitting tribute to Durbin. He had made Methodist missions effective by harnessing the main engine of Methodist life—the annual conference—to the missionary cause. By 1872, when Philadelphia elected him again and for the last time to General Conference, missions stood indeed first in conference affections. The *Minutes* registered its centrality with a new title page: *Minutes of the Eighty-Fifth Session of the Philadelphia Annual Conference of the Methodist Episcopal Church, Convened at St. Paul's M. E. Church, Philadelphia, Pa. Together with the Missionary Report.* The sessions brimmed with action about or statement concerning missions. Conferences had indeed responded to the overtures that Durbin had made in 1850.

At the General Conference that year, Durbin did not stand for reelection to the missionary helm. He took a timely departure. The same conference passed enabling legislation effectively transforming all its agencies from voluntary societies into denominational agencies. It did so by making their boards, not just the corresponding secretary, elective by and accountable to itself. From this action flowed the eventual nationalization and centralization of the denominational enterprise. Though the full development of bureaucracy would take some time, missions, like other denominational endeavors, would increasingly be run from the top. Durbin's career, and the Philadelphia Conference, over his nearly fifty-year association with it, illustrate an earlier chapter in the mission saga—one in which the church depended upon annual conferences to do its work.

Methodism had been no less a missionary movement in its initial penetration into American society. Indeed, in some respects in the earliest period, as Stevens intimated, Methodism possessed in its very structure, in its conference form, a missionary character. During the second phase, when Methodism found it necessary to mount missions to evangelize areas or peoples that/who could not be cared for with existing circuits and appointments, conference remained the main agent and context of missions. Durbin presided over yet another development: the harnessing of conference strength to raise funds for these special situations, at home and abroad. He also envisioned and encouraged the changes in conference life that would make such fund-raising possible. When he entered the Philadelphia Conference, it was a relatively informal body that had only recently begun to publish its own minutes. Its major responsibility was assessing the integrity of its members and those who sought to enter it. Durbin led Methodism and the conference into restructuring itself so as to garner resources for the missionary task. In so doing, wittingly or unwittingly, he facilitated and/or nurtured the subtle changes in Methodist life that would make Methodism less a mission than a body having missions. He can scarcely be blamed for the changes in Methodist missions that would make them engines of colonial or imperial conquest, the treating of the evangelized as an object to be converted rather than a brother or sister to be welcomed into the family. Yet those changes did come.

Throughout these transformations, did the Philadelphia Conference—indeed, did Methodism as a whole—remain "essentially a missionary movement, domestic and foreign"? Perhaps, but only if one concedes that both "missionary" and "movement" were effecting important changes on each other. Organizing for missions changed Methodism. And the missions that Methodism organized changed as well.

Self-Presentation—Ritually and Apologetically

CHAPTER 7

Connecting at the Table

In a Christmas-season Sunday school class a couple confesses how difficult the season has become now that their daughter has married a Muslim. Customs, seasonal observances, and family beliefs must be individually negotiated. They ask for the prayers and support of the class. The larger human family impinges on, indeed divides, their immediate family. A council of ministries meeting struggles over the priority to be given to witness, evangelism, and church growth over against new preschool ventures. Despite or without the oversight of the work area of education, classes proceed to order a wide variety of church school materials, including some from the Bristol Bible Curriculum. The liberal-evangelical division dramatizes itself locally. In her report to the council on ministries, the work area chairperson of church and society worries: Should all of the church's efforts in urban ministries be mediated through an interdenominational agency (which the church had itself brought into being)? Would it not be preferable for the church to undertake some missional efforts on its own? The agonies of ecumenism take local expression.[1]

United Methodism divides itself by ideals—ideals that aspire to unite it. Justice, evangelism, and ecumenism (to name but the obvious) each would pull Methodism together around itself. Each ideal, and the endeavor to press for it, however, produces not unity but divisions. And the competition on behalf of the three creates cacophony. How might the discord be lessened?[2]

Here we propose a metaphor for thinking about the three ideals and their relation—three meals eaten at early American camp meetings. The three, each requisite at Methodist camp meetings, were the *family meal* around the campfire or beside the tent, the Wesleyan *love feast*, and the *Lord's Supper* (Communion, Eucharist). Each meal had its own table, its own community, its own covenant, its own function, and if license be permitted, its own "grace." Methodists could not do without any. The camp meeting required the sustenance of each and all. Before exploring the three meals and the sustenance we might today draw from them or their counterparts, we need to essay the problem more fully.

The Search for Unity

To reiterate, United Methodism does find itself divided by ideals—ideals that aspire to unite it. Justice, evangelism, and ecumenism would each pull Methodism together around itself. Each offers itself as the priority in terms of which Methodism should conceive its mission. Each has its champions. And at every level of church life, the champions contest for position and priority on the denominational agenda. The contest is inescapable; it is built into the organizational fabric. Indeed, the church structures itself top to bottom with boards, agencies, committees, and caucuses committed to these ideals. The General Board of Church and Society, the General Commission on Religion and Race, the General Commission on the Status and Role of Women, and, to some extent, the General Board of Global Ministries pursue the various justice issues. The General Board of Discipleship, the General Board of Global Ministries, and the affiliate organization, Good News, raise the banner of missions, witness, and evangelism. The General Commission on Christian Unity and Interreligious Concerns labors for its ideals, with some encouragement from the Council of Bishops. Each agency and its counterparts on every level can be counted upon to press its agenda. But within each the other ideals emerge, spontaneously, reflexively, to vie for preeminence. The struggle for missional priorities in church, as in nation, has long since gone beyond the spirited give-and-take that warranted building these distinct ideals into United Methodist machinery.

In its most ferocious expression—in the caucuses—the struggle leads to anathemas. So, back in 1990, Good News pledged itself to the "DuPage Declaration," which delineated the lines of division and ideological rectitude sharply through affirmations and denials. Two of the latter bear citation:

> We deny that other religions are pathways to salvation, or that one can be in a right relationship with God apart from repentance and faith in Jesus Christ.
> We deny that the mission of the church is the self-development of exploited peoples or the political liberation of oppressed peoples.[3]

So on behalf of the one ideal of evangelism, the DuPage Declaration speaks to the other two ideals. And it speaks for evangelicals of many denominations, who conjointly drafted and subscribed it—an indication that the divisions within Methodism are replicated in other "mainline" denominations. It is worth underscoring this point, for both the above divisions and the search for a balm to heal them characterize much of the so-called mainline denominations. Indeed, one discerning observer has insisted that the divisions (primarily between evangelicals and liberals) that produce these contests have displaced "denominational" and "confessional" as the significant fault lines in American religious life.[4] Evangelicals from the several denominations feel themselves pulled together, as the DuPage Declaration certainly indicates. Liberals enjoy comity through ecumenical activities and working relationships between and among the professionals in the boards and agencies. Essentially the same fissures run through American politics and society. Not a denominationally fragmented Christianity but ideologically rent denominations constitute the present scandal of a divided Christianity (see chapter 13 and Conclusion).

It may seem naive to hope that the reimaging offered here would cure these divisions. A Methodist metaphor for thinking about the ideals? Surely a few words and a concept or two can do very little to heal divisions that run so deep. And yet several reasons suggest that a few words that evoke important Methodist commitments should not be inappropriate. First, it was Christ's wish for his disciples "that ye love one another, as I have loved you" and "that they all may be one; as thou, Father, *art* in me, and I in thee, that they also may be one in us: that the world may believe that thou has sent me" (John 15:12; 17:21, KJV, emphasis added).[5] Second, unity in mission was a central and motivating concern for John Wesley and early Methodism. Third, unity, and unity in mission, is a constitutional and constitutive mark of United Methodists, who, in the Preamble and initial articles to their Constitution, affirm:

> The church of Jesus Christ exists in and for the world, and its very dividedness is a hindrance to its mission in that world. . . . As part of the church universal, The United Methodist Church believes that the Lord of the church is calling Christians everywhere to strive toward unity; and therefore it will seek, and work for, unity at all levels of church life.[6]

Fourth, we live in Christ and in his church under an imperative to search for unity.

The Threefold Problem

Each of the three ideals—justice, evangelism, ecumenism—would present itself as the unitive solution. And even within the General Commission on Christian Unity and Interreligious Concerns (GCCUIC), all three ideals have standing as possible routes to the unity sought.[7]

Justice here will be construed as standing for the unity of the whole creation sought through struggles for "justice, peace and the integrity of creation,"[8] and also through the dialogue among and between representatives of the living religions. *Evangelism* will stand for the unity sought through missions and witness, bringing unity by the winning of souls to Christ; but it will also stand for the unity within the denomination between those who put such a premium on evangelism and those whose priorities lie elsewhere. This unity concerns the fissures between evangelicals and liberals with particular attention paid to the divisions those identities create within Methodism, but with obvious import for the lines drawn between those two parties in the larger arenas. *Ecumenism* will stand for the unity of Christians, the healing and renewing of Christ's body through the mutual recognition of ministers and members, inclusive eucharistic fellowship, and other forms of unity.[9]

The three "ideals" serve to heal as well as to divide and diagnose. As competing ideals, they divide the church. As a complex of assumptions and theory about reality, they diagnose the church's situation in the world. As a program, they offer the church a set of solutions. At every level in the connection, the three ideals divide, diagnose, and attempt to heal. What relief can be found for a troubled Zion?

Unifying the Schemes for Unity

The relation and priority among competing ideals of unity is an old and ongoing concern. *The Book of Discipline of The United Methodist Church*, as cited above, proceeds to specify several types of unity in which United Methodism should engage, specifically "world relationships with other Methodist churches," "councils of churches," and "plans of union." It does not indicate precisely how the church might hold those together or put them into priority order. Those tasks have been left to GCCUIC and the Council of Bishops, where discussion proceeds on both the kinds of unity just mentioned and those delineated by our three ideals. In such discussions, some hold out for a particular type of unity, for energetic participation in world Methodism, bilateral relations or COCU (Consultation on Church Union, the older and perhaps more familiar acronym for the unitive effort now named "Churches Uniting in Christ"),[10] for instance, to the relative neglect of the others. Other persons insist, as apparently do many within the World Council of Churches and the larger ecumenical arenas, on the interrelated character of the various kinds of unity.

In my own very limited observance of GCCUIC affairs, I have been troubled by such insistence on the seamless quality of ecumenism. I found myself especially perturbed by the enthusiasm lavished on interreligious dialogue, by the interjection of concern for other religions when items of Christian unity were on the table, and by the Commission's efforts to hold together the agendas represented in its name. How, I wondered, would this body really lead the denomination in reception of COCU, due for attention at the next General Conference, if its attention remains so fragmented? And with what theological rationale does the Commission insist on equating the unity of the body of Christ to dialogue with other religions? And why should Methodists, who know that if others' Christian hearts are as our hearts to give them our hands, extend ourselves in the same way for the Muslim or Hindu? I remained unconvinced that the justice or interreligious agenda, important though it might be, really belonged to Christian unity.

Something of a conversion occurred during a conference for United Methodist seminaries under the sponsorship of GCCUIC, the Division of Ordained Ministry in the General Board of Higher Education and Ministry, and the Association of United Methodist Theological Schools. What really brought a change of heart was Bishop

Roy Sano's insistence that global, interreligious, and ecumenical issues were preeminently local, that rural communities monitor the international economy on which their books balance, and that the opportunities and divisions represented abstractly by a term like *interreligious* manifest themselves immediately and concretely in neighbor and family.[11] During his talk, I made my own inventory and discovered, as I indicated through my opening remarks, that the various kinds of unity do impinge, as problem and opportunity, in the congregations. With that recognition came the realization that the several types of unity must be held together. They must be held together if the congregation is to be held together.

The Three Meals of Methodism

Conversions in both Scripture and the history of the church have often been portrayed as eye-opening experiences. Arminians, while holding grace to undergird the entire process, nevertheless believe that some eye opening precedes conversion even as conversion opens the eyes to the full realities of the human condition. My conversion proceeded in this fashion, impelled by the discovery (from my own research) of a Methodist way of seeing the problem, as also pulled by the realization that some such resolution needed to be found. From Methodist life came a metaphor that made it possible for me to see the several ideals as related and to understand the several kinds of unity as inseparable (though not indistinguishable or necessarily of the same importance). The metaphor derives from that staple of nineteenth-century Methodist life, the camp meeting.

As mentioned earlier, three meals sustained the camp meeting—each with its own table, community, covenant, function, and "grace." Many drew sustenance from all three meals; some partook of two; others would have been permitted only at one. The three meals were the Eucharist, or Communion; the love feast; and the family meal. Camp meetings required all three.

Communion could be said to have brought the camp meeting into being. The meetings had their spiritual origins in the large-scale sacramental meetings and quarterly conferences that characterized Pietism, and particularly Methodism, in the late eighteenth century.[12] When the stylized camp meeting eventually emerged, it continued to feature the Communion service. Also carried over into the camp meeting from the quarterly meeting were the love feasts—that Methodist borrowing from the Moravians that featured religious testimony sustained through a simple meal of bread and water. Camp meetings were camp meetings because families settled into rustic living on the grounds and therefore made provision for an extended stay. One such provision was eating, and the accounts of camp meetings recall the flickering campfires as well as the love feasts and Eucharists. Camp meetings, at least those under Methodist sponsorship, required all three. They could not exist without the family meal; they would have been unthinkable without the love feast; and they would have been incomplete without the Eucharist.

The family meals, though they divided the camp by kin (and race), were the most inclusive. The unregenerate spouse or child who came grumbling to the occasion and whose conversion highlighted the camp-meeting narratives would have been welcome—indeed, expected—at this meal. Here, as it were, the world partook. Slave families at such events rather especially suggest the worldly, even interreligious character of the camp meeting; for their Christianity reverberated with African pulses and their meals might well have included members whose religiosity remained essentially African. In the family meal, Methodism made table fellowship with the world, uneasily, perhaps testily (one can imagine a wife coaxing an unconverted husband or son over dinner with a firmness that made conviviality impossible and civility the only hope, or a teenager lampooning an exhorter who had made more wind than sense), but fellowship nonetheless.

Love feasts would have been the most exclusive, reserved theoretically for Methodist members of society in good standing. Disciplinary rules expressly limited the times that a nonmember might observe.[13] These were witnessing occasions. And here a society or circuit divided by some issue—not today's "liberal" and "conservative," but perhaps over the equally explosive matter of slavery—might find renewal and unity. For evangelicals, love feast returned to the basics—the recounting of conversion experiences and the simple meal, one uniting through the ear and memory, the other through taste, yet both employing the senses to renew and unite hearts. Love feasts dealt intradenominationally. Only Methodists need appear. The Presbyterian or Baptist at the camp meeting could simply sleep in. Methodists would be up at the crack of dawn for this simple meal, a fellowship well designed to hold the movement together.

Communion could be either inclusive or exclusive, depending on who celebrated. Baptists and Presbyterians, who often cooperated with Methodists in staging camp meetings, would reserve Communion to their own kind, a behavior paralleling Methodist policy on the love feast. Methodists, on the other hand, offered a more open Eucharist.[14] Then, as today, Methodist Communion would have welcomed the larger Christian family, "Ye that do truly and earnestly repent of your sins, and are in love and charity with your neighbors. . . ." Though non-Methodists did not always find this invitation compelling, here Methodists nevertheless made eucharistic fellowship possible.

In the three camp-meeting meals, then, early Methodists stylized the three ideals and the unity possible around each. At the common family table, all members justly received their fare, even though at other tables the family would divide. Justice, equity, and decency demanded that the whole family, even the worldly family, be fed. In the love feast, Methodists found unity through witness, a table designed for the household of faith. That spiritual intensity fed intradenominational unity and harmony. In Communion, Methodists offered a table that was open to the larger Christian family. The camp meeting required all three meals; it set three tables. Each and all provided sustenance for the camp meeting through which Methodism offered itself to and for the world.[15]

Three Covenants

Although we cannot and should not seek renewal by some repetition of the camp meeting and its meals, we might do well to reflect further on what those meals say about Methodist belief. I use the present rather than the past tense here to indicate that, in subjecting this metaphor to theological attention, we are proceeding beyond what early Methodism verbalized about the camp meetings. It is my conviction, elaborated in other chapters, that early Methodist theology was a theology of action, structure, and ritual. It needs to be exhibited in its fullness and respected for its texture. But then the action, structure, or ritual needs also to be analyzed if we would understand what Methodists believed. For their "thought," or theology, was imbedded in the forms by which Methodism lived. Of no event is this truer than the camp meeting. Methodists then and thereafter knew that it said something very important about themselves. But they found no good way of elaborating what it said, except by performing it. Their orthopraxy requires theological analysis from us if we would do them justice. Hence here we will speak of the meals and covenants as twentieth-century Methodist possibilities. This presumes, of course, that that earlier practice might be instructive to us today.

I do not intend to suggest that we ought to reinstitute the camp meeting, though it continues in many places even today. I *am* suggesting that we reclaim the three meals. The three tables call to mind three covenants. We Methodists do not typically formalize these covenants theologically in the manner of the Calvinists, or always give them the ritual expression they deserve. And yet, Methodists have a clear sense of each, and more important, an appreciation of the social bonds and realities that each entails, and at least some realization that they are brought into being and sustained by Christ.

Each table and meal depends upon its particular covenant. The family meal rests on the marriage covenant. The love feast, the missing rite in much of contemporary Methodism, belonged preeminently to the quarterly meeting and to the covenant that Methodists struck with one another. Its constitutional derivative today would be the charge or church conference, an organizational and business affair wanting the joy and intensity of the love feast and rendering the mutuality of that earlier covenant in fiscal and political terms. Communion, of course, derives from the church covenant, Christ's promise to be with us savingly in that meal.

Christ is not missing from the other meals, though the grace available differs. The family meal points to the creation, to God's sustaining of the natural order, to the divine ordering of the social and political realms, to the possibility that the common things of life—our meat and drink—might orient us to God's will. This prevenient grace works on and binds together those who do and those who do not call upon Christ's name. So we would understand the marriage covenant as holding together spouses who marry across religious boundaries (as well as families who share the same denomination) and pointing to the grace working throughout the human family.[16] Marriage is a gift to the human family. The grace that sustains it makes possible the good order of the world. It also makes possible a nurturing family life that redounds directly to the church. Hence our preference for a religious rather than civil marriage and for the church's blessing of the bonds that the couple accepts. But we do not typically limit the ceremony to believers and therefore do accept that the covenant thus created belongs to God's larger family. This covenant points especially to God the Father, the Lord of creation.

The love feast points particularly to the Spirit, at work in the Methodist faithful to make witness possible, to unite and renew, and give life to the church. In early Methodism, the love feast was routinely celebrated at quarterly conferences and quarterly conferences held in connection with camp meetings. Then the circuit gathered in witness to the commitment that held it together, to a peculiar covenant struck between a four-week road of preaching stops and a preacher, to connection that these people had made with one another. These powerful gatherings and experiences gave their testimony to the work of the Spirit with bodily expressions and sobbing and shouting. For such self-disclosures, love feasts needed intimacy and confidentiality. They also established intimacy and confidentiality; and they functioned when limited to those who had chosen to travel the Methodist road. So their sanctifying grace was limited to those justified. It is this grace that seems so missing in Methodism. The grace wanted to heal the chasm that divides evangelical and liberal, wanted to call Methodists thus united to that higher road of Christian perfection that has been our peculiar testimony, and wanted to give vibrance and spirit to our cause.

Communion, on the other hand, Methodists understood, and understand, as a saving ordinance. In it, Christ is available to those who would orient their lives to receive him. It points to him and joins in covenant all those who call upon his name. Of the meals celebrated at camp meetings, the Holy Meal has been the most fully and faithfully sustained in modern Methodism. Indeed, through the ecumenical liturgical renewal that has shaped our new rites, we have added eucharistic riches to the treasures that we, through Wesley, had derived from the Anglican tradition. Both old and new rites, because they belong really to the wider Christian heritage, point unmistakably to the wider covenant of Christ with his church. And the text and actions make that referent unmistakable.

Feast and Famine

Methodists drew sustenance from all three meals. Some partook of two; others would have been permitted only at one. Within United Methodism today we need the grace of all three.

Our family meals should always remind United Methodists of those who eat and those who do not eat across the globe; of those who by the common meal are made one even though we do not share a common witness; and of our responsibility to make sure that the bread is broken so that all may eat. We cannot do without our daily bread. In giving thanks for it, we accept in covenant all who share God's created order.[17] The ideal of justice and the unity of creation through justice belong to us as Methodists.

Nor can we do without Communion. And by our more frequent celebration, Methodists now recognize how vital this is to our life together. In remaining true to their understanding of Communion, Methodists need to proclaim their open table but also work zealously to make tables genuinely open. Our prayer is for real unity among Christians. We must be willing to accept the sacrifices that bring answers to that prayer. As Methodists we should be about the healing and renewing of Christ's body through the mutual recognition of ministers and members, inclusive eucharistic fellowship, and other forms of unity.

Unhappily, we have done without the love feast. The meal that comes closest is the dinner on the grounds or the church potluck. Something of the conviviality of the camp meeting affair survives in such meals and they may really be historically continuous with the camp meeting. But gone are its intimacy and grace. Methodism needs to reclaim this meal and its covenant.

The unitive ideal of evangelism belongs very much to Methodism. It cannot be the posture of one party. Real evangelical missions by Methodism require the commitment of the whole church. Such unity can come on the terms of neither party; and the posturing by the Good News movement, cited above, does little to achieve real commitment on the part of the denomination to the ideals for which Good News stands. Unity around the ideal of evangelism, no less than that around the other ideals, is costly. It is costly, but worth the cost, so that evangelicals and liberals can eat love feasts together.

The meals, families, and covenants need to be held together. And yet the several kinds of unity, though inseparable, are not indistinguishable. And Methodists need to know when and where to eat, how their eating binds them to others, and which dinner invitations take priority. We employ various stratagems for dealing with the invitations. Some would accept only one invitation, hold up the banner of only one of the ideals, and reject the other two. So, for instance, some believe that justice or evangelism is the United Methodist priority. Others would give priority to one and subsume the other two. A few, particularly in the ecumenical camp, would insist on holding all three together. The latter has been argued here, but with the realization that there will be occasions in which priority does have to be established.

To my own tastes, when invitations force some prioritizing, the ascending order would be family, Communion, love feast (justice, ecumenism, evangelism). We obviously cannot do without any. We cannot do without our daily bread. But for eternal well-being, the food of heaven, Communion takes priority. And when commitments to the two families come into conflict, when the two covenants divide our loyalties, when a choice has to be made between interreligious dialogue and Christian unity, the latter has precedence. Similarly, the unity in the Spirit takes highest priority.

It is important to underscore the point that love feast can have priority only insofar as it always depends upon and points to Communion. We do not here intend to undo the Reformation and establish another sacrament or in any way diminish the Eucharist. Rather, we would reclaim the distinctive Methodist commitment to perfection, holiness, and sanctification and understand that higher life as always fueled by the grace of Baptism and Communion but nevertheless aspire to the fullness of Christlike existence that Baptism and Communion make possible. Love feast symbolizes that fullness. It is worth recovering.

Love feast carries its full symbolic and salvific force when it depends upon, presumes, and evokes Communion. It does so not because ecumenism is irrelevant or misguided or liberal or whatever. Nor because our system works fine, thank you. Nor because United Methodism has something that would be lost were we to pursue COCU/CUIC. Rather, because of what we must attest, because our system does work, because ecumenism is not irrelevant, we need to be united so as to share our testimony. I have no misgivings about our zealous pursuit of the next stage in COCU/CUIC and other such ecumenical ventures; and I participate actively in the Episcopal-United Methodist bilateral dialogue. I favor ecumenical explorations by Methodism, by Methodism as a community confident of its own heritage, of what it brings to the table, of its peculiar grace, of the covenant it enjoys. So also renewal of the Methodist covenant in the Spirit makes genuine dialogue with persons of other faiths and accountability to the needs of the whole creation both possible and imperative. The three meals do belong together. All three are, in fact, necessary. Communion really is the basic meal, the one that makes it possible for us to enjoy the other two. Love feast provides a peculiarly Methodist accent to its own life and its involvement in the life of others. Within United Methodism today we need the grace of all three.

CHAPTER 8

A Study in Conference Self-Preoccupation

> And are we yet alive,
> And see each other's face?
> Glory and praise to Jesus give
> For his redeeming grace!
>
> Preserved by power divine
> To full salvation here,
> Again in Jesu's praise we join,
> And in his sight appear.[1]

"Ever since J[ohn] W[esley]'s later years," notes the bicentennial edition of *The Works of John Wesley*, "this has been the opening hymn for the sessions of the British Methodist Conference."[2] A similar claim frequently convenes North American conferences: "Now let's sing as has every conference since Wesley."[3] The latter assertion bears scrutiny; North-American Methodists established that "tradition" much later. This essay explores the making of a tradition and its import in the connectional self-consciousness of annual conferences.

Annual conferences in North America probably did open with a hymn, but they (1) initially did not bother to indicate which one; (2) at least from the time when the secretary bothered to record the choice, sang a wide selection; (3) did not initially select "And are we yet alive"; (4) rediscovered the "tradition" in the Southern church, and after the 1844 division, began to employ that hymn around the Civil War, during a period of intense self-preoccupation on the part of conferences; (5) found heightened liturgical awareness and new hymnbooks helpful in the making/revival of a tradition.

For its first seven meetings, the Ohio Conference did not make note of how it opened. In 1819, the secretary did so remark: "Saturday Morning Bishop McKendree and Bishop George both present, and after opening Conference by reading the Scriptures, singing and prayer, Bishop McKendree being much debilitated, desired Bishop George to attend to the business of Conference." The minutes do not record the opening of the next two conferences. By 1822 a formula emerged: "Thursday Morning Bishop McKendree and Bishop George present and after opening Conference with reading the Scriptures, singing & prayer it proceeded to Business."[4]

So also for Illinois in 1824: "Bishop McKendree opened the conference by reading a portion of the Sacred Scriptures, singing and prayer."[5] For the first half of the nineteenth century, this simple, common ritual opening—Scripture, singing, and prayer—served Methodist Episcopal conferences. Similar liturgical patterns pertained for sessions of Methodist Protestant and Methodist Episcopal South conferences.[6]

Christian Fellowship

One reason that conferences did not sing this particular hymn is that it belonged to another part of the organizational economy. It was, in fact, reserved for the family-like intimacies that pertained to close Christian friendship, and especially for class meetings. This was actually indicated in early hymnbooks. For instance, the 1837 *Hymn Book of the Methodist Protestant Church* identified "And are we yet alive?" as one of twenty hymns for "Class Meeting."[7] And "Class Meeting" constituted one of three subheadings under the heading of "Social Worship," the other two being "Prayer Meeting" and "Love Feast."[8] By rubrics, the Methodist Protestants recognized that "Are we yet alive?" belonged to Methodism on the local level. So also the Methodist Episcopal hymnbooks carried the hymn under the rubric of "Christian Fellowship."[9]

In the late 1840s, The Methodist Episcopal Church revised and The Methodist Episcopal Church, South, produced new hymnbooks. The former kept the hymn under "Christian Fellowship," maintained a category for "Love Feast," and created a new section for "Special Occasions," which included a rubric for Sunday schools.[10] The latter, the MECS, also established a section for "Special Occasions," and included Sunday schools under one of its seven subsections, "Education for Youth." Neither mentioned class meetings. The latter featured a very elaborate and detailed index. The index carried an entry for "Conference of ministers." Of the seven hymns so indicated, three carried the heading "Opening conference." They were "And are we yet alive," "Except the Lord conduct the plan," and "Our friendship sanctify and guide."[11]

In the Methodist economy, Sunday schools had displaced class meetings, and the special hymn for Christian fellowship would find a new niche at another organizational level. The Southern church recognized that first. It also made first use of the hymn for conference opening (discovered to date) but on General Conference rather than annual conference level. In 1850, the General Conference of The Methodist Episcopal Church, South, opened its session with 2 Corinthians 6 and the singing of #272, "And are we yet alive."[12] The 1846 conference had opened with "religious service." In 1858, the MECS returned to sing "And are we yet alive." But in 1854, they opened with #261, "High on his everlasting throne," which they sang again in 1866. In 1870, 1874, and 1878, two hymns were chosen, specifically, "Draw near, O Son of God, draw near" and "How rich thy bounty, King of kings" (1870); "Happy the souls to Jesus joined" and "O Thou, who camest from above" (1874); and again "O Thou, who camest from above" and "Try us, O God, and search the ground" (1878). General Conference, therefore, did not yet set the pattern for annual conference replication, at least as far as opening with "And are we yet alive" is concerned.[13] The Southern hymnal did not, by itself, a new tradition make. However, the dramatic events associated with the division of the church and the later division of the nation did have their part in the recognition/making of this tradition.

Minutes and Conference Organization

Just before the Civil War, conferences began to show a more intense self-preoccupation—a preoccupation indicated in procedure and structure, in how they preserved and presented their sittings, and in how they opened. This self-awareness derived, as we shall see, from several trends. The sectional crisis induced self-preoccupation by politicizing conferences, by making rules, procedure, and structure critical to legislative effectiveness, particularly when presiding bishops resisted conference initiatives. Parties to controversy demanded to be on the record.

Respectability also produced parliamentary awareness. Methodists, especially in the east and in towns and cities, increasingly drew middle-class adherents and consequently took their place within the social order. Methodists participated more in common evangelical Protestant efforts to Christianize society, fostering the appropriation of the organizational innovations then beginning to revolutionize American society, but in so doing also creating nostalgia for the simpler Methodism of an earlier day.

Both novelty and nostalgia focused attention on the conference as an entity. So did deaths and aging of "brothers," men made one in fraternity in the early nineteenth century when conferences had stabilized as geographic entities. Concern with itself derived, too, from conference divisions, boundary issues for conferences split North and South, and the transfer of "brothers" out. Conferences made a point of remembering who was still alive and who was not. The passion for remembering produced new histories, arrays of charts and tables, and the conference genre of a semicentennial sermon. Increased interaction with British conferences also focused attention on the common heritage, including matters of organization and order.[14]

Minutes reflect this greater self-consciousness. In 1851, the New England Conference diverted from the historic pattern of reporting its work under the Disciplinary questions. It restructured its minutes into chapters, the first of which served as a summary or digest of the workings of conference. It began with an address to the reader: "Will the readers of these 'Minutes' permit us to introduce them to the New England Conference, and its attendant religious exercise?"

This really quite striking presumption that the conference enjoyed a reading public led into a highly self-conscious effort at self-presentation. Chapter 1 described the rhythm of the week, touching on the structure of the work day, special services, the anniversary of the N.E. Conference Anti-Slavery Society, the meeting of the Conference Sunday School Union Society, important addresses (including on Saturday Bishop Janes's address to deacon candidates), the evening temperance meeting, Sunday's love feast and preaching, the Monday evening Missionary Meeting, and the closing devotional.[15] Chapter 2 covered the Disciplinary questions; chapter 3, Numbers in Society, and Finances; chapter 4, Officers of Conference

Societies, General Missionary, Domestic Missionary, Sabbath School, and Anti-Slavery; chapter 5, Reports and Resolutions; chapter 6, Appointments; chapter 7, Memoirs; and chapter 8, Visitors to Literary Institutions, the Course of Study, post office addresses of bishops, the presiding elders and superannuated.[16] These minutes reflected conference's self-preoccupation, indeed, its presumption that a wider Methodism shared in this preoccupation. This particular set was peculiar in its stage whisper of interpretation. However, the minutes from that period document annual conferences' concern with themselves, their workings, and their self-presentation—a concern that had gradually transformed the intense, communal, revival-like affairs of camp-meeting days into a business-like, legislative-judicial-executive organization.[17]

Ceremonial Opening

Two years later, New England recorded a significant divergence from the historic opening exercises of Scripture, hymn, and prayer: "Bishop Janes was present, and opened the Conference by reading the scriptures, singing, and prayer. After which the sacrament of the eucharist was administered."[18]

The 1853 eucharistic opening did not an immediate tradition create; but, beginning in 1860, New England did find that an appropriate ceremony.[19] And by 1867, New England recognized that it had established a tradition. Under the heading of "Opening Session," the secretary noted:

> The sacramental service, by common consent, has come to supersede the more formal mode of introducing the business of our Conferences (reading Scripture selections, singing, and prayer) which was in vogue so long,—and the effect of the change is undoubtedly for the best. On these occasions, ministers and people unite in commemorating the sufferings of our "blessed, blessed Master," with great spiritual profit.[20]

Still New England made no note of singing "And are we yet alive." Indeed, in the 1860s, it began to note what hymns were sung, and that one, #421, was not among them.[21]

The East Genesee Annual Conference went to a more discursive style of minutes in 1855, with paragraph summaries of each day's major actions (though modest in comparison with New England's). In that year, Bishop Beverly Waugh presided. He "conducted the opening religious service by reading 2d Tim., 2d Chapter, singing the hymn commencing, 'Except the Lord conduct the plan,' and prayer."[22] The following year, East Genesee made no indication of its initial hymn. The conference did receive an Irish delegate and took a special offering for that church. In 1857, again with an Irish delegate present and again with Waugh presiding, the conference opened with a reading of a selection from 1 Peter, "And are we yet alive," and prayer. One suspects that the international Methodist presence, perhaps reinforced by the British Methodist patterns so close by in Canada, may have been influential. At any rate, the following year, East Genesee introduced the sacrament and made no mention of its hymn selection. This set a pattern; the sacrament seems to be thereafter a tradition. No hymn choices are indicated again until 1876. In that year, Western New York and East Genesee met separately on October 4 and 5, the former opening with #266, the latter with #700. Then they met as a reunited body and sang "And are we yet alive."

Elsewhere also conferences evidenced similar self-preoccupation. In 1857, Baltimore[23] changed its style of recording and remembering its work. Instead of following the historic questions, it also adopted the minute form and identified actions day by day. The same conference called for historical sketches of the rise of Methodism. It still opened in the traditional fashion and with no indication of selections: "The Conference was opened with appropriate religious exercises, consisting of reading the Scriptures, singing and prayer, conducted by the president."[24]

Two years later, the Baltimore secretary specified the Scripture and opening hymn, #237, "I Love Thy Kingdom, Lord." The actual minutes, including the above notice, were prefaced by a list of "Names of Preachers and Date of Their Admission on Trial in the Traveling Connection": Joshua Wells (1789), Henry Smith (1794), Alfred Griffith (1806), and so on, continuing up to 1859.[25] Recollection of the names served perhaps to soften some of the pain caused by the division of the fraternity—the prior year conference had once again divided itself, this time into Baltimore and East Baltimore. Some of the enumerated brothers belonged now to a new fraternity.

Two years later, with the nation also dividing, the conference then meeting in Virginia heeded a memorial from the "Convention of Laymen which assembled in Baltimore in December last, relating to the action on Slavery by the General Conference . . . 1861" and effected yet another division.[26] These minutes were much more dramatic and detailed and still reverberate the tension over slavery. The secretary reverted to an older format, with rules first, then minutes, though the latter continued to be laid out in minute fashion. He did report the Scripture text and the actual hymn, #218, "Except the Lord conduct the plan." The plan they hoped "blest" declared the new General Conference chapter on slavery unconstitutional and declared itself as a conference "separate and independent . . . still claiming to be, notwithstanding, an integral part of the Methodist Episcopal Church."[27]

The next year, in 1862, the Baltimore Conference of the Methodist Episcopal Church met as two bodies, one in Harrisonburg as "separate and independent"; and the other in Baltimore, proclaiming loyalty to the MEC, disavowing the actions of the prior year, and regarding those not present as withdrawn.[28] The body meeting in Harrisonburg enjoyed a separate and independent existence through the war and thereafter voted to align with the MECS. In its first meeting (1862), and apparently only then, it opened with "And are we yet alive."[29]

This, the second use as an opening hymn (that I have yet discovered), was probably not known by other conferences and in itself could not have been all that influential. It does, however, nicely situate what would eventuate as a "new" tradition, amid the crises that called into question the very existence of things like "conference." Slavery, the continuing sectional crisis, war, and subsequent "religious" border warfare over turf accelerated conference preoccupation with itself, as conferences naturally cared for themselves in caring for the state of the church. In this context, the new tradition emerged.

The New England Conference of 1864 accounted for itself with an eight-page "Abstract of Daily Proceedings,"[30] a number of elaborate reports—including a long one on temperance—a list of "Deceased Members of the New England Conference," another listing of sessions of the New England Conference, a retrospective register of the New England Conference (alphabetically indicating successive appointments of each minister), and another alphabetical list of members.

The regular Baltimore Conference (MEC) continued to record the names of preachers and their dates of admission and to post offices. In 1864 (which, incidentally, opened again with "I Love Thy Kingdom, Lord"), it registered its work in far more formalized fashion: Contents, rules, officers, synopsis of the minutes (including the opening exercises of Scripture and hymn #237), introductions, committees of 1864, resolutions (including a request that William Prettyman preach a semi-centennial sermon), visit to the president, resolutions of thanks, fast day, and reports of committees.[31] By 1869, the Baltimore *Minutes* had become highly schematized. Included were:

- an elaborate table of contents
- a page of officers
- three pages listing members, in tabular display, including date of admission, present relation, appointment and residence
- committee lists for both 1869 and 1870
- questions of the General Minutes
- a page indicating appointments for 1869
- the journal, day by day, which indicated the opening as still Scripture, singing of hymn #707, prayer, singing of hymn #409, and another prayer
- motions of regret and blessing for seven persons being transferred out (71)
- a resolution of welcome to members of East Baltimore Conference, now reunited with Baltimore Conference
- an appendix, benevolent societies of the MEC (81–86); also general statistics on the church (87), and receipts of various denominational and voluntary agencies[32]

That year, amid all the formalization, Baltimore sang "And are we yet alive."

Baltimore sang the hymn again in 1872, in 1874, in 1875, in 1878; and by then it looked like a tradition. Or almost a tradition, for it was not to be unbroken. Baltimore sang "Draw near, O Son of God, draw near" in 1880 and again in 1884 and would select other hymns than "And are we yet alive" as late as 1890 and 1891. In the 1880s, specifically in 1886, Baltimore began New England's practice of celebrating the Lord's Supper at the opening. And in 1893, the tradition well established, it adopted a specific order prescribing that "[t]he Conference Session shall be opened with the administration of the Lord's Supper."[33]

New England apparently began singing "And are we yet alive" in the same year, 1872. Like Baltimore, New England settled into that as a tradition only gradually, singing different hymns in 1874, 1878, and 1882. They soon recognized it, though, as "that most appropriate and touching hymn."[34]

Rubrics in the Hymnal

The recognition of the hymn as "most appropriate and touching" came amid a surge of Methodist reclamations. The Northern church geared up for the 1866 centenary.

The 1864 General Conference authorized a gigantic, national financial drive, calling for two "departments of Christian enterprise . . . one connectional, central, and monumental, the other local and distributive." It connected fund-raising with denominational spiritual improvement achieved "by reviewing the great things God hath wrought for us, the cultivating of feelings of gratitude for the blessings received through the agency of Methodism."[35] It called each annual conference to "provide for the delivery of a memorial sermon"[36] and for "appropriate celebration" in principal churches.[37] It charged Abel Stevens with the task of producing a *Centenary of American Methodism*. Thus began a connection-wide season of remembering and reclaiming, a process that continued really through the 1884 centennial. Methodism went about the making and recovery of traditions. Histories and portraits of Methodism with a historical argument abounded. James Porter published his *Compendium of Methodism*.[38] Bishop Matthew Simpson produced his *A Hundred Years of Methodism*[39] and the monumental *Cyclopaedia of Methodism: Embracing Sketches of its Rise, Progress, and Present Condition, with Biographical Notices and Numerous Illustrations*.[40]

Similar remembering went on at conference level. Annual conferences called for semi-centennial sermons. Volumes appeared like *The Bishop's Council: With Reminiscences of an Annual Conference of the Methodist Episcopal Church*.[41] Baltimore produced *Crowned Victors. The Memoirs of Over Four Hundred Methodist Preachers, Including the First Two Hundred and Fifty Who Died on the Continent*.[42] The church looked ahead by looking back. "And are we yet alive" epitomized the church's mood.

The new tradition doubtless derived from a variety of influences—the Southern example, interaction with the British conference, the dissemination of new and good ideas by the itinerating general superintendents, an increased interest in liturgy. A change in the Northern hymnal both reflected and facilitated the new tradition of singing "And are we yet alive."[43] The hymnal in use as the conferences became more conscious of their opening was *Hymns For the Use of The Methodist Episcopal Church*.[44] Its index of subjects listed two batches of "Conference Hymns," #203–22 and 1119–29. The latter were "Close of Worship" hymns. The former deserve listing:

203 The Saviour, when to heaven he rose
204 Go, preach my Gospel, saith the Lord
205 How beauteous are their feet Who stand on Zion's hill

206 Let Zion's watchmen all awake
207 Lord of the harvest dear
208 Jesus, thy wand'ring sheep behold!
209 Comfort, ye ministers of grace
210 Jesus, the word of mercy give
211 Thus saith the Lord—'tis God commands
212 Sow in the morn thy seed
213 Draw near, O Son of God, draw near
214 Jesus, thy servants bless
215 Father of mercies, bow thine ear
216 Now, Lord, fulfil thy faithful word
217 High on his everlasting throne
218 Except the Lord conduct the plan
219 Jesus, the Name high over all
220 Lord, if at thy command the word of life we sow
221 And let our bodies part
222 O happy, happy place, Where saints and angels meet!

Not included in these conference hymns was #421, "And are we yet alive." The hymnal prescribed, and conferences would sing as conference, a variety of hymns. Focus did not fall on the one special hymn.

Hymnbooks did find such a focus and did feature the one special hymn after the Civil War. The MECS produced a new hymnbook in 1866.[45] It retained under its index of subjects the entry for hymns #272–78, namely, for "Conference of ministers," and the three for "Opening Conference," including #272, "And are we yet alive." The Northern church revised its hymnal in 1878.[46] Hymn #798, "And are we yet alive" carried the heading "Meeting, after absence," but under Index of Subjects, it was listed as "Conference Hymn" and was the only entry for that category. The tradition was "born."

Organization and Memory: A New Tradition?

In 1884, the Baltimore Conference met in a celebrative mood. Methodism was celebrating yet another anniversary and was doing so in a highly organized fashion. Bishop Edward G. Andrews made a statement on the centennial.[47] Lyttleton F.

Morgan preached his semi-centennial titled "The Centennial of the Methodist Episcopal Church, A Sermon." The conference produced and incorporated into the minutes a "Centennial Historical Manual of the Baltimore Conference M.E. Church."[48] The conference made a point of incorporating also the "Proceedings of the Baltimore Electoral Conference of Laymen of the Methodist Episcopal Church: Fourth Quadrennial Meeting." The church was feeling its way on the incorporation of the laity. It was also feeling its way on its own incorporation. The inclusion of the lay organization's meetings was entirely apt. The lay business "men" would not have found conference structure unfamiliar. It, too, had become business-like—with "corporate" officers; an array of distinct financial systems; an elaborate committee structure; rules; auxiliaries and societies through which the business of missions and higher education and Sunday school and church extension could be conducted; complex accounting systems that measured performance of churches, circuits, ministers, and Sunday schools; directories arrayed by mailing addresses; and a pension plan.

Conference drew on its organizational capacities also for memory. It completed the various charts and statistical sections with a "Roll of the Baltimore Conference."[49] It covered the period from 1797 to the present and used codes to indicate year of departure by:

d   death;
e   expulsion;
w   withdrawal;
l   location;
t   transfer;
also admission by:
a   on trial;
re-a   readmitted;
t   transfer.

The roll looked forward from 1797. A "Conference Roster" looked backward from the present. It listed the successive appointments of 1884 members.[50] So, with two elaborate charts that covered forty pages, Baltimore organized its memory.

Organization and memory went together. Indeed, Baltimore was well organized for memory, having established for itself and the denomination, "the American

Methodist Historical Society." In its memory, conference, and particularly the Baltimore Conference, loomed large in the Methodist saga:

> Here, then, in the Colony and State of Maryland, within the present Baltimore Conference, without doubt, was the first Apostle of Methodism in America; the first Society, the first Chapel, the first General Conference, which in 1784 organized the Church, the first school, Cokesbury College, the first native local preacher, Richard Owen, and the first native itinerant, William Watters. Moreover this was the field where its first fruits were most abundantly reaped, for the earliest statistics given (1773), show that it yielded more than half of the whole membership in America.[51]

When so highly organized for memory as for work; when organization delivered a detailed and "scientific" past; when the "fathers" and old Methodism lived through ceremony and charts; when elaborate Sunday schools and Akron Plan buildings (explained more fully in chapter 13) squeezed out class meetings; when organization transformed Methodism, threatening what it could now more clearly remember—then it became very important to create traditions to preserve as much as possible.[52] In 1884, Baltimore did not actually sing "And are we yet alive." But it had done so the previous three years, and it would do so frequently thereafter.[53]

As they sang, the preachers' memories cut through all the organized self-preoccupation to recall the fraternity into which they had been inducted, the covenant that had bound them together even as it had dispersed them to travel, the great relish with which they had gathered after a hard year, the "brothers" who had dropped from traveling or who had been dropped by death, the joy now in being with those "yet alive." A "conference hymn" indeed, "And are we yet alive" could not arrest time or time's toll on conference. It could not stop the dramatic organizational revolution that swept away the simpler Methodism the hymn recalled. It could not bring back the old days or those not "yet alive." It could not by legislation or exhortation recreate the love feast and class meeting in which this hymn had once resonated. But it could provide a moment when with lusty voice and teary eye conference could step outside of time.

CHAPTER 9

A Methodist Doctrine of the Church?

Do Methodists Have a Doctrine of the Church?" So Albert C. Outler queried in the title of a much-cited lead essay in a volume dedicated to precisely that question.[1] L. Harold DeWolf affirmed less ambiguously: "There has never been an official Methodist doctrine of the church excepting the brief and very general statements in the Articles of Religion and the General Rules. To this day such a Methodist doctrine remains unformulated." Durward Hofler concurred: "There is no Wesleyan doctrine of the church as such, for John Wesley unlike John Calvin did not undertake a systematic compilation of his theology or his ecclesiology."[2]

When Methodist theologians have worried over our ecclesiological poverty, they have sometimes drawn comfort from the deprivation's compensatory "apostolic" or missional vocation. So the Twelfth Oxford Institute of Methodist Theological Studies revisited Outler's query and frequently his essay/speech given at an earlier Institute by framing its purpose as "To Serve the Present Age, Our Calling to Fulfill: Ecclesiology, Mission, and Vocation." We Methodists, we infer, have denied ourselves a proper doctrine of the church in our concern for the world and other Christians (our evangelical catholicity).[3] We have been a life-and-work rather than a faith-and-order movement. Our mission to convert and our catholic spirit provided us with ecclesial sensibilities—the capacity to see the appropriate corporate Christian or churchly direction—that more than compensated for our lack of explicit ecclesial guidelines. The catholic spirit orients us toward the unity for which Christ prayed, toward shared Christian tradition, toward apostolic and creedal affirmations, and implicitly embraces the larger church's more detailed theologies of church and kingdom. Indeed, we have been modest enough to discern our initial ecclesial sensibilities as consonant with, perhaps productive of—certainly energizing of—twentieth-century ecumenism.[4] However, when the case for Methodist catholicity is stated, we appeal generally to John Wesley's sermons, to his conception of Methodist mission, to the peculiar relation of Methodist societies to the Church of England that he endeavored to sustain.

A Fall from Wesleyan Grace?

We American Methodists, and especially United Methodists, appropriately revert to Wesley for ecclesiology, as for our theology generally. His works, particularly the "Standard Sermons," "Explanatory Notes upon the New Testament," and "General Rules" remain authoritative, embraced by the *Discipline* as doctrinal standards. His Arminian theology undergirds our movement, and we forcefully set it forth as "Our Theological Task." His provisions for Christian living continue to provide guidance. His and especially his brother Charles's hymns continue on lips and in hearts. His discipline, commitment to mission, ordering of church and ministry, and balance of personal and social holiness take ever-new form. And now our epistemology—our endeavor to do theology quadrilaterally, relying on Scripture, tradition, reason, and experience—we affirm to be Wesley's. Theologically, we Methodists, certainly United Methodists, remain oriented to and by Wesley.

However, in doing theology by moving back and forth from the Wesleys, Methodist thinkers (unintentionally, perhaps) leave the impression that intervening Methodism did not sustain Wesleyan ecclesial commitments. A methodology that leaps back over two centuries to Wesley and then leaps forward implicitly interprets the intervening two centuries as theologically barren. Such theologizing posits a fall from Wesleyan truth and wisdom and its recovery only now—in the work of the author being read.

The theological move certainly is understandable. Early American Methodism, post- as well as pre-1784, when with Wesley's blessing and provisions The Methodist Episcopal Church was created, has not seemed to offer promising catholic foundations—indeed, theological moorings of any sort. By all appearances, and from its beginnings, the MEC lacked both an adequate doctrine of the church and the ecclesial, particularly catholic, sensibilities of Wesley's own commitments,[5] the indicators for which are numerous: the absence of theological capacity, not to mention leadership, among early American leaders; quite guarded acceptance of the highly trained and adept Wesley-designated superintendent (bishop), Thomas Coke; curious dependent relations upon Wesley; prior and unpersuasive efforts to remain within the colonial Church of England; pressures to produce church government and sacraments by revolution; an evangelical-pragmatic turn of mind; and persecution of American Methodists as Tories during the Revolution.

All of these factors conspired to press American Methodists, when gathered in the organizing Christmas Conference of 1784, to decision not reflection, to polity not doctrine. As Asbury confesses of that affair (which kept no minutes of its deliberations, except those implicit in the new *Discipline*): "We were in great haste, and did much business in a little time."[6] They accomplished much in this "business," transforming the strange guide for Wesley's movement, the Large Minutes, into a quasi-constitution for an episcopal church with a threefold ministry of superintendents (soon to be called bishops), elders, and deacons; adapting and revising the Anglican Articles of Religion for usage in a new republic; and accepting Wesley's recension of the *Book of Common Prayer*. With Wesley's blessing, his brother's hymns, their Arminian theology, the strong evangelical mission, and this new *Discipline*, the new MEC had work orders. Nevertheless, it was a polity without ecclesial warrant; or, to put it more charitably, a polity whose ecclesiology remained implicit. American Methodists seemed to want it that way. When faced with its first big schism, that of James O'Kelly and the Republican Methodists, bishops Thomas Coke and Francis Asbury gestured in the direction of a theology for Methodist polity by undertaking an exegesis of the *Discipline*. Their effort to provide scriptural warrant for Methodist polity—an important first step—*The Doctrines and Discipline of the Methodist Episcopal Church, in America, with Explanatory Notes*, itself created dissension and was not repeated or kept in print.

Controversy around Methodist polity continued. Having adopted an episcopal polity, relabeled their superintendents "bishops," lodged Wesley-like appointive power in their (particularly Francis Asbury's) hands, and created an office of presiding elder (now district superintendent) as an extension of the episcopacy, the young church had to contend almost immediately with external and internal criticism of its polity, some carping from the Wesleys, and pointed attacks from their American competition with a similar name, the Protestant Episcopal Church. Other denominations, too, found Methodist polity good sport. In this period of intense denominational competition, much of Methodist transaction with other religious bodies revolved around Methodist polity. Others attacked; Methodists defended. Defended, explained, gloried in. The Methodist view of the church became a divisive issue. American Methodists, it would seem, fell into a denominationalism that betrayed the ecumenical proclivities of their father in the faith. Was this a fall from the Wesleyan grace of catholicity?

The purpose of this chapter is to suggest that American Methodism retained far more of Wesley's catholicity than appearances would suggest. The thesis, conveyed by the title and hinted at above in relation to Wesley, is that while American Methodists (and I will confine myself for sake of convenience to the Methodist Episcopal Church) lacked an adequate and explicit doctrine of the church, they purposed accomplishments in God's world that implied a very rich sense of church.

What they lacked on a formal theological level, they often possessed on an operational or organizational level. In program, American Methodists sustained Wesley's catholic ecclesial sensibility to project a Protestant unity of affection (catholicity) and purpose (missions), providentially grounded, oriented toward the Kingdom, and expressed in a shared but denominationally differentiated faith and in a Christian nation.

As we have noted, these ecclesial sensibilities were not well integrated with the polity. They are not particularly striking in the *Disciplines*, *Minutes*, or *Journals*, for instance. Nor were they developed elsewhere into an explicitly coherent self-understanding. Hence Methodism rightly can be criticized for its want of an adequate doctrine of the church. However, it seems to me instructive to explore some of the intellectual and symbolic commitments out of which a more adequate ecclesiology might have been constructed. In a longer discussion, I would endeavor to show that these commitments suffused Methodist writings, appearing quite incidentally in journal, letter, sermon, or treatise.

Catholicity in Methodist Apologetics

The case for Wesley's ecclesial sensibilities in their mutuality and operation, even though not formally worked into doctrine, can be best made by discovering them together. And though one at first might suspect not, full expressions of Methodism's intimations of the church are even to be found in controversial works where its defenders were forced to think seriously about its purpose. By focusing on apologetical works in which Methodists sought to distinguish, defend, and provide warrant for their particularities and their orthodoxy—that is, where the temptation is greatest to be self-referential and self-aggrandizing—we can see that the commitment to Wesley's catholicity ran deep and true. Exchanges with Calvinists (Presbyterians especially), Baptists, and Episcopalians began early and continued through the Civil War. Apologetics with the latter two prove especially revealing, as they concern the polity in and through which Methodists enacted their ecclesiology.

Exchanges and debates with the Episcopalians were especially pitched, brought ecclesial issues to the fore, and endured well into the nineteenth century. To exhibit Methodism's ecclesial richness in the compass of this short paper I will restrict myself to work by two eminent spokesmen who summed up the controversy, Nathan Bangs's *An Original Church of Christ*, which appeared initially in 1837, and Abel Stevens's *An Essay on Church Polity*, which was published ten years later. These were influential and enduring statements by men who had shaped the church.[7]

Bangs and Stevens are best known today for the multivolume histories of Methodism by which they defined the church's historical self-understanding. Bangs's four-volume *History of the Methodist Episcopal Church* went through twelve editions. Abel Stevens's three-volume *History of the Religious Movement of the Eighteenth Century Called Methodism*, four-volume *History of The Methodist Episcopal Church*, and compressed version of the latter, *A Compendious History of American Methodism*, similarly enjoyed long lives.[8] Stevens's *History of the Methodist Episcopal Church* appeared on the "course of study" (the prescribed reading program for all those entering the ministry) in 1864, 1868, 1880, 1896, 1890, and then again in 1932. His *Compendious History* remained on the course from 1872 to 1908, with only a curious gap of 1900, when another of his works took its place.

These two men exercised a comparable role in their own day as media lords. Bangs edited *The New York Christian Advocate* and Stevens *Zion's Herald*. These publications aimed at the Methodist people and both were highly influential, the former a paper with one of the widest circulations and readership in American society. Bangs and Stevens also furthered scholarship, nurtured the ministry, and sought the cultured elite through serials *The Methodist Quarterly Review* and *The*

National Magazine. Bangs was editor, Stevens corresponding editor of the former; Stevens editor of the latter. These were men whose ecclesial views commanded respect and who merit our attention.

Indeed, Bangs had established himself as Methodist spokesperson with apologetical works that appeared in 1815, 1816, 1817, and 1820: *The Errors of Hopkinsianism Detected and Refuted, The Reformer Reformed, An Examination of the Doctrine of Predestination*, and *A Vindication of Methodist Episcopacy*.[9] These books, along with others like Asa Shinn's *An Essay on the Plan of Salvation* (1813), defended Wesleyan theology and Methodist ministry, orders, and episcopacy against the church's most powerful critics. In the first three, Bangs responded to Calvinists who derided its thought, and the last to Episcopalians who questioned its ecclesial legitimacy.[10]

Bangs and Stevens

In the two works under review the keen historical scholarship of Bangs and Stevens is very much evident. *An Original Church of Christ* and *An Essay on Church Polity*[11] are histories of ecclesiology undertaken to legitimate Methodist polity. What makes them important for our purpose is the combination of that historical sense and an acute self-consciousness about ecclesial issues for the church. They sought ecclesial self-understanding in the face of rather pointed external attacks upon and lingering divisive strains within Methodist polity. Both responded formally to Protestant Episcopal charges that Methodist orders (and, hence, sacraments) and indeed the entire system were spurious and therefore desecrated. They endeavored to do so without troubling the waters that had produced recent schisms (the Methodist Protestant Church for Bangs and the Wesleyan Methodist Connection for Stevens; Stevens was less concerned about the split between North and South). Stevens was especially intent upon explaining the Methodist system to local critics who found it un-American. He also intended "to comprehend the outline of the course of study on church polity, required of candidates for membership in our conferences" (Stevens, 4).

Bangs and Stevens provided quite competent expositions of Methodist polity and ably evidenced its fidelity to Scripture and tradition. It would be legitimate, I suppose, to take the polity expositions as the ecclesial statements of these authors. To do so would miss the catholic environment of Methodist polity. The liveliest sense of the church in these two inheres less in the formal historical and theological defenses of Methodism than in the exhortations to the Methodist faithful, in passing remarks, and in the sermonic portions of the text. They are in the order of commonplaces, assumptions, givens—I was to call them sensibilities—that are placed alongside of but not adequately integrated within the polity expositions. Yet Bangs and Stevens clearly envelop Methodism in the wider church in several ways. A statement by Bangs is worth reproducing at some length, for it touches on five of the six themes that, in my judgment, ought to be seen for their ecclesial significance:

> It is the wish of the present writer, that while we rally around our own standards, maintain our own peculiarities, and "contend earnestly for the faith once delivered unto the saints," as we understand it, we should needlessly give offence to none, but conform our love toward all men. It is possible, I think, to cleave to our own institutions, and yet exercise a catholic spirit toward all those who love our Lord Jesus Christ in sincerity. It is possible, indeed, to rise to that height in Christian experience, to be absorbed in the spirit of divine love, and so ardently drawn forth in quest of immortal souls, as to lose sight of sectarian differences and partialities, and to be wholly taken up in the more paramount interests of the Redeemer's kingdom. (Bangs, 381)

In this passage I would call your attention to (1) the spirit of catholicity and call for charity, a partaking in the unity of divine love; (2) unity founded in confidence and oriented toward the Kingdom; (3) a sense of a shared evangelical faith that transcends sectarian differences; (4) a perception of Methodist labors as part of the broader Protestant missionary quest for immortal souls; and (5) the acceptance, even celebration, of denominationalism as compatible with and conducive to common Christian purpose. Missing here but present elsewhere is the conferral of ecclesial significance on a Christian America.

It is theological sleight of hand, I guess, to subsume under ecclesiology themes that belong elsewhere in theological cyclopedia. Yet to fail to recognize these themes for their ecclesial significance would be a more grievous sin. It would imprison our historical perceptions in a sectarianism that our ancestors sought to escape. For a while, formal doctrines of the church had become part of the weaponry of sectarian warfare; many of the warriors felt impelled to moderate and modify their ecclesiological defenses and attacks by recognizing a broader (though limited) Christian unity in which all evangelical denominations were joined. To demean those efforts by dismissing their expositions as the branch theory of the church is unfair—not inaccurate but not adequate. Not inaccurate, for they used such language themselves (Bangs, 289), but inadequate because the phrase diverts attention to the divided limbs and away from the unity in trunk and roots. Early nineteenth-century Methodists were too intense about their commitment and not sufficiently latitudinarian or relativistic to regard one branch as good as another and implicitly to regard the branches as self-sustaining. They were better farmers and better churchpersons than to consider branches independent.

Bangs and Stevens, at any rate, took seriously Methodism's ecclesial unity with other evangelical Protestants. Both expressed unease about entering a potentially divisive controversy; both desired to carry it on without giving offense; both recoiled at Episcopal uncharitableness. Of apologetics predicated upon the doctrine of apostolic succession, Stevens complained, "It unchurches most of the Protestant world" (Stevens, 76). Aligning themselves with Wesley and a distinguished strain of catholic Christians, Bangs and Stevens sought to be avid Methodists imbued with a catholic spirit. They recognized that spirit inside and outside Methodism, confident that the catholic spirit informed institutional life:

> Now that efforts are making to spread the gospel of our common salvation to the ends of the earth, by the united instrumentality of all denominations of evangelical Christians, why should the breach be widened between any of them, by the utterance of those things which tend naturally to alienate affection? It is much more important, in my estimation, to exemplify the purity of true religion in our doctrine, spirit, and conduct, than it is to contend for mere forms and ceremonies. (Bangs, 23)

The unity enjoyed by evangelical Protestants required their cooperation and a civility in controversy, but it was not just of their agency. Unity rested on Providence. Methodist confidence in Providence was awesome; it suffused all their writings, including these two. The accent on the millennium here, however, is more muted. Still, appeal was made to both Providence and the millennium in legitimating Methodist polity. A chapter by Stevens titled "Methodism a Special System" simply overflows with trust in the divine provision for Methodist particularities. However, what gave the particularities their warrant was Methodist realization that the transformation of the world was a joint enterprise. The Providence that guided the Methodists oriented other denominations in the same direction and to the same end. So, in the chapter mentioned, Stevens projected a world mission for Methodism under "the universal idea of the church" in the morning of the latter day, preparing for the final battle and under a special Providence (Stevens, 204–6). It is possible to miss the unitive providential/millennial note amid the strains of Methodist triumphalism.[12] That would be a mistake.

Similarly, in the ferocity of the theological battles between Methodists and their adversaries, particularly the Calvinists, it is easy to lose sight of their belief that catholic unity and common guidance by Providence required and produced theological accord. Bangs corrected such mis-impressions:

> Indeed, the grand principle of Methodism from the beginning was, to lay fast hold of the cardinal doctrines of Christianity, with a determination never to unloose the hold, and then to adopt all those means to diffuse them among mankind, which the developments of time and circumstances should dictate to be necessary and expedient. (Bangs, 367)

Those doctrines—a Reformation credo plus holiness—were succinctly stated (Bangs, 364–65) and Methodists enjoined to adhere to them. In conserving a common evangelical faith, Methodists would preserve a "sacred deposit committed to our care by our fathers" (Bangs, 364).

The institutionalization of this providentially given, catholic, and theological unity was in a threefold manner dictated by the sociopolitical realities of a land of immigrant peoples launched on an experiment in religious and civil liberty and yet claiming the prerogatives of the covenant. Ecclesial significance was accorded the country itself, as well as missions and denominationalism (the voluntary system).

Methodist participation in a Christian America—in reforming the nation and spreading scriptural holiness over the land—is not a dominant motif in these two works. Overarching the national mission, as we will note below, was the imperative of the world. Nevertheless, it is present, as for instance in Stevens's affirmation of a providential linkage of Methodism and America:

> Its adaptation in this respect to our own country is worthy of remark. While the great moral revolution of Methodism was going on across the Atlantic, the greatest political revolution of modern times was in process on our own continent; and when we contemplate the new adaptations of religious action which were evolved by the former, can we resist the conviction that there was a providential relation between the two events?—that they were not only coincident

in time, but also in purpose? While Wesley and his co-laborers were reviving Christianity there, Washington and his compatriots were reviving liberty here. It was the American Revolution that led to the development of the resources of this vast country, and rendered it the assembling-place of all kindreds, tongues, and people; and Methodism commenced its operation sufficiently early to be in mature vigor by the time that the great movement of the civilized world toward the west began. It seems to have been divinely adapted to this emergency of our country. If we may judge from the result, it was raised up by Providence more in reference to the new than to the old world. (Stevens, 144)

Sidney Mead's formulation, *The Nation with the Soul of a Church*,[13] captures rather nicely the American transference of features of Christendom, church establishment, and churchly ecclesiology to the nation itself. Bangs and Stevens did not here develop a full-fledged theology of the nation, as might have their Presbyterian counterparts under a similar charge.[14] However, the elements of such a theology are present, as the above passage should suggest.

Much more pronounced was the Methodist recognition of an ecumenical missionary endeavor and pride in being its Protestant originator. Both the unitive and universal dimensions of Methodist missionary activity were obvious to Bangs, who taught that Methodist revivals had effected a reformation that "has spread less or more among all denominations" as "the radiations of Methodism" (Bangs, 301). He affirmed:

We believe, indeed, that God has made the Methodists, unworthy as they may be, instruments of reviving and spreading pure Christianity among mankind. We believe that the evangelical labors of Wesley, his coadjutors and followers, "have provoked very many" "to love and good works," and that thereby gospel light, love, and holiness have been extensively diffused among the different orders of Christians. With all those who are engaged in the solemn work of converting the world to Jesus Christ, we wish most heartily to co-operate, that we may unitedly carry on the warfare against the "world, the flesh, and the devil." (381)

Adding that Methodism is a missionary church, Stevens concurred:

Methodism is marked with a special character and a special purpose. Wesley said that its purpose was to "spread holiness over the land"; but it is greater; it is to "spread holiness over the world." It was raised up not merely to resuscitate the English Church, but to affect all Protestant Christendom, either by its direct influence or by its example. *It is a missionary church in its plans, a revival church* in its *spirit*; and such it promises to be until the world is redeemed, if we but preserve its peculiarities. (Stevens, 199)

In its essence, as a missionary, evangelical order Methodism was both most distinctive and most united with other Protestants.[15]

It was in that possibility of Christian unity despite denominational individuality that the ecumenical genius of the nineteenth-century denominational or voluntary system lay.[16] Bangs said it best: "While, therefore, the members of the Methodist Episcopal Church are exhorted to exercise a catholic spirit toward all Christian denominations, there is no inconsistency in urging them to a liberal support of their own institutions" (Bangs, 383). Unity in denominationalism, unity despite division, was feasible only when the preceding five understandings reigned. For then the denomination was a voluntary religious association, a compact of those who proposed together for the evangelization of society (Christian America) and the world (missions) in catholic and charitable accord with others who shared the essentials of the evangelical faith and sought providential guidance.

Catholic Spirit—Christian America

This vision of accord was a precarious vision, one even then being distorted by sectional divisions, slavery, the rising tide of confessionalism, and the rapid entry of new peoples who could not share in the Protestant vision. But for all its limitations, it was a noble attempt to see beyond disunity and to envision separate denominational ventures as part of a larger Christian purpose. Achieving unity of affection (catholicity) and purpose (missions), conceiving it in providential and theological terms, institutionalizing it denominationally and in the fabric of a Christian America, nineteenth-century American Methodists (and other Protestants) were ecumenical, though divided.[17]

One might draw quite opposite implications from this exploration. Recognizing the genius of a Methodist ecumenism that posits unity amid division and catholicity despite resolute maintenance of denominational structures, some would conclude that the nineteenth-century saga should content us with verbal ecumenism and structural denominationalism. Another, and opposite, reading would hold that a continuous legacy of Methodist ecumenism places a burden on its twenty-first-century heirs to take unity with utmost seriousness and to do so as Methodists. Various other constructions are possible.

My own conclusion differs from these and other views. Related to this difference is the program of this chapter—to examine the expression of Christian unity at a given time—without worrying over its departure from theological ground (Wesley) or its bearing on twenty-first-century unity (ecumenism). My judgment is that the appropriate (as well as actual) forms of Christian institutionalization differ; and that in consequence the appropriate (as well as actual) relation of unity and diversity also varies. Few would dispute the factual statement. When raised to an interpretive principle my judgment calls into question the teleology implicit in much history of Christian unity that measures previous unity by its approximation of the twentieth-century ecumenical movement and discerns the movement of past efforts toward fruition therein. That presentistic or Whiggish conception of history takes seriously the previous ventures in Christian unity but primarily as evolutionary stages whose fulfillment lies in their yielding to more recent and adequate unitive strategies. That mode of history is probably inevitable. Yet we should, I believe, strive to take each moment of history seriously in its own right. And that means respecting nineteenth-century American Methodist sensibilities for what they were and what they aspired to. To be sure, the Christian unity envisioned was limited to Protestants (and overly confident of even their cooperative spirit), focused excessively on a nation whose capacities for transcendence were quite limited, and construed racism as a sectional rather than pervasive trait. But for all that its evangelical catholicity was a significant venture in Christian and world unity.

The lessons that we draw from my construction are less programmatic than those of the other two readings. I do not expect a template for unity or denominationalism from historical inquiry. Rather, I would wish for reflection about the variety of Christian unity in our heritage; commitment to search for today's form; and appreciation for the imperfect, conditioned, partial character of our goal. Ecclesial sensibilities we might still require.

Conceptualizing the Connection

CHAPTER 10

Family Values: A Connectional Concern

A *United Methodist News Service* story, dateline June 23, 1997, Atlanta, announced an about-face by Emory's Board of Trustees in reaction to the North Georgia Annual Conference's protest of same-sex union ceremonies on the Emory campuses. According to UMNS:

> The agreement in effect prohibits same-sex covenant ceremonies from taking place in the churches and chapels since United Methodist clergy are bound to uphold the doctrine and polity of the United Methodist Church.
>
> "The board of trustees made it very clear," said North Georgia Bishop G. Lindsey Davis, "they want those sacred facilities, when they're used for religious services, rites, ceremonies, weddings, funerals, to be under the *Discipline* of the United Methodist Church and by United Methodist ministers."
>
> Neither he nor the church, Davis noted, wanted to "deprive gays and lesbians of their civil rights. But I do want the polity of our church to be respected, and I think this action does just that."
>
> The United Methodist *Book of Discipline* clearly states, "Ceremonies that celebrate homosexual unions shall not be conducted by our ministers and shall not be conducted in our churches."
>
> Should a chaplain or pastor allow a ceremony on campus that is contrary to United Methodist doctrine, he/she would be "accountable to an annual

conference and a bishop and a board of ordained ministry the same way any other United Methodist minister is," Davis said.[1]

Family Values?

The Emory board's action, in today's climate, might be interpreted as a victory for family values.[2] It might also indicate just how radically Methodism's family values have changed over the course of its life and how radically Methodism's relation to the social order has differed during the last two centuries. Indeed, the dramatic intervention required to effect Emory's compliance might well illustrate how tenuously Methodism now exercises influence on its most cherished institutions—not only Emory, nor just its other colleges and universities, but also its hospitals, homes, and various institutions. The church's values and its relation to culture and institutions have changed and in ways we might find surprising.

To put the matter bluntly, one might argue that in 1797 Methodism explicitly and formally created same-sex covenants as an essential part of its ministry and set those over against the family values of the day. A century later, in 1897, Methodism normed a patriarchy focused on the nuclear family and the family altar, patterns congruent with the Southern culture of the day. And, with the passing of yet another century, by 1997 Methodism, with much of American Protestantism, struggled to make moral and programmatic sense of sequential marriages, blended families, single-parent households, "segregated" old-age communities and institutions, a youth culture, families existing and children born out of wedlock, household roles and rules radically reconfigured by a quasi-egalitarian workplace, and, of course, gay and lesbian unions.

In its family values, Southern Methodism defined its relation to culture and its own. The Methodism of 1797, I will suggest, was *sectarian*, albeit with a combative and socially radical rather than withdrawing spirit. By 1897, Southern Methodism was clearly *denominational*, competitive, institution-creating, socially transformative, and aggressive, though accepting of much of the culture of the day. By 1997, Methodism still claimed title to Southern culture but had largely withdrawn into its household, content to clip its moral coupons, order its own affairs, and live off its *churchly* capital. Sectarian, denominational, and churchly—to speak of Methodism as having such phases is to employ sociological terms that we will have to give a rather full makeover to make sense of the Methodist experience.

Family Values

Caveats

Other chapters in this volume focus appropriately on limited topics and/or periods, often tracking these matters in relation to Northern Methodism (the Methodist Episcopal Church). This one looks at Southern Methodism by taking three snapshots, at 1797, 1897, and 1997, giving primary focus to 1797 and 1897. Its intent is to look at how Methodism understood and exercised its mission in society. By focusing on Southern Methodism we see more sharply transformations through which much of Protestantism and certainly much of Methodism were going. In that regard, and secondarily, this chapter concerns itself with the ways in which we construe Methodism as a social movement.

Further, we presume rather than treat directly what, perhaps, most shaped Methodism's social vision and what appropriately figure in most treatments of Southern Methodism, namely, race and regionalism. And it focuses upon episcopal Methodism, and really the white expressions of that. It employs the contrivance of these century-apart glimpses to suggest how very much Methodism has changed. That is not to deny that much about Methodism remained the same or that the intervening periods sloped only in the direction of these century-end profiles. Indeed, the nineteenth century in particular was dominated by major divisions—Civil War, the extrusion/departure into separate denominations of African Americans, and sectional/racial politics. The Southern Methodist churches went through stages of hyperactivity, mobilization, destruction, despondency, schism, and defensive rebuilding that fall outside normal denominational development. On the changes wrought by these nineteenth-century events more conventional treatments rightly focus. Still, these century-spaced snapshots, like those of family albums taken when periodic gatherings occur, allow us to see how we have grown and changed. They also permit us to think a little about how we conceptualize Methodism.

Around 1797

Early Methodism was a Southern affair.[3] In 1797 Methodism appointed six but held seven conferences. All but one of them were south of the Mason-Dixon Line. So also its membership was predominantly Southern (to the tune of 76 percent): 32,729 of its 46,445 white members and 11,627 of its 12,218 black members were in

Delaware and Maryland or farther south.⁴ Not surprisingly, the leadership also reflected Methodism's Southern proportions.

These Southern proportions have been noted by many, if not most, of Methodism's historians.⁵ None, as far as I know, called Methodism's Southern orientation "providential," though they applied that judgment liberally to other aspects of its character and development. Yet Methodism was peculiarly "fitted" to make its way in the South.

Methodism came as a late and highly developed form of Pietism, capitalizing on American familiarity—through the preaching of George Whitefield, the Tennants, and Jonathan Edwards—with Pietism's idiom, concern, and praxis. Methodism prospected in largely Anglican areas, areas not "claimed" by other Pietist movements: Southern areas. And it succeeded by representing itself as a reform impulse within Anglicanism, benefiting from the cooperation of, and endorsement by, like-minded spirits within the colonial church.⁶

Whether its timing was "providential" or not, Methodism emerged in the Revolutionary epoch, just as colonists recognized Anglicanism as implicated in Britain's "tyranny" and as party to the conspiracy to destroy the English liberties that Americans should enjoy. Methodism benefited from Anglican disarray as it had earlier from Anglican reception. And though at points persecuted as also Tory, Methodism lost most of its Tory aspect and leadership and, in the main, deported itself so as to emerge from the war cleared of charges of disloyalty and able to capitalize on Anglicanism's unmistakable Toryism and weakened state. Wesley's recognition of American Methodist independence came slowly for the Virginians and probably slowly also for Francis Asbury, but early as compared with other movements under trans-Atlantic authority. And in 1784, with its Anglican nomenclature and liturgy, Methodism made itself at home in areas where Anglicanism had prevailed, accenting its middle name, the Methodist *Episcopal* Church.

Methodism made itself at home in the South, however, not where Anglicanism had once nestled in—in the "big houses"—or, at least, not among the males of the big houses. Indeed, Methodism's rules and rhetoric oriented it against the predominant family values of the day, those of gentility. It appealed to the middling and lower sort, to women, to slaves, to the restless. And it condemned, viewed as worldly, and exercised discipline over the practices that defined the genteel world—fine apparel, dancing, gambling, horse racing, dueling, card playing, drinking.

Condemnation of this genteel code derived from Wesley and was beautifully modeled by Hester Ann Rogers, whose autobiography was widely read on this side of the Atlantic. Indeed, condemnation of the genteel code was shared among Pietists.[7] But opposition to gentility had a socially revolutionary aspect in the American South. Wesley's England was socially differentiated, and the gentry occupied only one rung among many in the ladder from peasant to crown. By contrast, the farming and plantation South had little in the way of merchant, craft, and professional classes, of course no nobility, and a huge slave population. The gentry reigned supreme, despite their small numbers. They were deferred to and aped by other whites, who aspired to that status.

Late eighteenth-century Southern males, particularly the gentry, but also others, experienced Methodism's moral code and practice as an assault on their family values—at least so argues Christine Leigh Heyrman in *Southern Cross: The Beginnings of the Bible Belt*. Some hint of this comes in a letter of 1802 from Hamilton Jefferson on the Fairfax Circuit, Alexandria District:

> At Pendleton there were nine professed to be converted, but not without opposition, for I never saw as much at a Quarterly Meeting in all my life. They dragged them away from us like d—ls. We pursued one fellow, and contested the matter with him; but as soon as we got hold of him, he dropped the poor woman, and looked like a d—l gagged. I asked him how he could act so much like the d—l, dragging souls away from God; [and told him] that he might rely on it that, if he continued in that way, God would make him an example of his displeasure. He got scared, and said he would do so no more.[8]

Such male opposition is well documented. But how widespread was white Southern male experience of Methodism as an assault on the genteel-normed family and whether this little movement created a pervasive sense of crisis, it is hard to say. What is clear is that Methodism offered Southerners an alternative family value system. At its heart stood covenants of fraternity and sorority, covenants that defined new values, covenants that established new families—same-gender and same-race unions. The language that Methodists employed to describe these could be highly affectionate, emotional, moving, even erotic. Terms of endearment, for instance, recur through the letters that itinerants exchanged. Nathaniel Harris, writing from Kentucky, called Stith Mead, "Dear Brother," and signed "Yours, in the best of bonds." A later letter he signed, "Yours in love."[9] John Kobler greeted Mead:

> My very dear Brother:—My heart is in heaven: the love that casteth out all fear fills my soul every moment. Since I saw your dear face last, my soul has been drinking daily into God. . . .
>
> O, Brother Mead, let us breathe the whole spirit of missionaries, and bring nothing but salvation on our tongues.

Later he wrote:

> My dear Brother:—I love you most tenderly in the bowels of Jesus Christ. . . .
>
> I much approve our agreement when together last, (to be in band). I do believe it will redound to the glory of God and the everlasting happiness of our souls.

The band agreement and bond to which he refers was described by Stith Mead as follows:

> The Rev. John Kobler, Presiding Elder of the Holstien District, condescended to receive me into Band Society with him, agreeable to the Rule found in the Discipline of the Methodist Episcopal Church, at a Quarterly Meeting for New River Circuit, Saturday and Sunday, 9th and 10th November, 1793; that a more particular minute of our lives when absent may be notice, and when personally present we may freely open our minds to each other; and continued prayer to be made for each other at the throne of grace.[10]

Similarly, Wilson Lee wrote Daniel Hitt:

> My very dear Brother:—I feel myself bound to write a few lines to you this morning, in token of love to you, and to let you know what God is still doing in the State of Maryland. . . .
>
> God bless you. I am in haste. Pray, and write to your loving brother.[11]

Not affectionate or erotic at all are the names by which we know these alternative family systems. We call them—they called them—class, quarterly meeting, and conference. When we hear those terms we think "polity."[12] Polity they were. But the class and the conference were also small same-sex (and racially segregated) communities where great intimacy, engagement, mutual accountability, and love prevailed. Note how Ezekiel Cooper described the male-only conferences (May 1791): "We still proceeded in our business. Great love and harmony reigned among us. Nothing of a sour or rough nature was seen." Or of a later conference that month:

> All the preachers were invited to breakfast at Mr. Rogers's at half after 7 OC. We had a long train of them near 30 in one room round a table. Great love and brotherly kindness subsisted among us. After breakfast we all retired into a room where conference was finished.[13]

Or of a 1797 conference:

> We had a glorious time. The Lord was with us, indeed. Peace, unity, and love reigned among the preachers, and great power attended their ministry. A number were converted. Almost every day and evening we had a shout among the people.[14]

Similar descriptions—both of the fraternity that prevailed and of the revival that resulted—recur through accounts of conferences, also of class meetings and quarterly meetings.[15] The latter, which brought together the classes into the larger family of the circuit and assembled the array of leadership from that and adjacent circuits, are among the best described of early Methodist meetings, particularly so because they were well attended by preachers who wrote one another letters or who left journals. A rich vein of such accounts can be found in a rare volume, *Extracts of Letters Containing Some Account of the Work of God Since the Year 1800: Written by the Preachers and Members of the Methodist Episcopal Church, to their Bishops.*[16]

Quarterly Meetings

The quarterly meetings, though an inherited part of the Wesleyan economy, had become in American hands an extended religious festival, anticipatory of later camp meetings. Bishop Coke immediately recognized their distinctive character:

> Their Quarterly-meetings on this Continent are much attended to. The Brethren for twenty miles round, and sometimes thirty or forty, meet together. The meeting always lasts two days. All the Travelling Preachers in the Circuit are present, and they with perhaps a local Preacher or two, give the people a sermon one after another, besides the Love-feast, and (now) the Sacraments.[17]

In their quarterly meetings, Methodists most fully and distinctively exhibited themselves as church—a gathering of the faithful to hear the Word, receive the sacraments, administer discipline, care for the needs of the church, and open their hearts

to those who would "flee the wrath to come." Not only did the quarterly meeting operationalize all of what Methodists had come to mean by church—from out of their Anglican as well as Wesleyan heritages. It was also the only such gathering that did. Quarterly meeting was church for early Methodism, an elaborate, staged affair of:
- the exercise of discipline, often on the first day, preferably Saturday;
- multiple sermons and exhortations;
- love feast, preferably early on the next morning;
- more sermons and exhortations;
- the Lord's Supper; and
- baptisms and memorial services, if needed.

It should come as no surprise, though it has been insufficiently appreciated, that many, if not most, of Methodism's early revivals had their seat or spring in quarterly meetings.[18] Many of these drew huge crowds—Ezekiel Cooper and Freeborn Garrettson give estimates in the thousands—and they were occasions for Methodists to hear the saving word but also to preach it to the world in a highly choreographed, dramatic, multi-act counterpart to Wesley's field preaching.

The scenes at quarterly meetings invite us to qualify what might be termed early Methodism's sectarian character. For, if Methodists withdrew to themselves in class and conference (and in same-sex communities), and if they preached and demanded of themselves an alternative lifestyle to that of the genteel world around them, then *they* also engaged the world in their preaching and preeminently in the quarterly meetings, seeking its transformation and certainly that of all who would listen. They would, they pledged in the *Discipline*, reform the continent. And Methodists, pragmatists from the start, measured their advances and conquests in the world by numbers, by body count. As did the United States in Vietnam, Methodists counted how many were slain, albeit in the Spirit.

Anti-Slavery

Early Methodism expressed its transformative gospel, its vision of new community, and its opposition and alternative to gentility in a highly controversial stance, namely, anti-slavery. To be sure, by 1797, they were in retreat from the advanced positions taken in the early 1780s. Nevertheless, some Methodists still preached against slavery, and they did so *as Southerners* and *in the South*.[19] This, too, tends to be overlooked and understated. Further, we need also to recall that in the late 1790s James

O'Kelly and the Republican Methodists bled off some of the anti-slavery spirit. The Republicans sought freedom for the preachers but also for the slave. We count them schismatic, but that does not mean that their views were, in every respect, unrepresentative. Asbury took them seriously. The witness and threat of the O'Kellyites can be read in the journals from the late 1790s of preachers stationed in the South. Henry Smith wrote Daniel Hitt from the Salt River Circuit in Kentucky:

> There is a certain Mr. Haw and a Mr. Kile, who have withdrawn from our order and Connection, and joined the Republicans; and two or three more of the local preachers, together with some of the members, are wavering. They speak much against slaveholders and Mr. Asbury's power; but there is not prospect of their drawing members away.[20]

Early Methodism, then, we can call sectarian, if we redefine the word to betoken a movement

- critical of the principalities and powers of the world and of the worldliness that invaded individual lives in immoral, frivolous, undisciplined living;
- structured into small same-sex groups that offered those who would flee the wrath to come new social relations and a new family;
- that drew the wrath of (some) men in power;
- that sought to engage even those men in its effort to transform the world.

It sought transformation mainly in and through itself, not with legislative act or with public campaigns, tentative efforts at both having been attempted to little effect. And it had virtually nothing in the way of institutions through which to effect its mission, its early efforts in education having quite literally gone up in smoke.

Around 1897

By the late 1890s Southern Methodism had become something radically different. It had, by then, substantially recovered from the war, defined its racial boundaries clearly, with the Cape May Accords of 1876 reestablished fraternal relations with the Northern church,[21] reentered a period of growth and prosperity, and reclaimed something of its earlier reformist spirit.[22]

In their address to General Conference in 1898, the bishops sounded an optimistic and positive note: "Surely the world is moving, and God is disencumbering and equipping it for progress." Celebrating progress, science, discoveries, technology, communications, commerce, and industry, they invoked a prophetic image long applied to Methodism—"of wheels within wheels"—and summoned conference to "take our bearings, inspect the field, adjust and modify and adapt the machinery of Methodism to altered conditions, and thus keep pace with the bewildering innovations and developments of the centuries."[23]

They celebrated education:

- the youth entering the ministry "whose scholastic and theological training fit them for the peculiar tests and demands of the times";
- the new hymnal for the Sunday schools and training programs for teachers;
- the "advanced course of study" represented by the Epworth League;
- the systematizing and centralizing role being played by the new Board of Education;
- the educational efforts being carried on through Paine and Lane Institutes for "the Colored People"; and
- Vanderbilt University "naturally and properly the center of our educational system, to which all our schools and colleges should be correlated."[24]

The bishops also celebrated missions—the advances, buildings, resources, and capitalization of missions worldwide; the missionary endeavor of annual conferences; the women's role as "helps meet" for men, just as meet in the church as in the family, and just as valuable, not to say indispensable—the accomplishments of the Scarritt Bible and Training School for Missionaries and Other Christian Workers; missions work of the Woman's Parsonage and Home Mission Society; the efforts to endow hospitals and homes; the role of the Department of Church Extension; the continued need for local preachers in unchurched situations; and the importance of publications.

Wheels Within Wheels: Denominationalism

The church's use of and confidence in its institutions, in structure, in organization, in machinery, in wheels within wheels strikes one as impressive, particularly for us today, now so critical of bureaucracy, of centralization, of taxation, of concentrated and focused power. By contrast, in 1897, Methodists, and particularly the bishops, welcomed the church's use of the technique and technology of the times to meet the new day. Throughout their state of the church, the bishops sustained a sense of Methodism's readiness for the new century, and nowhere better than in their attention to missions:

> Perhaps the most conspicuous feature of Episcopal Methodism is its aggressive character. Its history shows that it was framed with a view to the great commission to go "into all the world, and preach the gospel to every creature." It is inherently missionary in its spirit and aims. No ecclesiastical polity shows better adaptation to preach the gospel to the poor. By its very genius it is ever stretching out to the regions beyond, and can never be satisfied until it has compassed the ends of the earth.[25]

This aggressive, transformative, institution-creating spirit of Southern Methodism I would term "denominational." For the bishops invited the church to relinquish cherished notions of the spirituality of the church and slavery-and-war-induced inhibitions about involving itself in the sociopolitical order. The church, at least in the bishops' estimation, should now exhibit comfort with American denominationalism, accepting itself as:

- one among the many mainstream Protestant bodies about the Christianizing of American society and the world;
- comfortable with its place in the social order, though, hardly with the morality of the day (the bishops said little about temperance, but other voices raised that banner);
- ready for the competitive, voluntaristic, "free-enterprise" free-for-all with other denominations;
- confident of its place and that of other denominations in the larger church, with some notable exceptions, Roman Catholicism obviously being one;
- appreciative of the American experiment in religious liberty and separation of church and state; and
- missionary in nature.

Southern Methodism built itself up nationally and regionally by centralizing operations once locally undertaken, in machinery that we now call bureaucracy, through new organizations oriented to the cause at hand, each with its layers of structure, of networks, of media. One can see the new genius of Methodism, its creating wheels within wheels in the denominational boards but also in the Epworth League or The Woman's Board of Foreign Missions (founded 1878), or the Woman's Parsonage and Home Mission Society.[26] Southern Methodism's organization for work evidenced itself in the "DEDICATION OF THE SCARRITT BIBLE AND TRAINING SCHOOL" in 1892. The school and its work were termed a "splendid evidence of the vigor of modern Christianity. . . ." Miss Maria Layng Gibson, principal of the school, projected an institution dedicated "to the service of God and to the help of man" and "a living, active force." She said:

> Who has the prophet's tongue to tell to-day how great, how limitless may be the possibilities, the power of this institution? . . . If the King's business requires haste . . . shall not his messengers be trained to execute his bidding with wisdom and skill? Would an earthly king admit to his councils an untrained courtier? Were I to picture the ideal student of this and other training schools, she would be a woman who had completed the literary course of a college. If she had taught one or more years, she would meet the condition better. Such a woman the two years' course of study here would send forth well equipped for the service of the King. As we are said to live in two worlds, the spiritual and the physical, provision has been made in the course of study for the cultivation of the powers belonging to both. In its seven departments advantages are presented that can be appreciated only when enjoyed by a worker for Christ. The one end in view will be preparation for service.[27]

Scarritt and the new deaconess order looked forward to a new era of professionalism, of professionalized church work, of trained and skilled technicians, of networks (male and female) structured along vocational lines.[28]

This was still a very patriarchal time and a very patriarchal church. And Scarritt, of necessity, embraced and recognized the family values of the day. The new school looked forward to professional work for women, but did so under patriarchal constraints. It welcomed "mothers, wives and daughters" and offered training for roles allotted to women—roles in teaching, nursing, missions, and eventually social service. Southern Methodism respected, indeed celebrated, the family and like much of Protestantism had recognized the imperative of women's roles in the church because of family constraints, at home and abroad. Women would go, in service and witness, where only women were allowed. Hence the necessity for deaconesses and missionaries.

The Family as Nursery of Piety

And the family continued to be the nursery of piety. So thought the Committee on the Spiritual State of the Church and the General Conference of 1890, which, having outlined problems of corruption, including inordinate love of the world—wealth, fashion, and amusement—appealed as first remedy to the government of the family, which, in the nature of the case, is the most efficient ally of the church. Fathers and mothers, by both precept and example, can do much to restrain the young people of our church from the commoner forms of worldliness.[29]

So one can learn from Hilary Hudson, author of one of the manuals of Southern Methodism for the day, wonderfully titled, *The Methodist Armor or A Popular Exposition of the Doctrines, Peculiar Usages, and Ecclesiastical Machinery of the Methodist Episcopal Church South.* The book, which by 1897 had gone through fifteen printings/editions since its initial publication in 1882, and which would go through nineteen more until last published in 1927, devoted a substantial section to the Christian home as a nursery of piety. He affirmed:

> The homes of Methodists ought to be the brightest and happiest out of heaven. We have all the essential elements to make them such; the literature, the hymns, the tunes, the devotion, the social enjoyments—in fact, every thing to render them cheerful and attractive with living piety.
>
> Such homes would be nurseries for our churches—a perpetual means of grace to the children.[30]

The Congregational "Wheel"

Poised between the Christian home and the boards that organized the church's work nationally and regionally were what the *Discipline* still termed *circuits, stations,* and *quarterly conferences,* but which were imaged by tall-steeple edifices, sumptuous sanctuaries, Akron Plan education units, parsonages, and leaders now called "pastors." Disciplinese still spoke of "preachers in charge," but even the bishops conceded that the "pastorate is fundamental to our system."[31] The circuit rider had indeed dismounted,[32] and the Southern church had come to terms with the power of congregations. Presided over by a pastor, housed often in an elegant building, appealing increasingly to the middle class, the Methodist congregation had become now a highly structured, organizationally complex affair, particularly in the cities and towns.

The language of "local church" lay far in the future, but as early as 1866 the church had recognized that stations or congregations needed "church conferences." By 1894 the *Discipline* mandated them as monthly gatherings and assigned them key financial responsibilities.[33] Increasingly, the church put its emphasis on the congregation, as Bishop Holland McTyeire recognized in *A Catechism on Church Government: With Special Reference to that of the Methodist Episcopal Church, South*. Having summarized the work of General, annual, district, and quarterly conferences in a few sentences for each, he waxed eloquent:

> Last in the series comes the Church Conference assembled whenever there is cause and a call for it. Here the pastor comes down from the pulpit, and touches *the people*. He lays his hand on them, and they lay their hands to the work that is all around, level to every one's capacity. Here the individual member realizes his identity with the body of Christ and his relations to the brethren. Upon *this point*, finally the forces previously gathered must be delivered, or they are spent in vain. THE PEOPLE must be reached. All the gifts of the Holy Spirit, so freely and variously distributed among them, must be drawn out and stirred up in order to a full development of the New Testament Church. Life is more than law. If the work contemplated in the last of this series of Conferences be not accomplished by that or some other agency, then the great law-making Conference that heads the list will meet in vain, and the others will be held to little purpose.[34]

Having now delegated to the congregation responsibilities once the province of quarterly conferences, the denomination struggled to find roles for those persons and offices squeezed out of specifically congregational religious life. So the bishops and the church worried about what to do with local preachers, once the evangelistic outreach arm of the circuit; and what to commit to the presiding elders, once the sacramental and disciplinary officer of local Methodism. Many of the former were tempted into Holiness itinerancy. In the 1890s Holiness evangelists troubled the Southern Zion.[35] The church would counter, albeit ineffectively and belatedly, by creating the office of conference evangelist. In 1898, it reacted defensively, explicitly forbidding local preachers and others from holding services within a charge when so instructed by the preacher in charge.[36]

With the presiding elders the solution was easy enough. They became the tax collectors, receivers of the apportionments in the emerging new bureaucratic order. The Northern church would soon recognize the altered function with a new name, *district superintendents.* However named, they were key players in the building of Methodism, South as well as North, as a denomination. As much as any other office or officer, they kept in gear the wheels within wheels that made the machinery of Methodism hum and that made Methodism a builder of the new South.

And the Twenty-First Century?

We are living through decades in which United Methodism is struggling to undo the order built in the 1890s and recover the spirit that permitted the diversity of 1790.[37] Neither has come easily. The reordering seems less pulled by a new vision than driven by a sense of the burden of the old. Indeed, "reordering" seems less apt as a descriptor than "dismantling." We destroy rather than build. And the old order and its covenants we disparage. When we speak of "denomination" or "connection"[38] now, we reflexively utter something negative about boards, headquarters, bureaucracy, and apportionments. And when we speak of diversity, we tend to utter something about the organized form thereof, the caucuses, their causes, or their "several" family values. Our life together has become a problem to us. We seem overwhelmed by the diversity of values now brought within our common life.

Family values have become a problem. And not just in the sense that that phrase holds in conservative parlance. Individual families are indeed in disarray, but so also is the family of the church. Southern Methodism has been swept along by the currents in American society. Methodist capitulation to culture for some would be represented by same-sex unions. The virulent opposition to same-sex unions, the various strains in family life, and the various family values found within the church similarly represent culture's sway over religious life. The church accommodates culture on the right, as well as on the left, indeed quite across the spectrum.

And the overall values of the church are every bit as confused as its stance vis-à-vis the home. Indeed, one might argue that the basic covenants that define or at least have defined the church's life are at risk, those that establish:

- the values, purposes, and commitments of Methodist life together;
- the things for which we stand, the overriding purposes of our endeavor, and the goals for which we work;
- the way we organize ourselves;
- how we envision and structure religious life so as to pass on the faith from one generation to another;
- how we fashion congregational activities so as to deal with the structures of power in our society and matters of justice, peace, and order.

The concerns and activities around which Methodism for the last century has energized and organized itself seem, at the very best, grudgingly accepted. We support them with our apportionments, but with reluctance and sometimes anger. We would rather not be bothered. And have not recent General Conferences empowered us to ignore existing covenants and the structures by which we maintain them?

Our church seems comfortable in its buildings, though obviously troubled by the fewer and fewer who come to them and the many people of younger ages and other backgrounds outside of them. Southern Methodism has taken on what one might call a "churchly" mentality, a perspective like that of the established churches of Europe, a sense of enjoying (along with other mainstream or old-line denominations) a kind of proprietary role in Southern society. Methodism still has some claim to, some relation with, the great institutions that it has built—the Methodist hospitals, the homes, the orphanages, the camps, the schools, the colleges, the universities. If truth be told, what makes the connection is often not much besides the name. Genuine church relationships for these institutions may require something different than the nineteenth-century denominational bonds.

Methodism needs to be concerned about its college chapels and covenants therein, but the least of its concerns ought to be whether persons of the same sex make covenant there. Indeed, to the contrary, our problem may be that too few of the relationships among our people are grounded in and bonded by church covenants. If we cannot simply return to the institutional, denominational covenants of the nineteenth century, then we cannot return to the sectarian counterculturalism of the eighteenth century either.

New covenants, covenants reconstituting Southern Methodism for a new day, might be in order. We should, it might be argued, encourage rather than discourage covenants that bind Methodists together and in common endeavor for the Kingdom, covenants that establish United Methodists vis-à-vis the moral confusion across the entire social spectrum. We should be obsessed with the covenants:

- that give shape to our commitments;
- that institutionalize our ecclesial family values;
- that affect how we spend our money;
- that pass on the faith;
- through which we care for those in need.

Southern Methodism's problem today is that it has too few covenants rather than too many. We need covenants that will express our family values as Christian community.

CHAPTER 11

Methodism as Machine

Over machinery—the central, executive, decision-making apparatus of the denomination—American Methodists have *gloried* and *agonized* from the very beginning. The agonies focused initially on the power and authority exercised by the appointive office,[1] by John Wesley, founder of the movement, in his directives from Britain; by his assistants in the colonies, Thomas Rankin and Francis Asbury; and by the superintendents (bishops), Thomas Coke and Francis Asbury, after the church organized in 1784.

Methodists later agonized over the episcopal surrogates known as "presiding elders" (now termed *district superintendents*), who functioned regionally with much of the power of episcopacy, but who, as themselves episcopal appointees, lacked the authority, affirmation, and legitimacy enjoyed by the elected bishops. Recently, agonies have focused on the boards and agencies, the topic of other chapters. Over its machinery, Methodists have agonized. In it they have also gloried. This chapter charts the history of that ambivalence.

Schism over Machinery

The power and prerogative of its decision makers prompted Methodists to fight and even to divide, again and again. Other traditions experience turmoil over doctrine

Methodism as Machine

or liturgy. Such matters certainly do figure in Methodist squabbles. However, authority, its form, and exercise figure even more prominently. For instance, the schisms of Methodism's first century all concerned the superintending powers and authorities, typically those of bishops and presiding elders. The more important divisions were:

- the Fluvanna schism of 1779–81 that preceded the organization of the church;
- the separate organization of African Methodists, traditionally dated from 1787;
- the 1792 walkout of James O'Kelly and supporters to form the "Republican Methodists," and the coalescence of a Primitive Methodist movement around William Hammett in Charleston the same year;
- the New England-based Reformed Methodists organized by Pliny Brett in 1814;
- the Stillwellite and African Zion movements of the 1820s, both launched in New York City;
- the Methodist Protestants, whose reform efforts traumatized successive General Conferences in the 1820s and divided Methodism at its heart, in the border states (1830);
- the exiting of abolitionists to form the Wesleyan Methodist Church in 1842;
- the split of the Methodist Episcopal churches in 1844, North and South;
- the emergence of the Free Methodists in the late 1850s (formally organizing in 1860), and the Church of the Nazarene (in the 1890s).

In one or another, all of these divisions turned on the central decision-making power typically exercised by bishops or their surrogates, the presiding elders.[2]

Machinery as Missional

American Methodists also gloried over their organization, over the template sent them by John Wesley, over their improvements thereon, and over what they could and did achieve through its instrumentality. And they explicitly compared Methodism to a machine. Bishops Thomas Coke and Francis Asbury claimed their own role and that of the presiding elders "to preserve in order and in motion the wheels of the vast machine—to keep a constant and watchful eye upon the whole—and to *think deeply* for the general good."³ Editor Nathan Bangs, Methodism's spokesperson for his generation and the "inventor" of Methodism's early agency apparatus, did not use the "M-word" for Methodism. He spoke instead of "system," but he gloried in the machinery, nonetheless. His panegyric also functions as a good description:

> Let us now, that we may discover at one view the symmetry of the whole plan, glance at the different parts of the system. In the first place, there are the classes, consisting of from twelve to twenty members, under the inspection of leaders, who are responsible for their official conduct to the preacher from whom they receive their appointment. These meet together weekly for mutual edification and comfort, and to pay their weekly dues for the support of the poor and the ministry.
>
> Secondly:—There are the stewards, who take charge of the class, quarterly, and sacramental collections, and disburse them to the poor and the ministry, and are responsible to the quarterly meeting conference, from which they receive their appointment, on the nomination of the preacher in charge of the circuit.
>
> Thirdly:—There are the exhorters and local preachers, who, together with the leaders and stewards and travelling preachers on the circuit, compose the quarterly meeting conference, from which body exhorters and local preachers receive their license to officiate, and who recommend preachers to the annual conferences to be received into the travelling connection.
>
> Fourthly:—There is the travelling ministry, consisting of licensed preachers, deacons, elders, and bishops; and these compose the annual conferences, who have the power of receiving preachers, of trying their own members, of hearing appeals of local preachers, and of carrying into execution the rules of discipline, in relation to spreading the gospel by means of an itinerant ministry.
>
> Fifthly:—The general conference, which assembles quadrennially, and is composed of a certain number of travelling elders, elected by the annual conferences. This is the highest ecclesiastical body known in the Methodist Episcopal Church. Under certain restrictions which were imposed upon this delegated general conference at the time it was organized, in 1808, they have the power of revising the discipline, of electing the bishops, the editors and agents of the Book Concern, of hearing appeals from the decisions of annual conferences, and of reviewing the whole field of labor, whether it be included in the general work, or in the missionary department.

In the sixth place:—the bishops who derive their official existence from the general conference, superintend the whole work, preside in the annual and general conferences, perform the ceremony of ordination, and appoint the preachers to their several stations.

In addition to this regular work, in which we behold a beautiful gradation of office and order, from the lowest to the highest, there is the book establishment, which has grown up with the growth of the church, and from which are issued a great variety of books on all branches of theological knowledge, suited to ministers of the gospel, including such as are suited to youth and children, as well as those for Sabbath schools, and a great number of tracts for gratuitous distribution by tract societies, Bibles and Testaments of various sizes, a quarterly review, and weekly religious papers. This establishment is conducted by a suitable number of agents and editors, who are elected by the General Conference, to which body they are responsible for their official conduct, and, in the interval of the General, the New York Annual Conference exercises a supervision of this estimable and highly useful establishment.

In the last place, we may mention the Missionary Society of the Methodist Episcopal Church, which was organized in 1819, . . .

In the work of Sabbath schools, in the establishment of academies and colleges, though the latter have been but recently commenced with any thing like a determination to persevere, this church has taken an honorable stand among its sister denominations. . . .

This is a general outline of the system, the different parts of which have grown out of the exigencies of the times, suiting itself to the mental, moral, and spiritual wants of men, and expanding itself so as to embrace the largest possible number of individuals as objects of its benevolence. I may well be suspected of partiality to a system, to the benign operation of which I am so much indebted, and which has exerted such a beneficial influence upon the best interests of mankind; but I cannot avoid thinking that I see in it that "perfection of beauty, out of which God hath shined," and that emanation of divine truth and light, which is destined, unless it should unhappily degenerate from its primitive beauty and simplicity "into a plant of a strange vine," and thus lose its original energy of character, to do its full share in enlightening and converting the world.[4]

George Cookman, British-born, member of Philadelphia Conference, chaplain of the Senate and fervent abolitionist, viewed Methodism as a machine, the flywheel of which was itinerancy.[5] Employing the vision of Ezekiel, he conceded some of Methodism's agony over machinery but warranted its providential design:

The *great iron wheel* in the system *is itinerancy*, and truly it grinds some of us most tremendously. . . . Let us carefully note the admirable and astounding movements of this wonderful machine. You will perceive there are "wheels within wheels." First, there is the great outer wheel of episcopacy, which accomplishes its entire revolution *once* in *four* years. To this there are attached *twenty-eight smaller wheels*, styled *annual conferences*, moving around *once a year*; to these are attached *one hundred wheels*, designated *presiding elders*, moving *twelve hundred other wheels*, termed *quarterly conferences*, every *three* months; to these are attached *four thousand wheels*, styled *travelling preachers*, moving round *once a month*, and communicating motion to *thirty thousand* wheels, called *class leaders*, moving round *once a week*, and who, in turn, being attached to between *seven and eight hundred thousand wheels*, called *members*, give a sufficient impulse to whirl them round *every day*. O, sir, what a machine is this! This is the machine of which Archimedes only dreamed; this is the machine destined, under God, to *move the world, to turn it upside down*. But, sir, you will readily see the whole success of the operation depends upon keeping the *great iron wheel of itinerancy* in motion. It must be as unincumbered [*sic*] and free as possible.[6]

Writing during the Civil War, when Northern Methodism threw its machinery into gear for the Union cause, the historian and apologist Abel Stevens found his image for Methodist machinery not in the scriptural type but in the contemporary antitype. Looking forward rather than backward, he identified two engines that conquered the New World, the steam engine and Methodism. Stevens began his four-volume history of American Methodism with an imagined meeting in 1757 of John Wesley and James Watt in Glasgow. Watt, "the young artisan of Glasgow University, gave to the world the Steam Engine." Wesley fabricated a system, providentially suited, Stevens argued, for the New World, comparable in delivery of morality, values, belief, and commitment to that other engine and established a religious economy with its own factories, rails, steamship lines, and infrastructure. Stevens then described the Methodist system, showing how each feature of its machinery suited the American situation. By the conceit of the imagined meeting of Watt and Wesley, Stevens gloried in Methodist machinery: "Watt and Wesley might well then have struck hands and bid each other godspeed at Glasgow in 1757: they were co-workers for the destinies of the new world."[7]

Structuring for Accountability and Efficiency

On the eve of the war, the Southern bishop James O. Andrew (whose slaveholding, it should be noted, had occasioned the church's 1844 division), observed that Wesley's machine had over time acquired a complexity that now challenged the authority structures of the church: episcopacy and conference. Much of the change, particularly the establishment of institutions and agencies, had occurred during Andrew's career:

> When we first visited an Annual Conference, the most we had to do was to examine the characters of the preachers, take the numbers, attend to the finances, (a very small business about those times,) read out the appointments, and go home. We had no schools or colleges, no Tract, Missionary, or Sunday-school Societies, to manage. We had not a dozen associations whose complicated machinery requires several days to adjust and keep in proper order.[8]

What Andrew viewed as a challenge, the Northern church (the MEC), by the end of the war, began to recognize as a problem. The machinery, remarkable as it was, could run out of control. In particular, agencies set up as voluntary societies to manage the church's enterprises in publishing, education, missions, freedmen's aid, church extension, and Sunday schools—several of these with female counterparts—could operate remarkably independently. A committee set up to study the matter reported to the 1872 General Conference on the problem with the whole voluntary organizational plan:

> The members of the Board are elected by members of the Society, and the members of the Society are those persons who become such by the payment of twenty dollars or more to its fund.
>
> The General Conference has no legal connection with the Society, except only that by the charter it is provided that the Corresponding Secretaries of said Society shall be elected by the General Conference. . . .
>
> But as the whole management is vested in the Board elected by members of the Society, the Corresponding Secretaries are powerless to represent any interest of the Church or of the Conference independent of the will of the Board. It is evident, too, that the multitude of members of the Society, scattered widely in all parts of the country, either cannot or will not participate in the election of a Board of Managers. It is equally evident that local combinations are liable to be formed each year to change the management of the corporation, and

obtain control of its great resources. We do not express or intimate any doubt of the judicious and faithful management of the Society, but it is high time to close the door against the possibility of danger in the future. . . .

The General Conference, as the supreme legislative authority of the Church, and having in charge all its great interests for the diffusion of Christian civilization, should have a controlling power in all the missionary operations carried on in the name and behalf of the Church.[9]

So the Northern church, the MEC, in 1872, and the Southern church, the MECS, in 1874, acted to amend the charters of and reincorporate societies so as to make them denominational agencies, accountable to and with boards elected by General Conference. Over the next century, Methodist bodies sought various other efficiencies in machinery, as for instance, centrally determined budgets for all agencies and apportionments allocated to the annual conferences, as the MEC bishops advocated in 1912. They said:

As the head of a family anticipates and provides for the incoming year, as a business man estimates the capital required for his contemplated improvements as well as for conducting present enterprises, so should the church forecast her needs and consolidate her estimates for all connectional demands—not by the uncertain process of five or six boards and committees sitting apart and acting independently, if not competitively, but by a competent connectional board or commission—in which or before which all interests may be represented—and with final authority to fix the aggregate budget and properly apportion the total amount among the Conferences.[10]

In the 1939 union that brought together the two Methodist Episcopal churches and the Methodist Protestants, directors acquired the prerogative of selecting agency heads (general secretaries). And the 1968 union of the Methodist and Evangelical United Brethren churches, drawing on the experience of the latter denomination, established a program coordinating agency, the General Council on Ministries, to work alongside the General Council on Finance and Administration.

Wrenches in the Works

By the late twentieth century, the machine no longer enjoyed Methodist fascination. Steam ran fewer and fewer engines. The railroads clung on with subsidies. Factories folded and slunk off to the Third World. The industrial age gave way to that of the computer, electronics, media, and communications. Machinery in human affairs, bureaucracy, and red tape Americans disdained and denounced. George Wallace launched a presidential bid running against Federal machinery and pointy-headed bureaucrats. And subsequent campaigns for House, Senate, and presidency, both Democratic and Republican (but especially the latter), ran on Wallace's ticket. The same script worked famously on the regional and local levels, where candidates campaigned against state government or city hall.

So also in religious affairs, what had once been Methodist glory—national standards, centralized production, efficiencies of scale, common resourcing, proportional fiscal obligations, unified decision making, coherent denominational policy, easily recognized packaging, familiar products, dependable quality—Methodists pilloried. *Bureaucracy* has become a slur.

That negative reading surfaced powerfully after the 1960s—after the civil rights and anti-war campaigns and, for United Methodists, after the 1968 union and 1972 restructuring. It has continued ever since. One of the early denunciations came from two of my former Duke colleagues, Paul A. Mickey and the late Robert L. Wilson. Their *What New Creation? The Agony of Church Restructure* looked at bureaucracy and denominational reorganization efforts in the American Baptist, Episcopal, Presbyterian, United Presbyterian, and United Methodist churches. What they found were crises engulfing the denominations as a whole, which caused the denominations to focus on their agencies.[11]

Their findings or indictments have become something of a litany. National bureaucracies had been dismantled, reassembled, reshuffled, physically relocated with attendant chaos, confusion, and lowered morale among executives and staff. Funding had dropped as membership plateaued and dropped or as congregations withheld monies in anger over policies. Grassroots anger had indeed focused on a number of controversial and high-profile initiatives, programs had been cut, and distrust toward national and regional offices grew. Such pointed attacks on bureaucracy, sometimes concretized in term limits or other thinly disguised punitive efforts, produced morale problems in the agencies. Caucus attempts to gain footholds on boards and in their staffs intensified the political struggles by which leadership identification took place. Agencies evidenced confusion and lack of clarity about purposes and goals. The entire connectional scheme seemed in crisis—a crisis that Mickey and Wilson insist derived from underlying crises of denominational belief and purpose.

Since Mickey and Wilson wrote, we have witnessed a whole industry grow up producing books diagnosing the problems in mainline Protestantism and prescribing various antidotes. Many of these treat bureaucracy as a problem and echo the Mickey-Wilson indictments, if not always their vivid conspiratorial style. For instance, two of the volumes in the General Council on Ministries series "Into Our Third Century," *Images of the Future* by Alan K. Waltz, and *Paths to Transformation: A Study of the General Agencies of The United Methodist Church* by Kristine M. Rogers and Bruce A. Rogers, treated anti-centralization attitudes more as problem than as norm, but recognized the same problematic.[12] Bishop Richard Wilke, in *And Are We Yet Alive? The Future of The United Methodist Church*, found plenty of blame to spread around, but certainly called for overhaul, stripping down, streamlining, and reorienting of our structures.[13] Longtime church researchers Douglas W. Johnson and Alan K. Waltz, in their volume with the colorless title *Facts and Possibilities: An Agenda for The United Methodist Church*, pointed to the lack of coordination at the national level among the Council of Bishops, General Conference, and general agencies—and that despite the existence and efforts of the coordinating agencies, the General Council on Finance and Administration and General Council on Ministries (GCOM).[14] And then almost two decades ago, the whole Council of Bishops waded in with their prophetic study and episcopal letter, *Vital Congregations, Faithful Disciples: Vision for the Church: Foundation Document*.[15] They too treated central agency structures as problems.

New Machinery for a New Millennium?

The critics of Methodist bureaucracy sound like they oppose all machinery. To view their activities rather than listen to their tirades, one discovers, in many of these apparent Luddites, incredible institutional ferment, experimentation, creativity, and energy. They denounce old machinery to make space for new—assembled from below; freshly purposive; digital, technological, and media reliant; highly adaptive; and packaged for business. These Methodists glory over more local or adaptive machinery as they agonize over still official national structures.

This ambivalence runs deep in the Methodist psyche. It derives from habits and patterns and practices that Methodists are much better at doing than at explaining.[16]

The appointive machinery around itinerancy operationalizes a missional principle, namely, that ministry is sent, commissioned, missionary in character. The superintending or episcopal machinery, at its best, concerns itself with the Kingdom, the deployment of each for the good of the whole (earth). The conferences, which Methodists still regard as the basic body of the church, are now being reclaimed as "means of grace," a phrase Wesley himself applied to the conferencing tasks—conversations about growth in holiness for the whole body. And boards and agencies, even they display (as do these other systems) the deep Methodist conviction that connecting in the work of God is the church, that the church is connectional, that the connection displays God's will.

The United Methodist *Discipline* reads like a book of order or constitution; and that it is. But it derived from the series of conversations that Mr. Wesley conducted in conference about how to follow the path to holiness. This counsel about discipline the Americans decided to call *Discipline*. Over time discipline as calling, as response to the divine initiative, as a way of living into God's future has yielded power, structure, process. Its instrumental value has tended to obscure its missional, gracious, ecclesial character. Nevertheless, the machinery that the *Discipline* describes and calls for Methodists have typically established as an act of discipline. And from time to time, Methodists have seen fit to renew or refresh or augment their discipline by adding to or altering the *Discipline*. So as their machinery has evolved over time, the acts of discipline over which one generation glories has become the agonies of a later.

Connectional Reform?

Agonies over machinery—the central, executive, decision-making apparatus of the denomination—prompted three successive General Conferences to authorize the General Council on Ministries to lead the denomination in various studies and task force inquiries into national connectional structures and processes. Some critics viewed the assignment as at least ironic and perceived GCOM as itself a central if not *the* central problem, the most dysfunctional part of the whole machine. After countless meetings, considerable consultation, the tapping of wisdom from across the church and great expense, GCOM reported three times to the following General Conferences. On each occasion, GCOM brought in a vision for a new machine, a church reimagined for the new century. And each submission looked, at least to this observer, as though GCOM had reinvented the denomination like a giant GCOM. Rather than recommend its own demise—a difficult bureaucratic gesture—GCOM transformed itself three times and in three quite elegant designs into the whole church.

Three strikes is out. So deemed the 2004 General Conference committee at which the third swing came. Throwing out the study, the committee recommended the dismantling of GCOM and the creation of new coordinating machinery for a new age, coordinated by a Connectional Table. General Conference concurred. At this writing, the church has had only a quadrennium of experience with Connectional Table, but already generalized that organizational principle onto other levels. Judgment seems premature. Expect ambivalence. Over its machinery, Methodists have agonized. In it they have also gloried.

CHAPTER 12

Methodism and Providence

History and historical experience have told Methodists who they were. Of course, to some extent the same pertains to religious movements generally; all are historically conditioned by context, circumstance, events, personalities, conflicts, and environment. However, as I have endeavored to show, history has shaped American Methodism in very special ways. Inheritors of a Wesleyan system built piecemeal but freed suddenly from trans-Atlantic authority by the American Revolution, American Methodism found itself muddling into being a church without theologically trained leadership. Following John Wesley's pattern of experiential and experimental development, American Methodism gradually built a connectional church. In this aggregative church building they believed themselves led by the Holy Spirit and Providence, as we have seen and will note further below. Still Providence had not blessed them with an initial grand vision, the details of which only needed to be filled in. Instead, Methodists generated whom they were through the give-and-take, the conflicts, the inventions, the borrowings of history. And insofar as they grasped their new connectional order conceptually and theologically, they did so by looking at its unfolding, their history, by examining where the Spirit had led them. In this chapter, we look at Methodism's interpreters, her historians.

In a closely related but second sense, history has told Methodists whom they were. Methodists have employed history theologically when they needed to say whom they were, what goals they would pursue, from where they have come, how they were changing, and toward what ends they would proceed. They did so, as our first chapter shows and we note again below, in the *Discipline* through accounts of God's work in the Wesleyan revival. In such conversion narratives writ large, Methodists produced reflexively a naive, unreflective providential history. History served them doctrinally. However, The Methodist Episcopal Church did not refresh, update, and expand this providential historical preface to capture the sense that the Spirit's leadings were ongoing. Instead, they effectively froze that initial account, a kind of Methodist counterpart to the Protestant conviction that the age of miracles closed with the canon of Scripture. And the later Methodist movements, each prefacing their *Discipline* with a historical account of their beginnings, dwelled on power and authority, not on Providence or the Spirit.

The same desacralizing occurred, as this chapter shows, in Methodism's formal histories. The earliest accounts worked with a lively sense of God's presence in the American Methodist movement. Methodism's historians gradually muted the theological, the providential, the salvific dimension. The histories of Methodism grew in number, in scope, and in volume. History remained an important way of presenting the movement. What, though, would it mean for Methodists' religiosity or spirituality when the historical accounts muted the sense of God's presence with them? What would it mean for their doctrine, when history no longer functioned theologically? This chapter addresses these questions. It traces the growing sophistication and self-consciousness with which Methodists undertook their historical writing and their coming to terms with the late nineteenth-century "scientific" historiography that read God out of historical narratives.

Defining Church History

In 1884, the American Historical Association (AHA) was founded. Four years later, in 1888, the American Society of Church History (ASCH) came into being. These two events belong to the larger saga of late nineteenth-century professional formation.[1] In field after field, amateur and patrician endeavors fell before what seemed a common strategy to consolidate, standardize, resource, institutionalize, and professionalize. Yet, for my purposes, it is the relation of the ASCH to the AHA that is most instructive. The two organizations shared much. Both drew significantly upon the idiom and structures of German historical scholarship.

The guiding spirit of the AHA, Herbert Baxter Adams, plied his German training in a research seminar at Johns Hopkins University, whose methods and graduates swept historical efforts across the nation into the AHA orbit. His counterpart, Philip Schaff, conceived the ASCH in comparable instrumental and imperialistic terms. German-born, trained by Ferdinand Christian Baur and Johann A.W. Neander, Schaff put an indelible mark on the field of church history. The scholarship attests the leadership and legacy:

- a thirteen-volume American Church History series (1893–97);
- his own six-volume *History of the Christian Church* (1888–92);
- a three-volume *Religious Encyclopaedia* (1882–84), adapted from that of J.J. Herzog;
- the three-volume *Creeds of Christendom* (1877); and
- the Nicene and Post-Nicene Fathers, the two series of which ran to twenty-eight and fourteen volumes (1886–89; 1890–1900).[2]

Some around Schaff saw the purpose of the ASCH and the AHA as sufficiently identical to warrant merger. They formed a committee to pursue that end. In 1896, after Schaff's death, the ASCH, in fact, dissolved and transformed itself into a section of the AHA, only later to reestablish its independence. While he lived, Schaff fought such efforts, preferring to see the ASCH as having its own distinct mission.[3] Programmatic aspects of that mission, for instance the pursuit of Christian unity through history, clearly lay beyond the interests of secular historians. But Schaff also believed that the conception of history itself differed. The scientific lights by which colleagues, particularly in the AHA, increasingly found their paths, Schaff viewed as only partially illuminating the historical saga. He denounced the iconoclastic, empirical, and naturalistic tendencies of this new generation of scientific historians.[4] He considered rationalism an inadequate beacon for church history. On the contrary, he insisted that church history remain a sacred rather than a natural science. Premised on belief in God's operative control of history, church history required an appropriate definition of the church as a starting point and a method sensitive to the activity of the Spirit in human affairs. As a working maxim, Schaff affirmed: "The recognition of God in history is the first principle of all sound philosophy of history. . . . He who denies the hand of Providence in the affairs of the world and the church is intellectually or spiritually blind."[5]

The scientific historians were quite impatient with such views. They were especially so with their contemporaries from the older generation of American historians, who indulged themselves in such speculation, tracing, for instance, the finger of Providence in American affairs. Scientific history ought rather to confine attention to the human and natural realm, to cause-and-effect relations, to explanations that were objective, universal, and regular.[6] Even the church, they thought, should be treated as a human institution. With such an understanding, Herbert Baxter Adams taught a course in church history at Johns Hopkins.[7] Toward that understanding, the discipline of church history gravitated in the decades after Schaff's death. The standard-bearer was Ephraim Emerton, who taught church history at Harvard from 1882 to 1918. Trained at Harvard, Berlin, and Leipzig, Emerton sought to make church history scientific. He insisted that church history be pursued with the rules that govern all history: "Church History is nothing more or less than one chapter in that continuous record of human affairs which we give the name of history in general."[8] He rejected out of hand the older conception of church history, repudiating, for instance, the following as an unhistorical framing of the task: "To show when the divine force has controlled all human events, and made them subserve the steady progress of God's servants is the mission of him who treats the history of the Church."[9] Emerton functioned with the axiom that "the superhuman . . . is not a subject for the historical record."[10] Hence church historians had no business with the controlling hand of Providence, divine interpositions, and the divine presence in the life of the church.[11]

History and Providence

This chapter traces Methodism's shift from a providential (Schaff's) to a scientific (Emerton's) undertaking of its history. It amounts to an inquiry into the decline in belief in Providence. Or, perhaps I should say, a shift in the way in which God's activity in the world was envisioned; for I intend to monitor various claims to divine agency, not simply those that might be comprehended in a doctrine of Providence, strictly defined. My focus will be on a particular religious community, even a subvariety thereof, the body known as The Methodist Episcopal Church, perhaps the leading but certainly not the only bearer of the Wesleyan legacy in America.

I attempt to show that (1) a historical presentation of the movement functioned as an essential, if not *the* essential, mode of self-understanding; (2) the church permitted history that definitional and legitimating function because history served theological purposes; (3) for much of the nineteenth century those purposes placed Providence at the heart of Methodist history; (4) as the century wore on those claims about Providence changed; and (5) by the end of the century Methodist history began to approximate the views of Emerton.[12] On one level, and most explicitly, this inquiry traces the evolution of Methodist historical scholarship. However, since such scholarship shaped and was shaped by the self-understanding of the Methodist denomination, these historiographical changes also illustrate changes in the denomination. On that level, the inquiry concerns fundamental, paradigmatic shifts in Methodist consciousness. In several respects, this study opens the question of secularization. The relation of historical consciousness to institutional, popular, and societal consciousness (here treated in terms of the relation of Methodist history to Methodism); the specific changes in historiography (here Methodist historiography); and the changing character of denominations (here only The Methodist Episcopal Church)—all have been considered under the rubric of secularization.[13]

The motif of Providence is not the only window on these changes. And yet its transparency is not readily equaled. For in the movement's infancy, Methodists saw themselves in providential terms; they saw through their activities, beliefs, and rituals to the workings of God. In such claims, they entered to their own account a common vision. Most Americans in the eighteenth and early nineteenth centuries about whom we know believed fervently in Providence. And they saw in both public and personal events the clear tracings of the divine hand.[14] By the end of the century, as we have noted, those who could no longer see Providence disdained those who did. That shift altered the way historians envisioned the world. It produced no less dramatic changes in denominational consciousness. In a real sense, Providence was the issue of secularization.

History as Methodist Self-Definition

The Wesleyan movement understood itself in providential terms. Its revivals, preaching, structures, and ethos served to renew the church, so it thought, because they derived from the workings of the Holy Spirit. That premise made Methodists, as it made other movements who shared it (the Puritans and other Pietists, for instance), acutely sensitive to human experience. They looked within (the human heart) and looked without (in human affairs), expecting to detect God at work. What they found, they felt impelled to share, confident that God used even humble vessels to bear that which would save others. So men and women spoke of their religious experience in band and class meetings. So John Wesley broadcast those accounts in his *Arminian Magazine*. So he published journals, his own and others. And so he wrote his *A Plain Account of the People Called Methodists* and *A Short History of Methodism*, collective accounts of God at work. These were history-as-conversion narratives. Methodists turned to history, their own history preeminently, for redemptive purposes. History functioned not only as language about God—a theology—but, more important, as God's language, as the way God worked to achieve the renovation of the world.

Methodists generally gave history a prominent function. American Methodists, in particular, gave it a peculiarly salient place in their self-definition. As we noted in the first chapter, when American Methodists organized themselves as an independent church in1784, independent from Wesley (they thought) and independent from Anglicanism, they, like the nation, drew up a quasi-constitution. The document that resulted, commonly known as the *Discipline*, was one of three books (along with the Bible and their hymnbook) that defined and shaped the church. The latter two gave the movement its substance, the former its form. The initial version of the *Discipline* followed in style, substance, and order a loosely constructed, question-and-answer document derived from John Wesley's conferences with his preachers, the Large Minutes.[15] In 1787 the American Methodists put their own stamp and order on the *Discipline*—"Arranged under proper HEADS, and METHODIZED in a more acceptable and easy MANNER." They retained John Wesley's question-and-answer style. But they put up front a historical statement about themselves. Their introduction of themselves spoke first of history, before it said anything about what it believed, about Scripture or sacraments or authority or polity. They asked first, "What was the Rise of Methodism so called in Europe?"; second, "What was the Rise of Methodism, so called in America?"; and third, "What may we reasonably believe to be God's design in raising up the Preachers called Methodists?"

The first two answers sketched the very beginnings of Methodism in Britain and America on a human scale:

Answ. In 1729, two young Men, reading the Bible, saw they could not be saved without Holiness, followed after it, and incited others so to do. In 1737, they saw likewise, that Men are justified before they are sanctified: but still Holiness was their Object. God then thrust them out, to raise an holy People.

Answ. During the Space of thirty Years past, certain Persons, Members of the Society, emigrated from England and Ireland, and settled in various Parts of this Country. About twenty Years ago, Philip Embury, a local Preacher from Ireland, began to preach in the City of New-York, and formed a Society of his own Countrymen and the Citizens. About the same Time, Robert Strawbridge, a local Preacher from Ireland, settled in Frederick County, in the State of Maryland, and preaching there formed some Societies. In 1769, Richard Boardman and Joseph Pilmoor, came to New-York; who were the first regular Methodist Preachers on the Continent. In the latter End of the Year 1771, Francis Asbury and Richard Wright, of the same Order, came over.[16]

The answer to the third query spoke about the work of God, rendering a providential history of American Methodism. In the first clause, American Methodists customized a Wesleyan formulation. In the second, they placed a most significant theological construction on the first two questions and answers. "What may we reasonably believe to be God's design in raising up the Preachers called Methodists?"

To reform the Continent, and spread scripture Holiness over these Lands. As a Proof hereof, we have seen in the Course of fifteen Years a great and glorious Work of God, from New York through the Jersies, Pennsylvania, Delaware, Maryland, Virginia, North and South Carolina, even to Georgia.[17]

This, Methodism's purpose statement, was regularly cited and is still cited as defining what Methodists thought themselves about. Thus the *Discipline* gathered the entire Methodist movement into Providence, turned mundane into sacred history, conceived of history in redemptive terms.

In 1790, bishops Thomas Coke and Francis Asbury incorporated the providential account of Methodist origins into a prefatory episcopal address, where it would remain for the next century for the MEC. The MECS carefully incorporated the exact wording into its episcopal preface to warrant the claim that the separation of North and South into two episcopal connections was no schism and that it, as much as the MEC, remained a true part of the 1784 providential founding. Historical sections that followed in the MECS account dwelled on the very human factors that had split the church. And other denominations that took their rise out of the MEC stock did the same. So, although Methodists do not seem to have drawn out its implications, they carefully preserved both the precise wording and the placement of this providential historical formulation. It continued to be their first statement about themselves. By contrast, other denominations did not seem to rely on history in this fashion.[18] At any rate, Methodists, children of Providence by their own estimation, turned to history for the frame for their church, the *Discipline*.

Pure History of Religion in America

The historical imperative to view and document God's hand in Methodist affairs expressed itself in various ways other than in the Disciplinary account. The leadership clearly saw history's importance. John Wesley wrote the American Ezekiel Cooper in 1791: "We want some of you to give us a connected relation of what our Lord has been doing in America from the time that Richard Boardman accepted the invitation and left his country to serve you."[19] That sort of request generated the personal accounts with which Wesley filled his *Arminian Magazine* and that found their way into the initial, but short-lived American Methodist effort at serials. Wesley's overture also clearly prompted *The Experience and Travels of Mr. Freeborn Garrettson*,[20] the first of many American Methodist journals to be published.

Bishop Asbury, who oversaw the serialization of his own journal, issued a Wesley-like command to the American leadership, the presiding elders, requesting more of the same: "Once in every year I wish to hear circumstantially from the presiding elders, that we may collect, as in medium, the most pleasing and interesting things of the work of God, not only for the episcopacy, but the Conferences, and the press. I think we have paid but little attention to the work of God, or pure history of religion in America."[21]

Asbury's order resulted in the publication of *Extracts of Letters Containing Some Account of the Work of God Since the Year 1800. Written by the Preachers and Members of the Methodist Episcopal Church, to their Bishops*.[22] Here were the raw, undigested, immediate Methodist apprehensions of the movement of God—accounts of revivals, camp meetings, revivalistic quarterly meetings.[23] Here was a "pure history of religion" in Asbury's terms. A comparable perspective on a comparable document came from the book editors Daniel Hitt and Thomas Ware. They gathered into one volume *Minutes of the Methodist Conferences, Annually*

Held in America from 1773 to 1813, affirming: "[T]his publication must confessedly contain the best history (as far as it goes) of the Methodists and Methodist preachers in America, now extant; from the commencement thereof to the year 1813:—shewing to the reflective mind, what the Lord hath done for us, and by us, in the space of 40 years past." Noting the dramatic growth and prosperity of Methodism, the editors comment further, "With wonder and gratitude, we may exclaim, what hath God wrought?"[24]

The editors' claim for the *Minutes* is particularly interesting, because three years earlier Jesse Lee had published *A Short History of the Methodists*.[25] Apparently, Hitt and Ware preferred the uninterpreted legislative acts, statistical reports, listing of ministers and charges, and obituaries of the *Minutes* to Lee's more narrative account. His effort, however, resembled theirs more perhaps than they recognized.

The Methodist Historians

Jesse Lee (1758–1816)

Abel Stevens and J.M. Buckley ranked Jesse Lee next to Bishop Asbury in importance—"the most popular . . . and one of the most effective . . . of early American Methodist preachers." A national leader, Asbury's choice to be an episcopal colleague, nearly elected to that office, and "the founder of Methodism in New England," Lee lived the history he wrote, from his conversion in 1773 under Robert Williams, through pacificist alternative service in the Revolution, to chaplaincy to Congress.[26] On the title page of his *Short History of the Methodists*, Lee placed three verses from the Hebrew Scriptures. They suggested the essential continuity between this first, formal history and prior Methodist efforts at providential historical self-understanding: "The LORD hath done great things for us; whereof we are glad." (Psalm 126:3, KJV); "Come thou with us, and we will do thee good: for the LORD hath spoken good concern Israel." (Numbers 10:29, KJV); "We will go with you: for we have heard that God is with you." (Zechariah 8:23, KJV).

Lee sustained the providential theme from first to last, connecting it tightly to Methodism. In his preface, he affirmed:

> I desire to shew to all our societies and friends, that the doctrines which we held and preached in the beginning, we have continued to support and maintain

uniformly to the present day. We have changed the economy and discipline of our church at times, as we judged for the benefit and happiness of our preachers and people; and the Lord has wonderfully owned and prospered us. It may be seen from the following account, how the Lord has, from very small beginnings, raised us up to be a great and prosperous people. It is very certain, that the goodness of our doctrine and discipline, our manner of receiving preachers, and of sending them into different circuits, and the frequent changes among them from one circuit to another, not allowing them in general to stay more than one year in a station or circuit, and in no case more than two years, has greatly contributed to the promotion of religion, the increase of our societies, and the happiness of our preachers.[27]

Lee concluded on the same note, believing that his "collection of facts, and . . . clear, plain, and full account" would convince the reader "that the Lord has done great things for us."[28]

Not content to make vague, prefatory claims about general providential workings and leave the matter there, as would later historians, Lee found particular Providence far more important. Indeed, like John Wesley, Lee would probably have been not a little impatient with a sharp distinction between general and particular Providence.[29] Where Lee discerned the hand of God at work, he announced it. For instance, in analyzing Methodist growth in Petersburg in 1787, Lee stated forthrightly, "That town never witnessed before or since such wonderful displays of the presence and love of God in the salvation of immortal souls."[30] Lee made such providential judgments cautiously and selectively. There seem to be two factors that govern those conclusive claims: first, Lee's proximity to the events and, second, the presence of a revival. These criteria determine the point at which he begins to make providential calls. Although he began with Wesley and British Methodism and traced the early American developments, only when his narrative reached the 1770s, his native Virginia, and the labors of Robert Williams and Devereux Jarratt (after forty-three pages of earlier Methodist history) did Lee clearly discern "a considerable out-pouring of the spirit" and did he conclude that "many sinners were truly converted to God." Lee continued: "The revival of religion which first began under the ministry of Mr. Jarratt, was greatly increased by the labours of the Methodist preachers, who, uniting with Mr. Jarratt in the same blessed work, were greatly owned and honoured of God and had the pleasure of seeing the work of the Lord prospering in their hands."

Lee was himself one measure of that prosperity. He had been converted by Williams, whom he regarded as his spiritual father. Hence his confidence in God's activity.

At earlier points in the Methodist saga, where religious vitalities might have warranted a comparable providential discernment, Lee refrained from rendering the judgment himself. For instance, of a 1760 revival in Britain, Lee said, "Many persons, men and women, professed to be cleansed from all unrighteousness and made perfect in love in a moment." Then putting the providential discernment into other hands, he quoted Wesley, "Here began that glorious work of sanctification." So also Lee rendered an account of George Whitefield's 1740 revivals in New England by citing a passage from Whitefield's journal that advanced the claims about the work of God.[31]

Thereafter, Lee saw the hand of God primarily in the revivals and he saw it so clearly where he saw it close-up, directly, personally. For instance, Lee devoted some six pages to a major revival that occurred in 1775 in southern Virginia and in North Carolina. He spoke of God sending his word home upon hearts, of "the great power of God," of "the presence of God," of hundreds finding "the peace of God," of the work of God increasing on every side, and of the Lord raising up preachers. He concluded, "Such a work of God as that was, I had never seen, or heard of before." He then added, "I have spoken largely of this revival of religion; but my pen cannot describe the one half of what I saw, heard and felt. I might write a volume on this subject, and then leave the greater part untold."[32]

We might say that Lee did indeed write a volume on this subject. His history had as its subject "Methodism as revival." He wrote providential history with a narrow, revivalistic thrust. Or perhaps we should describe this as a conversion narrative expanded, a narration of a collective conversion. For really only in conversions and revivals did Lee see the hand of God. He did not ignore other aspects of the Methodist economy. Indeed, he structured the book around the periodic quarterly, annual, and General conferences, which functioned as the legislative, judicial, and executive of the Methodist movement. He attended to the evolution of structure and authority, taking care to cite important documents in full. He wrote essentially as an apologist for the system, even though he had his own differences with Bishop Asbury and made little use of Asbury's published journals.

Others before and after Lee—from John Wesley himself through most of the nineteenth-century Methodist historians—saw providential design in the entire

Methodist system, and particular features thereof, like its itinerant principle, its provision for small groups (classes), camp meetings, and the like. Lee would only hint at that general providential dimension.[33] Nor did Lee connect Methodism providentially with the American experiment. Perhaps, he saw too clearly what was central in God's intentions to be concerned with what seemed peripheral. At any rate, his successors put both Methodism and Providence in a larger context.

Nathan Bangs (1778–1862)

"Apologist for American Methodism" a study once described him, and that Nathan Bangs was.[34] Bangs wrote against Calvinists, who attacked Methodist doctrine, and against Episcopalians, who attacked its order. He also faced the critics within. But like Lee, Bangs was also a major creator of and actor in the script that he transcribed. Bangs led Methodism through the restructuring that made it a member of the nineteenth-century family of Protestant denominations, that voluntary establishment of Christianity. Most notably he had a hand in giving the denomination the rudiments of organization, by forming educational institutions, by creating a ministerial course of study, and by formally adopting the society principle through the creation of a missionary society (serving as its major officer). He also played a pivotal role in both *The Christian Advocate*, Methodism's national paper, and *The Methodist Magazine*, its first successful effort at theological journalism. Bangs was "American Methodism's first major historian, polemicist, and theological editor."[35]

From Bangs's pen came, in 1838–41, *A History of the Methodist Episcopal Church*, a four-volume work, each roughly 400 pages.[36] In certain respects, Bangs's providential views resembled Lee's. Bangs also termed the 1775 growth spurt "a remarkable revival of the work of God" and spoke of "these manifest displays of the power and grace of God."[37] He would not only see in the phenomenon of camp meetings "signal displays of the power and grace of God" but would analyze them with some care to defend that judgment.[38] Like Lee, Bangs recognized God's handiwork in conversions and revivals.

Bangs, however, also wrestled with the implications of Methodism's taking its place in American society and assuming a role in the Protestant endeavor to create a Christian society and state. That meant a conception of Providence put in a larger context and nuanced more carefully. Bangs conceded, for instance:

> We do not infer the blessing of God upon the labors of a ministry merely because proselytes are made. Mohammed made proselytes to his false religion by the power of the sword faster than Jesus Christ did by the power of his miracles and the purity of his doctrine. And any impostor, or mere formal minister, by the fascinating charms of his eloquence, or the cunning artifices to which he will resort, may succeed in proselyting others to his party without at all benefitting their souls, or reforming their lives. The mere multiplication of converts to a system is no proof, of itself, that it has the sanction of the God of truth and love.[39]

He continued,

> We have not, therefore, enumerated the communicants of the Methodist Episcopal Church as an evidence, of itself, that its ministry were moving in obedience to God's will, and in the order of his providence. Though they had been as "numerous as the sands upon the seashore," had they been destitute of righteousness, they would be no proof that the instruments of their conversion were sent of God.[40]

Bangs had directed much of his writing at critics who had, in various ways, implicitly or explicitly, suggested that Methodism was not of God. Bangs could not, with Lee, content himself with "providential" results and take those results as self-evidently attesting Methodism's providential character. He had to show the providential design. He did that in a variety of ways. First, and perhaps most important, he elaborated criteria that allowed him to make good the claim. To the rhetorical challenge just cited, Bangs proposed the following as sustaining the providential character of Methodism:

1. "[T]hese men preached the pure doctrine of Jesus Christ";
2. "[T]hose who were converted by their instrumentality were really 'brought from darkness to light, and from the power of Satan to God'";
3. [T]hose "born of the Spirit" then "brought forth the 'fruit of the Spirit, love, joy, peace, long- suffering, gentleness, goodness, faith, meekness, temperance.'"[41]

There could be no mistaking the maneuver. Bangs proposed as criteria of Providence precisely what Methodists took to be their hallmarks—faithful and efficacious preaching, the new birth, and holiness. However, he took care to locate the providential mark in the distinctiveness of Methodist commitment to orthodox belief, not in its theological novelty. Indeed, as a further criterion of Methodism's providential character, Bangs, in his *An Original Church of Christ*, elaborated the first point into a full-scale defense of the primitive, apostolic character of Methodism, a point that Methodists, following Wesley, had always made.[42] In his *History*, Bangs reiterated the apostolic claims on both doctrine and polity. With regard to the latter, he pronounced "the Methodist Episcopal Church Scriptural and apostolical in her orders and ordinances." On doctrine, he affirmed:

> The doctrine, too, which they principally insisted upon, had a direct tendency to produce the desired effect to heart and life. While they held, in common with other orthodox Christians, to the hereditary depravity of the human heart, the deity and atonement of Jesus Christ, the necessity of repentance and faith; that which they pressed upon their hearers with great earnestness was, the necessity of the new birth, and the privilege of their having a knowledge, by the internal witness of the Holy Spirit, of the forgiveness of sins, through faith in the blood of Christ; and as a necessary consequence of this, and as naturally flowing from it, provided they persevered, holiness of heart and life. On this topic they dwelt with an emphasis and an earnestness peculiar to themselves. The doctrine itself, though held by most orthodox churches . . . was allowed to sleep in their books.[43]

Because Methodists recognized that they emphasized doctrines, like holiness, the church generally had left dormant; because they saw themselves as reviving scriptural and "experimental" Christianity; because they recognized Wesley's own imprint in all they were about—they could not effectively establish a historical (i.e., human) connection between Methodism and the early church. So from 1784 on, they repudiated notions of uninterrupted apostolic succession.

Bangs concurred.[44] That wedded both him and Methodism generally to the doctrine of Providence. The connections between Methodism and primitive Christianity, between Methodism and Scripture—the connections that counted—were the Providence of God and Methodism's fidelity to the faith delivered to the saints. They saw John Wesley in those terms; they saw their church economy in similar terms.

Musing retrospectively about the historian's responsibility, Bangs asserted, "I might have conjured up a thousand fanciful theories to account for the success and influence of Methodism, without ascribing it to its true original cause, namely, the divine agency." Both the "entire structure" of Methodism and its introduction into this country, he thought, "originated without any foresight of man, without any previous design in the instruments to bring about such an event, and without any of those previously devised plans which generally mark all human enterprises."[45] This language, which echoed Wesley, pointed in Methodist minds to a Providence that was as practical and pragmatic in things structural as it was experimental in things personal. The providential claim covered the Methodist system generically. It applied particularly to engines of revival, most notably camp meetings. Bangs affirmed:

> [T]hese camp meetings were not the result of a previously digested plan, but like every other peculiarity of Methodism, were introduced by providential occurrences, and were embraced and followed up by God's servants because they found them subservient to the grand design they had in view, namely, the salvation of the world by Jesus Christ.[46]

Elsewhere Bangs spoke of the "gospel simplicity," "beautiful symmetry," providential character, and adaptation of means to ends of the Methodist machinery.[47] Hence perhaps the great Methodist fascination with their own history. It gave them God at work. Methodists knew Providence in history.

Bangs saw Providence in secular as well as sacred history. Unlike Lee, he began his history, not with Wesley but with Columbus. Bangs set Methodism within a republican and providential schema—one that honored the relation of civil and religious liberty, that depicted the unfolding American drama as providentially ordained, and that recognized a distinctive Methodist role in the construction of a Christian civilization. He insisted:

> And although it formed no part of the design of its disciples to enter into the political speculations of the day, nor to intermeddle with the civil affairs of the country, yet it is thought that its extensive spread in this country, the hallowing influence it has exerted on society in uniting in one compact body so many members, through the medium of an itinerant ministry, interchanging from north to south, and from east to west, have contributed not a little to the union and prosperity of the nation.[48]

Bangs developed this theme most explicitly in a several-page assessment of Methodist influence, predicated upon the common assumption that "a thoroughly reformed sinner cannot be otherwise than a good citizen, a good ruler, husband, brother, and friend." He asserted that revivals "had a most happy and conservative influence upon our national character."

Methodists rooted out infidelity that threatened the social order; they diverted attention from "mere secular and political affairs," which were divisive "to the momentous concerns of eternity"; and, most important, they instilled a "vital, experimental, and practical Christianity" that exerts a conservative influence "upon individual character, upon social and civil communities, and of course upon states and empires." Methodists did so, thought Bangs, because the entire system functioned well in the expanding country. The providential fit of church to nation applied to "camp and other meetings."

Their mode of preaching, too—plain, pointed, searching, extemporaneous, and itinerating from place to place, collecting the people in log houses, in school houses, in the groves, or in barns—was most admirably adapted to the state of society and calculated to arouse the attention of a slumbering world to the concerns of religion.[49]

Finally, Bangs argued that the cohesive, interactive, national character of Methodism had a nationalizing function, tending "in the natural order of cause and effect, to cement the hearts of our citizens together in one great brotherhood." Bangs recognized Methodism's cementing or cohesive value as particularly important given the divisive spirit abroad in the land. He said:

> It is well known that our civil organization, into several state sovereignties, though under the partial control of the general government, naturally tended to engender state animosities, arising out of local and peculiar usages, laws, customs, and habits of life. What more calculated to soften these asperities, and to allay petty jealousies and animosities, than a Church bound together by one system of doctrine, under the government of the same discipline, accustomed to the same usages, and a ministry possessing a homogeneousness of character, aiming at one and the same end—the salvation of their fellow-men by the same method—and these ministers continually interchanging from north to south, from east to west, everywhere striving to bring all men under the influence of the same "bond of perfectness?" Did not these things tend to bind the great American family together by producing a sameness of character, feelings and views?[50]

Not long after Bangs wrote this, the church divided, North and South; and not too many years after the Methodist, Baptist, and Presbyterian divisions, the nation itself divided.

Bangs, then, considered Methodism's relation to the nation a providential one and the nation itself providentially guided. And yet those were relatively minor themes, quite secondary to the far more prominently featured providences in individual lives and the even far more important providential role in the church itself. In his most important successor these priorities reversed themselves.

Abel Stevens (1815–97)

When American Methodism determined to make 1866 a centenary jubilee of its founding, it turned naturally to Abel Stevens to write a popular denominational history for the occasion.[51] Stevens had already completed standard histories under denominational sponsorship, *The History of the Religious Movement of the Eighteenth Century, Called Methodism*, a three-volume affair; and a *History of the Methodist Episcopal Church* in four volumes, then nearing completion.[52] He turned out a number of thematic, regional, and single-volume Methodist histories as well. His spokesperson role had been earned. Stevens guided *Zion's Herald*, Methodism's New England-based paper, for twelve years, beginning in 1848. In 1852, he assumed the editorial helm of *The National Magazine*, a Methodist venture into a more purely literary genre. In 1856, Stevens accepted denominational election to the national weekly *The Christian Advocate*, after having turned it down some years earlier. And in 1860, he moved on to serve as corresponding editor of *The Methodists*, another New York-based post, which he held until 1874.

Self-consciously and forthrightly committed to Methodism's unity and national influence, Stevens strove in the controversies leading up to the Civil War to play what he took to be a moderating role. In that stance, which often meant placating the South and countering abolition, he offered what we would now think unfortunate conciliation. In that, he rather faithfully represented and led the church.

Stevens's conception of American Methodist history cohered with and reinforced such a unitive mission. His was, in some ways, a more thoroughly and explicitly providential reading than either of his predecessors. Stevens elaborated the theory of general Providence toward which Bangs had struggled into a full-fledged historical vision. He also applied it continuously to the historical data so that the whole drama of Methodist history had an inner and consistent providential meaning. But it is a curiously attenuated Providence.

Stevens discerned Providence in the interconnecting missions of nation and church. Consistently, he pointed out how Methodism was providentially suited for America. For instance, summing up Methodism's pre-Revolutionary period, he affirmed, "In fine, the providential design and adaptation of Methodism, for the new nation, are revealed all through this period of its preparatory operations." He saw that in the way in which Methodism seemed peculiarly adapted, like some organism to its environment, to what would be the needs of the new nation, particularly as it expanded West:

> Obviously then the ordinary means of religious instruction—a "settled" pastorate, a "regular" clergy, trained through years of preliminary education—could not possibly meet the moral exigencies of such an unparalled condition. . . . A religious system, energetic, migratory, "itinerant," extempore, like the population itself, must arise; or demoralization, if not barbarism, must overflow the continent. Methodism entered the great arena at the emergent moment. . . . Methodism was not to supersede here other forms of faith, but to become their pioneer in the opening wilderness, and to prompt their energies for its pressing necessities. It was to be literally the founder of the Church in several of the most important new states, individually as large as some leading kingdoms of the old world. It was to become at last the dominant popular faith of the country, with its standard planted in every city, town, and almost every village of the land. Moving in the van of emigration, it was to supply, with the ministrations of religion, the frontiers from the Canadas to the Gulf of Mexico, from Puget's Sound to the Gulf of California. It was to do this indispensable work by means peculiar to itself.[53]

Then followed one of the most succinct descriptions of the Methodist denominational system and its functioning. The force of his analysis, there and throughout, was to show Methodism in the details of its structure and operation to be essential to the American experiment. So Stevens believed Methodism "to have been providentially designed more for the new world than for the old."[54] Obviously, the argument functioned apologetically.

Two Machines in the Garden

Stevens also believed that America had been providentially set aside, peopled, developed, and governed with Methodism in mind; or, to be more precise, with the Protestant Evangelicalism and the Protestant Evangelical social order in mind, which Methodism most fully embodied. Stevens registered both this claim about American society's religious purpose and that about Methodism's sociopolitical purpose with an arresting, initial metaphor. The metaphor makes the essentially providential character of Stevens's overall interpretation absolutely unmistakable. Stevens began both his four-volume history and the six hundred-page *Compendious History* with two figures whose paths he makes cross in a quadrangle at Glasgow and whose discoveries shaped American life.

The two men are James Watt and John Wesley, "co-workers for the destinies of the new world." Their machines—the steam engine and "Methodism, with its 'lay ministry' and 'itinerancy'"—are the forces that develop American society, two machines in the Garden, both more important for the new world than for the old.[55] In Stevens's presentation, Watt and the steam engine stood not only for the commercial and technological advances of his day but also for all that the century then named progress. For Stevens, the providential ordering concerned America as a whole—land, culture, peoples, society, economy, not just its democratic polity. So also the machine of Methodism served the entire moral order of the new nation, an order that he compared at one point to Augustine's city of God and to which he referred frequently.[56]

PROVIDENCE: WITHOUT TRANSCENDENCE OR IMMANENCE

American historians have long noted a subtle but important shift in Protestant relations to culture occurring around the mid-nineteenth century. One strand of Protestantism increasingly embraced culture, when appropriately Christianized, as the effective bearer of divinity. A Christian civilization, which in antebellum days had been recognized as a means to transcendent goals, symbolized in the kingdom of God, increasingly became an end in itself.[57] Stevens invited his Methodist readers into just such an inversion of means and ends. He did so by reversing Methodist providential priorities. As we have seen, he functioned with a consistent providential motif and connected Methodism with the nation providentially. Indeed, when he thought of Methodism and Providence, the nation seemed almost invariably to come to mind.[58] That combination in itself would not have alarmed his predecessor historians. Indeed, they would have found what he said congenial. It was what he did *not* say that would have alarmed them; that is, alarmed them, if they caught it. For Stevens put an incredible emphasis upon general Providence, but he slighted particular Providence.

The careless reader might not have caught the shift. God language in fact abounds. For instance, the reader who expected to hear extravagant claims for Methodist camp meetings and revivals would not be disappointed to hear of a Kentucky gathering that "the people fell under the power of the word like corn before a storm of wind," or to find said of a revival connected with the 1800 General Conference that "[t]he Lord . . . is at work in all parts of the town," and "Christ the Lord is come to reign."[59]

The attentive reader might have made an important discovery. Characteristically, Stevens would not make such direct claims about the presence of God in specific human affairs. Rather, for the recognition of God at work, the particular providences that dominated the works of Lee and Bangs, Stevens typically quoted, letting someone else make the call. Sometimes, as in those cited, he placed the discernment in quotation marks; more often he implicitly attributed them.[60]

Exceptions occur. For instance, Stevens declared that God summoned Freeborn Garrettson to Methodism. He also spoke of Jesse Lee as "endued with power from on high."[61] On occasion, Stevens asserted that individuals were providentially led (George Whitefield, for one) or that events were providential in character (the failure of the unpopular experiment with government by council).[62]

The pattern of foregrounding general and slighting particular Providence was nevertheless unmistakable. Providence became, for Stevens, not so much an active agent in history as an axiom about the nature of history. Or perhaps, one should say that Providence remained an active agent for Stevens's subjects, who spoke loudly from his pages permitting him a discreet silence. In a concluding chapter, Stevens addressed himself to the reasons for Methodism's phenomenal growth and influence. He found two causes. The first, Methodism's providential adaptation to the times and circumstances, he termed *primary*—a fitting notation for what had been the motif of the book. The second, the proximate cause, he called "the dispensation of the Spirit" and recognized in Wesley's Aldersgate experience and in the ethos of the movement generated therefrom. An afterthought at best.[63]

James Buckley (1836–1920)

For the Methodist volume in his American Church History series, Philip Schaff turned naturally to its most eminent spokesperson. No choice seemed more apt than that of spokesperson James Buckley, already author of a number of books and pamphlets on

Methodism, the long-term editor of the MEC's national paper, the *Christian Advocate* (1880–1912), and delegate to every General Conference from 1872 to 1912. His voice carried great weight in Methodist gatherings, and his editorials every bit as much in Methodist thought. That intellectual gravity was perhaps best illustrated by his later *Constitutional and Parliamentary History of The Methodist Episcopal Church*.[64] The extent of his influence can perhaps be gauged by the many apologetical and practical works that also came from his pen.[65] He was a formidable and conservative force in American Methodism.

Buckley's *History of the Methodists in the United States* appeared in 1896. He later issued it independently of Schaff's series in both one-volume and two-volume versions.[66] Buckley's work reflects some of the self-consciousness about historical method that Schaff and Adams espoused. He began the volume with a bibliographical preface and a bibliography of standard works. He concluded that section with a list of the official proceedings of the major Methodist denominations. In the course of his discussion, Buckley resorted to occasional footnotes to point the reader to the source or authority for a statement. In another preliminary statement, Buckley addressed himself to methodological concerns, and did so in a way that would have intrigued both Schaff and Adams. Schaff should have been pleased to find Buckley concerned with Providence and might have seen Buckley's apparent reticence in pronouncing judgment as more than offset by his professed obligation to set forth the record so that the reader might "estimate the relation of events to human and divine Providence—the factors in the development of every form of Christianity." For his part, Adams might well have been pleased with the following:

> Methodism is highly organized, and organization implies human centers of power. Hence the characteristics and work of individual men occupy a large place. The history of the body is but the history of those who have made it what it is.[67]

In actuality, Adams should have been the more satisfied. For in Buckley's hands, Providence effectively abandoned the Methodists. I choose the word *effectively* deliberately. In certain respects, Buckley was more explicit and extravagant in his theory about providential workings than his predecessors. Two significant passages, chapters 8 and 26, as we shall see, evidence that self-consciousness. And one can certainly find scattered here and there familiar providential claims. However, Buckley made neither general nor particular Providence integral or necessary to his account.

The reader might well draw his or her own inferences about providential workings. Buckley himself provided little assistance.

Particular Providences

Especially remarkable is that, for Buckley, particular providences no longer dominated Methodist history. Buckley continued Stevens's practice of quoting or paraphrasing statements made by historical figures. However, those turn out to be infrequent and primarily concentrated in the very earliest years of American Methodism. Equally rare was Buckley's own use of providential language. By my count, at only some seven places in his narrative did Buckley unambiguously identify the hand of God at work. He called Wesley "The Man of Providence,"[68] such a common designation that it almost could be considered Wesley's title. He spoke of Asbury refusing a call to a church and "justly regarding himself as providentially occupied." Similarly, at a later point, Buckley confirmed another Asbury judgment, "Well did Asbury conclude that 'the hand of God has been greatly seen in all this.'"[69]

The first discussion that broke decisively with this minimalist reading came at page 201, well into the narrative. There, in chapter 8, Buckley devoted twenty-four pages to the relation of the human and divine in eighteenth-century American Methodism. He examined the spiritual saga of several preachers, Benjamin Abbott, Caleb Pedicord, and Jesse Lee, among them, diagnosing their religious experience and practice in social-scientific and particularly psychological fashion. Buckley concluded that "natural" explanations, though important, were not sufficient.

There were not wanting those who constructed finely woven theories to explain the results of Methodist preaching upon natural principles; and there were others who denied that these principles had any influence. Both were in error; the former by predicating of nature effects that it never did or could produce, the latter by denying to nature the vast power that really exists to create influences that seem to many to be supernatural. Had there been no influence beyond unassisted nature, neither Christianity nor Methodism as a spiritual system could have become permanent.[70]

Here, then, Buckley insisted that "the preservation and growth of the fruits of the Spirit, and their correspondence with the plain teachings of God's Word, constitute proof of the divine origin of the movement."[71] So Buckley insisted upon the centrality of particular providences to historical reality, even though he did not or could not sustain that dimension in his historical analysis. He made his claim about Providence as a dogmatic or theological one, rather than as a reading of history.

General Providence

Virtually the same statement could be made about Buckley's views of general providence. He is the first of our historians, in fact, to abandon a providential framework for Methodist history. Neither Methodism as a providential force nor America as a providential construct shaped Buckley's narrative. In fact, the volume really lacks a unifying thread. Buckley hints at several threads that may have been operative in his thinking:

- a germ reading of American society and religion that located its genius in the earliest arriving European cultures, peoples, and traditions;
- a "great man" theory of history that, following Ralph Waldo Emerson, saw Methodism as "the lengthened shadow of one man";
- an Anglo-Saxonism that deemed this particular racial stock to be the bearer of civilization, progress, and liberty; and
- a fierce commitment to Methodist episcopacy that made him impatient with its detractors.[72]

The latter two points are implicit in Buckley's choice of a starting point, the English Reformation—not Wesley, nor the beginnings of American religion and society, nor the Reformation generally, but the beginnings of English religion. Of course, Wesley represents the fruition of those beginnings. It was a place to start that would not have led the Methodist reader to expect grand providential theory.

Indeed, though the volume hints at an overriding perspective, what really provides coherence is a historicist or scientific orientation to facts. Buckley refrained not only from providential judgments but really from interpretation altogether. He rarely permitted himself any distance from the historical process. Buckley the reporter, rather than Buckley the editorialist, charted the Methodist story. That dispassionate objectivity is particularly remarkable in the section on slavery and the sectional crisis and the division of Methodism.[73] After reporting the debates and events, Buckley did step back for what he called "A Calm Survey," an attempt to provide some perspective on that tragic episode in American and Methodist life. But even here he proceeded by identifying one figure in the maelstorm whom he thought afloat, Stephen Olin, and sketched Olin's views. Buckley's self-conscious commitment to historicism triumphed.

In a similar manner, Buckley stepped back from the historical process for some concluding and brief reflections about the spirit of Methodism. Here he concerned himself primarily with Methodism's future, but in so doing touched on the theme of general providence. What he said of Methodism in his own day, might well be said of his historical perspective as well: "The founders of Methodism had no enterprises that were not distinctly subordinate to the conversion of men and their spiritual training. Now its enterprises are many and complex, often pervaded by a distinctly secular element, which contends constantly with the spiritual." He followed with an exhortation to Methodists to keep the spirit, concluding with Wesley's prophecy that the movement would die if it had "the form of religion without the power," and lost "the doctrine, spirit, and discipline" with which it first set out.[74]

It may seem highly uncharitable to bring that prophecy down on Buckley himself. And yet, insofar as the historians gave Methodists their reality, insofar as history functioned to define the movement, insofar as theology required a historical presentation—could one not say that here in a historicist reading was "the form of religion without the power"? Indeed, what is striking about this theological excursus by Buckley, as well as that which touched particular providences, is that a person who wrote history as Buckley did could still hold those views or, to invert the statement, that someone who held those views could write as he did. Or to put the matter more charitably, Providence had become for Buckley a theological rather than a historical construct.

Conclusion

Buckley wrote for Schaff's series. He nodded also to Schaff's commitment to a providential reading of history. Providence, however, was but a facade. Underneath the historical process no Spirit operated. Buckley rendered a secular treatment. Adams and Emerton, not Schaff, ruled; though it was Schaff's series to which Buckley contributed.

Since Methodism accorded its history and historians great prominence, had called the latter to be the movement's spokespersons, had allowed them to define Methodism, Buckley's historicist interpretation was of great importance. Yet we must not make him a scapegoat for twenty-first-century Methodism's problems. For, as we have seen, the changes in Providence were a long time in the making. Lee had immediate experience of God's providences, discerning them in revivals he saw and/or in which he had a personal role. Bangs burdened Providence with the perfection of Methodist machinery and the adaptation of church to national republican order. Stevens shifted the emphasis even further toward a civil theology. Buckley completed the abandonment of particular Providence and rendered general Providence a postulate. Over the century, then, Providence changed radically. Burning conviction became historical theorem, experience became idea, agency became axiom.

But if we cannot scapegoat Buckley, we can nevertheless recognize that the interpretive trajectory that he represented came to dominate Methodism's historical self-understanding. The historicist spirit (not the Holy Spirit) came to inform the reading list for Methodist ministry, seminary instruction, and the preface to the *Discipline*. Insofar as history and historical experience continued to tell Methodists who they were, it left them on their own.

CHAPTER 13

United Methodism at 40: Taking Stock

Talk radio and conservative commentators blame much of America's ills on the 1960s—rampant permissiveness, teen pregnancy, divorce, drugs, poverty, homelessness, crime, urban decay, illegal immigration.[1] If not Franklin D. Roosevelt and the New Dealers, then blame Lyndon B. Johnson, the Great Society, Jimmy Carter, and the Liberal Left. Blame judicial activism, invasive government, policy by regulation, affirmative action, liberal elites. Of course, to the same period and to the same actors or actions other commentators can look appreciatively for societal repudiation of legalized segregation, for an end to back-alley abortions, for lifting cultural barriers to women and minorities in commerce and politics, for heightened environmental awareness.

Similarly, to the 1960s and the union of 1968 United Methodists look with both applause and blame. Some celebrate what 1968 achieved and/or symbolizes: empowering of women, minorities, and youth; recognizing the church's diversity; hearing the cries of the marginalized and oppressed; affirming difference of worldview and perspective; widening dialogues with Catholics, Jews, Muslims, Hindus, and Buddhists; orienting the church to its internal pluralism and its global nature. Others look back to blame the 1960s for hemorrhaging membership and doctrinal laxity; the church's embrace of abortion and temporizing on homosexuality; bureaucratic intransigence; suspect shibboleths like the "Wesleyan Quadrilateral"; and, of course, feminism and kindred radicalisms. To the latter group, the critics, 1968 symbolizes defective Christology, abandonment of missions, substitution of dialogue for evangelism, liturgical formalism, neglect of the Sunday school, and regulated inclusive language.[2] Of course, neither the plaudits nor the curses aim specifically at the Evangelical United Brethren. It is what happened around the union that earns the praise or blame. And both evaluations concern United Methodism in the United States and the predecessor Methodist denominations (Methodist Episcopal Church; Methodist Episcopal Church, South; Methodist Protestant Church, Methodist Church)—as will my discussion here.

Reasons to get worked up over the 1960s are obvious, as virtually any effort to image the decade should indicate. From that decade derive fragmentation around caucus and cause, the polarization of politics, campaigns against key institutions, deindustrialization, and urban decay. The changes in church and society wrought by the 1960s have been dramatic and catastrophic. So also has been the church's feeble coping. From that decade the church has been in steady decline. United Methodism's membership, around 11 million at merger, has dropped to under 8 million. Average worship attendance, hovering around 4 million in 1968, stood at 3.4 million in 2004. And the church school decreased from 6.2 to 3.5 million, a probable indicator of more bad news to come.[3]

Meanwhile, Pentecostal, conservative, and evangelical denominations and congregations built out the suburbs as the mainline once had the cities and experimented with televangelism as Methodism once had with print ministries. I return below to itemize further Methodism's woes and the competition's accomplishments. Here, I just take note of culpabilities. Of course, blame for all of United Methodism's decline and woes lay, and lie, at the feet of the "liberal elite" installed post-1968 at the helm of boards and agencies, just as Washington insiders could be charged with causing American industrial flight, economic woes, foreign policy debacles, and energy problems. So charged my friends and former Duke colleagues in attributing what they term the crises of belief and of program to bureaucracy and the post-1968 restructuring.[4] So Good News Movement and the Institute on Religion and Democracy also say.[5]

Which Birthday? Which Union to Celebrate? Which to Grieve?

Elsewhere I have examined some of the connection-enhancing and connection-straining aspects of the radical changes of the 1960s and 1970s.[6] Here I want to assume much of the assessment of 1968 and the 1960s and even the detailing of 1960-specific developments. Instead I will argue that those worried over United Methodism's ills—ills we Methodists share with mainstream Protestantism generally—should look for root causes in another union and in other birthdays. To 1884, the centennial birthday, we should look for great missional accomplishments that, *ironically*, also explain later failures of evangelism and mission, local and connectional inertias, leadership bent inward on institutional maintenance, and the church's comfort in society and culture. The year 1884 gave us taken-for-granted physical structures for local ministry, bureaucratic organization for mission, and management oriented toward maintenance—a scheme that eventually confined activity and decision making. And by 1884 Methodism, the MEC at least, was consolidating the educational apparatus—colleges, universities, seminaries—that would eventually orient toward social gospel and liberal directions. One century's initiatives would become another's burdens.

Similarly, to another union—1939, not 1968—we should look for explanations why the 1960s hit us so hard, why we failed to respond to its challenges, and why we find ourselves lacking the leadership and programmatic capacity to guide us into making disciples for Jesus Christ for the transformation of the world. That union wove regionalism into the fabric of the church, decentered authority, hobbled General Conference, and left boards and agencies as the primary connective realities. The year 1939 jurisdictioned our polity, laid the foundations for a diocesan episcopacy, and effectively limited horizons to region and conference. So hobbled and constrained, our leaders—no matter how gifted, energetic, dedicated, invested, and visionary—could lead their little society, class, or band but not The United Methodist Church. The last General Conference may have turned us around a corner, but what corner and toward what horizon we cannot yet discern.

1884: Main Streeted, Managed, and Mission-minded

By 1884, a Methodism once epitomized by camp meeting and horseback itinerant and once looked down upon by upper-crust Episcopalians and Presbyterians had muscled in beside them on Main Street. Not just muscling in and mimicking their Gothic architecture, Methodism showed its Protestant competitors a thing or two about program and facilities. Any religious body could build a sanctuary. Methodists taught the world that an effective church needed a Sunday school building of comparable size. At the national level, Methodists, Northern Methodists initially, modeled muscularity as well—in recreating the connection and making all missional and program entities accountable to General Conference. Between that bureaucratic level and the local church, Methodism gradually elaborated the role of a muscular middle manager, whose responsibility it was to oversee sales, inventory, personnel, and facilities—the presiding elder, fittingly later renamed "district superintendent." Main Street church, district superintendent, and board-and-agency structure—a vertically integrated, professionally managed, suitably housed system—epitomized 1884 Methodism. Or at the least it epitomized Methodism's next century. The pattern set by the organizational revolution is still very much with us.

Main Street Methodism

We treat the organizational revolution rightly on the denominational level and will do so momentarily (and briefly), but counterpart developments occurred throughout the system, including in local Methodism. The centennial General Conference, that of 1884, authorized the key organizational transformation that spelled an end to Methodist ordering through the quarterly conference and by the presiding elder. It permitted quarterly conferences to "organize, and continue during its pleasure, an Official Board, to be composed of all the members of the Quarterly Conference," to be "presided over by the preacher in charge," to discharge many of the duties of the leaders and stewards' meeting, and to "keep a record of its proceedings."[7] The creation of the official board brought to the local church what incorporation, consolidation, efficiency, bureaucratization, and professionalization brought to the church as a whole and, indeed, to American society—that is, corporate principles of finance, procedure, order, integration, governance, and cohesion. Bureaucratization at the top and business efficiency in the local church went together. Indeed, they were twins.

Decision making delegated from the elastic quarterly conference and the presiding elder to the intra-congregational official board and regularized on a monthly basis gave urban and small-town Methodists the organizational apparatus needed to manage complex new programs and to care for increasingly impressive physical facilities. The new program most requiring ordering and space was the Sunday school; and its demands derived from initiatives of preacher-educator John Vincent. As pastor in Chicago in the 1860s, Vincent spoke to Sunday school assemblies, produced model lesson plans, and organized teacher-training events—earning a national reputation that landed him as corresponding (general) secretary of the Sunday School Union in 1868.[8] Under Vincent's leadership, Methodism developed the uniform lesson plan (the Berean), promoted national training conventions, expanded a Sunday school teacher's journal, established a system of "normal schools" to convey best practices and theory, founded Chautauqua as a Sunday school teacher's assembly (1874), and took that assembly nationally in 1878 as the Chautauqua Literary and Scientific Circle. The uniform lesson plan, with its age-graded leaflets, Golden texts, pictures, teacher's materials, home readings, questions, and hymns did for the laity what the Course of Study achieved for the ministry, that is, put the entire denomination and all age groups on the same page scripturally and theologically. The uniformity and integration that this common lectionary achieved every Sunday depended on a cadre of teachers for each age group (women and men), functioning under the guidance and direction of a Sunday school superintendent—effectively the principal of a school system. And he (it was often "he") dramatized his high calling by leading the opening and closing assembly.

One superintendent realized that the highly regimented Sunday school system, when operating in its ideal form, required a very special building. An inventor and manufacturer of farm machinery, Lewis Miller, served as Akron (Ohio) Sunday school superintendent for over thirty-five years.[9] The inspiration for a building that would accommodate Vincent's Sunday school design and Miller's aspirations for both separate instructional and proximate assembly and worship spaces came, tradition holds, at a Sunday school picnic in a natural amphitheater or geological punch bowl.[10] The children, Miller noted, grouped themselves, but naturally faced the bowl center. He sketched a building that would achieve the same plan and persuaded architect and fellow church member Jacob Snyder to design a new complex to include a Sunday school and adjoining sanctuary. By 1870 the auditorium/classroom facility for the Akron Plan Sunday school was completed. Two stories high and capped by a dome, the building arrayed two tiers of classrooms opening into a large semicircular room. The desks in each class faced forward so that when its windowed door opened, the students had no need to move to hear or heed the superintendent.[11] With blackboards, piano, Scripture mottoes, stained glass, and carpet, the building achieved architecturally for the whole and its parts what the uniform lesson did instructionally—ordering, focusing, and facilitating a complex, extensive, inclusive, integrated church-embracing process.

Akron quickly became a Methodist pilgrimage site and the "Akron Plan" a distinctive American contribution to the grammar of architecture. Vincent used the *Sunday School Journal* to promote the model, as also his 1887 book *The Modern Sunday-School*.[12] And when his church in Plainfield, New Jersey, was built in the late 1880s, Vincent had it follow the Akron Plan.[13] It became a standard in church building and architectural catalogs, often adapted, sometimes copied, championed and idealized by the distinguished architect George Kramer (*MEA*, 1897); and, along with Gothic or Romanesque exteriors, it announced Methodism's Main Street status.

Around the turn of the century, Methodists (along with other Protestants) matured the Sunday school/sanctuary plant into a programmatically more complex facility, then known as the "institutional church" (think today's suburban church or even megachurch). A social gospel invention, called "central halls" in Britain, these large-scale church complexes indeed resembled the typical suburban or urban congregation of today, with sanctuary, educational wing, community service accommodations, kitchens, childcare facilities, and the like, and with a strong weekday as well as weekend program. Methodist life had fully moved from once simple worship houses into schools-cum-auditoriums-cum-sanctuaries. Here in multistory Gothic or Romanesque architecture was "the local church" we know today, a complex religious matrix incorporated or recognized as a single entity:

- functioning with a parish-like orientation to its geographical surroundings;
- channeling through its life the local mission efforts of the denomination;
- accommodating within its plant and covering with its governing umbrella a cradle-to-grave educational system—a full array of age-graded Sunday schools, including a huge men's Bible class composed of the Methodist share of the community's leaders;
- featuring one or more assemblies for weekly worship and a great variety of programs, groups, missionary associations, benevolent causes, and women's and youth organizations;

- understanding itself as a corporate religious body capable of (perhaps charged with) exercising communal leadership;
- raising by its stewardship and within its budget(s) monies needed locally for its own purposes and services and the lion's share of those required by conference, denominational, and ecumenical interests; and
- overseeing all this denominational/local apparatus and endeavor through lay and ministerial congregational leaders.

The turn-of-the-century "institutional church" consolidated and incorporated what for Methodism had been the dynamic, distinguishable, diverse expressions of local religiosity. Methodism congregationalized a piety that once met in class, assembled by appointment for preaching, congregated in quarterly meetings, and exploded in camp meetings.[14] And the prevalence of this "local church" form of the church today, reinforced by the American predilection for local rule and principled congregationalism, made the congregation as intellectual construct seem to be *the* and *the only* modality of local religiosity. Today, it just seems natural that local religious functions will center in a single congregation, "the local church."

The Methodist conceptual reorientation toward what we know now as "the local church" can be traced through successive twentieth-century *Disciplines*. The 1928 (MEC) *Discipline* indexed "The Local Church," but spread treatments of it over various rubrics. The 1930 (MECS) *Discipline* included a subsection titled "The Local Church," but lodged it under Christian education. The first *Discipline* of The Methodist Church, that of 1940, devoted a section to "The Local Church" and positioned it last under part 4, "The Conferences." So placed, it belonged still to the conference order of Methodist reality. By 1944, and from 1944 to 1960, "The Local Church" became part 2 of the (MC) *Discipline*, following immediately after "The Constitution" and preceding part 3, "The Ministry" and part 4, "The Conferences." Within "The Local Church" were embraced treatments of the quarterly conference and the church conference, as well as the official board. "The Local Church" entirely subsumed the once regional quarterly conference. Within that section as well was placed "Church Membership," once a major rubric in its own right. So change came gradually, by pulling together instructions and expectations about ministry in relation to local church and parish ministry, reflecting ways in which the church's mission came to center on congregations and buildings.

Organizational Revolution

Parallel developments at the national level had centered missions, education communication, evangelism, church development, and social concern in program boards. The key initiatives came in Northern Methodism between the 1866 Centenary and the 1884 Centennial. During the Civil War, religious community mobilization—by women and men—to supply, support, nurse, and minister had demonstrated the extraordinary delivery capacities of focused, popularly based, vertically integrated, nationally managed organization. Like Northern business, Northern Methodism had experienced firsthand in its war efforts the payoff of top-down control and corporate organization. In part emulating the business community, in part capitalizing on its own experience, Methodism and mainline Protestantism instituted a *corporate, board and agency system*, undertaking, in effect, a "managerial revolution."

This revolution—no conspiracy, but broadly supported by clergy and *laymen* alike (the *women* are quite another story)—aimed at checking the free enterprise, competitive, self-guided, trustee-accountable societies that previously had run ostensibly denominational programs. More positively, the revolution sought to increase the effectiveness of the array of enterprises being undertaken on the denomination's behalf, to achieve some coordination of their several efforts, and to bring the coordinated efforts under denominational authority. In 1872 (MECS, 1874), by legislative action and reincorporation, the MEC transformed voluntary societies into corporate boards accountable to General Conference.[15] Thereafter (until 1939), General Conference elected the boards as well as their general secretaries. And to board and general secretary General Conference entrusted the work of the church. No one symbolized that trust and resultant agency better than A.J. Kynett. Heading the Church Extension Society for thirty-two years, he helped the church build more than 11,000 churches, his associate C.C. McCabe boasting at one point that "we are building two a day."

Unlike official boards, General Conference could not, and thankfully did not, meet monthly. So over the years, General Conference elaborated procedures by which the boards coordinated programs, finance, communication, and publication between and among themselves. A similar coordination top to bottom ordered the entire church with a single organizational grammar. Every level of the church—from congregational to district to conference to national level—structured itself and functioned with the same bodies, the same names, and the same duties. The changes created national power centers, essentially bureaucratic in nature. Gradually the churches began staffing agencies with professionals, increasing their numbers dramatically, requiring higher degrees of specialization and expertise, and exploring new schemes of systematic finance.

Methodism modeled the mainstream denomination and participated actively in the collective system of Protestant denominationalism and Protestant ecumenism that effectively dominated American society and culture until the mid-twentieth century. Mainstream denominations ran the show in world missions, through new ecumenical orders (world, national, state, and local councils of churches), in war efforts, by control of the airwaves, through media coverage, by legislating temperance, and by sending members into every political office. Their several-fold authority systems, internal complexity, bureaucratic program structure, and professionalized leadership aligned them with American society generally, especially with business and government.

The Middle Manager—Presiding Elder/District Superintendent

By 1884, at the centennial birthday, Methodism was well on the way toward transforming what had been its strategy-creating, missional, evangelistic office—the presiding elder—into that of a middle manager. It took another couple of decades to retitle it in accord with its supervisory duties, but the change in responsibilities from an earlier day could readily be discerned. So Morris Crawford explained in an "Address by the Rev. M.D'C. Crawford at a Conference of Presiding Elders in New York City, Dec. 8, 1884, and published at the request of the Conference":

> I am requested to discuss the "*Changes in the Duties of the Presiding Eldership, and the Causes Thereof.*" That great changes have taken place in these duties—changes so marked as to give a new aspect to the office—must be apparent. It seems to me equally clear that all these changes have been caused by changes in the condition of the Church. No change has been made in the status of the office, or in its relation to the economy of Methodism, from the beginning until now. The section entitled "*Presiding Elders And Their Duty,*" was first framed and put in the *Discipline* in 1796. . . .
>
> But, notwithstanding the unshaken stability of the Presiding Eldership, great changes have taken place in its duties. . . . The Presiding Elder's visits,

however, are not now, as formerly, chiefly to preach and conduct other religious services, but much more to "*oversee the spiritual and temporal business*" of the various charges of his district. This means vastly more than in former days.

When Bishop Asbury in 1788 gave Freeborn Garrettson the Hudson River Valley for a district, with a dozen pious young men for preachers, among whom he divided the territory, this pioneer Presiding Elder traveled up one side of the river and down the other, meeting and encouraging all the preachers in turn, and by his ministrations making everywhere a profound impression. But certainly *supervision* was among the least of his duties, because there was little to supervise. Now how changed. We have everywhere large property interests, which the Presiding Elder is directed to promote by every means in his power. To see that the churches and parsonages are held by proper tenure, are well insured, and kept in repair, and freed from debt. To encourage generous provision for the support of the preachers. To urge liberality toward our great charities, missions, Church Extension, Conference claimants, Freedmen's Aid, education. To visit and foster Sunday Schools, and urge the formation of lyceums and reading circles, and all feasible methods for securing the religious training of our children and young people. He is never to lose sight of the evangelistic work of the Church, everywhere, and on all suitable occasions, exhorting preachers and people to seek directly the salvation of souls. There are many incidental duties. Frequently some pastor on his district will fail in health, when satisfactory provision must be made for the church, and the welfare of the pastor tenderly cared for. There are always embarrassed churches to be relieved, and discouraged workers to be helped. . . .

He needs to bring to his work all the power God has given him. He is a leader of preachers and of churches. He cannot escape responsibility if the spiritual and temporal interests of his district are not advanced. In this centennial year of our church but one watchword will save us from dishonor—*Speak unto the children of Israel, that they go forward*. We have received from our fathers, in our great denominational interests, a sacred trust which we are to study and guard and administer with intelligence and zeal. It will not answer to attempt to do over again the things they have done. We cannot bring back or repeat the past. The Church life of today must be distinctive of today. We must meet and grapple with the living problems of the present. But we shall triumph. God has not forsaken us. To him be all the glory.[16]

Although the *Discipline*'s paragraph explicitly describing the presiding elder may have been left unchanged, Crawford and his presiding elder colleagues did not want for instructions. The *Discipline* detailed six pages of duties for the district conference and eleven pages for the quarterly conference. And the work of the annual conference lay also in the laps of the presiding elders, given that the thirteen bishops had responsibility for over 100 conferences (eight of which were outside the United States).

Corporate but Conferencing

Urban pastor, presiding elder, and board or publishing house put the entire church to singing the same hymns, worshiping with common guidelines, reading age-graded Sunday school materials for the international lessons, conducting packaged mission-education programs, raising money on the same premises and with the same little envelopes. One could move from Washington, D.C. to California, step into the nearby MEC or MECS church, and know where to find the milk and the bread. And (to stay with the metaphor) grocery design, marketing, supply, and the like moved readily from headquarters in Nashville or New York to each and every store. Built to facilitate its mission, Methodism's organizational apparatus certainly bears comparison to the corporate and industrial machinery of the Gilded Age. And Methodists took pride in its machine-like character, even boasting of its machinery. So longtime editor of Methodist papers and magazines Abel Stevens began two of his several histories with a machine metaphor for American Methodism in its entirety. As mentioned in chapter 12, he started his four-volume MEC history and the 600-page *Compendious History* with an imagined encounter between James Watt and John Wesley in a Glasgow quadrangle. Terming them "co-workers for the destinies of the new world," he portrayed their machines—the steam engine and "Methodism, with its 'lay ministry,' and 'itinerancy,'" respectively—as the engines that developed American society, machines more important for the new world than for the old.[17]

But for all its mechanistic aspects—indeed, *in* its mechanistic aspects—Methodism remained a conferencing and conferring system. To grasp its responsive, interactive, collegial dimensions we need a biological as well as business metaphor. We need to speak of its mind, its heart, its diaphragm, its skeleton, its ligaments and tendons, and, yes, its muscles. And in a larger work we could distribute between and among bishops, general, annual, and district conferences, boards and agencies, circuits and stations, pastors and people the work of these human organs. Here it will have to suffice to focus upon ligaments, tendons, and sinews.

We who teach in seminaries or serve on boards of ordained ministry and worry about recruitment for ministry bemoan the fracturing of the old *vocational* pipeline. And we remember that it extended from baptismal register, to infant rolls, to vacation Bible school, to Sunday school, to Methodist Youth Fellowship, to summer camp, to youth rallies, to the Methodist Student Movement, to seminary, to probationary conference membership, and to first appointment. That pipeline, or to revert to a biological metaphor, that sinew, which yielded calls to ministry and to missions extended further and branched extensively. It served to train, mentor, place, and promote as well as to call. Talent and accomplishment took individuals (albeit primarily white males) into leadership in conference, onto an institution staff, and to the board of an agency. From these proven connectional servants, General Conference elected boards, editors, and general secretaries. And from these folks, who proved their connectional mettle, as well as from college and seminary heads, General Conference elected the bishops. An instance of such, already mentioned, was John Vincent, whose congregational-level Sunday school talent brought conference leadership that vaulted him to a general agency and then to the episcopacy. The system's responsiveness to talent, accomplishment, innovation, and creativity doubtless owed much to its widely circulated *Advocate*s and their ability to present the connection to itself.

Its responsiveness also owed much, perhaps more, to its circulating bishops. Although both the MEC and MECS found ways of dispersing episcopal residences—the MEC by fits and starts through General Conference legislation from the 1860s through 1916, and the MECS by the bishops' own discretion—bishops continued to revolve through annual conferences, to become aware of the gifts and grace of preachers in multiple states, to learn of experiments and failures, and to function individually and collectively as the church's talent agency.[18]

For instance, no bishop presided in the New Jersey Conference for more than three years successively until after the 1939 union. Until 1908 a different bishop presided each year. Then Luther Wilson served and returned in 1909. Joseph Berry began the first of three successive presidential assignments in 1912. He also returned from 1917 to 1918 and from 1920 to 1923. But note the succession of presiding bishops in the New Jersey Conference from 1884 through 1924: W. L. Harris, Henry Warren, John Fletcher Hurst, Randolph Foster, Cyrus Foss, Thomas Bowman, Daniel Goodsell, James Fitzgerald, John Vincent, John Walden, Edward Andrews, Stephen Merrill, Isaac Joyce, Warren again, C.C. McCabe, Foss again,

Hurst again, Willard Mallalieu, Andrews again, Foster again, Merrill again, Earl Cranston, Goodsell again, Warren again, Luther Wilson, Wilson again, Henry Spellmeyer/Thomas Neely, J.W. Hamilton, Joseph Berry (1912), Berry again, Berry again, Thomas Henderson, William Quayle, Berry again, Berry again, William Shepard, Berry again, Berry again, Berry again, Adna Leonard, Berry again.[19]

And even when Wilson began his two-year assignment to New Jersey in 1908, he presided as well over other conferences—his twenty-four U.S. and seven missionary episcopal colleagues having 132 annual conferences to care for. Indeed, that year Wilson presided also over Louisiana, Mississippi (black), Upper Mississippi (black), Central Pennsylvania, Puerto Rico, Norwegian-Danish, Minnesota, North Dakota, Dakota, Northern Swedish, and Northern Minnesota conferences. In the following year, 1909, when he returned to New Jersey, his assignment was less of a study in Methodism's ethnic and racial diversity. However, he itinerated through an entirely different set of other conferences—New England Southern, East Maine, Italian (meeting in Pittsburgh), Cincinnati, Kentucky, and West Virginia. Spellmeyer, who would follow Wilson in presiding over New Jersey, in 1908 chaired Newark, Florida (black), Saint Johns River (white Florida), South Florida (black), Northwest Iowa, Western Swedish (Upper Midwest), and Missouri. In 1909 Spellmeyer presided over Mexico, Arkansas, Saint Louis German, Iowa, Montana, North Montana, and Southern Illinois conferences. Some assignments were more geographically focused. Cranston, for instance, in 1908 presided in the east over Philadelphia, Delaware (black), Vermont, East Ohio, Central New York, Genesee, and Atlantic Mission (eastern North Carolina) conferences.

Such regional assignments made it easier to move preachers from one conference to another and from conference to agency and connectional leadership. Of course, itinerant general superintendents accommodated their talent purview to the prejudices and policies of the time no matter the conference or context over which they presided. But given those quite severe limitations of talent search and promotion—to white, English-speaking, male, full-connection preachers—their itinerations served to make the system responsive to gifts and experiments.

As important as, perhaps more important than, the connecting that the bishops effected through their itinerations and transfer of talent was the connectional perspective that the bishops developed from moving across the country; indeed, sometimes across the world. In 1908 Neely was sent to the Andes and South

America, presided over the Central Swedish (Western Pennsylvania and New York and the Midwest) and Chicago German conferences as also over West Wisconsin and Rock River. In 1909, he too had a different set of assignments, not global but another study in African American and Anglo Methodism—Louisiana (black), Newark, Upper Mississippi (black), Ohio, Central Ohio, West Texas (black), Southern German (Texas), Gulf (white), and Texas (black).

The itineration of general secretaries (or, as they were termed, "corresponding secretaries") to annual conferences and to speaking and listening activities across the connection served as well to keep boards and agencies engaged with pulpit and pew. Agencies also "corresponded" with one another and with other national or connectional leadership. Indeed, until 1939 or so, the boards and agencies, particularly in the MEC and MECS, were surrounded with other bodies, also active on a national level, that bound the connection together, interacted, and worked programmatically. These included, of course, the college or board of bishops and General Conferences but also other national organizations (women's, youth, reform, temperance, etc.), connectional *Advocate*s, clergy magazines, the seminaries (particularly Boston for the North and initially Vanderbilt in the South), and the publishing houses. The system was never tension free or conflict free. It was, after all, an earthen vessel. But it was a system, organic as well as machine-like.

So here we have it. By 1884 we Methodists were Main Streeted, managed, and mission-minded. The year 1884 gave us taken-for-granted physical structures for local ministry, bureaucratic organization for mission, and conference-level management oriented toward internal programs, fund-raising, nurture, and neighborhood outreach—offices and structures that effectively claimed, indeed required but also confined, activity and decision making. Methodism was big business, albeit Kingdom business and mission-minded—but business nevertheless. And the business had the capacity to incorporate innovation and capture talent but also developed incredible momentum. At this fortieth birthday of the church, it is to 1884, the centennial birthday, not to 1968 that we should look for explanations for the inertias that led eventually to failures of evangelism and mission, to local and connectional self-preoccupation, to leadership bent inward on institutional maintenance. Why did we not change? Why did not this system with its management and decision-making capacities effectively reorient the machinery when conditions in American society changed? Why the failure of leadership to lead us?

End of the Line? the Mainline?

Like the great passenger railroad network of a century ago, the vertically integrated, bureaucratically programmed, professionally led, Main Street-housed system has slowed, indeed has come to a crawl. Methodism and United Methodism hung on, stayed on the track of its business model, kept its machinery moving, even when like Amtrak, its passenger service eroded and/or required massive subsidies. Methodists shared in this strategy with mainstream or mainline Protestantism generally. And we share a common resultant plight. That plight, and the challenges to which Methodism ought to have responded, can be readily observed by looking backward from the present. From this perspective one can see that the American society and urban scene into which Methodism had settled in the 1880s had changed dramatically over the course of the twentieth century, and the religious ecology had shifted correspondingly; but our denomination had adjusted to these transformations only marginally. The changes, as the recent Pew study[20] and many commentators note, are astonishing:

- Membership in mainline Protestant denominations has eroded (and aged) over the last half-century; and the salience, prestige, and power of mainline denominational leadership is now contested, often bested (especially as symbolized in access to the White House, which, until recently, was occupied by a self-avowed but poorly practicing United Methodist).
- Conservative, evangelical, and fundamentalist bodies and their leadership have experienced corresponding growth, vigor, visibility, and political prowess, with their collective membership exceeding that of the mainline and constituting over a quarter of the overall American population.
- Membership growth outside the United States (for United Methodists, in Africa and Asia) and stagnation or decline in North America threatens long-standing patterns of assembly, governance, ethos, worship, and morality (on homosexuality especially).
- Methodist ethos, values, commitment, and cohesion now contend with the fact of switching, of adults shopping for a religious home after moves or childbearing, and of membership raised in other traditions or

denominations—a quarter of adults are no longer a part of the religion that nurtured them, a pattern that reaches 44 percent if switching among Protestant bodies is traced.
- Marriages across religious, confessional, and denominational lines (37 percent), persons retaining a sense of being Methodist but no actual membership, disaffiliation in younger age cohorts, and adherents experimenting with various individualistic, face-to-face, or media spiritualities and meditative practices also attest the weakening of denominational identity and allegiance.
- United Methodism contends with similar patterns of congregational independence or diffidence, reflected in the selection of nonstandard educational materials or hymnals, diversion of collections to local or nondenominational projects, resistance to denominational programs, and the removal of denominational signage.
- Competing for our congregations' business and competing with The United Methodist Publishing House, the General Board of Discipleship, and other general agencies are an array of independent and/or parachurch publishing houses, curricula suppliers, music licensers, bookstore chains, program franchisers, consultants, and training outfits.
- Megachurches, many independent or nondenominational, some loosely United Methodist, now boast resources comparable to small denominations, with sophisticated broadcast, Internet, and digital presence and the capacity to meet needs heretofore supplied by denominations (training, literature, expertise, missions, new church planting).
- Coalitions of mega-congregations and/or their church plantings coalesce into denomination-like entities or function more loosely as quasi-denominations, offering training events and inspiration gatherings that United Methodist wannabe clergy attend.
- Single-purpose, lobbying, humanitarian, and mission organizations and more occasional movements, gatherings, and events claim the interest, involvement, commitment, and resources once channeled through congregational structures and through denominations and denominational programs (Focus on the Family, Bread for the World, Habitat for Humanity).

- Similar single-purpose, struggle, ideological, or caucus groups within denominations, especially within mainline denominations, turn assemblies and conferences into contentious culture war gatherings, tend to align into broad progressive or conservative camps, and effect connections to similar camps in other denominations and/or through religious political action or coalition-forming entities like the Institute on Religion and Democracy.
- Older interdenominational organizations to which we still belong and that remain financially dependent on us—state and national councils of churches and the World Council of Churches—once harmonized the leadership of the mainline, but function now within the ambit of culture wars, and tend to retain the allegiance of the more progressive and to function as foil for the more conservative denominational leaders.
- Marginal membership attachment, congregational independence, culture war sentiments, and societal prejudices engender indifference, suspicion, sometimes hostility toward the centers and symbols of our denominational identity—the regional and national headquarters and leadership—sometimes resulting in tax resistance or other forms of revolt.
- Media ministries, newer virtual alliances, and political action efforts that trade on religious sensibilities enlarge the marketplace within which religious expression and affiliation occur, and induce consumption or invite appropriation of multiple beliefs, value systems, and ethical practices.
- Such public or digital visualizations of North America and of the world heighten awareness of American religious diversity, test tolerance levels, stimulate post-9/11 fears, and erode faith in or adherence to putative societal norms within which Protestant denominationalism has functioned (a "Christian culture," "public" or "civil" religion, "Judeo-Christian tradition[s]," and the like).
- And because denominational loyalty is tested on so many fronts, United Methodist leaders, boards of ordained ministry, and seminaries find themselves forced to accent confessional particularities, resulting in the strange phenomenon of hyper-denominationalism contending with post-denominationalism.[21]

Given its machinery, integrated programming, and management systems (bishops, boards, General Conferences, district superintendents, educational institutions, trained pastors), why did Methodism not respond effectively to the societal changes and demographic challenges? Why no leadership to lead us into dynamic adjustments? Why not a coordinated national strategy to cope with population shifts and suburban growth? Why not replication of earlier Methodist innovation—camp meetings, *Christian Advocate*s, Sunday schools, Chautauquas, Akron Plan facilities? For an answer, we must look not to 1968 but to 1939.

The Union of 1939

Methodism had been a system, an integrated system, a vertically integrated system, a horizontally integrated system. It could make decisions and implement them. It was also a segregated system, a sexist system, and a racist system. And the 1939 unification ratified its faults and undercut its strengths.

Jurisdictional Politics

Most notably, of course, the 1939 union gave us institutionalized racism in the jurisdictional system and in the all-black Central Jurisdiction.[22] And to its credit the 1968 union brought an end to the latter. But by 1968, the Methodists had lived too long with regional jurisdictions to question them and the EUB apparently made no great objection to them. After all, geographical division below the national or connectional level, whether into synods and presbyteries or conferences and districts, characterized American denominationalism. Nor was the principle of geographically larger ethnic conferences overlapping white English-speaking conferences new. Well into the 1920s the MEC featured Latin American, German, Chinese, Japanese, Swedish, Norwegian-Danish, and, yes, "Colored" conferences and conference groupings overlapping the white English-speaking.[23]

The jurisdictional system, if continuous in some respects with prior ordering, would, over time and in perhaps unintended ways, fundamentally damage the church's capacity for decisive, coordinated national strategy. It did so by creating what have turned out to be permanent regions, by granting the connection-making authority to these regional entities, and by the effective enlarging and empowering of the Southern church in the Southeastern and South Central jurisdictions. Earlier, one could argue, Methodism and specifically the MEC (and even including the "Colored" conferences, at least in their origin) had conceived ethnic or language conferences as, in a certain sense, self-willed, missional, and elastic. The 1939 jurisdictional scheme created a Central Jurisdiction that could by no stretch of the imagination be termed self-willed. Nor were jurisdictions missional or their boundaries more than theoretically elastic. But it was the powers granted to jurisdictions and removed from General Conference that regionalized the church and undercut its capacity to think and act strategically for the connection as a whole.

Federal-Style Connection

Among the drivers to the union of 1939 (MEC, MECS, MPC) was the belief that a united Methodism would be more effective in witness to American society. And one can point to evidential successes, preeminent of which might be the World War II Bishops' Crusade for a New World Order. This initiative coordinated relief efforts, supported the creation of the World Council of Churches, and endorsed the creation of the United Nations and the 1944–48 Crusade for Christ, which raised $2 million more than its $25 million goal, added a million members, and reversed previous losses in the Sunday school. Ironically, however, over time the 1939 union made concerted connectional efforts more difficult. Indeed, in the endeavor to create a more national church, the provisions of 1939 tore the sinews that held together the connectional fabric. Unification dropped power and authority into jurisdictional conferences, including particularly the power to elect bishops and to constitute boards. It made bishops regional not general superintendents.[24] It bloated General Conference by intention and regionalized seminaries and other teaching agencies by accident. It consolidated boards into even more significant bureaucracies, empowering those boards to select their professional staff.

 Did 1939 vault general secretaries into connectional visibility? Not really. Indeed, it seemed to make connectional leadership invisible. Who since then have been Methodism's Billy Grahams? Who the leader whom the laity and public would recognize? Where were the new Matthew Simpsons, Frances Willards, James Cannons, Francis J. McConnells, or G. Bromley Oxnams? Indeed, after Bromley Oxnam, what bishop had truly national stature? And which general secretary or editor? I speak here not of talent or ability but of the capacity of the Methodist system to forefront its leaders. And, to move beyond symbolism and image, I speak here of the incapacity of leadership to move the institution, to effect change, to launch new ventures. Of course, exceptions come to mind, as, for instance, Disciple Bible through Bishop Richard Wilke and The United Methodist Publishing House. But has not this wonderful program prospered as a stealth venture, its general agency sponsorship acknowledged, but minimally so?

If 1939 rendered our leaders faceless—no matter the gifts or grace—it proved even more destructive of accountability. The net effect of the 1939 changes was to leave the agencies as *the* connection-level or national powers *and* to undo the accountability that 1872 had achieved. Indeed, 1939 confused or diffused accountability. The general agencies remained the creatures of General Conference. Their general secretaries, however, were not. They labored, in effect, for jurisdictionally selected directors. And the bishops, once also nationally or connectionally elected, were jurisdictional officers and area leaders. Their connectional gathering in the Council of Bishops became initially something akin to a fraternity (and only recently has become an entity capable of acting in collective fashion).

In interposing jurisdictions between the boards and the conferences and congregations, in making board directors jurisdictional servants, and in removing or sidelining other national leadership, the 1939 scheme created what would eventually become communication gaps and occasions for mistrust. To be sure, much of the mistrust emerged only slowly, no small degree of it to be traced to the ideological and caucus politics of the 1960s. Yet, in the union of 1939, rather than that of 1968, lie the foundations for the concerns that trouble agency critics today.

The actions of 1939, of course, consolidated within Methodist governance patterns and practices that had long characterized American politics and been deemed good practice. In particular, 1939 established within Methodism:

- separation of powers and distinct legislative, executive, and judicial agencies;
- provision for judicial review;
- delimitation of national authority and reservation of powers and prerogatives to regional bodies (jurisdiction and conference);
- construal of Methodist conference structures at all levels as representative bodies and therefore to be inclusive of laity as well as clergy in accord with principles of equity and proportionality.

Concern to make Methodist polity behave according to American precept had begun when the first conferences convened. It had been made operative by Asbury's call for the Christmas Conference and elective episcopacy. It had found expression in the 1808 Constitution and provision for delegated representation. It had animated the reform efforts of African Methodists, Republicans, Methodist Protestants, Wesleyans, Free Methodists, and Nazarenes. It had encouraged women and blacks in their quest for representation, ordination, and episcopal orders. So while Methodists accommodated themselves to American political practice over the course of their history, only in 1939 did they accord American civil theory full Disciplinary status. The reunion of 1939 made federalism, political rights, representation, and separation of powers into Methodist principle. The linchpin in this federalism is the jurisdictional conference, an accommodation to Methodist racism and (Southern) regionalism, a federalism of a new sort, a structure of nullification between annual and General conferences. If I appear passionate in my brief against jurisdictions, it might help to know that I served as drafter for the Taskforce to Study the Episcopacy during the 2004–8 quadrennium and observed the disfunctionality of jurisdictions up close.

Professional Connections

Decisions in 1939 disguised but enhanced a long-term trend in Methodist life, namely, its reliance upon professions, professionalism, and professional association. What 1939 disguised with the new jurisdictional structures and its ratification of full laity representation was the way in which conference structures, particularly annual conferences, had evolved into professional organizations.[25] Increasingly, conferences functioned for clergy the way the state bar did for lawyers. They set standards, reviewed credentials, admitted to practice, guarded prerogative, pressed for compensation, contracted for healthcare, maintained pensions, and oversaw professional ethics. Ironically, conference professionalism continued, and grew even as conferences became representative and laity were included. Professional interests and concerns lodged themselves in boards or committees, particularly the board of ordained ministry, executive sessions, and various clergy-only affairs.

Professionalism extended beyond the clergy and the annual conferences. Methodist leadership generally aspired to professional recognition and prerogative.

Chaplains of various varieties, Christian educators, lay workers, evangelists, missionaries, information officers, large-church pastors, musicians, fiscal officers, church and society persons, and, after 1968, council directors—all developed professional or quasi-professional associations. Each role or vocational niche in the church seemed to acquire a professional aspect. Persons in that calling gathered together in regional and national meetings. And, once organized, they sought denominational recognition and/or relation to some board or agency. Through organization, training, and credentialing church professionals endeavored to become more effective in the particular service to which they had been called, to be better leaders, to offer the church the guidance or counsel that they alone could give. In many ways, the church was well served by such professionalism. *And* the church was connected in new ways through these professional networks, connected by the service they offered for the whole, connected in their very existence as the religious counterparts to the webs that held American society together, namely, the professional association.

But professionalism had its downside as well: elitism and self-absorption. Professionals exert influence and lead out of expertise, specialized skills, and privileged knowledge. The church certainly can and did make excellent use of its more polished preachers, more effective managers, more skilled teachers, and more compassionate counselors. However, the church needs charisma, giftedness, and grace in its leaders. And a little humility, commitment to the priesthood of all believers, awareness of the universality of sin, and aspiration for holiness help as well. Professionalism does not proscribe such vocational qualities, but it does not prescribe them either. Instead it features expertise. And expertise wants recognition, authority, acquiescence, and compliance.

And because of its expertise, professionalism offers a peculiar angle of vision on the needs, opportunities, challenges, and goods of the whole—of the whole society or the whole church. We are all too familiar with the tendency on the part of teachers or doctors or lawyers to equate professional wisdom, professional prerogatives, and professional interests with the needs and goods of education, healthcare, and justice. The same pertains in the church. Professionalized clergy and church professionals generally see the needs and good of the church in their own image. Of course, professionals did not invent idolatry—construing one's own desires as the will of God, confusing self and society, committing the original sin. Nor should this be seen as conspiracy or a set of conspiracies.

Nevertheless, as a prevalent, perhaps the dominant, mode of leadership, professionalism and the various professional elites riddle the church with competing, quite partial, visions and agendas for the church. Bishops know that superintendency of a single conference and longer tenure therein serve mission and evangelism. Deacons and elders offer competing notions of what ordination should mean. Church musicians know what we should sing. Liturgists order our worship. Christian educators map and stage the *via salutis*. And, of course, the professionals on our boards and in agencies or at conference headquarters push their wares as just what we all need. And since the 1960s the caucuses have added their special needs and concerns to the mix. They too view their particular agenda as crucial to the whole. African Americans claimed that explicitly in naming their cause Black Methodists for *Church Renewal* (emphasis mine). Each caucus—ethnic, theological, ethical, missional—functions with a comparable sense that it serves the well-being of the whole. Each makes a compelling case for its cause. But add the voice of every caucus to those of each professional cadre to those from Methodist machinery—and we have cacophony.

Meanwhile, who cares for the whole? How do these partial professional visions add up to coherent connectional policy?

Main Street Methodism and Mainline Denominationalism

Methodism empowered its various groups and interests, fragmented by cause and caucus, sidelined its leadership, and muted the voice of its once dominant middle. Without a capacity for effective connectional initiative, like its Protestant counterparts, it essentially just watched as the urban America that it had built and built into came apart in the 1960s. In witness to the city, Methodism had erected towers, like the Chicago Temple, boasting the highest cross in the world; or the fourteen-story Wesley Building in Philadelphia to accommodate bookstore, conference societies, bishop's office, general church agencies, and a hotel. Towns had their First Methodist Church, to which belonged the pharmacists, attorneys, grocers, bankers, shop owners, judges, and elected officials whose buildings nestled around the church. Teachers, also members, labored in the primary schools and high schools only several blocks farther away. Out-planted daughter churches served more distant neighborhoods, the mill, and the mine.

Like successive parson-owners of the "Wonderful One-Hoss Shay," Methodism, for a century and more, had united in tending, laboring through, and adding to its machinery—hospitals and homes, camps and orphanages, colleges and assemblies. Since its 1884 centennial, it had institutionalized itself in center-city Gothic churches, deployed its men's Bible classes on Mondays into downtown offices and department stores, positioned its ministers with its laity in Rotary and Kiwanis clubs, addressed the community through Sunday radio pulpits, trained up future civic leaders in vacation Bible school and Sunday schools, enjoyed friendly coverage from morning and evening papers, and depended on its mayors and council "men" to govern in its interest. Methodism was *At Home in the City*, as James Lewis demonstrates under that title for Gary, Indiana. The dream of City Church, as the Methodists fittingly named themselves, he affirms, "had filled the heart and mind of a pastor, had motivated a congregation, and to a considerable extent, had caught the imagination of a city." He continues: "The reality of a social gospel cathedral in the very heart of Gary witnessed to the continuing significance of progressive Protestantism in the industrial city. For a time, City Church was Gary's premier example of a church at home in the city." City Methodist Church, whose membership crested at over 3,000 in the 1950s, closed in 1975.[26]

Throughout the late 1960s and the 1970s, Methodism ministered through and out of its properties only to witness white flight scatter, and other churches follow, what had been its primary constituency into the suburbia of guarded cul-de-sacs and gated communities. A few Chicago Temples weathered the storm, held on, but only to watch—in cities large and small—American industries fly to the global South, department stores relocate to the suburbs, corporations build their own outlying campuses, deinstitutionalization fill parks with the homeless, blight and petty crime spread over the once vibrant business districts, transportation networks disappear as highways plowed through, urban renewal break apart neighborhoods, and remaining racial-ethnic communities struggle to reach retreating jobs and grocery stores. In places, riots finished the destruction.

"What's Ahead for Old First Church?" queried Ezra Earl Jones, at the time an executive at the General Board of Global Ministries, and my late colleague, the Duke researcher Robert Wilson.[27] But absent the capacity to envision—much less implement—an overall, coherent, and compelling denominational strategy, United Methodism left it to congregations and conferences to experiment with ways to minister in racially changing urban contexts. In many places, courageous members continued to commute into the downtown church to launch congregational or support conference initiatives: pantries, shelters, addiction clinics, training centers, AIDS ministries, tutoring programs, Meals on Wheels, day care, advocacy efforts.[28] In some cases, multiethnic or African-American United Methodism succeeded to sustain the Gothic facility, its maintenance often burdening effective ministry. Elsewhere, Methodism made Philadelphia's agonizing strategic decision to sell its aging, only partially occupied building and relocate to the Valley Forge Corporate Center.[29] All too often, however, the urban church dwindled, aged, hunkered down, just died, and left the conference a distressed sale.

The annual conference struggled as well, with apportionments plateauing as memberships plummeted, but typically succeeded in sustaining its incredible apparatus: retreat and camp grounds, conference centers, nursing and geriatric facilities, lay and clergy training ventures, orphanages and homes, short-term missions, plus all the ministries undertaken collaboratively with other denominations and its urban churches.[30] Its hands quite full, the conference nevertheless added or augmented ministries for the elderly, infirm, and indigent; undertook capital campaigns on its institutions' behalf; and faced similar challenges in closing funding gaps for pension and insurance programs. Although these were maintenance ministries, perhaps, as pop sociologists and organizational gurus charged, but clearly some saw the alternatives to constitute dereliction of duty, poor stewardship of ministry investment, and a betrayal of the Great Commandment. Nevertheless, keeping programs and ministries going and staying the course in the cities as long and as much as it did cost United Methodism in the scramble for suburban (white) religious loyalties. Symbolizing both commitment and its cost, North Georgia kept its conference headquarters in center city Atlanta—the cross and flame daily visible to every driver on the downtown connector—finally just a couple of years ago surrendering its witness to the city, building a conference center in the forest enclave of Simpsonwood, and redirecting the myriad conference gatherings to its sylvan retreat.

Is it surprising that Methodism proved unable to respond to the challenges of the twentieth century and of the cities? We have been a church of partial visions and fragmented leadership. Each board or agency functions independently, competing with the others, acting like it alone was the church. Board directors and committee members view themselves as representing their respective jurisdiction or caucus. Caucuses pursue their agendas. Bishops operate in diocesan fashion, serving their respective conference, acting as itinerant general superintendents only when they fly off to a meeting. Clergy-in-conference worry over pensions and health care. We have left it to individual pastors to try to deal with the big problems in American cities. Many responded creatively, heroically, stoically. No one, nobody, capitalized on experimental success, conceived a national strategy, and established new implementation procedures for Methodist and United Methodist witness to a changing American society. To be sure, a board policy here and a Key 73 (an ecumenical effort to spread the gospel) there imagined Methodism doing something coherent, extensive, coordinated, sustained. But to naught.

* * *

Whether the Council of Bishops can and will step into the leadership void we have yet to see. Holy conferencing will not birth leaders with the prerogative and the vision to transform a connection that 1939 jurisdictioned into disfunctionality. And tweaking Disciplinary language will not, I think, transmute an 1884 bureaucratized and congregationalized, and a 1939 federalized and professionalized denomination and denominational mission into disciple making for the transformation of the world. Arresting rhetoric, fresh ideas, and even proposed policies do not actualize or transform a system and structures in which the episcopacy is deeply implicated.

A connectional church? Or one cooped up in its institutions? We are jurisdictioned, congregationalized, bureaucratized, and professionalized—but leaderless. If we wish to move on as a church, if we really do want to reclaim our role as an ethical and social-ethical conscience for the nation, if we truly believe our disciple making to be world transforming, then we need to get beyond the game of mutual recriminations. We need to move past blaming one another over issues traced back merely forty years—to the liberalism or conservatism of the 1960s, the decade of merger, the appearance of caucuses—for our inertias. These are but symptoms. The underlying structural/praxis problems run deeper and further back. So we need more truly innovative praxis and more radical surgery on structure. And we need to trust leaders to exercise leadership, an issue to which we now turn.

CONCLUSION

Reforming the Connection: Breaching Four Walls

United Methodism in the United States—indeed, mainstream Protestantism—remains in trouble. We need no headlines or seer or prophet to tell us that. The signs abound. They appear at General Conference; they bedevil annual conferences; they polarize faculties; they sometimes traumatize congregations. Caucuses vie for attention, place, and priority. They divide us by agenda. Meetings fracture. We unite, not as a whole, but into warring parties, sometimes by ethnicity or gender, sometimes by status (laity, deacons, elders, local preachers), sometimes by region, and often under the general banners of liberal and evangelical. (We touched on the historical dimensions of this division in chapter 3,"General Conference: A Retrospective"; chapter 10, "Family Values: A Connectional Concern"; and chapter 11, "Methodism as Machine.") There we huddle, by caucus or commitment, our identity established by differentiation, prepared for the trench warfare between the two major camps.

Our divisions, especially between liberal and evangelical, run deeper and wider, we are told, than anything separating us from other Christian bodies; that is, separating denominations from one another.[1] The warring camps flail against each other and against what remains of established authority—the bishops, the boards and agencies, the seminaries, the clergy. Gatherings become tense, contentious, even mean-spirited affairs. Seemingly insignificant items become occasions for political grandstanding and symbolic warfare. And the true flash points—abortion, homosexuality, war—can bring the church's business to a halt. Highly politicized exchanges occur over ordination, representation, and funding.

Mainstream Protestantism is in trouble. It seems to have lost its way; fewer and fewer follow. Hemorrhaging membership losses beset United Methodists and other mainline denominations. A general malaise reigns. Leadership clutches desperately for panaceas and nostrums—anything to turn the numbers around. Numbers, numbers, numbers. We are preoccupied with them. And for solutions the two parties and the several caucuses chant their agendas. More effective presence in the urban areas! Move a board out of New York! Heed the authority of Scripture! More sustained witnessing! Greater commitment to love, peace, and justice! Recognize our truly global character!

Can we come to more penetrating analyses of our situation? The Lilly Endowment thought so, commissioned several major studies of mainline denominations, and invited several of my then-Duke colleagues and me to coordinate a major inquiry of the denomination. Drawing on scholars and church leaders from across the country, we undertook a major attack on the symptomologies of decline and division. Abingdon Press published the results of this study in five volumes as "United Methodism and American Culture."[2] What I outline below represents my own ruminations from this project, from other recent studies of mainstream Protestantism, from the recent Pew Forum on Religion and Public Life, from the *U.S. Religious Landscape Survey*, and from my own studies, some of which are gathered here.[3] I/we suggest that the perspectives of neither left nor right and the agendas of none of the caucuses reach quite deep enough.[4]

Let me begin at the beginning—at the Protestant beginning, that is—in 1520. At the start of this thing we call Protestantism, Martin Luther wrote a number of treatises demanding reform and denouncing the "woeful corruption" of Christendom, among them the 1520 trilogy *The Freedom of a Christian*, *An Open Letter to the Christian Nobility*, and *The Babylonian Captivity of the Church*.[5] Luther argued that the gospel was entrapped, the church imprisoned, the Christian tyrannized by principalities and powers. That entrapment walled off, cut off, separated the church from its own better self and from the gospel. As an evocative image for that self-alienation and its consequent corruption, Luther employed the notion of *walls*. Walls physically entrapped the gospel and church; walls stood between

Christians and the gospel. Beyond those walls, cut off from the Christians of his day, Luther saw what would be the great doctrinal treasures of the Reformation—the priesthood of all believers, the authority of Scripture, justification by faith, and the freedom of a Christian.[6] The walls blocked the Christian from the gospel itself. Walls of custom, walls of authority, walls of procedure, walls of privilege, walls of interpretation, walls of doctrine—in smashing them, Luther brought reform.

Have not we as United Methodists also erected walls that stand between us and the gospel, between us and faithful Christian practice, between us and true piety? Let me propose four walls, rather than three, that entrap United Methodism. Each of them blocks off the gospel, each divides United Methodism from the Wesleyan legacy, and each blocks our faithful witness. The four, covered here in various chapters, are bureaucratized polity, congregationalized itinerancy and connectionalism, regulatory discipline, and mission collapsed into influence and body count. Another way to describe these is:

- a polity suffocating from overstructure;
- connection and itinerancy collapsed into congregationalism;
- discipline transformed into a praxis of regulation and hyper-accountability; and
- mission confused with notions of Christendom and a Christian America.

For Methodists these should be very familiar topics. But do we not typically discuss them by blaming someone else: Nashville? New York? the bishops? conference headquarters? the other party in our culture war? The walls may—in fact, they do—stand between us and Nashville or New York. But the truth is we need not blame far-off antichrists. These walls, very high and very thick, may be found in our congregations. To understand the "four walls," we need to recall Pogo's profound insight, "We have seen the enemy and it is us." We have found its stronghold: walls of our design and construction.

Bureaucratized Polity

I need not dwell at great length on the first wall: bureaucratized polity. Overstructure in our denomination is no news to anyone at any level in the life of the church (see chapter 11, "Methodism as Machine"). The first complaint about denominations is bureaucracy: boards and agencies in far-off places running up the dollars for every meeting to concoct policy with which you and I disagree, to issue it in our name, to lavish our contributed dollars upon it, and then to insist that we act in solidarity. A similar but more muted refrain occurs on annual conference levels. There, too, the conference office functions as symbol and persons speak of "decades of focusing our missions through programs which originated in conference boards and agencies."[7] Congregations vent their unhappiness about apportionments and refer to them as "taxes." But Pogo was right: this same organizational bloat can be found with us, in many local congregations.

A complex of committees, elaborate decision-making procedures, tight control by small elites over resources and spending policies—this is ecclesiastical *Bleak House*, a bureaucratic labyrinth! That is what the *Discipline* has called for. Structure weighs us down. It does so at every level—congregational, conference, jurisdictional, general, and, yes, on the congregational level. Meetings consume congregational time and energy that ought to be devoted to outreach, to mission, to evangelism, to social reform. A good idea, perhaps some new venture in day care, dies before it has run the committee gauntlet—from proposers, to age-level coordinators, to education, to pastor- or staff-parish relations committees, to finance, to trustees, to church council. Bureaucracy in a local church wears a friendly face but involves no less bureaucracy—the church council (or earlier administrative board/council on ministries and still earlier the official board) overarches a series of committees and commissions every bit as impressive as far-off New York. To be sure, the 1996 and subsequent General Conferences have empowered local churches and annual conferences to address the bureaucratic morass and to adopt more flexible, missionally oriented structures.[8] Whether this feeds or cures the contagion we have yet to see. First responders—local churches and annual conferences—expended considerable effort in restructure and adjusting thereunto, effectively fixating the body on itself. The preoccupation with reform and political adjustments produced as much inwardness as the bureaucracy it replaced.

So we will have to see what becomes of the every-level bureaucratization, of our penchant for organization run amuck. Order, polity, and machinery has been a Methodist signature, part of the Wesleyan or the Methodist genius—indeed, it has been our contribution to American denominationalism, as chapters 2, 5, 6, 8, and 11 argue. What has become of the experimental, can-do, pragmatic spirit of earlier Methodism? Then we built structure for mission, for purpose, for evangelism, for the Kingdom, for reform. Where is our pride in institution creating, our building for mission, our innovation for evangelism, and our social reform? Now we experience our institutions as burdens or, as we see below in looking at the third wall, permit accountability and suspicion to govern our structuring and relations to structures.

Gone seems to be our capacity to make organization really serve purpose. We were Hester Ann Rogers, genteel women, who gave up our finery and quit the dance floor, who became servants of our mothers to win our spiritual freedom, who then broke the gender barrier as class leaders, and who so nursed others with the milk of Methodist gospel. We were Mary Masons who saw visions of mission to the outcast and needy and created new societies. We dared to defy convention. We experimented. We innovated organizationally. We were women and men who, in mission and missions, dared to create, to found new organizations, to cross boundaries, to move beyond our existing structures. We built structure to do something. Practical divinity, experimental divinity—that was our way.[9]

United Methodism, if we would now win our spiritual freedom, must recover our practical divinity, give ourselves permission to experiment, and give up our organizational finery. American society finds itself in the same plight as the church. Old corporate structures, old patterns of management, old formulas of inventory, old hierarchical styles do not work as they once did. Society too quests for new organizational models. Congress now endeavors to trash the old systems and to pass more costs and responsibilities as well as the organizational problem on to the states. Japan and its systems fixated us. Total Quality Management became a new religion, even for the religious. We put our faith in *Good to Great* or *Built to Last* or the contemporary business gurus' latest word. The society quests for forms. Yet forms alone will not suffice. A new spirit must animate the forms. And here United Methodism should prosper. Why can't United Methodists discover once again how things work, how practical divinity can be, how to experiment, how we ought to organize, how to put individuals together in society? That has been our genius. United Methodists can and should discover new ways of organizing to beat the devil.

Congregationalized Itinerancy and Connection

The wall of bureaucracy shuts us in. So does the wall of congregationalism. We are shut up in our congregations. We think of ministry as "parish." We construe everything else as "appointments beyond the local church" or as "extension" ministry. We make a fetish of the congregation. We construe disciple making to be a local church endeavor (see chapters 4 and 5).

Here, also, the concentration on the congregation derives from a variety of otherwise positive developments: the opening up of ordained ministry; longer, more stable pastorates; the Disciplinary provisions for consultation; two-career ministerial families; lay empowerment; encouragement of congregations to be in mission in their own setting.

The consequence of construing our mission as entirely mediated through local churches has been a great inversion. We think of persons who reach out to campus, or camp, or district, or military service, or teaching as "leaving the ministry."

Wesley thought the world his parish. Have we, as some quip put it, made our parish into the world? Parish we take to be the church;[10] congregation is the norm. Parish ministry we therefore assume to be the only form of ministry.

Methodists once had a more aggressive and dynamic view of ministry and church at local as well as translocal levels. Once we were German Methodists who met in great meetings; we assembled entire neighborhoods for sacramental gatherings. We punctuated our quarterly meetings and annual conferences with explosive love feasts, moving testimony, and powerful preaching. Crowds converted. Ministry, outreach, and testimony created their own assemblies. Conference became a means of grace. Several years ago I titled an address "Conference as a Means of Grace." Everyone thought it was an oxymoron. But this is just what I argue in chapters 1, 7, and 12.

Annual and General conferences became occasions for the revivals of early Methodism. The General Conference of 1800 stimulated widespread revivals. Revivals more typically grew out of annual and quarterly conferences. The church eventually programmed for conference revivals by scheduling camp meetings to coincide with their quarterly or annual sittings (see chapters 7 and 12).

We were a people who indeed made conference a means of grace. German and English, black and white—we made business a revival and revival our business. We did not coop ourselves up in parish, in congregation. Church was not parish; it was not congregation. It was the gathering out of the world of people who desired to flee the wrath to come, people who would deign to be called Methodist.[11]

Methodism was bigger and littler than parish. Methodists belonged to and had their membership in the most intimate of gatherings, the class meeting. And Methodism performed church. It offered the full array of services of Word, Order, and Sacrament in the large assemblies, the regional quarterly meeting or the exciting quarterly meeting-housing camp meeting. Conference said clearly what it meant to be church. Conference, quarterly meeting, class, mission society, Sunday school—those were Methodism at its best. Not congregation, not parish.[12]

Ministry also configured itself dynamically and corporately, not as parish ministry, not as ministry limiting itself to a congregation (see chapters 4 and 5). In thinking of that ministry we conjure up the image on The United Methodist Publishing House's datebook for clergy, the daily suggester, the one circuit rider in midstream braving storm, face masked against the elements. That image both helps and misleads. It helps by reminding us of the circuit and of the fact that the appointment was to the connection, not to a congregation. But the singularity of the image misleads. We offered ourselves as a collective ministry—class leaders, exhorters, local preachers, traveling preachers, presiding elders, bishops.

We rode together, with preachers' journals or diaries recording "We rode . . ." day after day. We preachers made appointments for one another (and for presiding elders [district superintendents] and bishops when the leaders rode through our circuit). We functioned together, rode together, and gathered frequently. Quarterly meetings brought together not just the traveling preachers, local preachers, exhorters, and class leaders from the one circuit but typically also those from the neighboring circuits (see chapters 4 and 7). And the gesture was reciprocated.

We itinerants did not box ourselves up in parish. Methodism conferenced and feasted in love. As ministers, we were more collective than individual, more connectional than congregational.

Methodism must recover the fluidity and dynamism of its historic sense of ministry and church. Methodism must again extend its ministry and spill its life beyond the walls of our buildings. We must not wall ourselves up in our congregations. We must reclaim our connectional ministry.

Regulatory Discipline

Less familiar in name, but very familiar in practice, is our reflexive regulatory discipline.[13] This third wall of regulation shuts us in. Regulation, accountability, accusing attitudes, and elaborate criteria have become our way of life. This behavior in the church is hardly strange; indeed, it is very familiar. Our society seems to run itself by regulation. By executive order, judicial decree, congressional or state legislative action, we fill our lives with rules, protections, and procedures. Business folk cry over the protocols. Doctors quit in disgust over governmental and insurance intrusions. Local governments protest unfunded mandates. Campaigns against regulation and regulators capture our imagination and votes. But, ironically, the foes of regulation move quickly to impose new, more subtle forms of regulation. The Reagans, Gingriches, and Bushes promise to cut back on regulation and to overturn affirmative action and environmental safety rules, but then would impose their own regulations with regard to families, schools, abortion, homosexuality, and the like. They prove less against regulation than against *certain forms* of regulation. So also the Democrats. In such inconsistency, the politicians represent us well. As a people, we both protest regulation and organize to make sure that our own interests remain protected (by regulation). Special-interest groups prosper. They press for regulation—reduce emissions, stop abortions, impose the death penalty, remove the death penalty, do not harass, do not discriminate, recycle, reimpose school prayer, save the turtles and dolphins, drink with paper not Styrofoam cups, do not smoke. Monitoring groups, some self-appointed, others legislated, watchdog our behavior. We transact business in a hermeneutic of suspicion.

The same tactics work remarkably well in the church. Within United Methodism the most adroit at caucus politics are the evangelicals. Organizing around their causes—doctrine, missions, seminaries, church funding, feminism, abortion, homosexuality—they have generated impressive caucus organization/machinery: the Good News movement, the Confessing Movement, the Mission Society for United Methodists, Aldersgate Renewal Fellowship, A Foundation for Theological Education (AFTE), Lifewatch, RENEW, Transforming Congregations, the Association for Church Renewal, and United Methodist Action. From the latter, the United Methodist wing of the Institute on Religion and Democracy (IRD), which seems to orchestrate political action for the several conservative caususes, Democratic or Republican political action committees could take a lesson or so.

Hermeneutics of suspicion rule on the left as well as the right, as much with COSROW (Commission on the Status and Role of Women) as with Good News, as much with the Northeastern Jurisdiction as with the Southeastern Jurisdiction. The church finds regulation the easiest way to do business. Every committee constitutes itself by category—female and male, diaconal and ordained, white and ethnic, challenged and able, youth and adults, and on some occasions straight and gay—and jurisdiction. We structure for symbolism. So also we pray, listening for verbal offenses, such as sexist language or feminine imagery. We measure program by whether it attends appropriately to deacons' as well as elders' interests. We monitor and watchdog through caucuses on the Left and on the Right. We turn budgets into reward systems, doling out "grants" to groups and individuals who measure up. By criteria, by norm, by regulation, by reward, we do business.

Boards and agencies, having suffered tremendous cuts in budget and staff, find regulation to be the primary power left. They increasingly look like secular regulatory agencies. Annual conferences increasingly find the same tactics necessary. They legislate lavish expectations for local churches. Even local churches find accountability to be an easy way to do business. It comes naturally, automatically, instinctively.

I could illustrate from personal experience just how very naturally, automatically, and instinctively churches do business—with memories of a local church's creation of regulations after receiving an endowment, or with a recent stint on a conference board of higher education and campus ministry, or with recollections of the behaviors of two different boards of ordained ministry. Instead, let me use experience with a national agency. Some years ago I found myself on a committee of a general commission. We—staff, theological educators, clergy and lay directors—concerned ourselves with that agency's relation to the seminaries. We did so motivated by a genuine concern for the education of the next generation of ecumenical leadership and with the apprehension that it was not happening. As a first order of business, we gathered information to assess the situation, that is, we monitored the seminaries for their ecumenical involvement. A second impulse came equally instinctively. We began to elaborate criteria, expectations, and regulations to elicit, even enforce education for ecumenism. Only after we had proceeded quite far into developing regulatory protocols did we step back. We resisted this impulse with great difficulty, and only after I indicated how unfriendly and unhelpful the proposal would be to the seminaries. We resisted the impulse to regulate because I—then a seminary administrator and faculty member—realized that I was putting myself in the position of one to be thereafter regulated. A conflict of interest saved the day. Regulation seemed to be so much the way to do business that I had come close to regulating myself.

Similar calls to resist regulation, resolution passing, and legislating on controverted issues come now from bishops and others concerned with the atmosphere of suspicion and recrimination that we have created. At times and in places conferences have so restrained themselves. But such self-limitation proves difficult. The petitions pour in, caucuses strategize, and politicking for legislation continues. Less interested in *what* we do than *how* we do it, the church continues to make accountability rather than program its first priority.

This is not Methodist discipline at its best. This is not why we called our constitutional book *Discipline*. This is not why we made discipline one of the marks of the church. We have let the social fractures of the world consume our order. We have let the adversarial politics of the United States dictate our discipline. We once thought that our order—our Methodist discipline—could triumph over the world. That is why we committed ourselves, at the very start, to fight the curse and sin of slavery. We knew the social distinctions of the world to be wrong.

We are "brothers" (*Wir sind Brüder*)—we, with William Otterbein, said to Martin Boehm.[14] So we named each other brother, sister, mother, father. Whether white or black, slave or free, rich or poor, we claimed one another as family. Women in leadership we called "Mothers in Israel." Our early records minuted action by "brother" this and "brother" that. So, for instance, the General Conference of 1808 recorded critical actions as taken by "brother" this and that:

> Thursday, May 12, 1808
>
> Brother M'Claskey and brother Cooper asked leave to withdraw the motion for seven additional bishops; which was refused.
>
> Brother George Pickering moved, and was seconded by brother Joshua Soule, that the conference decide on the motion now before them, whether there shall be seven additional bishops or not. Carried.
>
> Brother Ostrander's motion for two additional bishops, being put to vote, was lost.
>
> Brother Roszel's motion, for one additional bishop, to be elected or ordained at this conference, being put to vote, was carried.[15]

Less formally and more intensely, we embraced our brothers and sisters in classes, society, and quarterly meeting. There, we sisters/brothers were accountable to one another, watched over one another, reproved one another. But in such accountability, we dealt with one another directly, personally, honestly, frankly, not through the mediation of regulation; and we held ourselves over against the world. Accountability pitted our Methodist order against that of the world.

Such accountability recognized that we were male and female, black and white, German and English, young and old, rich and poor. But we claimed those equal in

God's sight and not to be disdained with the world's distinctions—slave and free, property owner and not, gentility and the poorer sort.

In our language of the day, we Methodists spoke about diversity, pluralism, multiculturalism, ethnicity—but we did so firm in the conviction that gospel liberty triumphs over the enslaving distinctions of the world. We sang "I got shoes, you got shoes" in the belief that though divisions ran through the world, Methodists could not let the world's distinctions divide and define us.

Have we today forgotten that gospel and let worldly status divide and define us? We need ways of relating to one another that do not blur our differences but nevertheless move us beyond the regulatory mode, beyond trying to turn our agenda into law for others. We need discipline, not accommodation. *Regula*, not regulation.

Mission: Influence and Body Count

The fourth wall shuts up mission. We, or at least some of us, remain fixated by the late nineteenth-century colonial/imperial strategies and images for winning America and the world.[16] And, in consequence, we remain internally conflicted about the nature and purpose of mission.

Our movement was missionary from the start. Indeed, mission was constitutive of Methodism. Early Methodism understood its mission—understood itself—in Wesley's terms, namely, to reform the continent and spread scriptural holiness over the land (see chapters 1, 10, and 12). In so doing Methodists labored on Zion's behalf. Zion represented the object of our mission—not a worldly imperium, but an imperium over the world. So one of our earliest papers called itself *Zion's Herald* (lately renamed *The Progressive Christian*). So one of the African Methodist churches embedded Zion in its name. Zion, we then recognized, stood over against the kingdoms of this world. Asbury affirmed:

> All the prospects of this world are dead to me. I feel not a wish for creatures or things. The glory of the Kingdom of Christ, the organization of a primitive Church of God, these are all my objects; was it possible to set a glass to my heart, you should see them engraven there by the word & spirit of the living God.[17]

Asbury and Coke explained Methodist disorientation to the world in their commentary on the *Discipline*. Explicating Methodist behavior, they proclaimed: "[O]ur one aim, in all our economy and ministerial labours, is to raise a holy people, crucified to the world and alive to God." Speaking of ministry, they asserted, "Our original design in forming our religious Society. . . [is] [t]o raise a holy people. . . . We will have a holy people, or none. In every part of our economy, as well as doctrine, we aim at crucifixion to the world and love to God."[18]

"Crucified to the world" in the course of our history we forgot. Methodists, especially Northern Methodists, increasingly associated their "Zion" and America. The Civil War proved to be especially transformative. Newly empowered, Methodists joined the Protestant establishment, sought the Christianization of American culture, and claimed culture as itself a primary vehicle of such Christianization. Methodists lost their critical distance from culture. With Protestants generally, they dreamed that America could be made a Christian society. By the early twentieth century, they hoped also that the world could be Christianized "in this generation." And "in this generation" we sought both evangelical and social gospel transformations of the world. Both evangelicals and liberals sought dominion; they differed in their strategy and weaponry. Dominion proved seductive.

Those hopes lost some of their luster in the 1920s and 1930s when world war, the failure of prohibition, depression, industrialization, secularization, and genuine pluralism (to mention just the obvious) shattered Protestant illusions. My teacher Robert Handy spoke of this disillusionment as the "second disestablishment."[19] Just as the constitutional epoch brought a new day for the church in disestablishing and severing the legal tie with the state, so depression brought a new day for the church in disestablishing and severing the informal tie with culture. Christian America was, and is, over! Dawn brought an ecumenical and interreligious future.

We don't seem to want to hear this word about the new day for the church. Ronald Reagan and George Bush have run the country by not hearing. Pat Robertson acquired a network so that more will not hear. Talk radio shouts its deafness. One major news channel specializes in not seeing or hearing. Parts of our church want to make sure that the rest of us don't hear. They genuinely believe Methodism to be committed to a Christian America. They genuinely believe that Methodism loses something of itself if it gives up the hope of Christianizing America and the world. And when evangelizing prospects for United Methodism in the United States seem dim, we take solace in the church's growth elsewhere and especially when we gain by the incorporation of entire conferences.

The folks worked up over influence and numbers have it only half right. They are absolutely correct in believing that Methodism is about mission. But they are speaking late nineteenth-century civilization, not genuine Wesleyanism in equating mission with soul conquest, winning, domination, and control—the colonial or neocolonial style. We are walled in by that understanding, and ironically, walled in by the embrace of culture that it entailed. Culture religion entraps us; a colonial mentality entraps us. We confuse Americanism with the gospel and numbers with faithfulness.

We can well return to Asbury and Coke's formulation. With them, we once said: "Our original design in forming our religious Society . . . [is] [t]o raise a holy people. . . . We will have a holy people, or none. In every part of our economy, as well as doctrine, we aim at crucifixion to the world and love to God."[20] We must reclaim a Wesleyan sense of mission: aggressive, dynamic, and evangelistic—but on Zion's behalf.

Four Walls

Four walls entrap us. That is the bad news. And they entrap us in our congregations, in our weekly lives. We may image the walls with our distant Nashville or conference headquarters bureaucrats. But the walls also run through even small local churches. They entrap us because *we* are our enemy. *We* choose to do business this way—to overstructure, to bottle ourselves up in our buildings, to program by watchdogging one another, and to confuse Zion with the nation. That is the bad news.

We cannot simply move the walls—for instance, from the general boards and agencies to annual conferences; or, as some conferences propose to do, from annual conferences to districts. We cannot simply move the walls and expect anything to change. Bureaucracy and congregationalism and regulatory discipline and capitulation to culture come every bit as easily at a district level as at a national level. My special counsel to reorganizers is that simply moving the walls won't really help. That is more bad news.

The good news is that cooped up within these walls are 8 or 9 million United Methodists who need and want out. In our congregations can be found loyal, effective, and committed leaders. Energy, vision, and dynamism abound. We have tired our people out with too much structure, too much business, too much skirmish, and too much regulation. But the Wesleyan spirit, though walled in, remains very much alive.

We United Methodists need to find ways to breach these walls. It is easier said than done. We need structure. We cannot abandon our existing congregations and

Conclusion

buildings. We must not give up our wonderful institutions. We cannot wish away the diversities and the differences. And we cannot simply dismiss a century of imperial missions. The walls had their purpose. Each of them indeed represents an ideal, a good, a Methodist characteristic—but a good gone to excess. And they are there. We have trained up a generation of leaders who use and depend upon them. The walls are there.

They do wall us in. We are entrapped, imprisoned, and tyrannized. Through that dominion we fall under the principalities and powers of this age. We succumb, because Pogo is right: "The enemy is us."

We need *reformation*! But Luther knew that "though this world" be "with devils filled" and "the Prince of Darkness grim," "We tremble not for him . . . / For lo, his doom is sure; / One little word shall fell him."

One little word fells the prince of darkness and these walls. It did for Luther. It can for us. That word is the *Word*—and faith and trust in that Word. Trust in the Word is especially essential. That word is the Word. That Word and the faith, hope, and love made possible in him is what we need. Trusting in him we can love one another, look forward to a common hope, and recognize one another as sharing in the apostolic faith. Trust in the Word breaches walls.

Holding up each of these walls amounts to mistrust. Each wall expresses a fundamental mistrust of our Methodist gospel. Each separates us from our real, our better, Methodist nature. That is our papacy; that is the enemy within; that is our anti-Christ.

- We fail to claim our liberty in the gospel, our pragmatic spirit, and our experimental divinity. We mistrust ourselves and one another to carry through obligations and so we overstructure for everything. *An excess of our organizational prowess!*
- We fail to claim our connectional ministry, our historic openness to new deployment, our appointive system, and our leadership. So we fix upon the congregation and collapse connection into parish. *Consultation gone to excess!*
- We fail to claim the triumph of the gospel over the world. So we let the worldly differences and their spirit rule. So caucus rules in the place of discipline, of brotherhood and sisterhood. *A hermeneutical excess—too much suspicion!*

- We fail to claim our calling to be "a holy people, crucified to the world and alive to God." So some still contrive for missionary dominion. *Excessive identification with the culture!*

Trust may require doing more by congregations, clusters, and districts but also doing more beyond congregations and districts. It may also require doing with less structure—and so seeking genuine connectionalism. It may require some other formula for representation than the formula of the ark—two of every kind, two from every district, conference, and caucus. It may require:

- trusting our ministry enough to give up the salary ladder of appointments;
- trusting our bishops and trusting them to lead;
- trusting persons in our conferences and congregations with whom we fundamentally disagree;
- trusting ourselves to experiment, to dare, to start afresh, to create some things new;
- trusting enough in the gospel to launch out afresh in mission;
- trusting our Methodist liberty enough to flaunt the world's distinctions;
- moving through and beyond the hermeneutics of suspicion, not to naïveté or a new patriarchy but to a hard-won trust.

And then, agreeing to disagree, we find ourselves:

- praying for one another, particularly those with whom we disagree;
- experimenting, daring, starting afresh;
- launching new missions;
- legislating less and suggesting more;
- turning our conferences again into gracious affairs.

Trust will bring the four walls tumbling down. One little word. One little word opens a big project and a great future. Trust in God, trust in one another, trust in our mission. "A Mighty Fortress Is Our God."

Notes

Introduction: History, the Methodist Mode of Self-Identification

1. Sweet, *Methodists*, 691–706. For full details on this and other abbreviated references, see the Abbreviations, vii-xi.

2. *Minutes of the Methodist Conferences, annually held in America from 1773 to 1784, inclusive* (Philadelphia: Printed by Henry Tuckniss; sold by John Dickins, 1795), (5)-7; reprinted in *MEA* 2:56.

3. "To Dr. COKE, Mr. ASBURY, and our Brethren in *NORTH-AMERICA*," in Wesley, *Letters* (Telford), 7:237–38. Reproduced in *MEA* 2, 1784a, 72.

4. *John Wesley's Sunday Service of the Methodists in North America*, with an introduction by James F. White (Nashville: Quarterly Review, 1984).

5. Lee, *Short History*, 107.

6. *Minutes of Several Conversations Between the Rev. Thomas Coke, LL.D., the Rev. Francis Asbury and others, at a Conference, Begun in Baltimore, in the State of Maryland, on Monday, the 27th of December, in the Year 1784* (Philadelphia: Charles Cist, 1785). For the text of the first *Discipline* in parallel columns with the "Large Minutes," see Tigert, *History*, 532–602.

7. See Carlton R. Young, *Companion to The United Methodist Hymnal* (Nashville: Abingdon, 1993), 94–95.

8. See Wesley, *Works* 7, *A Collection of Hymns for the Use of the People called Methodists*, ed. Franz Hildebrandt and Oliver A. Beckerlegge, with the assistance of James Dale.

9. To some extent, it would function for Methodists as did the *Book of Common Prayer* (*BCP*) for Anglicans.

10. MEC *Discipline* 1787, 3–7.

11. *Minutes*/MEC/1773, 5.

12. Tigert, *History*, 58–59.

13. Donald T. Kauffman, *The Dictionary of Religious Terms* (Westwood, N.J.: Fleming H. Revell, 1967); Bill J. Leonard, "Baptists in the South: A New Connectionalism," *American Baptist Quarterly* 21 (September 2002): 208–21; Bill J. Leonard, "Baptists in the South: A New Connectionalism," *Review and Expositor* 95 (Winter 1998): 75–85; Scott M. Gibson, "Theological Connectionalism: A Perspective from American Baptist Evangelicals," *American Baptist Quarterly* 21 (June 2002): 173–79; Richard R. Hammar, "Judicial 'Connectionalizing' of Congregational Polities," *Governmental Intervention in Religious Affairs* 2, ed. Dean M. Kelley (New York: Pilgrim, 1986), 199–217; John Maust, "Connectional Denominations Try Retying Their Slipknots," *Christianity Today* 22/23 (September 21, 1979): 50–51; Lyle E. Schaller, "Connectionalism: The New Polity?" *Christian Century* 81 (July 1964): 858–61.

14. UMC *Discipline* 2008, ¶ 131, 90–91.

15. UMC *Discipline* 1988, ¶ 112, 116–18.

16. UMC *Discipline* 1992, ¶ 112, 111–13.

17. Sweet, *Methodists*, 680–709; James Penn Pilkington and Walter Newton Vernon, *The Methodist Publishing House: A History*, 2 vols. (Nashville: Abingdon, 1968, 1989).

18. For further elaboration of this, see Russell E. Richey, *Doctrine in Experience: A Methodist Theology of Church and Ministry* (Nashville: Kingswood, 2009).

Chapter 1: The First Word about Methodism: History in the *Discipline*

1. (Philadelphia, 1785). For comparison of the American with the Wesleyan minutes, see Tigert, *History*, appendix 7, which puts the two in parallel columns. Consult this volume; Frank, *Polity*; and Nolan B. Harmon, *The Organization of The Methodist Church*, 2nd rev. ed. (Nashville: The Methodist Publishing House, 1962) on constitutional matters.

2. *A Form of Discipline, For the Ministers, Preachers, and Members of the Methodist Episcopal Church in America* (New York, 1787), 3–4. For sustained reflection on the import of the changes that the Americans made, see the first seven essays in *Reflections upon Methodism during the Bicentennial* (Dallas: Bridwell Library Center for Methodist Studies, 1985; papers presented at the 1984 Regional Conference of the World Methodist Historical Society).

3. An accessible version of the early Methodist *Discipline*s is *The Methodist Discipline of 1798, Including the Annotations of Thomas Coke and Francis Asbury*, facsimile edition, ed. Frederick A. Norwood (Rutland, Vt.: Academy, 1979). Designed for apologetic purposes to address critics from other denominations and critics from within, like James O'Kelly, the annotations bear on the argument of this chapter. They appeal consistently to Scripture, and, as appropriate, to tradition. And they make a reasoned case for the rubrics of the *Discipline*. Here, then, in the notes—after the fact, as it were—the bishops become self-conscious about the nature of Methodist authority. Why, one might ask, had they and the church not been more self-conscious in their prefatory statements? Or, perhaps had they?

4. For Wesley's "A Plain Account," see *Works* (Jackson) 8:248–68.

5. See *The Doctrines and Discipline of the African Methodist Episcopal Church* (Philadelphia, 1817); *The Doctrines and Discipline of the Wesleyan Methodist Episcopal Zion Church in America*,

Established in the City of New-York, October 25th, 1820, 2nd ed. (New York, 1840); *The Doctrine and Discipline of the Evangelical Association, Together with the Design of Their Union, translated from the German* (New-Berlin, 1832); *Origin, Constitution, Doctrine and Discipline, of the United Brethren in Christ* (Circleville, Ohio, 1837); *Constitution and Discipline of the Methodist Protestant Church* (Baltimore, 1830); *The Discipline of the Wesleyan Methodist Connection of America*, particularly in the 2nd (New York, 1845) and 3rd (New York, 1849) versions, which include a preface by a committee appointed "to prepare a short account of the Wesleyan Methodist Connection of America, to be inserted in the Discipline" (1845, iii); *The Doctrines and Discipline of the Methodist Episcopal Church, South* (Richmond, 1846); *The Doctrines and Discipline of the Free Methodist Church* (Rochester, 1870); *The Doctrines and Discipline of the Colored Methodist Episcopal Church in America* (Louisville, 1874). All were consulted in The Archives and History Center of The United Methodist Church, General Commission on Archives and History, Drew University, Madison, New Jersey.

6. For a fascinating study of the contrasts, see David Little, *Religion, Order, and Law: A Study in Pre-Revolutionary England* (New York: Harper & Row, 1969).

7. See, for instance, part 1, "Book of Confessions"; part 2, "Book of Order," *The Constitution of the Presbyterian Church (U.S.A.)* (New York: Published by the Office of the General Assembly, 1985); and *Constitution and Canons for the Government of the Protestant Episcopal Church . . . Adopted in General Conventions 1789–1987, Together with the Rules or Order* (Printed for the Convention, 1985).

8. See Lee, *Short History*, especially the preface.

9. See Abbreviations, Asbury/Coke *Discipline*.

10. For elaboration of the Quadrilateral (Scripture, tradition, reason, and experience), see 1972 and later versions of *The Book of Discipline of The United Methodist Church*. Also note Thomas A. Langford, "The United Methodist Quadrilateral: A Theological Task," in *Doctrine and Theology in The United Methodist Church* (Nashville: Kingswood, 1991), 232–44.

11. To recognize these historical prefaces as deriving from experience is not quite the same as to posit that the *Discipline* made experience (rather than Scripture, tradition, or reason) normative and its point of theological departure. To reiterate a point made earlier, these prefatory essays were more instinctive than reflective; they indicate the priority of conversion narrative and historical account in Methodist genre. These prefaces do not present themselves as premises of the *Discipline* as a whole. The present debates concern the shape and internal priorities of those premises and appropriately appeal to the legislative record of early Methodism. To identify the premises, one does have to look to those factors, beliefs, and commitments that informed the "Book." In that sense, the debates in conference have at least as much theological bearing on the *Discipline* as the prefaces.

12. MEC *Discipline* 1932, 9. The brief apology and self-conscious attention to doctrine set important precedents for what would follow in 1972.

13. In an interesting reflexive moment, the Historical Statement indicated consciousness of its high calling, of its obligation to tell the story, of its function as an authoritative statement about the movement. On mention of The Methodist Protestant Church, it said, "The history of this movement may be read in the last DISCIPLINE of the Methodist Protestant Church" (MC *Discipline* 1940, 6). The Methodist Protestant *Disciplines* always carried a much fuller and expressive historical account, some ten pages by the 1930s. Even so, it only detailed origins.

14. This particular function is especially interesting since constitutional continuity was formally and legally cared for elsewhere in the *Discipline*.

15. The listing of bishops had actually begun in the 1964 Methodist *Discipline* and was carried over into United Methodist practice.

16. One significant addition to the initial historical statement of the *Discipline* was made in 1976 and continues to the present. It is titled "Black People and Their United Methodist Heritage." It functions, as does the rest of the historical statement, and as have the prefaces over the years, to confer legitimacy. In this case, it symbolizes within the *Discipline* the end to the segregated Central Jurisdiction, the end to *de jure* marginal status for blacks, the end to *de facto* racism.

17. As an aside, I would concede perplexity at the church's dramatic revision of the 1972 historical account. I made this point to Richard Heitzenrater when outside comment was invited. It strikes me that radical changes to constitutional and quasi-constitutional documents tend to induce skepticism and doubt. The advocates of change to the 1972 *Discipline*, persons wanting greater doctrinal clarity and commitment, may have set in process a self-defeating stratagem.

18. Here, the 1988 *Discipline* does not diverge radically from the 1972 version. That account also portrayed Methodist doctrinal development in Wesleyan terms.

19. See, in particular, Thomas A. Langford, *Practical Divinity: Theology in the Wesleyan Tradition* (Nashville: Abingdon, 1983), which struggles with the issue of whether such a tradition exists and how it might be conceptualized. Langford devotes an early chapter to "The Americanization of Wesleyan Theology," and there attends to matters raised here.

20. For instance, the focus upon Wesley, and upon Methodism's loyalty or disloyalty to his literary corpus, obscures the way that other features of the Methodist ethos have affected doctrinal development. A compelling case can be made for rather considerable impact upon Methodist doctrine of Methodist practice, polity, and worship. Camp meetings and revivalism are only the most obvious of a variety of influences that deserves mention. So also the powerful influences of American culture and also of both Pietism and the Enlightenment could readily be acknowledged. This point seems to be conceded in the text but not explicitly developed. Obviously, there are severe limits as to what can be included in such a brief account. Still, can the church afford to depict the heritage as a self-contained Wesleyan stream?

21. A jeremiadic construction of reality comes easily to Americans who have, according to Sacvan Bercovitch, defined their very being and construed their national self-understanding in such terms. For discussion of the genre and its uses, see Bercovitch, *The American Jeremiad* (Madison: University of Wisconsin Press, 1978).

22. Heitzenrater's argument has been advanced in several places. See, for instance, "At Full Liberty: Doctrinal Standards in Early American Methodism," *Quarterly Review* 5 (Fall 1985): 6–27. Thomas C. Oden responded in "What Are 'Established Standards of Doctrine'?: A Response to Richard Heitzenrater," *Quarterly Review* 7 (Spring 1987): 41–62; and more extensively in *Doctrinal Standards in the Wesleyan Tradition* (Grand Rapids: Francis Asbury, 1988).

23. The issue is raised as a matter of principle. I happen to concur in Heitzenrater's reading.

Chapter 2: Connectionalism: Defined in Conflict

1. *JLFA* 3:114, letter dated December 1792, "To Jesse Nicholson." The presiding elder was the counterpart to today's district superintendent. The short titles employed here for standard Methodist reference items, as this one for volume 3 of Asbury's *Journal and Letters*, are those now recognized by Abingdon for the Kingswood Press productions and are listed below.

2. On O'Kelly and the movement, see Edward J. Drinkhouse, *History of Methodist Reform*, 2 vols. (Baltimore, 1899); Charles Frank Kilgore, *The James O'Kelly Schism in the Methodist Episcopal Church* (Mexico City: Casa Unida de Publicaciones, 1963); Wilbur E. MacClenny, *The Life of Rev. James O'Kelly* (Raleigh, 1910); Milo T. Morrill, *A History of the Christian Denomination in America* (Dayton, Ohio: The Christian Publishing Association, 1912).

3. "James O'Kelly: Francis Asbury's Pain and Methodism's Growth" is a title I employed humorously but not inaccurately in the conference version of this paper.

4. See the first published collection, *Minutes of the Methodist Conferences Annually Held in America, from 1773 to 1794, Inclusive* (Philadelphia, 1795); the *Minutes*/MEC (1813) or the standard *Minutes*/MEC.

5. *Minutes*/MEC/1779 (1813), 19–20. See "The Leesburg Minutes of the Methodist Connection, 1775–1783," *Virginia United Methodist Heritage* 5 (Fall 1977): 5–43, especially 19–20. Mss. owned by the Reverend Melvin Lee Steadman Jr., and cited with his permission. See also "Minutes of Conference from the year 1774 to the year 1779 [from minutes kept by Philip Gatch]," *Western Christian Advocate* 4/5 (May 26, 1837): 18–19.

6. *Minutes*/MEC/1779 (1813), 19–20; "The Leesburg Minutes," 19–20. The Leesburg Minutes added, "What provision shall be made in case of Br. Asbury's Death or absence? Ans. Let Br. Ruff, B. Garrettson and Br. McClure act as general Assistants for the Northrin Stations." Asbury noted, "We appointed our next conference to be held in Baltimore town, the last Tuesday in April next."

7. The bold parentheses here refer to documents in our *MEA 2* (*The Methodist Experience in America*).

8. "The Leesburg Minutes," 24.

9. The Leesburg Minutes made the stipulations clearer: "as contained in the notes of New Testament, and four Volumns of Sermons, and . . . Set forth in the Original minutes of conference."

10. For the procedures by which the *Minutes* were expurgated, see Tigert, *History*, 130. The 1782 *Minutes* stipulated (Quest. 18) the erasure of items dealing with the ordinances; see *Minutes*/MEC/1782 (1813), 37.

11. John A. Vickers, *Thomas Coke: Apostle of Methodism* (London: Epworth, 1969), 99n, 114; Wesley, *Letters* (Telford), 7:339; Lee, *Short History*, 124–27; *American Methodist Pioneer: The Life and Journals of the Rev. Freeborn Garrettson, 1752–1827*, ed. Robert Drew Simpson. Published under sponsorship of Drew University Library (Rutland, Vt.: Academy, 1984), 132, 133, 254–55; Wesley, *Journal* (Curnock), 7:300n. Though termed a "General Conference" by Wesley, this 1787 event was not properly a general conference in the sense that that of 1792 and those quadrennially called thereafter would be. For an exhaustive canvassing of this point, see Tigert, *History*, 237–39.

12. See the letter of April 1787 from O'Kelly in *JLFA* 3:49–54; *Minutes*/MEC/1786 (1813), 61; 1787, 62–68; Thomas Ware, *Sketches of the Life and Travels of Rev. Thomas Ware* (New York: G. Land & P. P. Sandford, 1842), 129–31; Lee, *Short History*, 125.

13. Lee, *Short History*, 149–50. Thomas Ware shared Lee's opposition: "A minority, however, opposed it from the first; and I happened to be one of that number. I had ventured to say, if there must be a council to consist of bishops and presiding elders, the latter should be chosen, not by the bishops, but by the conferences, and every thing done in council should be by a simple majority" (*The Life and Travels of Rev. Thomas Ware*, 181–82). The discussion in the remainder of this essay follows the treatment in *MEA*, 42–49.

14. Tigert noted that unanimity "virtually gave Bishop Asbury—for Bishop Coke was not present at either of the sessions held—an absolute veto on all proposed legislation" (Tigert, *History*, 244). Of course, it gave every member such a veto, but since the elders ("presiding elders," in the language of the plan) served at the bishop's pleasure, the power of the bishop was effectively magnified. The legislation on concurrence read: "Provided, nevertheless, that . . . nothing so assented to by the council, shall be binding in any district, till it has been agreed upon by a majority of the conference which is held for that district" (Lee, *Short History*, 150). Tigert used the term *nullification* to describe the potential effect of this provision (see *History*, 245). Lee excerpts liberally from the minutes of the 1789 and 1790 meetings of the council (*Short History*, 151–59). See also the published versions, seven- and eight-page documents, titled differently each year: *The Proceedings of the Bishop and Presiding Elders of the Methodist-Episcopal Church, in Council Assembled, at Baltimore, on the First Day of December, 1789* (Baltimore, 1789); and *Minutes Taken at a Council of the Bishop and Delegated Elders of the Methodist Episcopal Church: Held at Baltimore in the State of Maryland, December 1, 1790* (Baltimore, 1790).

15. Lee, *Short History*, 151–55. Legislation so passed "shall be re-ceived by every member of each conference" (153). Thomas B. Neely, *A History of the Origin and Development of the Governing Conference in Methodism, and especially of the General Conference of the Methodist Episcopal Church* (Cincinnati: Cranston & Stowe, 1892), 304.

16. *JLFA* 1:620, for Tuesday, January 12, 1790. Asbury registered his own sense of the constraints on his power and influence.

17. *JLFA* 1:625, for February 14, 1790; *JLFA* 1:642, for June 14, 1790; "Journals" 4 for September 1, 5, 1790, in James Meacham Papers, 1788–97. Manuscript Department, Duke University Library, Durham, N.C. Used with permission; Robert Paine, *Life and Times of William M'Kendree*, 2 vols. (Nashville: Publishing House of the Methodist Episcopal Church, South, 1874), 1:61, 113, 129; *JLFA* 3:87, Commentary on letter "To the Virginia Preachers," dated Autumn 1790; *JLFA* 1:649, Wednesday, August 25, 1790. Sentiment against the council was far from uniform. Most of the conferences supported the plan. Asbury noted for the conference on the eastern shore of Maryland, "One or two of our brethren felt the Virginia fire about the question of the council, but all things came into order, and the council obtained" (650), Monday, September 13, 1790. Affection for O'Kelly extended beyond that region. William Colbert reported for Tuesday, September 1, 1791, "Met with Br. O'Kelly, at (Jm. Ps.) My [bones?] was much refreshed in once more seeing this dear servant of Christ" (*A Journal of the Travels of William Colbert, Methodist Preacher: Thro' Parts of Maryland, Pennsylvania, New York, Delaware and Virginia in 1790 to 1838*, 1:130. 10 vols. Typescript, Methodist Library, Drew University.

18. The framing legislation for the council had begun: "Whereas the holding of general conferences on this extensive Continent would be attended with a variety of difficulties, and many inconveniences to the work of God" (Lee, *Short History*, 149; *JLFA* 1:687, for July 1, 1791). Compare the account in Leroy M. Lee, *The Life and Times of The Rev. Jesse Lee* (Louisville: John Early, for the Methodist Episcopal Church, South, 1848), 268–71. Jesse Lee had made a similar proposal when the council met (though he was not a member of that body). He had been sharply rebuffed. The council responded: "Very dear Bro.: We are both grieved and surprised to find that you make so many objections to the very fundamentals of Methodism. But we consider *your want of experience* in many things, and therefore put the best construction on your intention" (*Life and Times of The Rev. Jesse Lee*, 282; see also, Lee, *Short History*, 177).

Coke's commitment to a general conference was posited by William Hammett, who cited a letter, allegedly summarizing a circular printed by Coke asserting: "Five things we have in view: 1st, The abolition of the arbitrary aristocracy. 2dly, The investing of the nomination of the presiding elders in the conferences of the districts. 3dly, The limitation of the districts to be invested in the general conferences. 4thly, An appeal allowed a preacher on the reading of the stations: And 5thly, a general conference of at least two thirds of the preachers, as a check upon every thing." Coke was also alleged to have said with respect to the then-deceased Wesley, "I doubt much, whether the cruel usage he received in Baltimore, in 1787, when he was excommunicated (wonderful and most unparalled step!) did not hasten his death. Indeed I little doubt it. For from the time he was informed of it, he began to hang down his head, and to think he had lived long enough." *The Impartial Statement of the Known Inconsistencies of the Reverend Dr. Coke, In His Official Station as Superintendent of the Methodist Missions in the West-Indies: With a Brief Description of one of his Tours through the United States* (Charleston, 1792), 6–7.

19. On O'Kelly, see Charles Franklin Kilgore, *The James O'Kelly Schism in the Methodist Episcopal Church* (Mexico City: Casa Unida de Publicaciones, 1963); Lee, *Short History*, 178–79.

20. *The Life and Travels of Rev. Thomas Ware*, 220–21.

21. The literature on republicanism is extensive. See, for instance, James H. Hutson, *Religion and the Founding of the American Republic* (Washington, D.C.: Library of Congress, 1998); Margaret A. Nash, "Rethinking Republican Motherhood: Benjamin Rush and the Young Ladies' Academy of Philadelphia," *Journal of the Early Republic* 17/2 (1997): 171–91; Ralph Lerner, "Rattling the Iron Cage," *Law and History Review* 15/1 (1997): 145–58; Gordon S. Wood, *The Radicalism of the American Revolution* (New York: Knopf, 1992); Michael P. Zuckert, *Natural Rights and the New Republicanism* (Princeton, N.J.: Princeton University Press, 1994); Patricia U. Bonomi, "'Hippocrates' Twins': Religion and Politics in the American Revolution," *History Teacher* 29/2 (1996): 137–44; Joyce Appleby, *Liberalism and Republicanism in the Historical Imagination* (Cambridge, Mass.: Harvard University Press, 1992); Milton M. Klein, Richard D. Brown, and John B. Hench, eds., *The Republican Synthesis Revisited: Essays in Honor of George Athan Billias* (Charlottesville: University Press of Virginia; Worcester, Mass.: American Antiquarian Society, 1992); Alan Craig Houston, *Algernon Sidney and the Republican Heritage in England and America* (Princeton, N.J.: Princeton University Press, 1991); Paul A. Rahe, *Republics Ancient and Modern: Classical Republicanism and the American Revolution*, rev. ed. (1992; repr., Chapel Hill: University of North Carolina Press, 1994); J.R. Pole, "In Machiavelli's Fading Footprints," *Historical Journal* [Great Britain] 38/3 (1995): 707–13; Peter S. Onuf, "Republicanism, Sectionalism, and Union: Political Development in the Early Republic," *Reviews in American History* 22/3 (1994): 418–23. For discussion of this ideology and its play in American Methodism, see Russell E. Richey, "The Four Languages of Early American Methodism," *Methodist History* 28 (April 1990): 155–71.

22. Paine, *William McKendree*, 1:64. McKendree's return to the connection had much to do with the excesses in this republican rhetoric. In particular, he found Asbury not to be the tyrant that O'Kelly alleged him to be.

23. *JLFA* 1:734, for Thursday, November 8, 1792.

24. *Journals* 6 for November 6, 1792, in James Meacham Papers, 1788–97. Manuscript Department, Duke University Library, Durham, N.C. Used with permission.

25. Other individuals, parties, and actors contributed materially as well. Here we focus specifically on a Virginian in the construction of Methodism.

26. *JLFA* 2 for April 5, 1802, 332–33. He noted, while editing another portion in 1798: "I have well considered my journal: it is inelegant; yet it conveys much information of the state of religion and country. It is well suited to common readers; the wise need it not. I have a desire that my journals should be published, at least after my death, if not before" (*JLFA* 2:153, for February 6, 1798).

27. See the first published collection, *Minutes of the Methodist Conferences Annually Held in America, from 1773 to 1794, Inclusive* (Philadelphia, 1795; repr. Strawbridge Shrine Assn.); the *Minutes*/MEC (1813); or the standard *Minutes*/MEC.

28. Philadelphia, 1792; republished in 1817 and 1849.

29. *The Doctrines and Discipline of the Methodist Episcopal Church in America with Explanatory Notes, by Thomas Coke and Francis Asbury* (Philadelphia, 1798; facsimile edition, ed. Frederick A. Norwood [Rutland, Vt.: Academy, 1979]).

30. (New York, 1805). The subtitle read "Written by the Preachers and Members of the Methodist Episcopal Church to their Bishops." Asbury elicited these letters with directives such as the following to George Roberts:

"Once in a year all the presiding elders ought to write to the Episcopacy, to collect into a focus the work of God, for the press, and I wish the preachers of [today] would write a brief of their conviction, conversion and call to preach and where they had laboured. I will select all the most spiritual parts of letters to print and to keep a history of what God is doing in the South. . . . Would the presiding elders write to me one letter only of the state of the work, I should rejoice and the city preachers also of the cities. We could give great personal information to the conference and individuals of the work of God." See *JLFA*, 3:199, letter to George Roberts, February 4, 1801. Compare the letter two days later to Thomas Morrell, 3:202: "You will favour me with a letter to Norfolk, the last of March. If the presiding elders, in the cities and towns and country would give once a year circumstantial accounts of the work. I would—annually of Methodism, like Prince's History for a select collection of original papers."

31. (Richmond, 1798). O'Kelly's other works included *Divine Oracles Consulted* (Hillsboro, N.C., 1820); *Essay on Negro Slavery* (Philadelphia, 1789); *Hymns and Spiritual Songs Designed for the Use of Christians* (Raleigh, 1816); *Letters from Heaven Consulted* (Hillsboro, N.C., 1822); *The Prospect Before us by Way of Address to the Christian Church* (Hillsboro, 1824); *A Vindication of the Author's Apology* (Raleigh, 1801).

32. (Philadelphia, 1800) and (Philadelphia, 1802).

33. The themes are further developed in *The Methodist Conference in America*.

34. *The Doctrines and Discipline of the Methodist Episcopal Church in America with Explanatory Notes*.

35. I want to express appreciation to James Becker, who shared with me the analytical categories he is employing to define and interpret Wesleyanism—categories that suggest that he and I understand the movement in a very similar fashion. I thank him for nuances from his reading that may now influence mine.

Chapter 3: General Conference: A Retrospective

1. *JLFA* 1:472; Lee, *Short History*, 93; Tigert, *History*, 180–94; and *The Making of Methodism* (Nashville: Publishing House of the Methodist Episcopal Church, South, 1898), 86.

2. The 1787 gathering refused Wesley's bidding, and Whatcoat would be elected only in 1800.

3. (Philadelphia: Charles Cist, 1785). For the comparison of the two—the Large Minutes and the first *Discipline*—see Tigert, *History*, 532–602.

4. Published at the desire of the conference. (Baltimore, 1785; repr., New York: T. Mason and G. Lane, 1840).

5. J. B. Wakeley, *The Patriarch of One Hundred Years; Being Reminiscences, Historical and Biographical, of Rev. Henry Boehm* (New York: Nelson & Phillips; Cincinnati: Hitchcock & Walden, 1875), 180–84, 395–98, especially 397.

6. MEC *Discipline* 1785, Q. 42–43. See Tigert, *History*, 554–56; or *MEA* 2, 1785a. The *Discipline*, unhappily, also made provision for white oversight of black gatherings.

7. See Tigert, *History*, 464–65.

8. I explore this dimension at some length in *Conference*.

9. For an analysis of the conference, see Frederick A. Norwood, "A Crisis of Leadership: The General Conference of 1792," *Methodist History* 28 (April 1990): 129–201, and specifically 193. See also Tigert, *Making of Methodism*, 145; James M. Buckley, *Constitutional and Parliamentary History of the Methodist Episcopal Church* (New York: The Methodist Book Concern, 1912), 68–69; and Tigert, *History*, 263.

10. Lee, *Short History*, 180.

11. *JGC*/MEC 1804, 51.

12. For discussion of these developments, see J. Bruce Behney and Paul H. Eller, *The History of The Evangelical United Brethren Church*, ed. Kenneth W. Krueger (Nashville: Abingdon, 1979).

13. *JGC*/MEC 1804, 48. This tally differs slightly from the enumeration given by Lee in *Short History*, 297.

14. *JGC*/MEC 1816, 148–52, 166–69.

15. See Edward J. Drinkhouse, *History of Methodist Reform*, 2 vols. (Baltimore and Pittsburgh: The Board of Publication of the Methodist Protestant Church, 1899), 2:275–76.

16. *JGC*/MEC 1864, 485–86. On Burns, see James E. Kirby, Russell E. Richey, and Kenneth E. Rowe, *The Methodists* (Westport, Conn.: Greenwood, 1996), 45–47, 272–73.

17. See William B. McClain, *Black People in The Methodist Church: Whither Thou Goest?* (Nashville: Abingdon, 1984), 65–68. On Jones and Clair, see Kirby, Richey, and Rowe, *The Methodists*, 46–47, 279–80, 311–12.

18. On the admission of women, see Jean Miller Schmidt, *Grace Sufficient: A History of Women in American Methodism, 1760–1939* (Nashville: Abingdon, 1999), especially 213–31. Note that MPC conferences recognized the ordination of women beginning in 1880 but the church as a whole concurred only in 1892. See Schmidt, 194.

19. *JGC*/MEC 1816, 126, 128–29.

20. *JGC*/MEC 1872, 295–98, "Report of Committee on Benevolent Societies." The committee's commentary on the Missionary Society indicated the nature of the problem:

> The management and disposition of the affairs and property of the corporation known as "The Missionary Society of the Methodist Episcopal Church" are by its charter vested in a Board of Managers to be annually elected at a meeting of the Society, to be called for that purpose, and held in the City of New York at such time and on such notice as the Board of Managers, for the time being, shall previously prescribe.

The members of the Board are elected by members of the Society, and the members of the Society are those persons who become such by the payment of twenty dollars or more to its fund.

The General Conference has no legal connection with the Society, except only that by the charter it is provided that the Corresponding Secretaries of said Society shall be elected by the General Conference; and shall hold their offices for four years, and until their successors are elected, and that in case of vacancy the Bishops shall elect their successors to hold till the ensuing General Conference.

But as the whole management is vested in the Board elected by members of the Society, the Corresponding Secretaries are powerless to represent any interest of the Church or of the Conference independent of the will the Board. It is evident, too, that the multitude of members of the Society, scattered widely in all parts of the country, either cannot or will not participate in the election of a Board of Managers. It is equally evident that local combinations are liable to be formed each year to change the management of the corporation, and obtain control of its great resources. We do not express or intimate any doubt of the judicious and faithful management of the Society, but it is high time to close the door against the possibility of danger in the future. . . .

The General Conference, as the supreme legislative authority of the Church, and having in charge all its great interests for the diffusion of Christian civilization, should have a controlling power in all the missionary operations carried on in the name and behalf of the Church. The act of incorporation is subject to a general law, which declares that "the charter of every corporation that shall hereafter be granted by the Legislature shall be subject to alteration, suspension, and repeal, in the discretion of the Legislature." To place this corporation under the control of the General Conference, it will be proper to procure an act of the Legislature to amend the charter so as to provide that the Board of managers shall be elected by the General Conference. In this respect the charter of the Board of Education furnishes a model which would seem to secure stability and proper management.

21. *JGC/*MECS 1854, 356.
22. *JGC/*MEC 1884, 74.
23. See the concise discussion of the evolution and nature of this plan in Nolan B. Harmon, *The Organization of The Methodist Church*, 2nd rev. ed. (Nashville: The Methodist Publishing House, 1962), 167–82.
24. For discussion of the effects of these several changes, see Richey, *Conference*, 175–84.

Chapter 4: Itinerancy in Historical Perspective: "A Wandering Arminian Was My Father . . ."

1. As the title suggests, this essay will explore the baseline from which itinerancy evolved. On the title itself, compare Deuteronomy 26:5. Lee so introduced himself on April 1, 1790. See Minton Thrift, *Memoir of the Rev. Jesse Lee. With Extracts from his Journals* (New York: N. Bangs and T. Mason for the Methodist Episcopal Church, 1823), 145.

2. Asbury/Coke, *Discipline*, 42.

3. And that notwithstanding the initiatory and critical role played by laity and lay preachers from the start and thereafter, a point made frequently and eloquently by Frederick Norwood. See his "The Americanization of the Wesleyan Itinerant," *The Ministry in the Methodist Heritage*, ed. Gerald O. McCulloh (Nashville: Department of Ministerial Education, 1960), 33–66; and *The Story of American Methodism* (Nashville: Abingdon, 1974), especially 61–69, "Lay Beginnings."

4. Edgar M. Bacon and Andrew C. Wheeler, *Nation Builders: A Story* (New York: Eaton & Mains, ca. 1905), 20–21.

5. Robert Paine, *Life and Times of William M'Kendree*, 2 vols. (Nashville: Publishing House of the Methodist Episcopal Church, South, 1874), 1:115. Concurring that "our plan is Providential" was the author of *The Bishop's Council: With Reminiscences of an Annual Conference of the Methodist Episcopal Church By an Ex-Presiding Elder* (Saint Louis: P.M. Pinckard, 1867), 16.

6. Wallace G. Smelter in *Methodism on the Headwaters of the Ohio* (Nashville: Parthenon, 1951), 82; and E. Dale Dunlap, "The United Methodist System of Itinerant Ministry," in *Rethinking Methodist History*, ed. Russell E. Richey and Kenneth E. Rowe (Nashville: Kingswood, 1985), 18–28.

7. *Cyclopaedia of Methodism*, 5th rev. ed. (Philadelphia: L.H. Ewerts, 1882), 487.

8. James Porter, *The Revised Compendium of Methodism* (New York: Hunt & Eaton, 1875), 350.

9. Gerald Kennedy, "The Genius of the Methodist Itinerancy," *Forever Beginning. 1766–1966*, ed. Albea Godbold (Lake Junaluska, N.C.: Commission on Archives and History, 1968), 195. Without it, Kennedy suggested, there would be no connectionalism. It was Methodism's uniqueness and genius (194, 195).

10. *MQR*, 25 (1843): 278, quoted by James David Lynn in *The Concept of the Ministry in the Methodist Episcopal Church, 1784–1844* (PhD diss., Princeton Theological Seminary, 1973), 223.

11. Minutes/MEC/1773 (1813), 6.

12. Other contextual constellations vital for understanding itinerancy but impossible here are: (5) the range of ministerial tasks deemed vital for the church and society of the day and the priorities established among them; (6) the procedures for selection, preparation, and nurture of the preachers, including both the Course of Study and theological education; and (7) the theology of church and ministry, both explicit and implicit, in terms of which itinerancy was both understood and exercised. On the latter, see Thomas A. Langford, *Practical Divinity* (Nashville: Abingdon, 1983); Dow Kirkpatrick, ed., *The Doctrine of the Church* (New York: Abingdon, 1964); Dennis M. Campbell, *The Yoke of Obedience* (Nashville: Abingdon, 1988); Leon O. Hynson, *To Reform the Nation* (Grand Rapids: Francis Asbury, 1984); and M. Douglas Meeks, ed., *The Future of the Methodist Theological Traditions* (Nashville: Abingdon, 1985). For (6) above, see Gerald O. McCulloh, *Ministerial Education in the American Methodist Movement* (Nashville: United Methodist Board of Higher Education and Ministry, 1980).

13. For suggestive treatment of how the Awakening and Whitefield revolutionized American rhetoric, see Harry S. Stout, *The New England Soul: Preaching and Religious Culture in Colonial New England* (New York: Oxford University Press, 1986).

14. See Russell E. Richey, "The Southern Accent of American Methodism," *Methodist History* 27 (October 1988): 3–24.

15. *The Carolina Backcountry on the Eve of the Revolution: The Journal and Other Writings of Charles Woodmason, Anglican Itinerant*, ed. Richard J. Hooker (Chapel Hill: University of North Carolina Press, 1953).

16. See F. Ernest Stoeffler, ed., *Continental Pietism and Early American Christianity* (Grand Rapids: Eerdmans, 1976).

17. Behney/Eller, *History*, 31–45, 52.

18. E. Brooks Holifield, *A History of Pastoral Care in America* (Nashville: Abingdon, 1983); and *God's Ambassadors: A History of the Christian Clergy in America* (Grand Rapids: Eerdmans, 2007).

19. See Russell E. Richey, "Evolving Patterns of Methodist Ministry," *Methodist History* 22 (October 1983): 20–37; and *Doctrine in Experience: A Methodist Theology of Church and Ministry* (Nashville: Kingswood, 2009).

20. Frederick A. Norwood, "The Americanization of the Wesleyan Itinerant," in *The Ministry in the Methodist Heritage*, ed. Gerald O. McCulloh (Nashville: Board of Education, The Methodist Church, 1960); and Luther W. King, *An Historical Study of Ministerial Authority in American Methodism: 1760 to 1940* (PhD diss., Columbia University, 1981).

21. Nathan O. Hatch, *The Democratization of American Christianity* (New Haven, Conn.: Yale University Press, 1989). For an illustration of Methodist evaluation of itinerancy's cultural impact, see Bangs, *History*, 1:362–63.

22. Daniel H. Calhoon, *Professional Lives in America* (Cambridge, Mass.: Harvard University Press, 1965); Sidney E. Mead, "The Rise of the Evangelical Conception of the Ministry in America (1607–1850)," in *The Ministry in Historical Perspective*, ed. H. Richard Niebuhr and Daniel D. Williams (San Francisco: Harper & Row, 1956; repr. 1963), 207–49. Stephen Olin opines: "It is true, and must often be repeated, that the itinerancy is a missionary system. To the efficiency of the missionary principle, inherent in her constitution, is the Methodist Episcopal Church indebted for her extension and prosperity, and to it, more than to all other causes combined, is this nation indebted for that timely interference which has saved the whole region west of the Alleghany Mountains from the ineffable curse of an infidel and semi-heathen population. . . . What by other Churches are denominated domestic missions, constitute, to a large extent, the regular field of labor of the Methodist ministry in the new states and territories. The Indian missions have many of them been formed by a similar process. . . . The conversion of the slaves has likewise been effected by the ordinary operation of the system" (*The Life and Letters of Stephen Olin*, 2 vols. [New York: Harper & Brothers, 1853], 1:172–73).

23. Campbell, *The Yoke of Obedience*, 47–68.

24. Wesley, *Works*: 4, *Sermons*, 4:79–80.

25. Parallel presentation of the 1780 Large Minutes and the first American *Discipline* can be found in appendix 7 of Tigert, *History*, and p. 550 for the items cited. See also Wesley, *Works* (Jackson), 8:309. The twelfth Rule of a Helper is worth particular note (this stylizing of the Rule is from the first *Discipline*):

> Act in all Things, not according to your own Will, but as a Son in the Gospel. As such it is your Part to employ your Time in the Manner which we direct: Partly in Preaching and visiting from House to House: Partly in Reading, Meditation, and Prayer. Above all, if you labour with us in our Lord's Vineyard, it is needful you should do *that Part* of the Work which we advise, at *those Times and Places* which we judge most for his Glory.

26. One gets a sense of that process by following the legislative additions to the *Discipline.* See, for instance, Emory, *Discipline,* which itemizes changes by Disciplinary paragraph. Note especially 152–206.

27. See Behney/Eller, *History,* 114–17, 131–33.

28. See Donald K. Gorrell, "'Ride a Circuit or Let it Alone': Early Practices That Kept the United Brethren, Albright People and Methodists Apart," *Methodist History* 25 (October 1986): 4–16. Gorrell indicates that differences in discipline, including differing commitment to itinerancy, disrupted union negotiations between the German and English Methodists.

29. *JLFA,* 3:491–92.

30. C.C. Goss, *Statistical History of the First Century of American Methodism: With A Summary of the Origin and Present Operations of Other Denominations* (New York: Carlton & Porter, 1866), 169–70. Goss designated this the "Self-sacrificing Spirit of Its Ministry": "The spirit of self-sacrifice lies at the foundation of all moral achievement . . . [illustrated with example of Christ]." "The Methodist ministry are perhaps sharers with Christ in this respect to a greater degree than others. It is a part of the system with which they are identified. As they have no certain dwelling-place, they are rightfully styled itinerants" (168).

31. Thrift, *Memoir of the Rev. Jesse Lee,* 42.

32. Dunlap, "The United Methodist System of Itinerant Ministry," 18.

33. Asbury Coke/*Discipline,* 34.

34. "Up until the year 1828 all the Annual Conferences sat with closed doors, none being admitted except full members. This was convenient and almost necessary considering the extremely close and searching personal examination to which the members were subjected and the rigid scrutiny of all the candidates for admission or orders. But as the numbers grew larger and customs changed a little the rigidity of the rule was gradually relaxed." James Mudge, *History of the New England Conference of the Methodist Episcopal Church, 1796–1910* (Boston: Published for the Conference, 1910), 98.

35. Ibid., 66. Compare William Warren Sweet, ed., *The Rise of Methodism in the West, Being the Journal of the Western Conference 1800–1811* (New York and Cincinnati: The Methodist Book Concern, 1920), 100–109. These minutes take special note of the "profession of religion" of those admitted on trial. The following notation indicates the ease with which conference moved from scrutiny to testimony and the close relation of those processes: "The Conference spent a few hours, this evening, in speaking of the work of God in their souls and Circuits" (107).

36. "Autobiography of Rev. William Burke," in James B. Finley, *Sketches of Western Methodism: Biographical, Historical, and Miscellaneous,* ed. W.P. Strickland (Cincinnati: The Methodist Book Concern, 1854), 27. Burke registered his expectation for and value of companionship when later he lacked it: "I traveled this year alone, and had not the pleasure of seeing the face of a traveling preacher through the entire year" (Finley, *Sketches,* 52). Of course, the image of the lonely itinerant drew from reality as well. Here it is captured by local preacher Thomas S. Hinde, writing as "Theophilus Arminius," in *The Methodist Magazine* (5, [1822]: 393):

"That the preachers suffered much in forming these new Circuits is unquestionable; having often to swim the deep and large Creeks on their horses, and to ride from twenty to thirty miles through the wilderness from one settlement to another, and not infrequently had to take up their lodgings in the woods, amidst the howling wolves and screaming panthers. It was not uncommon occurrence for the scattered members of Society, on hearing of a preacher, to travel ten or twenty miles through the woods to invite him to come and preach at their cabin, and to mark for him a way by blazing the trees" (quoted by Wallace G. Smeltzer in *Methodism on the Headwaters of the Ohio* [Nashville: Parthenon, 1951], 87).

37. Thrift, *Memoir of the Rev. Jesse Lee*, 224–25.

38. The flavor of conference and its fraternal character is summarized by Mudge, *History of the New England Conference*, in a section titled "Life in the Conference," 177–208. See 177–78 on conference's gathering.

39. "The pioneers of Methodism in that part of western Virginia and the Western territory suffered many privations, and underwent much toil and labor, preaching in forts and cabins, sleeping on straw, bear and buffalo skins, living on bear meat, venison, and wild turkeys, traveling over mountains and through solitary valleys, and sometimes, lying on the cold ground; receiving but a scanty support, barely enough to keep soul and body together, with coarse home-made apparel; but the best of all was, their labors were owned and blessed of God, and they were like a band of brothers, having one purpose and end in view—the glory of God and the salvation of immortal souls. When the preachers met from their different and distant fields of labor, they had a feast of love and friendship; and when they parted, they wept and embraced each other as brothers beloved. Such was the spirit of primitive Methodist preachers" (William Burke in Finley, *Sketches*, 58).

40. Will B. Gravely, "African Methodisms and the Rise of Black Denominationalism," *Rethinking Methodist History*, 111–24; *Women in New Worlds*, ed. Hillah F. Thomas, Rosemary Skinner Keller, and Louise L. Queen. 2 vols. (Nashville: Abingdon, 1981; repr. 1982), especially 1: Rosemary Skinner Keller, "Creating a Sphere for Women: The Methodist Episcopal Church, 1869–1906," and the four essays in 2, section 4.

41. See Jean Miller Schmidt, *Grace Sufficient: A History of Women in American Methodism, 1760–1939* (Nashville: Abingdon, 1999).

42. Bishops modeled ministry for Methodists, and the prerogatives they claim and demands they make soon thereafter are to be sought by the ministers.

43. *Sketches of The Life and Travels of Rev. Thomas Ware*. Most major figures enjoyed national careers like that of Ware. One of the most celebrated was Martin Ruter, whose career went from New England to Texas (Bangs, *History*, 4:288–91; Mudge, *History of the New England Conference*, 76). Less prominent ministers also labored nationally. For instance, John Sales, born in Virginia in 1769; admitted on trial in Virginia in 1795; appointmented to Virginia in Swanino, 1795?, and Mattamuskeet lowlands; then appointed to Holston on Russell (1799), Salt River, Shelby, and Danville circuits; next appointed to the North-Western territory (1803) on the Scioto and Miami circuits, and to Kentucky (1805) on the Lexington circuit; next appointed to Ohio on the Miami circuit, and then to Kentucky for four years (see Finley, *Sketches*, 185–89). Compare "A Sketch of the Labours and Travels of Ira Ellis," *JLFA*, 2:460–61.

44. *JLFA*, 3:475. The Asbury policy that made for a national itinerancy was clear to William Burke: "The year 1799 I expected would terminate my labors in the western country. At the request of Bishop Asbury, all the preachers that had been in the west for any considerable time were to leave the country and attend the General conference at Baltimore, on the sixth day of May, 1800, and to receive their appointments in the old states, and a new set to be sent to the west" (see Finley, *Sketches*, 55).

45. C.C. Goen, *Broken Churches, Broken Nation: Denominational Schisms and the Coming of the American Civil War* (Macon, Ga.: Mercer University Press, 1985). A contemporary perspective

comes from Jacob Lanius: "The Missouri Annual Conference commenced its session in the city of St. Louis, September 13th, 1837. . . . The session continued nine days incessantly. A great deal of weighty and important business was transacted. A spirit of brotherly love prevailed to a considerable extent interrupted only very slightly or by very slight and unimportant events. I am rather afraid that a feeling rather serious is originating in the conference. The preachers of the north and south seem to look upon themselves as distinct or as members of different ecclesiastical bodies. I may be too suspicious in this matter but I think the signs of the times are too ominous of an evil of this kind. To prevent this I think the preachers of these two points ought to be changed and changed frequently. This would prevent local interest and selfish feelings from entering the ministry, a thing necessary in order to preserve ministerial peace and harmony, without which the cause of Christ cannot prosper in our hands. 'United we stand divided we fall.' How fearfully true is the old National adage" (*The Journal of The Reverend Jacob Lanius*, ed. Elmer T. Clark [1918], transcribed and re-edited by Theodore H. Holff [1963], typescript, Methodist Library, Drew University, 237–38).

46. The office is recognized in the 1789 *Discipline*.

47. The evolution of the office from an ordinary to an extraordinary one, the addition of the appointive office to its sacramental functions, is most clearly seen in the successive Disciplinary legislation in Emory, *Discipline*, 136–42.

48. MEC *Discipline* 1792, in Emory, *Discipline*, 138.

49. MEC *Discipline* 1786, in Emory, *Discipline*, 137.

50. One of several quarterly meetings on Redstone circuit detailed by Robert Ayres, *Mss. Journal*, cited by Wallace Guy Smeltzer in *Methodism on the Headwaters of the Ohio, the History of the Pittsburgh Conference of the Methodist Church* (Nashville: Parthenon Press, 1951), 61–62.

51. Bangs, *History*, 3:304.

52. Emory, *Discipline*, 191–202.

53. Mudge noted: "The locations from the breaking down of health or from family necessities, and the early deaths, were incessant and ruinous to the work. Of 600 who belonged to the itinerant ministry prior to 1800, about 500 located permanently, besides very many who, after an interval, reentered the traveling connection. Of the fifty-five young men who entered the New York Conference in 1801, twenty-nine retired from the ministry within the short period of ten years. During the first fifty years more than half of all who entered the ministry were obliged to locate. During the quadrennium ending in 1840 the locations reached 546, or more than one-fourth of the whole number in the itinerant ranks at its commencement." He continued, "The places of those who retired, often men of cultivated talent and experience, had to be supplied with ever fresh drafts of untried men, a portentous evil" (Mudge, *History of the New England Conference*, 110).

54. *JLFA*, 2:474, July 9, 1805; Finley, *Sketches*, 180–81. Preachers nevertheless married and located. The continuing seriousness of this prompted a study and report at the 1816 General Conference by the Committee of Ways and Means on the loss to the church through locations of its experienced, trained, and pious "ornaments" (*JGC/* 1816, 148–52).

55. Lee, *Short History*, 255.

56. Mudge, *History of the New England Conference*, 239–40. Mudge observed: "The lay or local preachers and exhorters have formed, from the beginning, a very important factor in the work. The great extent of the early circuits would of itself imply this. . . . We have no way of ascertaining accurately the number of these early local preachers, for the statistics of the Minutes do not recognize them till 1837, when the number in the whole church is given as 4,954 as against 2,933 in

the itinerant ranks. Only eighty-five are reported at that time from the New England Conference, or about half the number of those traveling. In 1850 the local preachers of this Conference were eighty as compared with 113 traveling, and in the whole church 5,420 as compared with 3,777. In 1870 there were 10,340 local, and 8,830 traveling. In 1890 the numbers were practically equal, 14,072 local and 14,792 traveling. At present there are 14,743 local and 19,421 traveling."

57. Ibid., 241.

58. Frederick A. Norwood, *The Story of American Methodism*, 132. See the pages following for Norwood's discussion of the local ministry.

59. *Minutes*/MEC/1774 (1813), 8, 147.

60. See Dunlap, "The United Methodist System of Itinerant Ministry," 23–26.

61. The changes in itinerancy relate also to evolution in other contextual constellations itemized in note 11 above but not analyzed here.

62. UMC *Discipline* 1988, 80–84, 7–18, 40–60. See chapter 1 above.

Chapter 5: Extension Ministries

1. *Discipline*/UMC 1996, 206; compare UMC *Discipline* 2008, ¶¶ 343, 254; compare UMC *Discipline* 1996, ¶¶ 334, 206.

2. The argument of this chapter is greatly expanded in my *Extension Ministers: Mr. Wesley's True Heirs* (Nashville: General Board of Higher Education and Ministry, 2008), but the latter's recommendations are refined and elaborated here.

3. *Minutes*/MEC/1799 (1813), 1801, 259. For the intervening year for some reason, the *Minutes* reverted to the earlier form.

4. On the evolution of the office, and especially the role of John Dickins, in or around 1783 made publisher, see James P. Pilkington, *The Methodist Publishing House* (Nashville: Abingdon, 1968), 1:43–116.

5. *Minutes*/MEC/1802, 278. For similar earlier treatment, see *Minutes*/MEC/1789, 82–83; 1790, 93; 1791, 104; 1792, 113, 116; 1793, 129; 1794, 144; 1795, 157–62; 1796, 182; 1797, 194–95.

6. *Minutes*/MEC/1803, 297, 300.

7. *Minutes*/MEC/1804, 322.

8. *Minutes*/MEC/1809, 459, 458, 454–55, 460.

9. *Minutes*/MEC/1809, 459.

10. *Minutes*/MEC/1773, 6.

11. *JGC*/MEC 1796, 17.

12. *Minutes*MEC/1797, 198–99.

13. "Journal of a Conference Held in New York, Tuesday 12th June 1804" (typescript, Drew University), 22/52.

14. *Minutes of the Philadelphia Conference of the Methodist Episcopal Church*, 1862, 22–26.

15. *Minutes of the Philadelphia Conference of the Methodist Episcopal Church*, 1865.

16. *Minutes of the . . . Philadelphia Conference of the Methodist Episcopal Church*, 1886, 39.

17. William Phoebus, *Memoirs of the Rev. Richard Whatcoat, Late Bishop of the Methodist Episcopal Church* (New York: Joseph Allen, 1828), 30.

18. Ibid., 37.

19. Ibid., 39.

20. This is a point that I cover in *Conference*. See especially chapters 6 and 8. The assertions in the preceding and following paragraphs derive also from that volume.

21. Abel Stevens, *The Centenary of American Methodism: A Sketch of its History, Theology, Practical System, and Success*. With a statement of the plan of the Centenary Celebration of 1866 by John M'Clintock, DD (New York: Carlton & Porter, 1865), 180, 185–87.

22. William F. Warren, "Ministerial Education in Our Church," *MQR* 54 (April 1872): 246–67, 260.

Chapter 6: Organizing for Missions

1. Abel Stevens, *The Centenary of American Methodism: A Sketch of its History, Theology, Practical System, and Success*. With a statement of the plan of the Centenary Celebration of 1866 by John M'Clintock, D.D. (New York: Carlton & Porter, 1865), 180, 187. For a similar succinct estimate today, pertaining to Protestant missions generally, see Alvyn Austin, "Loved Ones in The Homelands: The Missionary Influence on North America," *Evangelical Studies Bulletin* 14 (Spring 1997): 1–5.

2. Compare the judgment of George G. Cookman in *Speeches Delivered on Various Occasions, by George G. Cookman, of the Baltimore Annual Conference, and Chaplain to the Senate of the United States* (New York: George Lane, 1840), 127–37:

"*What is Methodism?* Methodism, sir, is a *revival of primitive New Testament religion*, such as glowed in the bosom and was seen in the lives of the apostles and martyrs.

It is a *revival of the vital, fundamental doctrines of the Christian faith*.

It is a *revival of the original New Testament organization*, particularly in restoring the itinerancy and brotherhood of the ministry, and the *right* administration of church discipline.

It is a *revival of the social spirit*, the free and ancient manner of social worship.

It is, above all, a *revival of the missionary spirit*, which, not content with a mere *defensive* warfare upon Zion's walls, goes forth *aggressively*, under the eternal promise, to the conquest of the world."

3. *History of the Methodist Episcopal Church in The United States of America*, 4 vols. (New York: Carlton & Porter, 1864–67); *The History of the Religious Movement of the Eighteenth Century Called Methodism* (New York: Carlton & Porter, 1858–61); *A Compendious History of American Methodism* (New York: Eaton & Mains; Cincinnati: Curts & Jennings, n.d., but 1867/68); *Supplementary History of American Methodism* (New York: Eaton & Mains, 1899); *Memorials of the Introduction of Methodism into the Eastern States* (Boston: Charles H. Pierce, 1848); *Memorials of the Early Progress of Methodism in the Eastern States* (Boston: C.H. Pierce, ca. 1851); *An Essay on Church Polity* (New York: Carlton & Porter, 1847); *The Women of Methodism* (New York: Carlton & Porter, 1866). Many of these items went through several editions. Stevens also produced a variety of other works.

4. See, especially, J.M. Reid, *Missions and Missionary Society of the Methodist Episcopal Church*, 2 vols. (New York: Phillips & Hunt, 1879); see also the revised and extended edition with J. T. Gracey, 3 vols. (New York: Eaton & Mains, 1895, 1896); Barclay, *Missions*; and Dana L. Robert, *American Women in Mission: A Social History of Their Thought and Practice* (Macon, Ga.: Mercer University Press, 1996).

5. No one captured the machine aspect of American Methodism better than George Cookman. He conceived of the entire movement as a set of "wheels within wheels." See Cookman, *Speeches Delivered on Various Occasions*, 134–37.

6. What, even today, constitutes the basic structure of the church? To non-Methodists that might seem to be the congregation. Not so. In Methodism, the annual conference is "the basic body in the Church" or "the fundamental" body of the church. See UMC *Discipline* 2008, ¶¶ 11, 33. Annual conference enjoys that distinction constitutionally, operationally, theologically, and historically. It was, and is, prior to ministries, members, lay officers, and congregations. Prior to conference, of course, was Mr. Wesley, but then by Stevens's day he was with Methodists only in spirit. Conference carried on his role.

7. *Minutes*/MEC/1773, 5–6.

8. I cover this point in Richey, *Conference*. See especially chapters 6 and 8.

9. Stevens, *Centenary of American Methodism*, 187.

10. "Circular address, and Constitution of the Missionary and Bible Society, of the Methodist Episcopal Church in America," *The Methodist Magazine* (June 1819): 277–79. (Note: The name of the society was subsequently simplified to Missionary Society.)

11. See *Consecrated Talents: Or, The Life of Mrs. Mary W. Mason* (New York: Carlton & Lanahan, 1870), 82–85.

12. On the development and role of auxiliaries, see Barclay, *Missions*, 1:291–303.

13. Barclay, *Missions*, 1:280. Nathan Bangs, one of the architects of the new society, its principal head in early years, the drafter of its reports through 1837, and thereafter "Resident Corresponding Secretary" until 1844, in his retrospective on its creation, quotes an endorsement made by the Reverend Thomas L. Douglass (Tennessee Conference), who reassured his readers, "The men to be aided and sanctioned as missionaries are to be approved by our annual conferences, and to act under the direction of our bishops" (*A History of the Methodist Episcopal Church*, 8th ed., 4 vols. [New York: Carlton & Porter, 1860; originally published 1838–41], 3:179). On the role of Bangs, see Reid, *Missions and Missionary Society of the Methodist Episcopal Church*, 1:28–30.

14. Reid, *Missions and Missionary Society of the Methodist Episcopal Church*, 1:19–24.

15. MEC *Discipline* 1832, 22, 24.

16. The 1836 General Conference dedicated in that year's *Discipline* a section to "Support of Missions," which delegated the preponderance of the agency for missions to the annual conferences, both through the directives it gave about the establishment and use of conference auxiliaries and the guidance it offered concerning launching new conference missions. See MEC *Discipline* 1836, 174–78.

17. *Annual Report of the Missionary Society of the Methodist Episcopal Church*, 1837, 17, 22. At this point, the Society divided its missions into three categories: "Foreign and Aboriginal," "Domestic Missions Among the Destitute White Settlements," and "Missions for People of Colour." The Philadelphia Conference missions fell among the middle category. Among the few foreign efforts then drawing support were Liberia and South America.

18. Francis H. Tees et al., *Pioneering in Penn's Woods: Philadelphia Methodist Episcopal Annual Conference Through One Hundred Fifty Years* (n.p.: The Philadelphia Conference Tract Society of the Methodist Episcopal Church, 1937), 98.

19. *Minutes*/MEC/1829–39, 194, 254, 318, 378, 450, 534, 622. The conference would also report that item, by individual collections or receipts, and initially it did not aggregate the amounts.

See for 1834 Question 17, "What has been contributed for the support of Missions, and what for the publication of Bibles, Tracts, and Sunday school books?" rendered in simple summary table (*Minutes of the Philadelphia Conference of the Methodist Episcopal Church*, 1834, 10, 34 [typescript version of apparently printed minutes at Duke University]). Note: The titles of the minutes or proceedings of this and other conferences vary over time and are standardized in the above manner.

20. *Minutes*/MEC/1839–45, 42, 135, 229, 333, 440, 568. Items marked with an asterisk were identified as "very imperfect." Their imperfection can be confirmed at the receiving end. The *Annual Report of the Missionary Society of the Methodist Episcopal Church*, 1844, listed 1843 receipts from Philadelphia as $1,985.35 in contrast to the $4,403.23 reported by the conference in the *Minutes*.

21. *Minutes*/MEC/1846–51, 12, 102, 200, 312, 421, 556. The *Annual Report of the Missionary Society of the Methodist Episcopal Church*, 1849, listed receipts from Philadelphia as partially from 1848 and from 1849 and the amount as $4,373.85.

22. *Minutes*/MEC/1852–56, 16, 166, 339, 505. The *Annual Report of the Missionary Society of the Methodist Episcopal Church*, 1854, listed 1852–53 Philadelphia receipts as $11,783.89.

23. *Minutes*/MEC/1856–57, 19, 227. Beginning in 1857, the *Minutes* rendered the accounts from the conferences in elaborate tables that specified the receipts from the various benevolences by charge, that is, by each circuit or station.

24. *The Methodist Centennial Year-Book for 1884*, ed. W. H. De Puy (New York: Phillips & Hunt; Cincinnati: Walden & Stowe, 1883), 129, 124. The *Year-Book* tracks the total receipts from 1820 through 1882. Philadelphia's percentage of the whole does not vary that dramatically, but its steadiness as the major supporter was achieved despite the dramatic growth in the number of conferences and of the population of the whole MEC. There were, for instance, only twenty-two conferences from 1832 to 1836, as opposed to ninety-nine in 1882.

25. *Minutes of the Philadelphia Conference of the Methodist Episcopal Church*, 1839, 13.

26. Ibid., 14–15. By 1841, the conference added lines for elders, deacons, "colored preachers," schools, and scholars. See *Minutes of the Philadelphia Conference of the Methodist Episcopal Church*, 1841, 10–11.

27. *Minutes of the Philadelphia Conference of the Methodist Episcopal Church*, 1842, 14. The conference passed two other resolutions pertaining to Bible societies and one stipulating days for fasting and prayer—the first Friday in October and Good Friday.

28. "Report of the Committee on an Uniform Plan of Finance,"ibid., 18–19.

29. *Minutes of the Philadelphia Conference of the Methodist Episcopal Church*, 1846, 13.

30. *Minutes of the Philadelphia Conference of the Methodist Episcopal Church*, 1848, 10. The *Discipline* specified that such dates be set, mandating with regard to missions, "It shall be the duty of each annual conference to appoint some month within the conference year, in which missionary collections shall be taken up within their respective bounds, and also to make such arrangements concerning branch societies as may be deemed expedient" (MEC *Discipline* 1848, 179).

31. In 1839 the denomination reorganized the Missionary Society, incorporating it through an act of the New York Senate and Assembly. Its affairs were vested in a board of managers "of not less than thirty-two lay members, and of so many clerical members, not exceeding that number . . . to be annually elected at a meeting of the Society to be called for that purpose, and held in the city of New York" (*Annual Report of the Missionary Society of the Methodist Episcopal Church*, 1854, 5–6).

32. "The resident corresponding secretary shall, by virtue of his office, be a member of the New-York conference, to which, in the interval of the General Conference, he shall be held responsible for his conduct, and the New-York conference shall have power by and with the advice of the managers of the Missionary Society of the Methodist Episcopal Church and consent of the bishop presiding, to remove him from office: and in case of removal, death or resignation, the New-York conference with the concurrence of the presiding bishops, shall fill the vacancy until the next ensuing General Conference" (MEC *Discipline* 1836, 177–78).

33. *Minutes of the Philadelphia Conference of the Methodist Episcopal Church*, 1847, 6.

34. Ibid., 5.

35. *Minutes of the Philadelphia Conference of the Methodist Episcopal Church*, 1848, 5–6.

36. MEC *Discipline* 1848, 177–85. General Conference expanded the largely passive, permissive eight-point program of the 1836 *Discipline* into a seventeen-paragraph venture that assigned major responsibilities for conferences, both in themselves and as overseers of the circuits and stations. The major points in this program are elaborated in discussion of John Durbin's work.

37. Reid, *Missions and Missionary Society of the Methodist Episcopal Church*, 1:32–39.

38. For further information on Durbin, see the entry in James E. Kirby, Russell E. Richey, and Kenneth E. Rowe, *The Methodists* (Westport, Conn.: Greenwood, 1996), 291–92; see also the estimates of him by John A. Roche, *The Life of John Price Durbin* (New York, 1889), and "John Price Durbin," *MQR* 69 (May 1887): 329–54.

39. *Minutes of the Philadelphia Conference of the Methodist Episcopal Church*, 1835 (typescript version of apparently printed minutes), n.p., but 10.

40. J. P. Durbin was, for instance, listed first as delegate to the 1844 General Conference. See *Minutes of the Philadelphia Conference of the Methodist Episcopal Church*, 1844, 10.

41. *Minutes of the Philadelphia Conference of the Methodist Episcopal Church*, 1845, 12.

42. *Minutes of the Philadelphia Conference of the Methodist Episcopal Church*, 1846, 14.

43. *Minutes of the Philadelphia Conference of the Methodist Episcopal Church*, 1849, 5. This office is now known as the district superintendent. By that time the *Minutes* listed a North German Mission in North Philadelphia District and a South German Mission in South Philadelphia District (*Minutes of the Philadelphia Conference of the Methodist Episcopal Church*, 1849, 5–6).

44. Tees et al., *Pioneering*, 117–19.

45. *Minutes of the Philadelphia Conference of the Methodist Episcopal Church*, 1850, 6.

46. *Minutes of the Troy Conference*, 1851, 21–22. Troy outlined the program, derived from a communiqué from Durbin, in a set of eight resolutions that specified agency, action, calendar, and follow-up procedures.

47. "Minutes Erie Conference for the Year 1850," *Minutes of the First Twenty Sessions of the Erie Annual Conference* (Published by Order of the Conference, 1907), 257.

48. For Erie, see *Minutes of the First Twenty Sessions of the Erie Annual Conference*, 257. Compare *Minutes of the Maine Annual Conference*, 1850, 10–11; and *Minutes of the New England Annual Conference*, 1851, 30–31.

49. *Minutes of the Philadelphia Conference of the Methodist Episcopal Church*, 1851, 12.

50. Ibid., 8.

51. *Annual Report of the Missionary Society of the Methodist Episcopal Church*, 1854, 9. As an interim step, the General Conference of 1844 had empowered the bishops to take such action (Curts, *General Conferences*, 367–68).

52. *Annual Report of the Missionary Society of the Methodist Episcopal Church*, 1854, 33.

53. *Minutes of the Philadelphia Conference of the Methodist Episcopal Church*, 1856, 14, 1. At this point Philadelphia created thirteen standing committees. Missions was third on the list, being preceded by Public Worship and Necessitous Cases. To the latter, incidentally, the Conference stewards were appropriately appointed.

54. *Minutes*/MEC/1859, 1. The preceding year it had begun to include tables, one of "Appointments of Preachers, With Their Post Office Address," another listing names of all preachers by year of admission to the conference, with 1806 being the first. See *Minutes of the Philadelphia Conference of the Methodist Episcopal Church*, 1858, 9–12, 19–20. By 1859, Philadelphia added a very interesting "Plan of Statistics for Annual Minutes" to those two items.

55. See the *Minutes* for various actions, including memorials on the New Chapter on Slavery, which were referred to "Committee on the State of the Church." For instance, "A memorial from a Convention of laymen, held at Cambridge, Md., March 5th, 1861, also the action of the male members of the Cambridge Station, upon the subject of the New Chapter on Slavery, were presented and referred to the same Committee." The report proposed, and conference passed, a resolution calling for repeal of New Chapter. Then the conference directed "the printing in tract form of 5,000 copies of the report of the Committee on the State of the Church; also, its publication in the Christian Advocate and Journal, Methodist, and Baltimore Christian Advocate" (*Minutes of the Philadelphia Conference of the Methodist Episcopal Church*, 1861, 8–12).

56. *Minutes of the Philadelphia Conference of the Methodist Episcopal Church*, 1864, 15, 44–45.

57. Ibid., 47–48.

58. *JGC*/MEC 1864, 485–86.

59. Tees, *Pioneering*, 102.

60. *Minutes of the Philadelphia Conference of the Methodist Episcopal Church*, 1862, 13.

61. *Minutes of the Eightieth Session of the Philadelphia Conference of the Methodist Episcopal Church*, 1867. The minutes also include "Forty-Sixth Annual Report of the Missionary Society of the Methodist Episcopal Church, within the Bounds of the Philadelphia Conference, for Promoting Domestic and Foreign Missions," 65–116.

62. Ibid., 6–7.

63. Ibid., 65.

64. Ibid., 10, 47.

65. Ibid., 10.

66. *Minutes of the Philadelphia Conference of the Methodist Episcopal Church*, 1868, 12.

Chapter 7: Connecting at the Table

1. All of these examples are drawn from my personal experience with one local United Methodist church.

2. Here we make the assumption that advocates of any one ideal are unlikely to triumph, thereby producing that model of unity. Unity by victory would probably result in a major division or significant membership losses, depending on whether the losing party or parties exited collectively or individually.

3. *Good News Magazine* 23 (May/June 1990): 41. These points, III and VII, included also affirmations of justification by grace and the imperative of Christian witness and discipleship.

4. Robert Wuthnow, *The Struggle for America's Soul: Evangelicals, Liberals, and Secularism* (Grand Rapids: Eerdmans, 1989); and *The Restructuring of American Religion* (Princeton, N.J.: Princeton University Press, 1988).

5. John 17:22–23: "The glory that you have given me I have given them, so that they might be one, as we are one, I in them and you in me, that they may become completely one, so that the world may know that you have sent me and have loved them even as you have loved me."

6. UMC *Discipline* 2008, "Part I: The Constitution: Preamble" and "Division One—General: ¶ 6. Article VI: Ecumenical Relations," 21, 23. For an illuminating discussion of Christian unity as constitutive of Methodism, see John Deschner, "Globalization in Theological Education: United Methodism's Basic Ecumenical Policy," *QR* 11/3 (Fall 1991): 41–57.

7. The rationale for this threefold schematization of the United Methodist problematic and of its resolution will be found below. There are other and more conventional ways of outlining the vying priorities and conceptions of the unity to be sought. For instance, the Center for Ecumenical Dialogue in Longwood, Florida, orders its work into three dialogues—with the Christian Community, with the Religious Community, and with the Human Community—thus distinguishing in its first two dialogues what we have combined in our first. The Center subsumes our second under its first. Our threefold delineation indicates an explicit concern with the disunity within denominations, and not incidentally sets up the Methodist metaphor that is the burden of the paper. The proof is, I hope, in the pudding and I beg the reader's patience in its preparation here.

8. This is the title of one of the World Council of Churches' processes, a world convocation that met in Seoul, South Korea, in March 1990. Efforts to tie this concern to faith and order are being carried on through a formal study project titled "The Unity of the Church and the Renewal of Human Community."

9. Observers of GCCUIC and of United Methodist ecumenical endeavor will recognize the first and third as not only appropriately assigned to—indeed, mandated of—GCCUIC but also as embodied in its very name. The middle conception will seem less clearly GCCUIC's. The recognition by that agency of the importance to its officially given instructions of the unity within the denomination can be seen in its efforts to work more effectively with the World Methodist Council, in attention within its meetings to the larger agenda of conversations with the church's evangelical wing, and in an effectively sounded call by Bishop Roy Sano to work toward that end. For the latter, see Roy I. Sano, "Globalization in Theological Education: Ecumenical and Interreligious Agenda of the United Methodist Church," *QR* 11 (Spring 1991): 82–97.

10. I will use the acronym COCU or COCU/CUIC, since the earlier acronym may be more familiar than later names for the unitive efforts, namely, "The Church of Christ Uniting" and now "Churches Uniting in Christ." The older referent was for "Consultation on Church Union," which produced a plan for structured union. However, the plan failed. Now, GCCUIC envisions unity via covenanting. For particulars, see the descriptive documents, *The COCU Consensus: In Quest of a Church of Christ Uniting*, ed. Gerald F. Moede (Princeton, N.J.: COCU, 1985); and *Churches in Covenant Communion: The Church of Christ Uniting* (Princeton, N.J.: COCU, 1989); or consult the Web site, http://www.cuicinfo.org.

11. Sano, "Globalization in Theological Education."

12. See Leigh Eric Schmidt, *Holy Fairs: Scottish Communions and American Revivals in the Early Modern Period* (Princeton, N.J.: Princeton University Press, 1989); Russell Richey, "From

Quarterly to Camp Meeting," *Methodist History* 23 (July 1985): 199–213; Kenneth O. Brown, "Finding America's Oldest Camp Meeting," *Methodist History* 28 (July 1990): 252–54; and Charles A. Johnson, *The Frontier Camp Meeting* (Dallas: Southern Methodist University Press, 1955). For treatment and bibliography, see Kenneth O. Brown, *Holy Ground, Too: The Camp Meeting Family Tree* (Hazleton, Pa.: Published by Holiness Archives, 1997); and Michael J. McClymond, ed., *Encyclopedia of Religious Revivals in America.* 2 vols. (Westport, Conn.: Greenwood, 2007).

13. The first *Discipline* queried: "How often shall we permit strangers to be present at our love feasts?" and stipulated "*Ans*. Let them be admitted with the utmost caution; and the same person on no account above twice, unless he becomes a member." The first *Discipline* and Large Minutes are conveniently compared in Emory, *Discipline*, 29, and in an appendix in Tigert, *History*.

14. The first *Discipline* specified a controlled invitation: "Let no person who is not a member of the society be admitted to the communion, without a sacrament ticket, which ticket must be changed every quarter. And we empower the elder or assistant, and no others, to deliver these tickets" (Emory, *Discipline*, 45).

15. I have not attempted here to treat the camp meeting as a whole and so therefore slight the other offices, particularly preaching, that played such an important role in Methodism's spreading scriptural holiness over the land and reforming the continent. The point of this chapter is not to propose the modality of Methodism's engagement with the world or even the means by which unity might be achieved. Were I to do so, certainly other means of grace would take more prominence and preaching would receive its due. The point rather is to discover how, as Methodism went about its work, it managed to hold itself together.

16. By limiting marriage within the faith community, some traditions and most sectarian movements place the marriage or family covenant within the church covenant. The more expansive notion outlined here would seem more in keeping with Methodist thought.

17. Even our meals around the TV, though they rob the nourishment that we give one another, by mediating the world to us could serve to point to this larger covenant. Obviously, the TV dinner would need some creative attention and interpretation before it could function in this way.

Chapter 8: A Study in Conference Self-Preoccupation

1. Wesley, *Works* 7, *A Collection of Hymns for the Use of the People called Methodists*, ed. Franz Hildebrandt and Oliver A. Beckerlegge (Nashville: Abingdon, 1983), #466, p. 649. In *The United Methodist Hymnal* (Nashville: The United Methodist Publishing House, 1989, #553), the first stanza is the first half of the above and reads:

>And are we yet alive, and see each other's face?
>Glory and thanks to Jesus give for his almighty grace!

2. Wesley, *Works* 7:649.

3. "From John Wesley's later years to the present, this piece has appropriately served as the opening hymn for the Methodist annual conferences," says James I. Warren Jr., in *O For A Thousand Tongues: The History, Nature, and Influence of Music in the Methodist Tradition* (Grand Rapids: Francis Asbury, 1988), 51.

"This is one of the author's '*Hymns for Christian Friends*.' It is preeminently *the Conference hymn* of Methodism. It is sung at the opening of Methodist Conferences the world over, and has been so used for a hundred years. All branches of Methodism alike use it for this purpose" (Wilbur F. Tillett and Charles S. Nutter, *The Hymns and Hymn Writers of the Church: An Annotated Edition of The Methodist Hymnal* [Nashville: Smith & Lamar; New York: Eaton & Mains, 1915], 293).

4. William Warren Sweet, *Circuit-Rider Days Along the Ohio: Being the Journals of the Ohio Conference from its Organization in 1812 to 1826* (New York & Cincinnati: The Methodist Book Concern, 1923), 173, 216. Compare for the following conferences to 1826: 228, 242, 262, 275.

5. See "The Journals of the Illinois Annual Conference," in William Warren Sweet, *Religion on the American Frontier 1783–1840: The Methodists, a Collection of Source Materials* (New York: Cooper Square, 1946; repr. 1964), 263. In 1825: "Bishop McKendree opened the Conference by reading, singing, & prayer" (282). And in 1831: "Conference was opened by reading a portion of the Sacred Scriptures, Singing and prayer" (352).

6. See *Minutes of the . . . Annual Conference of the Maryland District of the Methodist Protestant Church*, 1840–62. Typically, the minutes did not initially indicate what constituted religious services. In 1844 the secretary noted "Scripture and prayer"; in 1846, he recorded "Scripture, singing and prayer." Beginning in 1863, specific hymns are noted and for five times in the next fifteen years #557 is sung. The pattern in the Southern church was similar. The typescript *Minutes of the Holston Annual Conference*, 1824–62, described openings with "religious services." *Minutes of the . . . Virginia Annual Conference of the Methodist Episcopal Church, South*, 1868, indicated that Bishop William M. Wightman "opened with religious services." As late as 1879, the North Georgia Conference, MECS, observed the same formula, "Scripture, singing and prayer" (*Minutes of . . . North Georgia Annual Conference of the Methodist Episcopal Church, South*, 1879). Prior minutes that I examined did not indicate what was done. The following year, a specific hymn was indicated, #533. If that conference used the 1866 or 1880 new MECS hymnal, it did not then sing "And are we yet alive," which was #272.

7. *Hymn Book of the Methodist Protestant Church*, 4th ed. (Baltimore: Book Committee of the Methodist Protestant Church, 1842), 313–27, hymns #404–23. It was the second hymn, #405.

8. There were separate headings for "Public Worship," "The Ordinances," "Admission to Membership," "Revival," and so forth.

9. See *A Collection of Hymns for the Use of the Methodist Episcopal Church* (New York: N. Bangs and T. Mason for the M.E.C., 1821), #411, 356; and *A Collection of Hymns . . . Revised and Corrected* (New York: G. Lane & P. P. Sandford for the M.E.C., 1842).

10. *Hymns for the Use of the Methodist Episcopal Church*. Rev. ed. (New York: Carlton & Lanahan, 1849), 411, 575–626, 603.

11. Pages 199–200, #272–74. Another hymn was labeled "Before receiving Appointments" and three were labeled "Closing Conference." The one sung before receiving appointments was #275, "Jesus, the truth and power divine." The three hymns for closing were #276, "Jesus, accept the praise That to thy name belongs!"; #277, "Bless'd be the dear uniting love"; and #278, "And let our bodies part."

12. *JGC*/MECS 1850, 125.

13. The MEC indicated its hymn selection in 1844 (#461); did so explicitly thereafter; also went to two hymns in 1852; and sung a variety of selections, most frequently, "I love thy kingdom, Lord."

14. This came through formal delegates from the English and Irish conferences at American conferences, and vice versa. It also came especially for the Genessee Conference through interaction with British Methodists in Canada, a point to which we return below.

15. *Minutes of the New England Conference of the Methodist Episcopal Church . . . 1851*, 3–15.

16. The latter section included also Bishop Janes's remarks spelling out reasons why he continued the four (rather than three) districts and presiding elders, apparently a recent innovation—essentially because of workload and despite appeals to return to three districts.

17. On this character of early conferences, see Russell E. Richey, *Early American Methodism* (Bloomington: Indiana University Press, 1991). It should be noted that the processes that we label "self-preoccupation" had begun in the very early nineteenth century and the focus on mid-century captures only a portion of the larger saga.

18. *Minutes of the New England Conference of the Methodist Episcopal Church . . . 1853*, 3.

19. *Minutes of the New England Conference of the Methodist Episcopal Church . . . 1860*: "Bishop Janes, assisted by Rev. G.F. Cox, introduced the religious services, by reading the Scriptures, singing, and prayer, after which the holy sacrament was administered" (3).

1862: Introduction . . . "The religious services were opened with the reading of the Scriptures by the Rev. Bishop Janes, who presided at the Conference, and the singing of a hymn; after which Rev. Chas. Baker offered prayer. The Holy Sacrament was then administered to the members of the Conference, a large number of whom were present, and also to the members of the church who were in attendance" (3).

1863: "Levi Scott, presiding . . . Scripture, hymn, communion."

1866: "The Holy Sacrament . . . several of the preachers assisting therein" (3).

20. *Minutes of the New England Conference of the Methodist Episcopal Church . . . 1868*, 8.

21. *Hymns For the Use of The Methodist Episcopal Church*, rev. ed. (New York: Nelson & Phillips, 1849). New England noted the singing of #280 in 1865 and #218 in 1867.

22. *Minutes of the Eighth Session of the East Genesee Annual Conference of the M.E. Church*, 1855, 3.

23. On the Baltimore Conference(s), see Gordon Pratt Baker, ed., *Those Incredible Methodists: A History of the Baltimore Conference of the United Methodist Church* (Baltimore: Commission on Archives and History, The Baltimore Conference, 1972).

24. *Annual Minutes of the . . . Baltimore Annual Conference of the Methodist Episcopal Church*, 1857.

25. *Annual Minutes of the . . . Baltimore Annual Conference of the Methodist Episcopal Church*, 1859.

26. *Annual Register of the Baltimore Conference of the Methodist Episcopal Church*, 1861, 5. "Register" represents a reversion to an earlier name for the minutes.

27. *Annual Register of the Baltimore Conference of the Methodist Episcopal Church*, 1861, 49.

28. *Register of the Baltimore Annual Conference of the Methodist Episcopal Church*, 1862, 22–23. These actions came in the adoption of the report of a Special Committee of Seven.

29. *Minutes of the Sessions of the Baltimore Annual Conference of the Methodist Episcopal Church, Held at Harrisonburg . . . 1862, Churchville . . . 1863, Bridgewater . . . 1864, Salem . . . 1865, Rev. John S. Martin, Sec.* (Staunton: Stoneburner & Prufer, 1899).

30. *Minutes of the New England Conference of the Methodist Episcopal Church . . . 1864*, 3–11.

31. *Register of the Baltimore Annual Conference of the Methodist Episcopal Church*, 1864.

32. *Minutes of the . . . Baltimore Annual Conference of the Methodist Episcopal Church*, 1869.

33. *Minutes of the . . . Baltimore Annual Conference of the Methodist Episcopal Church,* 1893, 15, 80.

34. *Minutes of the New England Conference of the Methodist Episcopal Church . . . 1879,* 5.

35. Abel Stevens, *The Centenary of American Methodism: A Sketch of Its History, Theology, Practical System, and Success. Prepared by Order of the Centenary Committee of the General Conference of The Methodist Episcopal Church* (New York: Carlton & Porter, 1865), 248.

36. For an example, see the appendix of George R. Crooks, *The Life of Bishop Matthew Simpson* (New York: Harper & Brothers, 1891), 471–512.

37. Ibid., 256.

38. *The Revised Compendium of Methodism. Embracing The History and Present Condition of its Various Branches in All Countries; with A Defence of its Doctrinal, Governmental, and Prudential Peculiarities* (New York: Hunt & Eaton; Cincinnati: Cranston & Stowe, 1875).

39. (New York: Phillips & Hunt, 1876).

40. (Philadelphia: L.H. Ewerts, 1882).

41. By an ex-presiding elder (Saint Louis: P. M. Pinckard, 1867).

42. Compiled by J.W. Hedges (Baltimore: Methodist Episcopal Book Depository, 1878). This is a Baltimore Conference compilation that subsumed episcopal Methodism in its own history.

43. Please note the discussion above, describing the Southern church's earlier recognition of "And are we yet alive" as a conference hymn.

44. Rev. ed. (New York: Nelson & Phillips, 1849).

45. I refer to *A Collection of Hymns for Public, Social, and Domestic Worship* (Nashville: Southern Methodist Publishing House, 1880; but apparently a reissue of the 1866 edition).

46. *Hymnal of the Methodist Episcopal Church* (Cincinnati: Hitchcock & Walden, 1878; also New York: Nelson & Phillips, 1878).

47. *Minutes of the . . . Baltimore Annual Conference of the Methodist Episcopal Church,* 1884, 52–55.

48. Ibid. It follows p. 106 but is freshly paginated as 3–16 and was "Published by the American Methodist Historical Society."

49. Ibid., 136–50.

50. Ibid., 151–75.

51. Ibid., 127.

52. It is worth noting that the hymn became established as a conference hymn at the point when the love feast and class meeting had become more memories than vital practices. With this hymn, conference perhaps sustained the memory of its own intimacies, its earlier class-like character, even as it jeopardized such intimacies with the new organizational apparatus.

53. *Minutes of the . . . Baltimore Annual Conference of the Methodist Episcopal Church,* 1884. The hymn that year was #815, "Draw near, O Son of God, draw near." "And are we yet alive" was sung in 1885, 1888, 1889, and 1892. The hymn was not indicated for 1886. Others hymns were sung in 1887, 1890, and 1891.

Chapter 9: A Methodist Doctrine of the Church?

1. Albert C. Outler, "Do Methodists Have a Doctrine of the Church?" in *The Doctrine of the Church,* ed. Dow Kirkpatrick (New York: Abingdon, 1964), 11–28. But see Scott J. Jones, *United*

Methodist Doctrine: The Extreme Center (Nashville: Abingdon, 2002); Ted A. Campbell, *Methodist Doctrine: The Essentials* (Nashville: Abingdon, 1999); Thomas C. Oden, *Doctrinal Standards in the Wesleyan Tradition* (Grand Rapids: Francis Asbury, 1988); Thomas A. Langford, ed., *Doctrine and Theology in The United Methodist Church* (Nashville: Kingswood, 1991); W. Stephen Gunter et al., *Wesley and the Quadrilateral: Renewing the Conversation* (Nashville: Abingdon, 1997); Scott J. Jones, *John Wesley's Conception and Use of Scripture* (Nashville: Kingswood, 1995); Walter Klaiber and Manfred Marquardt, *Living Grace: An Outline of United Methodist Theology*, trans. and adapted by J. Steven O'Malley and Ulrike R.M. Guthrie (Nashville: Abingdon, 2001); Kenneth J. Collins, *John Wesley: A Theological Journal* (Nashville: Abingdon, 2003); and Russell E. Richey, *MARKS*.

2. L. Harold DeWolf, "The Doctrine of the Church," in *Methodism*, ed. William K. Anderson (Cincinnati: Methodist Publishing House, 1947), 217; Durward Hofler, "The Methodist Doctrine of the Church," *Methodist History* 6 (October 1967): 25.

3. Outler, "Do Methodists Have a Doctrine of the Church?" 25–27. Compare Outler, "Methodism's Theological Heritage," in *Methodism's Destiny in an Ecumenical Age*, ed. Paul M. Minus Jr. (Nashville: Abingdon, 1969), 67–68.

4. Colin W. Williams, *John Wesley's Theology Today* (New York: Abingdon, 1960). See particularly the preface, chapter 1, and the conclusion.

5. But see Hofler, "The Methodist Doctrine of the Church," 25–35.

6. *JLFA* 1:476, December 18, 1784.

7. On the role of Bangs and Stevens as historians, see chapter 12.

8. Bangs, *History* (New York: Carlton & Porter, 1860); Abel Stevens, *The History of the Religious Movement of the Eighteenth Century Called Methodism*, 3 vols. (New York: Philips & Hunt, 1858–61); Bangs, *History*; Stevens, *A Compendious History of American Methodism* (New York: Carlton and Porter, 1868, c. 1867).

9. *The Errors of Hopkinsianism Detected and Refuted* (New York, 1815); *The Reformer Reformed: or A Second Part of the Errors of Hopkinsianism Detected and Refuted* (New York, 1816); *An Examination of the Doctrine of Predestination* (New York, 1817); *A Vindication of Methodist Episcopacy* (New York, 1820).

10. See Thomas A. Langford, *Practical Divinity: Theology in the Wesleyan Tradition*. 2 vols. (Nashville: Abingdon, 1983), 1:70–88.

11. I am using the second, or 1840, revised edition of Bangs (New York: T. Mason and G. Lane); and the 1852 edition of Stevens (New York: Lane & Scott). Hereafter, to ease identification of which author I am referencing to, I will cite author and page in parentheses in the text.

12. I am accenting the unitive value of aspects of American religion that have sometimes been seen as divisive. See Walter G. Muelder's ambivalence on such themes in "Methodism and Ecumenism in the United States," in Minus, *Methodism's Destiny in an Ecumenical Age*, 156–74. Compare Sidney Mead, *The Lively Experiment* (New York: Harper & Row, 1963), 103–33. A unitive valuation is given by many of the participants in the discussion of Christian America and civil religion. See, for instance, Robert Handy, *A Christian America* (New York: Oxford University Press, 1971).

13. See the title essay in Sidney E. Mead, *The Nation with the Soul of a Church* (New York: Oxford University Press, 1971).

14. See Fred J. Hood, *Reformed America* (Tuscaloosa: University of Alabama Press, 1980).

15. Outler, "Do Methodists Have a Doctrine of the Church?" 24–25.

16. See Winthrop S. Hudson, "Denominationalism as a Basis for Ecumenicity: A Seventeenth Century Conception," in *Denominationalism*, ed. Russell E. Richey (Nashville: Abingdon, 1977), 19–42; and the several essays in R. Bruce Mullin and Russell E. Richey, ed., *Reimagining Denominationalism* (New York: Oxford University Press, 1994).

17. Compare Lefferts A. Loetscher, "The Problem of Christian Unity in Early Nineteenth-Century America," *Church History* 32 (March 1963): 3–16.

Chapter 10: Family Values: A Connectional Concern

1. Alice M. Smith,"Emory University announces compromise agreement regarding use of campus churches, chapels," *United Methodist News Service* (June 23, 1997).

2. "Family Values" is a chapter title in Christine Leigh Heyrman's *Southern Cross: The Beginnings of the Bible Belt* (New York: Knopf, 1997), and the argument and perspective of that volume decidedly influence the shape of this presentation. So also do the works of Donald G. Mathews, particularly *Religion in the Old South* (Chicago: University of Chicago Press, 1977); and *Slavery and Methodism: A Chapter in American Morality, 1780–1845* (Westport, Conn.: Greenwood, 1965; repr. 1978). I am influenced as well by A. Gregory Schneider in *The Way of the Cross Leads Home: The Domestication of American Methodism* (Bloomington: Indiana University Press, 1993); Dee E. Andrews, *The Methodists and Revolutionary America, 1760–1800: The Shaping of an Evangelical Culture* (Princeton, N.J.: Princeton University Press, 2000); Cynthia Lynn Lyerly, *Methodism and the Southern Mind, 1770–1810* (New York and Oxford: Oxford University Press, 1998); William H. Williams, *The Garden of American Methodism: The Delmarva Peninsula, 1769–1820* (Wilmington, Del.: Scholarly Resources for the Peninsula Conference of The United Methodist Church, 1984); John H. Wigger, *Taking Heaven by Storm: Methodism and the Rise of Popular Christianity in America* (New York: Oxford University Press, 1998); and David Hempton, *Methodism: Empire of the Spirit* (New Haven: Yale University Press, 2005).

3. See Russell E. Richey, *Early American Methodism* (Bloomington: Indiana University Press, 1991), especially 47–64.

4. *Minutes*/MEC/1797 (1813), 190–99. See Lee, *Short History*, 249, for explanation. The next year more Northern conferences were held.

5. Holland N. McTyeire observed: "[T]his is not a history of Southern Methodism, but of Methodism from a Southern point of view. In the South, Methodism was first successfully planted, and from thence it spread North, and East, and West. If all the members claimed by all the branches be counted, there is a preponderance of American Methodism now, as at the beginning, in the South" (*A History of Methodism* [Nashville: Southern Methodist Publishing House, 1884], 3). Of his three historian predecessors, Jesse Lee, Nathan Bangs, and Abel Stevens, he observed, "The first wrote when there was no North and no South in Methodism; the second, when these began to be; the third, when they were realities" (4).

6. See Williams, *The Garden of American Methodism*.

7. *A Short Account of the Experience of Mrs. Hester Ann Rogers* was available in English versions very early, in an American printing in the first decade of the nineteenth century (New York, 1804), and was frequently reprinted. For the documentation of impressive and steady sales of subsequent editions by Methodist itinerants (book agents), see William Warren Sweet, "The Preacher

as Book Agent in the West," *Religion on the American Frontier, 1783–1840: The Methodists* (New York: Cooper Square, 1946; repr. 1964), 4:698–706. For instance, in 1812 Benjamin Lakin sold thirteen different items, including twelve catechisms, eighteen copies of the minutes, twelve of Nelson's *Journal*, two of Wesley's *Journal*, and nine of Mrs. Rogers's book (700).

8. *MQRS* (July 1860): 472–73. Compare this account by Ezekiel Cooper from December 1790 and Maryland: "Had a serious conversation with Miss BRB who has been obliged to leave her father's house for religion and he obstinately refuses to let her return unless she will quit the Methodists entirely, which she is resolved not to do if she never is received into his favor. May the Lord help her and provide in his mercy for her. 'Tis a blessing she has friends out of her . . . obstinate father's house" (The Ezekiel Cooper Collection, GETS Library, Journal 2, 1790–1802).

9. "Old Letters," *MQRS* (April 1860): 308. The letters are from 1793.

10. Ibid., 308–10. These letters are also from 1793.

11. "Old Letters," *MQRS* (July 1860): 470–75.

12. For an effort to correct and enlarge our understanding of polity, see Thomas Edward Frank, *Polity, Practice, and the Mission of The United Methodist Church* (Nashville: Abingdon, 2006), especially 39–62.

13. The Ezekiel Cooper Collection, GETS Library, Journal 2, 1790–1802, for May 3, 9, 1791.

14. *Beams of Light on Early Methodism in America*, compiled by Geo. A. Phoebus (New York: Phillips & Hunt; Cincinnati: Cranston & Stowe, 1887), 234.

15. For instance, another part of the letter of 1802 from Hamilton Jefferson on the Fairfax Circuit, Alexandria District, reported, "At Rockingham there were twenty or upwards converted to God, and seven or eight professed sanctification. The meeting held three days and nights until two or three o'clock: the last day and night was the most powerful time. I am clear for three days at Quarterly Meetings" (*MQRS* [July 1860]: 472–73).

Compare accounts by Richard Whatcoat, in 1789 presiding elder, later bishop:

> The 26th of April, 1789, at a quarterly meeting, held at the old meeting-house, near Cambridge, Dorset county, the Lord came in power at our Sacrament; the cries of the mourners, and the ecstasies of believers were such, that the preacher's voice could scarcely be heard, for the space of three hours; many were added to the number of true believers. At our quarterly meeting, held at St. Michael's, for Talbot circuit, the power of the Lord was present, to wound and to heal. Sabbath following, our quarterly meeting, held at Johnstown, for Caroline circuit, was yet more glorious; the power of the Lord came down at our love feast. The house was filled with the members of our societies, and great numbers of people were on the outside; the doors and windows were thrown open, and some thronged in at the latter. Such times my eyes never beheld before!
>
> May 5th and 6th, we held quarterly meetings for Dover circuit, at Duck Creek Cross Roads; the 7th and 8th, at Dudly Church, for Queen Ann's circuit; and on the 10th and 11th, at Georgetown, for Kent circuit. The power of the Lord spread from circuit to circuit.

Note also his account of general and annual conferences:

> At our General Conference held at Baltimore, in Maryland, May the 6th, 1800, I was elected and ordained to the Episcopal office. We had a most blessed time and much preaching, fervent prayers, and strong exhortations through the city, while the high

praises of a gracious God reverberated from street to street, and from house to house, which greatly alarmed the citizens. It was thought that not less than two hundred were converted during the sitting of our Conference.

On the 1st of June we held a Conference at Duck Creek Cross Roads, in the state of Delaware. This was a glorious time; such a spirit of faith, prayer, and zeal, rested on the preachers and people, that I think it exceeded any thing of the kind I ever saw before. O, the strong cries, groans, and agonies of the mourners! Enough to pierce the hardest heart; but when the Deliverer set their souls at liberty, their ecstasies of joy were inexpressibly great, so that the high praises of the Redeemer's name sounded through the town, until solemnity appeared on every countenance: the effect of which was, that on the Thursday following, one hundred and fifteen persons joined the society in that town, while the divine flame spread greatly through the adjacent societies.

Our Conference began at New-York, the 19th of June, 1800, and closed the 23d; a few souls were converted.

"Experience and Travels of the Rev. Richard Whatcoat. Written by Himself," in William Phoebus, *Memoirs of the Rev. Richard Whatcoat, Late Bishop of the Methodist Episcopal Church* (New York: Joseph Allen, 1828), 24–25, 30.

16. (New York: Ezekiel Cooper and John Wilson, for the Methodist Connection in the United States, 1805). Another rich vein is *American Methodist Pioneer.*

17. *Extracts of the Journals of the Rev. Dr. Coke's Five Visits to America* (London: Printed by G. Paramore, 1784), 35–36.

18. But see Lester Ruth, *A Little Heaven Below: Worship at Early Methodist Quarterly Meetings* (Nashville: Kingswood, 2000).

19. Especially outspoken was James Meacham. See his Journal in the Special Collections Library, Duke University Library, Durham, N.C. See also the Edward Dromgoole Papers, Southern Historical Collection, University of North Carolina Library, Chapel Hill, N.C.

20. "Old Letters," *MQRS* (1859): 618–23, especially 622. The letter is dated March 23, 1796. Several other letters in this little collection speak of O'Kelly's competition and with less confidence.

21. *The Year Book of the Methodist Episcopal Church, South, for the Year 1898* (Nashville: Publishing House Methodist Episcopal Church, South, 1898) added a substantial section on "Fraternal Relations" (51–58), outlining the various relationships then recognized and included from the Cape May Accords the "Declaration and Basis of Fraternity" and "Rules for the Adjustment of Adverse Claims to Church Property" (52–53).

22. See Hunter Dickinson Farish, *The Circuit Rider Dismounts: A Social History of Southern Methodism, 1865–1900* (Richmond: Dietz, 1938); Robert Watson Sledge, *Hands on the Ark: The Struggle for Change in the Methodist Episcopal Church, South, 1914–1939* (Lake Junaluska, N.C.: General Commission on Archives and History, 1975). And on the processes leading up to this "adjustment," see Mathews, *Slavery*; C.C. Goen, *Broken Churches, Broken Nation: Denominational Schism and the Coming of the Civil War* (Macon, Ga.: Mercer University Press, 1985); Donald G. Jones, *The Sectional Crisis and Northern Methodism: A Study in Piety, Political Ethics and Civil Religion* (Metuchen, N.J.: Scarecrow, 1979); Reginald F. Hildebrand, *The Times Were Strange and Stirring* (Durham, N.C.: Duke University Press, 1995); Katharine L. Dvorak, *An African-American Exodus: The Segregation of the Southern Churches* (Brooklyn: Carlson, 1991); Clarence E. Walker, *A Rock in a Weary Land: The African Methodist Episcopal Church during the Civil War and*

Reconstruction (Baton Rouge: Louisiana State University Press, 1982).

23. "Bishops' Address," *JGC*/MECS 1898, 18–31, 19. For an earlier use of this image, see Phoebus, *Memoirs of the Rev. Richard Whatcoat*, 5–6: "The Methodist Episcopal Church is one; is truly federal; in all its stations and circuits it exhibits this same feature: as a wheel within a wheel. No annual or general Conference can alter it, without such a departure as would be considered a breach of trust."

24. Ibid., 21–23.

25. Ibid., 23–24.

26. On the latter two organizations and especially the last's contribution to the new aggressive spirit of Southern Methodism, see John Patrick McDowell, *The Social Gospel in the South: The Woman's Home Mission Movement in the Methodist Episcopal Church, South, 1886–1939* (Baton Rouge: Louisiana State University Press, 1982).

27. "Dedication of the Scarritt Bible and Training School," *Woman's Missionary Advocate* (November 1892): 136–40.

28. The school's professional mandate was clearly spelled out by *The Year Book of the Methodist Episcopal Church, South, for the Year 1897* (Nashville: Publishing House of the Methodist Episcopal Church, South, 1897): "The need for an increased number of trained laborers in all the fields of Christian beneficence is apparent to any intelligent observer. In every other department of human effort, where any degree of intelligence is required, some special training is supposed to be necessary; certainly where instruction and counsel are expected, and where professional knowledge is demanded, special training is essential. This training the Scarritt Bible and Training School is prepared to give, and at moderate cost." A seven-point program was then spelled out (30–31).

29. *JGC*/MECS 1890, 160–63.

30. Hilary Hudson, *The Methodist Armor*, rev. and enl. (Nashville: Printed for the Author, Publishing House of the Methodist Episcopal Church, South, 1892), 301. The section is found on 294–311, and is apparently excerpted, at least in part, from an Address of Rev. Joseph Wood, in the *Ecumenical Methodist Book*.

31. "Bishops' Address," *JGC*/MECS 1898, 29.

32. Of course this is the title of the study by Farish, *The Circuit Rider Dismounts: A Social History of Southern Methodism, 1865–1900*.

33. "Of the Social Church Meetings," MECS *Discipline* 1866, 93. Compare MECS *Discipline* 1894, 51–53. See Holland N. McTyeire, *A Manual of the Discipline of the Methodist Episcopal Church, South* (Nashville: Publishing House of the Methodist Episcopal Church, South, 1902), 36–38; and also P. A. Peterson, *Revisions*, 48–49.

34. H.N. McTyeire, *A Catechism on Church Government: With Special Reference to that of the Methodist Episcopal Church, South* (Nashville: Publishing House of the Methodist Episcopal Church, South, 1899), 40–41.

35. See especially "Bishops' Address," *JGC*/MECS 1894, 23–26.

36. *JGC*/MECS 1898, 176. See *Discipline*, chap. VI, Sec. V, Quest. 4, An. 3.

37. For fuller discussion of the late twentieth-century developments, see Robert Bruce Mullin and Russell E. Richey, eds., *Reimagining Denominationalism: Interpretive Essays* (New York: Oxford University Press, 1994), especially Richey, "Denominations and Denominationalism: An American Morphology," 74–98.

38. In 1902, the bishops addressed themselves to "Connectionalism" and the "connectional character of our Church." They saw connectionalism in the conference structure, in itinerancy, in appointments, in the episcopal mandate to care for the needs of the whole church. They noted that "it is the genius of our system and the law of our Church that the bishops, as General Superintendents of the Church, make such disposition of the itinerant preachers as in their judgment will best serve the whole Church. The itinerancy of a preacher does not mean his traveling only in one Conference, and that of his own selection, but in any Conference of the Connection, when in the judgment of the appointing power it is needful that he change his mere Conference relation." See "Bishops' Address," *JGC/*MECS 1902, 26.

Chapter 11: Methodism as Machine

1. The meaning of this phrase will emerge in the course of this essay. It refers to the power in Methodist episcopacy or superintendency—power first exercised by John Wesley—to assign preachers.

2. These divisions figure prominently in virtually every history of Methodism. For a short review of the issues and actors, see Russell E. Richey, "Is Division a New Threat to the Denomination?" in *QTCC*, 105–16.

3. "SECTION V. *Of the Presiding Elder, and of their Duty,*" in Asbury/Coke, *Discipline*, 52, the only annotated version of the Methodist *Discipline*.

4. Nathan Bangs, D.D., *An Original Church of Christ: Or, A Scriptural Vindication of the Orders and Powers of the Ministry of the Methodist Episcopal Church* (New-York: J. Collord, 1837), 348–51.

5. *Itinerancy,* or *itineracy,* the hallmark of Methodist ministry, was the system designed by John Wesley of appointing preachers, of putting them traveling on a circuit of preaching places, and of moving them periodically from circuit to circuit. The long quotation above from Nathan Bangs describes this system, as does the following statement from George Cookman. The best way to view the itinerant system is by reading the journal of a traveling preacher; and those abound. See, for instance, David L. Kimbrough, *Reverend Joseph Tarkington, Methodist Circuit Rider: From Frontier Evangelism to Refined Religion* (Knoxville: University of Tennessee Press, 1997).

6. George G. Cookman, *Speeches Delivered on Various Occasions* (New York: George Lane for the Methodist Episcopal Church, 1840), 127–37.

7. Abel Stevens, *History of The Methodist Episcopal Church in the United States of America*, 4 vols. (New York: Eaton & Mains; Cincinnati: Jennings & Pye, 1864–67), 1:16, 18, 26–28, 15–46.

8. James O. Andrew, "Bishop Asbury," one of a series of review biographical statements in commentary on Thomas O. Summers, found in *Biographical Sketches of Eminent Itinerant Ministers*, *MQRS* 13 (January 1859): 10–11.

9. "The Report of the Special Committee on the Relation of Benevolent Institutions of the Church to the General Conference," *JGC/*MEC 1872, 295–99.

10. "Episcopal Address," *JGC/*MEC 1912, 198–202.

11. Paul A. Mickey and Robert L. Wilson, *What New Creation? The Agony of Church Restructure* (Nashville: Abingdon, 1977).

12. Alan K. Waltz, *Images of the Future* (Nashville: Abingdon, 1980); and Kristine M. Rogers and Bruce A. Rogers, *Paths to Transformation: A Study of the General Agencies of The United*

Methodist Church (Nashville: Abingdon, 1982).

13. Richard Wilke, *And Are We Yet Alive? The Future of The United Methodist Church* (Nashville: Abingdon, 1986), especially 57–64.

14. Douglas W. Johnson and Alan K. Waltz, *Facts and Possibilities: An Agenda for The United Methodist Church* (Nashville: Abingdon, 1987).

15. The Council of Bishops of The United Methodist Church, *Vital Congregations, Faithful Disciples: Vision for the Church: Foundation Document* (Nashville: Graded Press, 1990).

16. On the following themes, see other chapters and the several volumes in the United Methodism and American Culture series, particularly the introductory essay in *CEMI*, 1–20.

Chapter 12: Methodism and Providence

1. See John Higham, *History: Professional Scholarship in America* (Baltimore: Johns Hopkins University Press, 1965; repr. 1983); Peter Dobkin Hall, *The Organization of American Culture, 1700–1900: Private Institutions, Elites, and the Origins of American Nationality* (New York: New York University Press, 1984); and the centennial issue of *The American Historical Review* for October 1984 and in that issue, particularly David D. Van Tassel, "From Learned Society to Professional Organization: The American Historical Association, 1884–1900," *The American Historical Review* 89 (October 1984): 929–56. Van Tassel distinguishes a learned society and a professional organization in these terms: "A learned society, therefore, may be defined as an organization, often exclusive in membership, dedicated to the preservation, advancement, and diffusion of knowledge solely through the publication of papers read at periodic meetings. While pursuing some of the same goals as a learned society, a professional organization usually distinguishes itself from other groups, sets standards of professional performance as well as guidelines for professional training programs, enhances communication among the members, serves and protects special interests of the profession by promoting legislation, among other things, and enforces a degree of conformity to professional practices and standards among its members. Indeed, a professional organization is the product of a community of people with a common sense of purpose" (930). In these terms the ASCH remained a learned society long after the AHA had achieved professional status.

2. See Henry W. Bowden, *Dictionary of American Religious Biography* (Westport, Conn.: Greenwood, 1977). In this discussion I follow Bowden's *Church History in the Age of Science: Historiographical Patterns in the United States, 1876–1918* (Chapel Hill: University of North Carolina Press, 1971); and Higham, *History*.

3. Bowden, *Church History*, 59–61; Higham, *History*, 17.

4. This formulation of history as science can be found in Bowden, *Church History*, 17 passim.

5. Quoted by Bowden, *Church History*, 52, from Philip Schaff's *Theological Propaedeutic: A General Introduction to the Study of Theology* (New York: Charles Scribner's Sons, 1893), 236.

6. Higham, *History*, 92–103.

7. Bowden, *Church History*, 26.

8. Ibid., 106n. From Emerton's "A Definition of Church History," *Papers of the ASCH*, 2nd ser. 7 (1923): 55–56. Emerton affirmed, "Historical evidence concerns only such things as are perceptible to human powers and can be recorded by human means. Miracles—all miracles—are to be excluded from the historian's function, because no human evidence can establish the fact of a mir-

acle" (Bowden, *Church History*, 109; Emerton, "A Definition of Church History," 63).

9. Bowden, *Church History*, 103; Emerton, "A Definition of Church History," 57.

10. Bowden, *Church History*, 108; Emerton, "A Definition of Church History," 62. Emerton continued: "The belief in the superhuman . . . because it is a fact of human experience, has its historical record and can be studied historically."

11. Bowden, *Church History*, 103; Emerton, "A Definition of Church History," 57.

12. For related efforts to show how Methodists use history for theological and definitional purposes, see Russell E. Richey, "History as a Bearer of Denominational Identity: Methodism as a Case Study," in *Beyond Establishment: Protestant Identity in a Post-Protestant Age*, ed. Jackson Carroll and Wade Clark Roof (Louisville: Westminster/John Knox, 1993), 270–95; and "American Methodism: A Bicentennial Review," *The Drew Gateway* 54 (Winter–Spring 1984), in a double issue titled "Methodism and Ministry: Historical Explorations," special editors J. Brian Selleck and Russell E. Richey, 130–42. See also Kenneth E. Rowe, "Counting the Converts: Progress Reports as Church History," in *Rethinking Methodist History: A Bicentennial Historical Consultation*, ed. Russell E. Richey and Kenneth E. Rowe (Nashville: Kingswood, 1985), 11–17. This effort builds on Rowe's findings.

13. Christian Smith, ed., *The Secular Revolution: Power, Interests, and Conflicts in the Secularization of American Public Life* (Berkeley and Los Angeles: University of California Press, 2003); Karel Dobbelaere, "Bryan Wilson's Contributions to the Study of Secularization," *Social Compass* 53/2 (June 2006): 141–46; idem., "Assessing Secularization Theory," in *New Approaches to the Study of Religion: Textual, Comparative, Sociological, and Cognitive Approaches*, ed. Peter Antes, Randi R. Warne, Armin W. Geertz, and R. Geertz (Berlin: Walter de Gruyter, 2004), 2:229–53; and idem., "Secularization: A Multi-Dimensional Concept," the full issue of *Current Sociology* 29 (Summer 1981); and Karel Dobbelaere, "Secularization Theories and Social Paradigms," *Social Compass* 31 (1984): 2–3, 199–219; Larry Shiner, "The Concept of Secularization in Empirical Research," *Journal for the Scientific Study of Religion* 6/967: 207–20. See also the several works of Bryan Wilson and David Martin.

14. On Providence as an American commonplace, see especially John F. Berens, *Providence and Patriotism in Early America, 1640–1815* (Charlottesville: University Press of Virginia, 1978); Paul C. Nagel, *This Sacred Trust: American Nationality 1798–1898* (New York: Oxford University Press, 1971); Henry F. May, "The Decline of Providence?" in *Ideas, Faiths and Feelings: Essays on American Intellectual and Religious History, 1952–1982* (New York: Oxford University Press, 1983), 130–46; Joanna Bowen Gillespie, "'The Clear Leadings of Providence': Pious Memoirs and the Problems of Self-Realization for Women in the Early Nineteenth Century," *Journal of the Early Republic* 5 (Summer 1985): 197–221; Fred J. Hood, *Reformed America: The Middle and Southern States, 1783–1837* (Tuscaloosa: University of Alabama Press, 1980); Lewis O. Saum, *The Popular Mind of Pre-Civil War America* (Westport, Conn.: Greenwood, 1980); Sacvan Bercovitch, *The American Jeremiad* (Madison: University of Wisconsin Press, 1978).

15. See notes on the Large Minutes in chapter 1.

16. MEC *Discipline* 1787, 3–4.

17. Ibid.

18. A tentative claim, based on a small sample of constitutions: *A Summary of Church Discipline . . . by The Baptist Association* (Charleston, 1774); *The Canons and Constitution of the Protestant Episcopal Church* (1789); *The Constitution of the Reformed Dutch Church* (1793); *The Constitution of the Presbyterian Church* (1821).

19. Wesley, *Letters* (Telford), 8:259. The letter was dated February 1, 1791.
20. *The Experience and Travels of Mr. Freeborn Garrettson* (Philadelphia, 1791). Republished as *American Methodist Pioneer*.
21. *JLFA*, 3:197. To Daniel Hitt, dated January 30, 1801. Compare the letter to Stith Mead ten days earlier, 3:195–96.
22. (New York, 1805).
23. See Russell E. Richey, "From Quarterly to Camp Meeting: A Reconsideration of Early American Methodism," *Methodist History* 23 (July 1985): 199–213. Republished in Richey, *Early American Methodism*.
24. *Minutes of the Methodist Conferences, Annually Held in America from 1773 to 1813, Inclusive* (New York: Daniel Hitt & Thomas Ware for the Methodist Connexion in the United States, 1813), iii, iv.
25. Jesse Lee, *A Short History of the Methodists* (Baltimore, 1810; facsimile edition, Rutland, Vt.: Academy, 1974).
26. Abel Stevens, *A Compendious History of American Methodism* (New York: Eaton & Mains, n.d.), 517–18, 143–46; J.M. Buckley, *A History of Methodists in the United States*, 4th ed. (New York: Charles Scribner's Sons, 1890), 354, 353, 191, 213–16.
27. Lee, *Short History*, v-vi.
28. Ibid., 362.
29. The distinction between general and particular Providence was a common one. John Wesley examined the issue in his sermon "On Divine Providence," in Wesley, *Works* (Jackson), 6:313–25. Wesley asked the reader, "You say, 'You allow a *general* providence, but deny a *particular* one?' And what is a general, of whatever kind it be, that includes no particulars?" (322). "What becomes, then, of your general providence, exclusive of a particular?" (323). However, both in this sermon and in "Spiritual Worship" (Wesley, *Works*, 6:424–35), Wesley did attend to both. This series of statements (each of which is elaborated) summarizes his position on general Providence:

> "He is the true God, the only Cause, the sole Creator of all things."
> "And as the true God, he is also the Supporter of all the things that he hath made."
> "As the true God, he is likewise the Preserver of all things."
> "[H]e is the true Author of all the motion that is in the universe."
> "The true God is also the Redeemer of all the children of men."
> "The true God is the Governor of all things." (426–28)

Wesley distinguished God's "providential government over the children of men" by a "threefold circle of divine providence": "The *outermost circle* includes all the sons of men; Heathens, Mahometans, Jews, and Christians. He causeth his sun to rise upon all. He giveth them rain and fruitful seasons. He pours ten thousand benefits upon them, and fills their hearts with good and gladness. With an *interior circle* he encompasses the whole visible Christian Church, all that name the name of Christ. He has an additional regard to these, and a nearer attention to their welfare. But the *innermost circle* of his providence encloses only the invisible Church of Christ; all real Christians, wherever dispersed in all corners of the earth" (428).

30. Lee, *Short History*, 129.
31. Ibid., 43, 44, 21, 37; Stevens, *Compendious History*, 49.

32. Lee, *Short History*, 54–59. For other revival accounts, see 43, 49, 51, 74, 77, 82, 129–34, 138–40, 145, 218, 271–75, 277–80, 283–87, 289–94, 300–304, 308, 311–15, 344, 351, 356.
33. Ibid., iv, v.
34. Richard E. Hermann, "Nathan Bangs: Apologist for American Methodism" (PhD diss., Emory University, 1973).
35. Leland Scott, "The Message of Early American Methodism," *HAM*, 2:347; Stevens, *Compendious History*, 367–68.
36. I am using the 6th edition, 4 vols. (New York: Carlton & Porter, 1860).
37. Bangs, *History*, 1:89.
38. Ibid., 2:101, 109–19.
39. Ibid., 1:360.
40. Ibid., 360–61.
41. Ibid., 361. The specification of three criteria and the numbering are mine.
42. Nathan Bangs, *An Original Church of Christ* (New York: T. Mason and G. Lane, 1837; 2nd ed. rev. 1837, 1840). I am using the 1840 edition.
43. Bangs, *History*, 1:165, 364. Chapter 3 of this volume recounts the organization of The Methodist Episcopal Church and effectively summarizes the defense that Bangs had mounted in *An Original Church of Christ*. See particularly his twelve points on 159–63.
44. Ibid., 160. Thomas Coke made this point at the organization of the church and in specific reference to the church order being adopted. See his *The Substance of a Sermon Preached at Baltimore . . . Before the General Conference of the Methodist Episcopal Church . . . at the Ordination of the Rev. Francis Asbury to the Office of a Superintendent* (Baltimore, 1785).
45. Bangs, *History*, 4:456; 1:46.
46. Ibid., 2:111–12. In "A Plain Account of The People Called Methodists," Wesley said of "the whole economy of the people commonly called Methodists": "[A]s they had not the least expectation, at first, of any thing like what has since followed, so they had no previous design or plan at all; but every thing arose just as the occasion offered. They saw or felt some impending or pressing evil, or some good end necessary to be pursued. And many times they fell unawares on the very things which secured the good, or removed the evil. At other times, they consulted on the most probable means, following only common sense and Scripture: Though they generally found, in looking back, something in Christian antiquity likewise, very nearly parallel thereto" (Wesley, *Works* [Jackson], 8:248).
47. Bangs, *An Original Church of Christ*, 346–47. Compare 347–48. Note the curious anomaly in Bangs and early Methodism. Providential leadings yielded a dynamic view of structure and a static view of doctrine. However, that anomaly disappeared as Bangs and others insisted that what had been dynamically given should be left alone. See ibid., 370.
48. Bangs, *History*, 1:20–33, 46, 280–88; 2:146–50. Quotation from 46.
49. Ibid., 2:148, 146, 147.
50. Ibid., 148–49. In *Broken Churches, Broken Nation* (Macon, Ga: Mercer University Press, 1985), Clarence Goen, echoing Bangs's sentiments, has carefully argued what others have intimated, that the first divisions largely determined the latter.
51. See Abel Stevens, *The Centenary of American Methodism: A Sketch of Its History, Theology, Practical System, and Success* (New York: Carlton & Porter, 1865).
52. Abel Stevens, *The History of the Religious Movement of the Eighteenth Century, Called Methodism*, 3 vols. (New York: Philips & Hunt, 1858–61); and *History of the Methodist Episcopal*

Church, 4 vols. (New York: Carlton & Porter, 1864–67).

53. Stevens, *Compendious History*, 146, 22–23. Compare Stevens, *History of the Methodist Episcopal Church*, 1:26–27. I will follow the one-volume, condensed version of Stevens's narrative. He worked these essential points into whatever scale analysis he undertook. Compare, for instance, *The Centenary of American Methodism*, 147–53, with the sections just cited. There Stevens also concluded, "It would indeed appear that the Methodist movement was thus a providential intervention for the new nation" (151).

54. Stevens, *Compendious History*, 24; *History of the Methodist Episcopal Church*, 1:28.

55. Stevens, *Compendious History*, 18, and chapter 1; Stevens, *History of the Methodist Episcopal Church*, 1:18 and chapter 1. Stevens does not call Methodism a machine, though some of his contemporaries did. See Leo Marx, *The Machine in the Garden: Technology and the Pastoral Ideal in America* (London: Oxford University Press, 1964).

56. Stevens, *Compendious History*, 176. See also 199–200, 262, 506, 578–80, and indeed the entirety of this concluding chapter (chapter 36), as well as the entirety of chapter 1.

57. This particular formulation comes from my teacher, Robert T. Handy, *A Christian America*, 2nd ed. (New York: Oxford University Press, 1984). Compatible but differently nuanced readings prevail in more recent critical literature.

58. Stevens, *Compendious History*, 46, 55, 107–9, 146, 199–200, 262, 266, 424–25, 506.

59. Ibid., 404, 419.

60. Ibid., 39, 49, 81, 84, 85, 91, 257, 442.

61. Ibid., 96, 143.

62. Ibid., 55, 263.

63. Ibid., 578–82.

64. James Buckley, *Constitutional and Parliamentary History of The Methodist Episcopal Church* (New York: Eaton & Mains, 1912).

65. See Kenneth E. Rowe, ed., *Methodist Union Catalog: Pre-1976 Imprints* (Metuchen, N.J.: Scarecrow, 1975–), 2:207–11.

66. James Buckley, *History of the Methodists in the United States* (New York: The Christian Literature Co., 1896); *A History of Methodism in the United States*. 2 vols. (New York: The Christian Literature Co., 1897). I am using *A History of the Methodists in the United States*, 4th ed. (New York: Charles Scribner's Sons, 1900).

67. Buckley, *History of the Methodists*, xvii.

68. Ibid., 49, the title of chapter 3; 170–73, 176–77, 179, 203, 205, 248.

69. Ibid., 173, 188. See also 533, 655.

70. Ibid., 221.

71. Ibid., 220–21.

72. Ibid., 97, 1.

73. Ibid., 407–63, chapter 17. Buckley titled the chapter "Bisection of The Methodist Episcopal Church," perhaps a further indication of his effort at "objectivity," and implicitly a recognition of Southern claims that both branches represent genuine episcopal Methodism and that neither is a schism.

74. Ibid., 685, 686.

Chapter 13: United Methodism at 40: Taking Stock

1. This chapter originated as a keynote address delivered at a conference titled *The United Methodist Church at 40: Considering Our History, Teaching Our Traditions, Anticipating Our Future,* held August 14–17, 2008, at the Crowne Plaza Hotel Atlanta Airport, in Atlanta, to celebrate the fortieth anniversary of the formation of The United Methodist Church.

2. See Riley B. Case, *Evangelical and Methodist: A Popular History* (Nashville: Abingdon, 2004).

3. Charles Yrigoyen Jr., John G. McEllhenney, and Kenneth E. Rowe, *United Methodism at Forty* (Nashville: Abingdon, 2008), 40; statistics derived from the *General Minutes.*

4. Paul A. Mickey and Robert L. Wilson, *What New Creation? The Agony of Church Restructure* (Nashville: Abingdon, 1977).

5. James V. Heidinger II and Steve Beard, eds., *Streams of Renewal: Welcoming New Life into United Methodism* (Wilmore, Ky.: Living Streams Publications, 2004); and Case, *Evangelical and Methodist.*

6. See Richey, *MARKS* and the other four volumes in the UMAC series. The first four are collections of essays on the UMC, *CEMI, PCM, DD, QTCC*. See also Frank, *Polity.*

7. *JGC*/MEC 1884, 337.

8. This discussion draws on *MEA* 1 and particularly on the research and writing of Kenneth Rowe on the Sunday school and its architecture. See also Edward A. Trimmer, *John Heyl Vincent: An Evangelist for Education* (PhD diss., Columbia University, 1986). The vintage biography is Leon H. Vincent's *John Heyl Vincent: A Biographical Sketch* (New York: Macmillan, 1925); see also "Autobiography of Bishop Vincent," *North Western Christian Advocate* 58 (April 13, June 1, June 22, June 29, July 13, July 20, August 3, and August 24, 1910). For Vincent's role in Methodist Sunday school publishing, see Walter N. Vernon, *The United Methodist Publishing House: A History* (Nashville: Abingdon, 1989), 2:70–77. Volume 1 by James Penn Pilkington appeared in 1968.

9. Ellwood Hendrick, *Lewis Miller* (New York: G. P. Putnam's Sons, 1925). On the Akron Plan Sunday school, see A. Robert Jaeger, *The Auditorium and Akron Plans* (Master's thesis, Cornell University, 1984), chapter 4. See also Lewis Miller's own essay, "The Akron Plan," in *Seven Graded Sunday Schools,* ed. Jesse L. Hurlbut (New York: Hunt & Eaton, 1893), 11–32. An older and briefer study is Marion Lawrence, "The Akron Plan—Its Genesis, History and Development," in *Housing the Sunday School; or, A Practical Study of Sunday School Buildings* (New York: Eaton & Mains, 1911), 83–92. An abbreviated version of Lawrence's chapter on the Akron Plan was reprinted by The Methodist Episcopal Church, South, Board of Church Extension in its *Thirty-Second Annual Report, 1913–1914,* 268–71.

10. Hendrick, *Lewis Miller,* 144–47.

11. For early description and floorplan, see "The Model Sunday-School Room," *Sunday School Journal* (new series) 2/1 (October 1869): 11. Jaeger's detailed description is based on a description of the building in the *Akron Daily Beacon* at the time of the dedication, 1870. See Jaeger, *Auditorium,* 150–54.

12. "The Model Sunday-School Room," *Sunday School Journal* (new series) 2/1 (October 1869): 11; John H. Vincent, *The Modern Sunday-School* (New York: Hunt & Eaton; Cincinnati: Cranston & Curts, 1887), 160–61.

13. Architect Oscar S. Teale was also secretary of the Sunday school. See "A Model Sunday School Room," in *Seven Graded Sunday Schools*, ed. Jesse L. Hurlbut (New York: Hunt & Eaton, 1893), 113–20; and "Building of Vincent Chapel," [First Methodist Episcopal Church, Plainfield, N.J.] *Program of the 100th Anniversary Exercises October 16–23, 1932 and Historical Sketch* (Plainfield, N.J.: The Church, 1932), [8–9]. For a description and floorplan, see Marion Lawrence, *Housing the Sunday School* (New York: Eaton & Mains, 1911), 59–63.

14. See Lester Ruth, *A Little Heaven Below: Worship at Early Methodist Quarterly Meetings* (Nashville: Kingswood, 2000); and Russell E. Richey, *The Methodist Conference in America*.

15. See *MEA* 2:370–73.

16. Morris D'C. Crawford, "Changes in the Duties of the Presiding Eldership," *CA* (New York) (February 12, 1885): 4. Italics in original. Reproduced in *MEA* 2:419–21.

17. Abel Stevens, *A Compendious History of American Methodism* (New York: Eaton & Mains, n.d.), 17–19; and *History of the Methodist Episcopal Church*, 4 vols. (New York: Carlton & Porter, 1864–67), 1:15–18.

18. See Nolan B. Harmon, *The Organization of the Methodist Church*, 2nd rev. ed. (Nashville: The Methodist Publishing House, 1962), 63–65. See also James E. Kirby, *The Episcopacy in American Methodism* (Nashville: Kingswood, 2000).

19. See Robert B. Steelman, *What God Has Wrought: A History of the Southern New Jersey Conference of The United Methodist Church* (Pennington, N.J.: Commission on Archives and History of the Southern New Jersey Annual Conference, 1986), 320–22.

20. "U.S. Religious Landscape Survey," *Pew Forum on Religion and Public Life* (2009); online: http://religions.pewforum.org.

21. For the bulleted list, I draw on my essay on "Denominationalism" in *Encyclopedia of Religion in America*, ed. Charles H. Lippy and Peter W. Williams (Washington, D.C.: CQ Press, forthcoming).

22. See Morris L. Davis, *The Methodist Unification: Christianity and the Politics of Race in the Jim Crow Era* (New York: New York University Press, 2008).

23. See *MEA* 2:26.

24. In recent years, the Council of Bishops has begun to take important leadership initiatives as a council—that is, collectively.

25. See Richey, *Conference*, 145–74.

26. See James W. Lewis, *The Protestant Experience in Gary, Indiana, 1906–1975: At Home in the City* (Knoxville: University of Tennessee Press, 1992), 201, 150. On mainline denominationalism, see Richey's article in the *Encyclopedia of Religion in America*; and the "Bibliography of Scholarly Writing about Denominations," http://hirr.hartsem.edu/denom/biblio.html.

27. Ezra Earl Jones and Robert L. Wilson, *What's Ahead for Old First Church* (New York: Harper & Row, 1974).

28. See, for instance, Mildred Morse McEwen, *First United Methodist Church, Charlotte, North Carolina* (published by the church, 1983); and Herchel H. Sheets, *Methodism in North Georgia: A History of the North Georgia Conference* (Milledgeville, Ga.: Boyd Publishing Company for the Commission on Archives and History and the Bishop and Cabinet of the North Georgia Annual Conference, 2005), 322–38. For parallels in an urban Presbyterian congregation, see James K. Wellman Jr., *The Gold Coast Church and the Ghetto: Christ and Culture in Mainline Protestantism* (Champaign: University of Illinois Press, 1999). For perspective on congregations,

see James P. Wind and James W. Lewis, *American Congregations*, 2 vols. (Chicago: University of Chicago Press, 1994).

29. Joseph F. DiPaolo, "From Methodist Bookstore to Valley Forge Conference Office," *Annals of Eastern Pennsylvania* 4 (2004): 57–76.

30. Sheets, *Methodism in North Georgia*.

Conclusion: Reforming the Connection: Breaching Four Walls

1. See Nancy Tatom Ammerman, various works, including *Pillars of Faith: American Congregations and Their Partners* (Berkeley and Los Angeles: University of California Press, 2005); C. Kirk Hadaway and David A. Roozen, *Rerouting the Protestant Mainstream* (Nashville: Abingdon, 1995); James Davison Hunter, *Culture Wars: The Struggle to Define America* (New York: Basic, 1991); Milton J Coalter, John M. Mulder, and Louis B. Weeks, eds., *The Mainstream Protestant "Decline"* (Louisville: Westminster/John Knox, 1990); Wade Clark Roof and William McKinney, *American Mainline Religion* (New Brunswick, N.J.: Rutgers University Press, 1987); and Robert Wuthnow, various works, beginning with *The Struggle for America's Soul* (Grand Rapids: Eerdmans, 1989); and *The Restructuring of American Religion* (Princeton, N.J.: Princeton University Press, 1988). There is no question but that United Methodism experiences the division that these scholars discover. There is some question as to whether Methodism is as cleanly and sharply divided as other denominations. There is certainly a question as to whether such a division has typified Methodism and as to whether treating the division as *the* social reality within the denomination is self-actualizing prophecy or sociology.

2. Russell E. Richey, Dennis M. Campbell, and William B. Lawrence, editors and coauthors, *Connectionalism: Ecclesiology, Mission, and Identity*; *The People(s) Called Methodist: Forms and Reforms of Their Life*; *Doctrines and Discipline*; *Questions for the Twenty-First Century Church*; and *Marks of Methodism: Practices of Ecclesiology*.

3. (Washington, D.C.: Pew Research Center, 2008). See also the several volumes titled *The Presbyterian Presence*, under the joint authorship of Milton J. Coalter, John M. Mulder, and Louis B. Weeks, from Westminster/John Knox, particularly *The Re-Forming Tradition: Presbyterians and Mainstream Protestantism* (Louisville: Westminster/John Knox, 1992); *A Case Study of Mainstream Protestantism: The Disciples' Relation to American Culture*, ed. D. Newell Williams (Grand Rapids: Eerdmans; St. Louis: Chalice, 1991); Steven M. Tipton, *Public Pulpits: Methodists and Mainline Churches in the Moral Argument of American Life* (Chicago: University of Chicago Press, 2007); and the various publications by Robert Wuthnow, including *America and the Challenges of Religious Diversity* (Princeton, N.J.: Princeton University Press, 2005).

4. My observations seem also to track judgments being made across the church—and clearly evident in conference after conference—that the church needs more than palliatives, that our problems run fairly deep, that we must discover fundamentally different ways of doing and being the church.

5. See Martin Luther, *Three Treatises* (Philadelphia: Fortress, 1960), or with slightly varying English renderings, *Martin Luther*, ed. John Dillenberger (Garden City, N.J.: Anchor, 1961).

6. See *An Open Letter to the Christian Nobility*.

7. This indictment was voiced in a Wisconsin Annual Conference self-study and planning document *Shape to the Future*.

8. For discussion of this, see Frank, *Polity*, 185–94.

9. See Thomas A. Langford, *Practical Divinity: Theology in the Wesleyan Tradition* (Nashville: Abingdon, 1983); and *Wesleyan Theology: A Sourcebook* (Durham, N.C.: Labyrinth, 1984); Robert E. Cushman, *John Wesley's Experimental Divinity: Studies in Methodist Doctrinal Standards* (Nashville: Kingswood, 1989); and Richey, *MARKS*.

10. Even the superb episcopal initiative *Vital Congregations/Faithful Disciples* tends to view church as congregation.

11. This discussion draws on Russell E. Richey, *Early American Methodism* (Bloomington: Indiana University Press, 1991).

12. On the emergence of the "local church," see Frank, *Polity*, chap. 6.

13. See the introduction by both editors and the concluding essay by the second in Roozen and Nieman, *Church, Identity, and Change: Theology and Denominational Structures in Unsettled Times* (Grand Rapids: Eerdmans, 2005), 1–34 and 625–53; also see Craig Dykstra and James Hudnut-Beumler, "The Ecology of Denominational Organization: A Query," in *The Organizational Revolution: Presbyterians and American Denominationalism*, ed. Milton J. Coalter, John M. Mulder, and Louis B. Weeks (Louisville: Westminster/John Knox, 1992).

14. J. Bruce Behney and Paul H. Eller, *The History of the Evangelical United Brethren Church*, ed. Kenneth W. Krueger (Nashville: Abingdon, 1979), 38–39.

15. *JGC*/MEC 1808, 80–81. Such language seems to be wholly absent from 1812, when D. Hitt served as secretary. One finds an occasional occurrence in 1816 (Lewis Fechtig, sec.) and 1820 (Alexander M'Caine, sec.), almost wholly absent from 1824 (Robert R. Roberts, sec.) except as imbedded in a motion; very occasional in 1828 (Martin Ruter, sec.), 318–19, and the same in 1832 and 1836.

16. I use *fixated* rather than a word like *captive* to suggest that even those of us who no longer think of a Christian America or winning the world for Christ retain elements of those visions.

17. *JLFA* 3:566 (August 2, 1806).

18. Asbury/Coke *Discipline*, 159, 167.

19. Robert T. Handy, *A Christian America*, 2nd ed. (New York: Oxford University Press, 1984).

20. See Asbury/Coke *Discipline*, 159, 167.

Index

Abbott, Benjamin, 204
abolition, 75, 173
abortion, 235
accountability, 97, 227, 242, 243
   conference structures of, 90-93
   of extension ministries, 86-88
   of General Conference, 59
Adams, Herbert Baxter, 185, 186, 203, 206
African Americans, 55-56, 59, 74, 110-11, 157, 228
African Methodist Episcopal Church, 21, 46, 55, 173, 228
African Methodist Episcopal Zion Church, 21, 46, 55, 56, 112, 173, 244
agencies, 215, 221, 242
Akron Plan, 140, 212-13, 225, 286n9
Albright, Jacob, 28
Aldersgate Renewal Fellowship, 241
Allen, Richard, 46
America, as Zion, 245, 246. *See also* Christian America

American Historical Association, 184-85, 281n1
American Methodist Historical Society, 139-40
American politics, and Methodist practice, 227-28
American Revolution, 2, 9, 22, 42, 143, 150, 158, 183
American Society of Church History, 184-85, 281n1
"And Are We Yet Alive" (Wesley hymn), 11, 129-31, 133, 134, 135, 136, 137, 138, 140
Andrew, James O., 177
Andrews, Edward G., 138
Anglican Articles of Religion, 30, 51, 143
Anglicanism, 158, 188
annual conferences, 50, 52, 54, 72, 129-30, 174, 176, 242, 266n6
   and missions, 101, 113
   opening service of, 133-34
   as professional organization, 228
anti-slavery, 35, 47, 162-63

apologetics, 45, 144-46
apostolic succession, 37, 66, 196
appointments, beyond the local church, 95, 238. *See also* extension ministries
apportionments, 169, 170, 237
aristocracy, 48
Arminianism, 47-48, 122, 142, 143
Arminian Magazine, 21, 44, 188, 190
Asbury, Francis, 6, 25, 36, 47, 49, 52, 88, 143, 158, 163, 172
    as American counterpart to Wesley, 37-38
    and American style of governance, 9
    on council, 52-53
    encounter with O'Kelly, 35, 43
    on itinerancy, 76, 262n44
    on Kingdom, 244
    on marriage, 79
    on Methodism as machine, 173-74
    monarchical tendencies in, 44
    power of, 40, 42, 254n14
    on Providence, 189, 204
Ashton, J. Y., 89
Association for Church Renewal, 241
Association of United Methodist Theological Schools, 121
Atlanta, 232
Augustine, 201
Ayers, Robert, 77

Baltimore Conference, 134, 135-36, 138-40
Bangs, Nathan, 11, 68, 78, 145-48, 174, 194-99, 202, 207, 266n13, 276n5, 280n5, 284n47
baptism, 128
Baptists, 145
Barrett, Patricia, 94
Baur, Ferdinand Christian, 185
Baxter, Richard, 38
Bercovitch, Sacvan, 252n21
Berry, Joseph, 219
bishops, 27-28, 39-41, 50, 72, 143, 175, 218, 219-20, 226, 230, 232, 280n38
    and General Conferences, 58
    as itinerating general superintendents, 75, 95
    and missions, 100, 102
    ordination and consecration of, 50
Bishops' Crusade for a New World Order, 226
Black Methodists for Church Renewal, 60, 230
Boardman, Richard, 190
Board of Education, 164
boards, 215, 219, 221, 226, 227, 242
Boehm, Henry, 50-51, 86
Boehm, Martin, 28, 69, 243
bonding, of itinerancy, 73-74
book agents, 86, 87
Book Concern, 7, 87-88, 104
Book of Common Prayer, 3, 143
Book of Discipline of the United Methodist Church (1988), 17
Book of Resolutions, 61
Bostwick, Shadrach, 85
Bread for the World, 223
Brett, Pliny, 173
British Methodism, 69
brotherhood. *See* fraternity
brothers and sisters, 243
Buckley, James, 191, 202-6, 285n73
bureaucracy, 113, 165-66, 179-80, 209, 211, 216, 226, 246
Burke, William, 74, 261n36, 262n44
Burns, Francis, 55
Bush, George, 245

Calvinists, 125, 145, 146, 149, 194
Calvin, John, 141
camping ministries, 95
camp meetings, 77, 91, 101, 161, 197, 202, 225, 252n20, 271n15
    as business-like organization, 133
    meals in, 118, 122-24
campus ministries, 95, 96
Cannon, James, 226
Cape May Accord, 163, 278n21
Carter, Jimmy, 208
catholicity, of Methodism, 46-47, 141-42, 144, 147, 148

Index

caucuses, 60, 118, 169, 179, 224, 230, 232, 233, 234, 241, 247
Centennary of 1866, 136, 199, 215
Centennial of 1884, 137, 210-11, 215
centralization, 40, 94, 96-97, 100, 113, 165
Central Jurisdiction, 59-60, 226, 252n16
chaplains, 88, 96, 110
character, review of, 92, 93, 97, 113
Chautauqua Literary and Scientific Circle, 212, 225
Chicago Temple, 230, 231
Chichester, Elijah, 85
Christendom, 13, 150, 236
Christian Advocate(s), 7, 57, 99, 108, 194, 199, 203, 225
Christian America, 13, 147, 149-51, 165, 236, 245, 246, 275n13, 289n16
Christian civilization, 132, 201
Christmas Conference (1784), 10, 38, 49-52, 53, 61, 143, 228
church
    as a connection, 5
    holiness, catholicity, and apostolicity, 13
    Methodist doctrine of, 141-52
church covenant, 125, 271n16
church history, 184-86
churchly Methodism. *See* "congregational" Methodism
circuit rider, 1, 167, 240
circuits, 167
civil religion, 224, 275n13
civil rights movement, 179
civil theology, 207
Civil War, 11, 110, 130, 131, 134, 145, 157, 176, 177, 215, 245
Clair, Matthew W., 55
Clarendon Code, 68
Clark, Laban, 85
class, 100, 158
class collectors, 106
class leaders, 176
class meetings, 130-31, 140
Coate, M., 86
COCU/CUIC, 121, 128, 270n10

Cokesbury College, 51
Coke, Thomas, 2, 20, 25, 38-39, 41, 42, 44, 47, 50, 88, 143, 161, 172, 173-74, 198, 244, 255n18
Collection of Psalms and Hymns for the Lord's Day, 3
collections, for missions, 106-7, 112
colleges and universities, 92, 156, 175
colonialism, 114, 244
Colored Methodist Episcopal Church, 21, 56
Commission on the Status and Role of Women, 241
commissions, of General Conferences, 58
Committee on the Spiritual State of the Church, 167
Communion, 118, 122-28, 133
conference evangelists, 168
conference hymns, 137-38, 140
Conference Missionary Society, 112
conferences, 39, 48, 240
    and connectionalism, 90-93
    as distinctively Methodist, 62
    as fraternal experience, 72-75, 160
    hierarchy of, 72
    as means of grace, 62, 181, 239
    and missions, 101-3, 107, 114
    oversight of special ventures, 88
    professionalization of, 229
Confessing Movement, 241
confessionalism, 151
congregationalism, 12, 68, 214, 223, 238-40, 246
"congregational" Methodism, 156, 167-69
connectionalism, 5-7, 45
    bishops on, 280n38
    as centralization, 84, 90
    and conferences, 90-93
    vs. structure, 247
Connectional Table, 7, 182
conservative bodies, 222
consumerism, 224
conversion narrative, 23, 26, 122
Cookman, George G., 175, 265n2, 265-66n5, 280n5

Cooper, Ezekiel, 85, 86, 87, 160, 162, 190, 277n7
corresponding secretaries, 221
councils, 39-41, 48, 53 118, 121
covenants, 73, 125, 159, 170-71
Crawford, Morris, 216-17
creation, 125, 126
Cromwell, James O., 51
culture, accommodation to, 169, 244, 247
culture war divisions, 12, 224

Daily Christian Advocate, 59, 61
Davis, G. Lindsey, 155-56
deaconesses, 166-67
deacons, 78, 96, 143, 230
democracy, 70
denominationalism, 147, 151-52
    as fall from catholicity, 144
    hostility toward, 12, 223, 224
"denominational" Methodism, 156, 164-67
denominations, 6
    bureaucratization of, 216
    crises in, 179-80
    as negative, 169
    switching, 222-23
Department of Church Extension, 164
desacralization, of Methodist history, 184
DeWolf, L. Harold, 141
Dickinson College, 89, 108
discipleship, as dimension in conferences, 97
Discipline, 3, 4, 6, 25, 28-32, 45, 48, 50, 61, 181
    historical preface, 17-20, 24, 184, 188
disciplining, 73
district conference, 217-18
district superintendents, 95, 169, 172, 211
diversity, 208, 224, 244
Division of Ordained Ministry, 121
doctrine, and history, 28-32
Doctrines and Discipline of the Methodist Episcopal Church, in America, with Explanatory Notes (Coke and Asbury), 45, 143

Douglass, Thomas L., 266n13
Dunlap, E. Dale, 66, 73
DuPage Declaration, 118-19
Durbin, John Price, 89, 90, 108, 109, 111, 112, 113-14,

East Genesee Annual Conference, 133-34
ecclesiology, 8-9, 11, 31
ecumenicity, 127-28, 151-52, 216, 242
ecumenism, 11, 117-20
education, 164, 210
Edwards, Jonathan, 158
efficiency, 211
elders, 76, 96, 143, 230
elitism, 229
Emerson, Ralph Waldo, 205
Emerton, Ephraim, 186-87, 206, 281n8
Emory University, 155-56
English Reformation, 205
Enlightenment, 252n20
episcopal authority, 72
Episcopalians, 21-22, 144, 145-46, 194
    constitution of, 21-23
episcopal Methodism, 157
Epworth League, 164, 166
Essay on Church Polity (Stevens), 145, 146
ethics, 11
ethnic conferences, 225-26
ethnicity, 100, 244
Ethnic Minority Local Church, 60
Evangelical Association, 21, 53, 56
evangelicals, evangelicalism, 119, 148-51, 200, 222
Evangelical United Brethren, 27, 60, 178, 209, 225
evangelism, 11, 117-20, 127-28, 209, 237-38
experience, 23-26, 251n11
experimental divinity, 238, 247
expertise, 216
extension ministries, 10, 83-97, 139, 238
    as beyond the local church, 94
    as "leaving the ministry", 84

extraordinary office, itinerancy as, 70-71, 77-78, 80

faculty, in Methodist schools, 88
family, as nursery of piety, 167
family meal, 118, 122-28
family values, 156, 159, 169-71
federalism, 228, 233
Female Bible Society of the M.E. Church, 111
feminism, 209
Fernley, T. A., 89
Finley, James B., 79
Fluvanna Conference (1779) 35-37, 45, 173
Focus on the Family, 223
forms, 238
Foundation for Theological Education, 241
fraternity, 48, 72-75, 140, 159, 161
freedom. *See* liberty
Free Methodist Church, 21, 72, 173, 228
free will, 47
frontier, 66, 91, 102
fundamentalism, 222
fund-raising, 137
    for colleges, 88

Garrettson, Freeborn, 51, 162, 190, 202, 217
Gary, Indiana, 231
Gatch, Philip, 36
gender, 100
General Board of Church and Society, 118
General Board of Discipleship, 118
General Board of Global Ministries, 118
General Board of Higher Education and Ministry, 121
General Commission on Christian Unity and Interreligious Concerns, 118, 120, 121, 270n9
General Commission on Religion and Race, 118
General Commission on the Status and Role of Women, 118
General Conference, 10, 44, 45, 48, 49-62, 174, 176, 215, 219, 237, 253n11, 257n20
    accountability of, 58-59
    on extension ministries, 83
    hobbled in 1939 union, 210
    membership of, 53-56
    oversight of, 56-58
General Conference (1792), 41, 53
General Conference (1800), 239
General Conference (1844), 59
General Council on Finance and Administration, 178, 180
General Council on Ministries, 178, 180, 181-82
general providence, 205-6, 207, 283n29
general secretaries, 221, 226-27
gentility, 100, 158-59, 162
German Methodism, 69, 71
German scholarship, 185
Gibson, Maria Layng, 166
Goen, Clarence, 284n50
Good News movement, 118-19, 127, 209, 241
Gorrell, Donald K., 261n28
gospel, entrapment of, 235-36
Goss, C. C., 261n30
governance, 48
grace, 125-26
Great Awakening, 68
Great Society, 208

Habitat for Humanity, 223
Hammett, William, 46, 173, 255n18
Handy, Robert, 245
Harris, Nathaniel, 159
Harrisonburg Conference (MECS), 135
Hatch, Nathan O., 70
"headquarters", revolt against, 12
Heidelberg Catechism, 30
Heitzenrater, Richard, 31, 252n17, 252n22
hermeneutics of suspicion, 241
Heyrman, Christine Leigh, 159
Higgins, S., 89
higher education, 139
higher life, 128
Hinde, Thomas S., 261n36
historicism, 206, 207

histories, of Methodism, 12, 137
history, 9
    appeal to, 17-21, 28-29, 32-33
    and corporate identity, 24
    and doctrine, 28-32
    justifies union, 26-27
    and Providence, 186-90
    shaped American Methodism, 183-84
    Wesleyan character of, 30-31
Hitt, Daniel, 190-91, 289n15
Hofler, Durward, 141
Holifield, E. Brooks, 69
holiness, 128, 150, 181
holiness evangelists, 168
Holy Spirit, 183, 185
    and revivals, 187
homosexuality, 209, 222, 235
hospital ministries, 95
hospitals, 156
Hudson, Hilary, 167
Hymn Book of the Methodist Protestant Church, 130-31
hymnody, 1, 3, 11, 137, 138
Hymns for the use of the Methodist Episcopal Church, 137-38
hyper-accountability, 236
hyper-denominationalism, 224

idolatry, 229
inclusive language, 209
inclusiveness, 70
industrialization, 179, 218, 245
innovations, of Methodism, 225
Institute on Religion and Democracy, 209, 224, 241
"institutional" church, 213-14
institutionalization, 151-52, 221
Internet, 223
interreligious dialogue, 121-22, 208
itinerancy, 10, 12, 43-44, 65-82, 95, 240, 280n5
    as extension ministry, 83
    and machine of Methodism, 175-76, 218

Janes, Edmund, 111, 132, 133, 273n16, 273n19
Jarratt, Devereux, 192
Jefferson, Hamilton, 159, 277n15
jeremiadic history, 31, 252n21
Johns Hopkins University, 185, 186
Johnson, Douglas W., 180
Johnson, Lyndon B., 208
Jones, Ezra Earl, 231
Jones, Robert E., 55
Judiciary Committee, 59
jurisdictional politics, 59-60, 210, 225-26, 228, 231
justice, 11, 117-20, 126-28

Kennedy, Gerald, 66, 259n9
Key 73, 233
Kingdom, 144, 147, 170, 181, 244
Kirby, James, 55, 58
Kobler, John, 159-60
Kramer, George, 213
Kynett, A. J., 215

laity, 52, 55, 56, 139, 239
Lakin, Benjamin, 79
"Landmark" documents, 28
Lanius, Jacob, 263n45
Large Minutes, 2, 3, 5, 18, 50, 51, 143, 188
lay ministry, 218
leadership, 69, 226-27, 228-30, 232-33
Lee, Jesse, 3, 37, 39, 40, 41, 42, 49, 53, 54, 65, 68, 73, 74, 79, 191-94, 202, 204, 254n18, 276n5
Lee, Wilson, 160
Lewis, James, 231
liberalism, 208, 210
liberty, 42-43, 47-48, 70
Lifewatch, 241
Lilly Endowment, 235
liquor, 51
local church, 94, 168, 214
local ministry, 78-80
local preachers, 168-69, 174
Lord's Supper, 118, 136. *See also* Communion

Lore, D. D., 108
love, 119, 147
love feasts, 118, 122-28, 132
Lutheran Church, 112
Luther, Martin, 12, 235-36, 247

machinery, of Methodism, 172-82, 218-21
mainline Protestantism, 12, 119, 180, 210, 222, 234-35
"Main Street" Methodism, 211, 221, 230
managerial revolution, 215-16
Manship, A., 89
marriage, 79, 125, 156, 271n16
Mason, Mary W., 103, 238
McCabe, C. C., 215
McConnell, Francis J., 226
McCullough, J. B., 89, 112
McKendree, William, 28, 40, 42, 56-57, 79, 130
McTyeire, Holland N., 168, 276n5
Meacham, James, 40, 42-43, 278n19
Mead, Sidney, 150
Mead, Stith, 159-60
media, 24, 180, 216
media ministries, 224
meetings, 237
megachurches, 223
memory, 82
Merwin, Samuel, 85, 86
Methodism
    and America, 149-50
    and Anglicanism, 51
    as aural/oral movement, 1-2, 4
    catholicity of, 46-47, 141-42, 144, 147, 148
    as a "connection", 5-7
    declension of, 31
    early history as southern affair, 157-58
    fluidity and dynamism of, 240
    on history, 17-21, 23-24
    lack of self-consciousness, 25-26
    as machine, 172-82, 218
    as missionary movement, 91, 98-99, 101-2
    organizational transformation of, 139-40
    and Providence, 201
    as revival, 193
    rise of, 19-20
    as social movement, 157
Methodist Episcopal Church, 59, 158, 209
Methodist Episcopal Church, South, 21, 56, 59, 131, 135, 138, 173, 178, 189, 209
Methodist Magazine, 7, 44, 194
Methodist Protestant Church, 21, 55, 59, 72, 146, 173, 178, 209, 228
Methodist Quarterly Review, 57, 145
Methodists Associated Representing the Caucus of Hispanic Americans, 60
Mickey, Paul A., 179-80
middle judicatory, 99
middle manager, 216
millennium, 148-49
Miller, Lewis, 212
ministry
    care and regulation of, 51
    at translocal levels, 239
missional, 95, 118, 181
Missionary Advocate, 108, 109
Missionary Society of the Methodist Episcopal Church, 57, 89, 103-4, 107, 108, 109, 175, 257-58n29, 267n31, 268n32
missions, 10, 51, 88, 98-114, 139, 164, 165, 216, 237-38
    as conference-based, 100-101
    confused with numbers, 13
    ministry as, 91
    nature and purpose of, 244-46
Mission Society for United Methodists, 241
mistrust, 247
Moravians, 122
Morgan, Lyttleton F., 138-39
Mudge, Enoch, 79, 263n53, 263n56
Mudge, James, 73
multiculturalism, 244
mutual accountability, 160

narrative, 27, 32
National Fellowship of Asian American United Methodists, 60

nationalization. *See* centralization
National Magazine, 99, 146, 199
Native American International Caucus, 60
Nazarenes, 228
Neander, Johann A. W., 185
Neill, James, 89
New Chapter on Slavery, 110, 269n55
Newcomer, Christian, 28
New Deal, 208
New England Conference, 132, 133, 135, 136
New Jersey Conference, 219
new machinery, 180-81
new organizational models, 238
New York Christian Advocate, 145
Northern Methodism, 111-12, 157, 163, 176, 177-78, 245
Norwood, Frederick A., 79

offices, 71
    ordinary and extraordinary, 77-78
Ohio Conference, 130
O'Kelly, James, 10, 34-35, 37, 38, 39, 40-41, 42, 43, 45, 46-48, 53, 143, 163, 173
Olin, Stephen, 260n22
ordinary offices, 77-78, 80
organizational revolution, 215-16
Original Church of Christ (Bangs), 145, 146
orthopraxy, 124
Otterbein, Philip William, 28, 69, 243
Outler, Albert, 11
Oxford Institute of Methodist Theological Studies, 141
Oxnam, G. Bromley, 226

Paine, Robert, 66
parachurch organizations, 222, 223
parish minister, 78, 81, 83
parish ministry, 67, 71, 81, 95, 100, 238-40, 247
particular providence, 204-5, 207
pastors, 167-69
patriarchy, 156, 166
Patton, John, 94
Pedicord, Caleb, 204

Pepper, E. I. D., 89
perfection, 128
Pew Forum on Religion and Public Life, 235
Philadelphia City Home Mission, 111
Philadelphia Conference, 103-7, 108, 111, 114
Pietism, 122, 158, 159, 187, 252n20
Pitman, Charles, 108
plans of union, 121
pluralism, 31, 208, 244
polity, 12, 143, 236-38
Porter, James, 66, 137
post-denominationalism, 224
power, concentration of, 165
pragmatism, of Methodism, 13, 162, 197, 237-38, 247
preaching, 1, 50-51, 196
Presbyterians, 6, 21-23, 112, 145, 150
presiding elders, 76-77, 80, 110, 112, 168-69, 172, 176, 211, 218, 255n18
Prettyman, William, 135
Primitive Methodists, 173
primitivism, 31, 47
professionalism, 211, 228-29, 233
progress, 164
prohibition, 245
Protestantism
    divisions within, 234
    unity with, 149-51
Providence, 12, 20, 21, 28, 32, 148-49, 151, 175, 183, 282n14
    Bangs on, 194-99, 284n47
    Buckley on, 203-6
    as facade, 206
    and history, 186-87, 189-90
    Lee on, 191-94
    Stevens on, 199-202
publications, denominational, 2, 44-45, 87, 88, 223
Puritanism, 68, 187

Quadrilateral, 17, 25, 31, 47, 209, 251n10
quarterly meeting, 76-77, 78, 80, 101, 125, 161-62, 167, 176, 218, 240
Quigley, G., 110

Index

race, 100, 157
racism, 59-60, 74, 225, 228, 252n16
radicalisms, 209
Rankin, Thomas, 172
rationalism, 185
Reagan, Ronald, 245
reason, 25
Reformation, 235-36
Reformed Methodists, 173
regionalism, 157, 210, 219-21, 225, 228
regulation, 236, 240-44, 246
RENEW, 241
republicanism, 37, 42, 47, 255n21
Republican Methodists, 34, 72, 143, 163, 173
Restrictive Rules, 10, 30, 31, 56
retired bishops, 97
revival, revivalism, 46, 50, 76, 91, 161, 162, 187, 192-93, 197, 202, 207, 238, 252n20
Robertson, Pat, 245
Rogers, Bruce A., 180
Rogers, Hester Ann, 159, 238
Rogers, Kristine M., 180
Roman Catholicism, 165
Roosevelt, Franklin D., 208
Rowe, Kenneth, 33

sacred history, 20, 32, 189, 197
Sales, John, 262n43
same-sex communities, 159-60, 162, 163
same-sex unions, 155-56, 169, 170
sanctification, 128
Sano, Roy, 122, 270n9
Scarritt Bible and Training School, 164, 166
Schaff, Philip, 185, 186, 202-3, 206
schism, 10, 45, 44, 46, 48, 143, 146, 173
scientific history, 185-86
Scripture, 25
    in Methodism, 31
    Presbyterians on, 23
"second disestablishment", 245
sectarian Methodism, 156, 162-63
secularization, 187, 245
segregation, 111
seminaries, 226

separation of church and state, 165
Shinn, Asa, 146
Simpson, Matthew, 66, 137, 226
Simpsonwood (Atlanta), 232
single-parent households, 156
Sixties, 208, 227
slavery, 47, 51, 55, 58, 75, 100, 110, 134-35, 159, 269n55
Smelter, Wallace G., 66
Smith, Henry, 163
Snethen, Nicholas, 45, 86
Snyder, Jacob, 212
social gospel, 210, 231, 245
social ministries, 95
social reform, 157, 237-38
social worship, 130
society, 6
sorority, 159
Southern Methodism, 12, 156-71
"special appointments", 88, 90. *See also* also extension ministries
special-interest groups, 241
specialization, 57, 216
special providence, 283n29
Spirit, 125-26, 128
spirituality of the church, 165
stations, 77-78, 167
steam engine, 176, 201, 218
Stevens, Abel, 11, 91, 98-99, 101, 102, 104, 108, 114, 137, 145-48, 176, 191, 199-202, 207, 218, 276n5, 285n53, 285n55
stewards, 174
Stillwellite movement, 173
structure, 246-47
suburban church, 213
Sunday school, 24, 131, 139, 140, 209, 211, 212-13, 219, 225, 240
Sunday School Union, 212
superintendents, 143, 175, 280n1. *See also* bishops

taxation, apportionments as, 65, 237
teaching office, 44-45
Teale, Oscar S., 287n13

technology, 180
temperance meeting, 132
Tennants, 158
testimony, 1, 32
theological education, 92-93, 96
Tigert, John, 5, 49, 254n14
Tories, 143, 158
Total Quality Management, 238
tradition
  creation of, 140
  in Episcopalianism, 22
  in Methodism, 25
Tranforming Congregations, 241
traveling bishops, 65
traveling companions, for bishops, 85-86
traveling preachers, 71, 72, 174, 176. See also itinerancy

uniform lesson plan (Sunday school), 212
union of 1939, 26-27, 178, 210, 225-30
union of 1968, 27, 178, 208-9
United Brethren in Christ, 21, 53, 56
United Methodist Action, 241
United Methodist Church, 6, 8, 27, 209
  divisions within, 117-19, 234
  fortieth anniversary of, 12
  legitimacy of, 27-28
  membership decline of, 209
  unity in missions, 119-20
United Methodist Publishing House, 223, 227
United Nations, 226
unity, types of, 121, 127
urban churches, 230-33

Valley Forge Corporate Center, 232
Vanderbilt University, 164
Van Tassel, David D., 281n1
Vasey, Thomas, 52
Vincent, John, 212-13
voluntarism, of denominations, 149, 151, 165
voluntary societies, 103, 107, 177, 215

Wallace, George, 179
walls, 235-36, 246-47

Waltz, Alan K., 180
war, 235
Ware, Thomas, 39, 75-76, 190-91, 253n13, 262n43
Warren, William F., 92
Watt, James, 176, 201, 218
Waugh, Beverly, 133-34
Wesleyan Female College, 89
Wesleyan Methodist Church, 21, 146, 173, 228
Wesley Building (Philadelphia), 230, 232
Wesley, Charles, 1, 2, 11, 142, 143
Wesley, John, 1, 2, 51
  Aldersgate experience, 202
  on appointing preachers, 280n5
  authority of, 38-39
  catholicity of, 144, 145
  ecclesiology of, 141, 142
  on history, 21, 188
  and James Watt, 176, 201, 218
  on itinerancy, 67-68, 69, 71
  in Methodist history, 30-31
  missionary scheme of, 101
  offices held by, 88-89, 93, 172
  on Providence, 204, 283n29
  on unity in mission, 119
Western Book Concern, 59
Whatcoat, Richard, 28, 38-39, 49, 52, 90, 257n2, 277-78n15
Whiggery, 42, 152
Whitefield, George, 67-68, 69, 158, 193, 202
White, Thomas, 35
Wilke, Richard, 180, 227
Willard, Frances, 226
Williams, Robert, 2, 87, 192-93
Wilson, John, 85
Wilson, Luther, 219, 220
Wilson, Robert L., 179-80, 231
Woman's Parsonage and Home Mission Society, 166
women
  at General Conferences, 56
  and missions, 102-3
  ordination of, 75, 228, 257n18

role in the church, 166-67
in traveling ministry, 74-75
Women's Board of Foreign Missions, 166
Women's Parsonage and Home Mission Society, 164
Woodmason, Charles, 68
World Council of Churches, 121, 224, 226, 270n8
worldliness, 100, 167

World War II, 226
Wyandots, 92, 99, 103

Young Men's Central Home Mission, 111
Young Men's Christian Association, 112
youth culture, 156

Zion, 244-45, 246
Zion's Herald, 99, 145, 199

LaVergne, TN USA
27 October 2010

202558LV00001B/164/P